The Confident Student

The Confident Student

Seventh Edition

Carol C. Kanar

WADSWORTH
CENGAGE Learning

Australia • Brazil • Japan • Korea • Mexico • Singapore • Spain • United Kingdom • United States

The Confident Student, **Seventh Edition**
Carol C. Kanar

Senior Publisher: Lyn Uhl

Director: Annie Todd

Senior Sponsoring Editor: Shani Fisher

Development Editor: Beth Kaufman

Assistant Editor: Daisuke Yasutake

Editorial Assistant: Cat Salerno

Media Editor: Emily Ryan

Senior Marketing Manager: Kirsten Stoller

Marketing Coordinator: Ryan Ahern

Marketing Communications Manager:
Martha Pfeiffer

Associate Content Project Manager:
Sara Abbott

Art Director: Jill Haber Atkins

Print Buyer: Julio Esperas

Senior Rights Acquisition Account Manager,
Text: Katie Huha

Production Service: Elm Street Publishing
Services

Text Designer: Janet Theurer/Theurer
Briggs Design

Rights Acquisition Account Manager,
Image: John Hill

Cover Designer: RHDG/Brie Hattey

Cover Image: Janet Theurer/Theurer
Briggs Design

Compositor: Integra Software Services Pvt. Ltd.

For product information and technology assistance, contact us at
Cengage Learning, Customer & Sales Support, 1-800-354-9706

For permission to use material from this text or product,
submit all requests online at **www.cengage.com/permissions**.
Further permissions questions can be emailed to
permissionrequest@cengage.com.

Library of Congress Control Number: 2009932923

ISBN-13: 978-1-4390-8251-5
ISBN-10: 1-4390-8251-0

Wadsworth
20 Channel Center Street
Boston, MA 02210
USA

Cengage Learning is a leading provider of customized learning solutions with office locations around the globe, including Singapore, the United Kingdom, Australia, Mexico, Brazil and Japan. Locate your local office at **international.cengage.com/region**

Cengage Learning products are represented in Canada by Nelson Education, Ltd.

For your course and learning solutions, visit **www.cengage.com**.

Purchase any of our products at your local college store or at our preferred online store **www.ichapters.com**.

Printed in the United States of America
1 2 3 4 5 6 7 13 12 11 10 09

BRIEF CONTENTS

BRIEF CONTENTS

CONTENTS

Thank you for choosing *The Confident Student*, Seventh Edition. This book is special for several reasons. It has grown with the times to reflect pedagogical changes, technological advancements, and students' needs. Yet *The Confident Student's* core values of individual responsibility and confidence through accomplishment remain at its forefront. Providing a solid foundation in academic skills, *The Confident Student's* pragmatic approach helps both the first-time college student and the older returning student make the transition to academic life and work. Most important, students tell us that they like this book, find it worthwhile, and actually enjoy reading it—a plus for any instructor.

Today's college students are busy. They attend classes, they work, some have families, they have a wide variety of interests, and they are involved in many activities. They take their education seriously. Their goals are to master their course materials so they can perform well in class, get good grades, graduate, and land the job or career of their dreams. Today's students are technologically literate, often outpacing their instructors in their use of the Internet and communications technology. They are a diverse group, not only in their backgrounds but in the ways they learn. Some learn best by reading, some are more graphically oriented than print oriented, and some learn best through practice and assessment. *The Confident Student*, Seventh Edition, appeals to student readers by answering their needs in the following ways:

▛ The tone is open, engaging, conversational, and student centered.

▛ The writing style gets to the point quickly and is easy to understand without being oversimplified.

▛ A user-friendly format includes boldfaced key terms, boxed features, and headings that are color coded to chapter objectives.

▛ A prereading (color-coded Chapter Objectives, Awareness Checks) and postreading (Summary Check, Chapter Review Quiz, Show Your Confidence, Your Reflections) apparatus encourages active reading.

▛ The design's use of color and graphics has a visual impact that not only engages students' interest but helps reinforce key concepts.

▛ Pedagogical features include self-assessments, themed exercises, and confidence-building activities that keep students motivated and their attention focused.

▛ A strong supporting website provides students with additional materials for practice, self-assessment, and inspiration (www.cengage.com/success/Kanar/Confident7e).

Every new edition of a book inspires the addition of some new material and a few major changes. *The Confident Student*, Seventh Edition, is no exception.

What's New in *The Confident Student*?

The Seventh Edition has a new design. Special design elements promote active reading and learning. These elements include the chapter-opening photograph that reflects a central concept or chapter theme, clearly stated objectives, and a chapter-opening quotation that addresses one of the 14 traits of confident students explained in the text. Section headings are color coded to the objectives they address. Key terms and definitions are called out in the margins. Icons designate Confidence Builder, Awareness Check, Computer Confidence, and Critical Thinking features. Photographs and other graphics reinforce key concepts. These textual aids promote student interaction with the text and enhance instructional delivery as well, by serving as reference points for both students and instructors.

A more intentional focus on the theme of confidence is evident in every chapter, beginning in Chapter 1 with Figure 1.1: Are You a Confident Student? This figure lists and defines 14 traits of confident students. A chapter-opening quotation addresses a trait for students to reflect on as they read about and apply chapter concepts. The **Confidence Builder** feature now follows the chapter introduction so that students begin each chapter on a positive note that inspires and motivates. **Show Your Confidence**, a post-reading feature, invites students to apply what they have learned.

Awareness Checks in each chapter are now numbered 1.1, 1.2 etc. to coincide with the chapter number for easy reference.

New end-of-chapter materials include several features: The **Summary Check** is a chapter review checklist of concepts and key terms. The **Chapter Review Quiz** can be used as an open-book self-assessment or as a graded review (answer key included in the Instructor's Resource Manual). **Show Your Confidence** is a critical-thinking exercise that asks students either to apply, analyze, synthesize, or evaluate information from the chapter and then share what they have learned in writing or class discussion.

Problem solving has been moved back into Chapter 4 to more clearly address the connection between setting goals and writing an action plan to achieve those goals. Decision-making and problem-solving skills are essential to the goal-setting process.

A new Chapter 12, Building Skills for Confident Communication, addresses the skills of listening, speaking, writing, and researching, as well as the group interaction skills of successful collaboration and conflict resolution. Relationship management is also included, as is a section on the effective use of communication technology.

An improved chapter organization serves two purposes. First, the new order flows logically from global skills such as motivation and critical thinking to more specific skills such as reading actively and studying from textbooks. Second, the chapters covering academic skills are now grouped together, as are the chapters covering life skills. Specific organizational changes include the following: The coverage on active reading has moved from Chapter 13 in the Sixth Edition to Chapter 7 in the Seventh Edition. Similarly, the coverage on attention and memory has moved from Chapter 10 to Chapter 8. Both these changes respond to reviewers' requests that coverage of reading skills and the memory process appear earlier in the text. Chapters 11 and 12 on preparing for tests and reducing test anxiety are now combined in the new Chapter 11 so that students can more easily see the relationship between these topics. Of course, instructors are free to teach the chapters in whatever order best meets the requirements of their courses.

The Computer Confidence content in Chapters 1, 5, 9, 10, 13, and 14 has been revised to reflect new technological developments and concerns about the use of technology. Professor Mario Núñez from Erie Community College served as a consultant on these changes, as well as on changes made to the computer exercises in some chapters.

Features Retained from the Sixth Edition

The Confident Student, Seventh Edition, continues to be a highly visual student-centered text with a strong academic base. The new design enhances these qualities. In addition, the text's signature features that promote active learning have been retained.

Awareness Checks in every chapter are brief checklists or assessment questionnaires that orient students to a chapter concept or discussion topic. Many of the Awareness Checks are cast in a Likert-type format, followed by a brief explanation that helps students assess their attitudes, skills, and prior knowledge.

Confidence Builders in every chapter address learning strategies, attitudes, and career skills. Their purpose is to broaden students' understanding and build confidence by extending the discussion of chapter topics into related areas of interest or research. Students are encouraged to pursue these topics further by visiting *The Confident Student* premium website to do related online searches.

Computer Confidence is a feature that provides students with an opportunity to build confidence in using technology. Computer Confidence has been updated to reflect new trends and concerns about the use of technology.

Critical Thinking exercises enhance the text's pedagogical foundation. Through this feature, students learn to integrate critical thinking naturally into their approach to studying and interacting in the classroom as they are asked to question, more fully process, and consider different viewpoints surrounding the issues and concepts presented in each chapter.

Your Reflections is a journaling activity that poses several questions or statements for students to think about and respond to in writing. The Reflections provide an excellent opportunity for students to assess their progress, reflect on what they are learning, and plan ways to apply their new skills. The Reflections can also be used as a personal log or as a springboard to discussion.

Exercises in every chapter—designated by icons—address learning styles, collaborative activities, and computer/Internet applications. Many of the exercises both in the text and online have been revised, and some are new.

A Personal Message from Author to Student

This message is just between me and you. I once sat where you are now. I was fresh out of high school, a little bit nervous about being on my own, wondering if I had what it takes. College was difficult for me at first. You see, I was not prepared. When I was in college, there were no student success courses. We were expected to know things like how to take notes, how to manage our time, and how to read a textbook. Unfortunately, many of us didn't, and I was one of them. I struggled during my first year, but with a lot of effort and the help of one very special teacher who taught me how to study, I persisted and was able to graduate with honors. This is why I believe that if you want anything bad enough and are willing to work hard enough, you can accomplish whatever you set out to do. Now is your time.

The Confident Student, Seventh Edition, is my gift to you. This book contains everything I know about how to achieve success in college and in life. This is the book that I wish someone had written for me when I was in college. Please read it and enjoy it, and feel free to write to me and tell me how you are doing. I would also be grateful for any ideas you can share with me that would help me to help other students. Please send your comments to the following email with the subject line "The Confident Student 7e": CSWeb@cengage.com.

Sincerely,

Carol C. Kanar

Ancillaries for Instructors

The Instructor's Resource Manual that accompanies *The Confident Student* contains an answer key for the exercises and chapter-by-chapter suggestions for using the text. Also included are sample course syllabi, a brief bibliography, and handouts to use as supplementary materials. Information on portfolio assessment in student success courses has been retained from the Sixth Edition. You can find the Instructor's Resource Manual and PowerPoint slides, as well as materials you may have previously used, by visiting www.cengage.com/success/Kanar/Confident7e.

Additional Ancillaries

New Course Cartridge Materials in WebTutor: If you're taking your class online, you'll want to check out the new course cartridge materials in WebTutor. The WebTutor offers a number of instructor resources to complement the main text, including grade book content. Instructors have the option of using the electronic grade book, receiving assignments from students via the Internet, and tracking student use of the communication and collaboration functions. WebTutor content is available in Blackboard, WebCT, and Angel platforms, and an access code is required for purchase by your students to reach this material. This resource is available for packaging with a Printed Access Code (PAC), or students can purchase an Instant Access Code (IAC) online at www.ichapters.com. Talk to your Cengage Sales Representative for more information. Need help finding your rep? Visit http://academic.cengage.com.

Assessment Tools: If you're looking for additional ways to assess your students, Cengage Learning has additional resources for you to consider. For more in-depth information on any of these items, talk with your sales rep, or visit the *Confident Student* website.

▶ **College Success Factors Index:** This pre- and post-test determines students' strengths and weaknesses in areas proven to be determinants of college success.

▶ **CL Assessment and Portfolio Builder:** This personal development tool engages students in self-assessment, critical-thinking, and goal-setting activities to prepare them for college and the workplace. The access code for this item also provides students access to the Career Resource Center.

▶ **Noel-Levitz College Student Inventory:** *The Retention Management System*™ *College Student Inventory* (CSI from Noel-Levitz) is an early-alert, early-intervention program that identifies students with tendencies that contribute to dropping out of school. Students can participate in an integrated, campus-wide program. Cengage Learning offers you three assessment options that evaluate students on 19 different scales: Form A (194 items), Form B (100 items), or an online etoken that provides access to Form A, B, or C (74 items). Advisors are sent three interpretive reports: The Student's Report, The Advisor/Counselor Report, and The College Summary and Planning Report.

▶ **The *Myers-Briggs Type Indicator*® *(MBTI*®*) Instrument*[1]** is the most widely used personality inventory in history—and it is also available for packaging with *The Confident Student*. The standard Form M self-scorable instrument contains 93 items that determine preferences on four scales: Extraversion-Introversion, Sensing-Intuition, Thinking-Feeling, and Judging-Perceiving.

College Success Planner: Package your textbook with this 12-month week-at-a-glance academic planner. The College Success Planner assists students in making the best use of their time both on and off campus, and it includes additional reading about key learning strategies and life skills for success in college.

Cengage Learning's TeamUP Faculty Program Consultants: An additional service available with this textbook is support from **TeamUP Faculty Program Consultants.** For more than a decade, our consultants have helped faculty reach and engage first-year students by offering peer-to-peer consulting on curriculum and assessment, faculty training, and workshops. Our consultants are educators and higher education professionals who provide full-time support helping educators establish and maintain effective student success programs. They are available to help you establish or improve your student success program and provide training on the implementation of our textbooks and technology. To connect with your TeamUP Faculty Program Consultant, call 1-800-528-8323 or visit www.cengage.com/teamup.

---

[1] MBTI and Myers-Briggs Type Indicator are registered trademarks of Consulting Psychologists Press, Inc.

For Students

The Confident Student Premium Website
www.cengage.com/success/Kanar/Confident7e
New features on the website include a **Chapter Summary of Topics** for every chapter that students can use either for previewing or reviewing a chapter's content or as a study guide for a quiz. Exercises titled **Thinking Ahead About Career** help students apply chapter concepts to workplace situations.

Features retained from the Sixth Edition include a **Skillbuilder Library** where students can read articles and do exercises to improve proficiency in math, writing, science, vocabulary, and research skills. The **Confidence Builder Web Search** is a feature that allows students to investigate the concepts from the textbook in online search activities.

Students can use the **Interactive Skill Finder** to help determine their confidence index: a measure of what they already know about the skills covered in the textbook and what needs improving. This website also includes various interactive materials for review and practice: additional chapter exercises, articles, self-tests, a journaling activity, and a glossary of key terms and definitions.

Acknowledgments

First of all, I thank my husband, Stephen P. Kanar, for being the person he is and for steadfastly providing me encouragement and support through seven editions of this book. Second, I want to dedicate *The Confident Student*, Seventh Edition, to my dad, James C. Cooper, 1920 to 2008, who was ever my loyal defender and confidant.

A book is the product of many people's efforts, and I am indebted to everyone at Cengage-Wadsworth Learning Systems who contributed to the development and production of the Seventh Edition. I especially want to thank the following people: Shani Fisher—we have been together in this venture through five editions. We have grown and changed through the years, yet in all the important ways we remain the same. How do I thank you for all you have been and done? You are my champion and inspiration. Beth Kaufman, your editorial help, imagination, and wit have been invaluable, and it shows in the Seventh Edition. Thank you, Beth. Daisuke Yasutake, for all you do, every day, and for your efforts, which have seen this book through to completion, I thank you. To Danielle Urban who managed the production: Thanks for making this easy and for listening to all my little complaints. Kudos to Sara Abbott for your work on the production of this book. Thank you, Katie Huha, for your work in securing permissions, and thank you, too, Jen Meyer Dare and Kelly Franz, for finding the photographs that added visual interest to each chapter. For a beautiful cover and design, I can't thank Brie Hattey, Yvo Riezebos, Linda Jurras, and Janet Theurer of Theurer Briggs Design enough. I also want to remember Mario Núñez for his contributions as well to the success of this book. Thank you all, again.

As always, I remain deeply grateful to the many students whose hopes and accomplishments inspire each new edition of *The Confident Student*. Wherever you are today, I wish you the fulfillment of your dreams.

Finally, to the reviewers, listed below, who read my manuscript and provided me with many fine suggestions for developing the Seventh Edition: You were a guiding light, giving me the direction I needed to move ahead with this edition. Thank you for your help and also for the dedication you show in serving your students.

Jackie T. Cohen
Augusta State University

Dan Foltz-Gray
Roane State Community College

Dale S. Haralson
Hinds Community College

Amy R. Hopkins
Georgia Perimeter College

Lynn Ingraham
Erie Community College

Shiela P. Kerr
Florida Community College

Jean Layne
Blinn College

Karen S. Mayse
Central Christian College of Kansas

Tamra Ortiges Young
Georgia Perimeter College

Joy-Ann Perard
Miami Dade College

Rebecca Samberg
Housatonic Community College

Brian Stroup
Oregon State University

Melissa Woods
Hinds Community College

SKILL FINDER

This questionnaire will help you determine your *confidence index*: a measure of what you already know about the skills covered in this book and which skills need developing or improving. Read each statement. How confident are you that you possess the skill or knowledge that the statement describes? Check the column that best expresses your level of confidence: *Very Confident*, *Fairly Confident*, *Not Very Confident*, or *Not Confident*. Give yourself 3 points for a check in the *Very Confident* column, 2 points for a check in the *Fairly Confident* column, 1 point for a check in the *Not Very Confident* column, and no points for a check in the *Not Confident* column. Add your points and write your score in the space labeled *Section Total*. When you have completed your Skill Finder, transfer your section totals to Table 1 on page xxvii, add them, and write your score in the space labeled *Grand Total*. Use your section totals and grand total from Table 1 to help you find your confidence index for each section (Table 2, p. xxviii) and your overall confidence index (Table 3, p. xxviii). A more detailed explanation of how to calculate and interpret your confidence index follows at the end of the Skill Finder.

Words in italics identify some of the key terms explained in each chapter. *The Confident Student* premium website has an online glossary to help you remember these key words. You can also print out a list of the key terms and their definitions.

The complete Skill Finder is also available in an interactive format. To access it, log on to *The Confident Student* premium website.

Very Confident
Fairly Confident
Not Very Confident
Not Confident

3 2 1 0   **Success is a matter of choice, not chance.**

☐☐☐☐ 1. I know the difference between *elective courses* and required courses.

☐☐☐☐ 2. I have a *mentor* I can turn to for advice.

☐☐☐☐ 3. I have a college catalog, and I know what kinds of information it contains.

☐☐☐☐ 4. I know what services my college offers to help students financially, academically, and in other ways.

☐☐☐☐ 5. I have an academic support group.

☐☐☐☐ 6. I use email and am aware of its benefits.

☐☐☐☐ 7. I am flexible and able to adapt to change.

☐☐☐☐ 8. I am comfortable in a culturally diverse environment.

☐☐☐☐ 9. I do not hesitate to ask questions when I need answers.

☐☐☐☐ 10. I know what it means to be an active learner.

Section Total: _____

Motivation and learning are connected.

☐☐☐☐ 11. I know what my basic skill strengths and weaknesses are.

☐☐☐☐ 12. I know what my *learning style* is and how to use it to my advantage.

☐☐☐☐ 13. I adapt easily to others' teaching and learning styles.

☐☐☐☐ 14. I understand how motivation and learning are connected.

☐☐☐☐ 15. I am aware that people may have *multiple intelligences*.

☐☐☐☐ 16. I know what *critical thinking* is, and I am able to think critically.

☐☐☐☐ 17. I take personal responsibility for my learning and its outcomes.

☐☐☐☐ 18. I know where and how I learn best, and I try to create those conditions for myself.

☐☐☐☐ 19. I am usually able to manage my own feelings and behavior.

☐☐☐☐ 20. I am aware that there are different ways to learn and that it is up to me to choose appropriate strategies.

Section Total: _____

Very Confident	Fairly Confident	Not Very Confident	Not Confident	
3	**2**	**1**	**0**	**Thinking critically and reading are lifelong learning skills.**
☐	☐	☐	☐	21. Before reading or listening to lectures, I first examine my own *assumptions* about the topic.
☐	☐	☐	☐	22. I know how to predict test questions from reading and lectures.
☐	☐	☐	☐	23. I am able to determine an author's or speaker's *purpose.*
☐	☐	☐	☐	24. I am able to find my own purpose for reading and studying.
☐	☐	☐	☐	25. I am able to use *creative thinking* to meet many challenges.
☐	☐	☐	☐	26. I know how to evaluate what I am learning for its *reliability, objectivity,* and *usefulness.*
☐	☐	☐	☐	27. I am an *active reader* rather than a passive reader.
☐	☐	☐	☐	28. I know how to find main ideas, identify supporting details, and make inferences.
☐	☐	☐	☐	29. I am able to calculate my reading rate so that I can manage my reading and study time more effectively.
☐	☐	☐	☐	30. I use a textbook marking system.

Section Total: _____

				Goal setting and problem solving are keys to your future.
☐	☐	☐	☐	31. I know the difference between a *short-term* goal and a *long-term* goal.
☐	☐	☐	☐	32. Setting goals is an important part of my planning.
☐	☐	☐	☐	33. When things get difficult, I am not inclined to give up.
☐	☐	☐	☐	34. I usually do not have trouble making decisions.
☐	☐	☐	☐	35. I know why I am in college.
☐	☐	☐	☐	36. I am able to tell when a goal is a realistic one.
☐	☐	☐	☐	37. I have a *positive attitude* toward others, myself, and the future.
☐	☐	☐	☐	38. I am aware of different types (categories) of goals.
☐	☐	☐	☐	39. When I have a problem, I am able to identify its causes.
☐	☐	☐	☐	40. I solve problems through planning rather than by relying on time or chance to take care of them.

Section Total: _____

Very Confident
Fairly Confident
Not Very Confident
Not Confident

3 2 1 0   **Listening and note taking are cornerstones of classroom success.**

☐☐☐☐ 41. Most people would describe me as a good listener.

☐☐☐☐ 42. I know the difference between *active listening* and *passive listening*.

☐☐☐☐ 43. I am not usually distracted when I am listening to a lecture.

☐☐☐☐ 44. I recognize the *signal words* that are clues to a speaker's important ideas.

☐☐☐☐ 45. I have a note-taking system that usually gives me good results.

☐☐☐☐ 46. I consider myself to be an effective speaker or presenter.

☐☐☐☐ 47. I am able to use my computer for organizing my notes.

☐☐☐☐ 48. My interpersonal skills make it easy for me to participate in group activities.

☐☐☐☐ 49. I am almost always prepared for class.

☐☐☐☐ 50. I use my course *syllabus* to keep up with assignments.

Section Total: _____

Time management is essential to college, life, and career success.

☐☐☐☐ 51. I realize that time is a *resource* I must use efficiently and wisely.

☐☐☐☐ 52. I usually have no trouble making time for studying.

☐☐☐☐ 53. I almost always arrive on time for classes.

☐☐☐☐ 54. I hand in projects and assignments on time.

☐☐☐☐ 55. I rarely miss class for any reason.

☐☐☐☐ 56. I am aware of different types of schedules and how they can help me manage my time.

☐☐☐☐ 57. As a student athlete, or the friend of one, I know the challenges athletes face and how they can manage their time more effectively.

☐☐☐☐ 58. I know what causes *procrastination* and how to avoid it.

☐☐☐☐ 59. I have a positive attitude toward my courses and toward studying.

☐☐☐☐ 60. I understand the connection between time management and study environment.

Section Total: _____

Very Confident Fairly Confident Not Very Confident Not Confident

3   2   1   0   Attention and memory are linked.

☐☐☐☐   61. I am able to control both *internal distractions* and *external distractions*.

☐☐☐☐   62. I know how to find or create an appropriate study environment.

☐☐☐☐   63. I understand how having a regular time and place for study helps me focus my attention.

☐☐☐☐   64. Neither the instructor's style nor the subject matter interfere with my ability to pay attention.

☐☐☐☐   65. I understand how the mind processes information.

☐☐☐☐   66. I know what *selective attention* is.

☐☐☐☐   67. I know how *sensory memory*, *short-term memory*, and *long-term memory* differ.

☐☐☐☐   68. I know what causes forgetting and how to combat it.

☐☐☐☐   69. I understand the connection between active learning and memory.

☐☐☐☐   70. I use a variety of memory-enhancing techniques.

Section Total: _____

Know how to read and study from textbooks to maximize learning.

☐☐☐☐   71. I am able to tell what is important in a textbook chapter.

☐☐☐☐   72. I know how to use the common parts of textbooks and chapters.

☐☐☐☐   73. I have my own reading-study system, such as *SQ3R*, that I use consistently.

☐☐☐☐   74. I have no trouble maintaining interest in what I read.

☐☐☐☐   75. I use mapping and diagramming techniques to organize information.

☐☐☐☐   76. I know the purpose of graphics, and I know how to read and interpret them.

☐☐☐☐   77. I have a system for learning new words and terms.

☐☐☐☐   78. I use different strategies for learning the material in different courses or disciplines.

☐☐☐☐   79. I know how to *survey* websites to find the resources I need.

☐☐☐☐   80. I am *proactive* about studying by taking control of what I learn and how I learn it.

Section Total: _____

Very Confident	Fairly Confident	Not Very Confident	Not Confident	
3	**2**	**1**	**0**	**Be well prepared for tests to reduce anxiety and ensure success.**
☐	☐	☐	☐	81. When it comes to tests, I know what, when, and how to study.
☐	☐	☐	☐	82. I am almost always well prepared for a test.
☐	☐	☐	☐	83. I know when it is appropriate to use guessing strategies.
☐	☐	☐	☐	84. I am able to control my feelings and attention during tests.
☐	☐	☐	☐	85. I review my errors and learn from my mistakes.
☐	☐	☐	☐	86. I am good at taking several different types of tests.
☐	☐	☐	☐	87. I know what *test anxiety* is.
☐	☐	☐	☐	88. I know the common causes of test anxiety and how to eliminate them.
☐	☐	☐	☐	89. I understand how *positive self-talk* can build my confidence and reduce my anxiety.
☐	☐	☐	☐	90. I use my *self-management* skills to help me prepare for tests.

Section Total: _____

				Effective communication is your key to good interpersonal relationships and career success.
☐	☐	☐	☐	91. I have no trouble communicating with others.
☐	☐	☐	☐	92. I am a good speaker and presenter.
☐	☐	☐	☐	93. I am an active listener who uses different types of listening for different purposes.
☐	☐	☐	☐	94. I use communication technology in appropriate ways.
☐	☐	☐	☐	95. I can work effectively with others in small groups.
☐	☐	☐	☐	96. I am good at resolving conflict within a group.
☐	☐	☐	☐	97. I am usually able to manage my interpersonal relationships effectively.
☐	☐	☐	☐	98. I have no trouble gathering information from printed or online sources.
☐	☐	☐	☐	99. I know what *plagiarism* is, and I know how to avoid it.
☐	☐	☐	☐	100. I know how to plan, research, and write a paper.

Section Total: _____

Very Confident	Fairly Confident	Not Very Confident	Not Confident		
3	**2**	**1**	**0**		**Manage your life, health, and finances for a confident, successful future.**
☐	☐	☐	☐	101.	I have personal goals for my life in the future.
☐	☐	☐	☐	102.	I have already chosen a major or course of study.
☐	☐	☐	☐	103.	I have begun thinking about or have already chosen a career.
☐	☐	☐	☐	104.	I know what the essential skills are that employers expect.
☐	☐	☐	☐	105.	I am in control of my emotions.
☐	☐	☐	☐	106.	I know how to manage my diet and exercise to stay fit.
☐	☐	☐	☐	107.	I am not addicted to harmful substances or activities.
☐	☐	☐	☐	108.	I have found ways to manage stress.
☐	☐	☐	☐	109.	Through budgeting and living within my means, I am able to manage my finances.
☐	☐	☐	☐	110.	I use credit cards wisely and understand their advantages and disadvantages.

Section Total: _____

INTERPRETING YOUR SCORE AND CONFIDENCE INDEX

Now that you have completed the Skill Finder, transfer your *Section Totals* to Table 1, page xxvii. Table 1 lists the chapters in *The Confident Student*, Seventh Edition, that address the skills covered in each section. There are no good or bad scores. The reasons for calculating your score are to find out which skills need developing or improving and to calculate your Confidence Index.

Your Confidence Index (CI) is a number on a scale from 1 to 10 based on how confident you are about your skills as identified by this questionaire. Use your CI to help you determine which skills you already possess and which skills you need to develop. For example, take your section total for statements 1–10 from Table 1. This number will be somewhere between 0 and 30. Suppose your section total is 24. Find this number in the column labeled *Score Ranges* on Table 2. Read across to the second column where you will see a CI of 8. This high CI means that you already possess some background for the skills covered in Chapter 1. However, suppose your CI for section 1 is below 5. A CI in the lower ranges may indicate a lack of confidence or some unfamiliarity with the skills covered in Chapter 1. In the first case, you can build on your background to take your skills to a higher level. In the second case, you can use your new self-knowledge as motivation for developing new skills. Finding your CI for each section of the Skill Finder will give you a brief overview of the skills covered in *The Confident Student*, Seventh Edition, and will show you where you are in your skill development.

Calculate your overall CI by taking your grand total from Table 1 and using it to find your score range on Table 3. For example, if your grand total is 270, locate this number in the *Score Ranges* column and read across to find your CI of 8. An overall CI of 8 means that you may already possess a number of essential skills, which you can develop to even higher levels.

Whatever your Confidence Index, this book will help you build the skills you need to be successful in college and your career. Complete the Skill Finder again at the end of the course to see how much your CI has improved.

TABLE 1

Score and Correlation Chart

STATEMENTS BY NUMBER	YOUR TOTAL POINTS PER SECTION	CHAPTER WHERE SKILLS ARE COVERED
1–10		Chapter 1
11–20		Chapter 2
21–30		Chapters 3 and 7
31–40		Chapter 4
41–50		Chapter 5
51–60		Chapter 6
61–70		Chapter 8
71–80		Chapters 9 and 10
81–90		Chapter 11
91–100		Chapter 12
101–110		Chapters 13 and 14
Grand Total		

TABLE 2

Your Confidence Index per Section

SCORE RANGES	CONFIDENCE INDEX
29–30	10
26–28	9
23–25	8
20–22	7
17–19	6
14–16	5
11–13	4
8–10	3
5–7	2
2–4	1
0–1	−1

TABLE 3

Your Overall Confidence Index

SCORE RANGES	CONFIDENCE INDEX
330	10
297–329	9
264–296	8
231–263	7
198–230	6
165–197	5
132–164	4
99–131	3
66–98	2
33–65	1
0–32	−1

1 Becoming a Confident Student

i love images(RF)/Jupiter images

This chapter encourages you to:

- Use honest self-assessment to make the choices that will help you plan for a successful academic future.

- Form a network of helpful people who will support your academic and career goals.

- Reach out to all students in a spirit of cooperation, understanding, and acceptance.

- Use the strategies that will keep your mind active and engaged in the process of learning.

Confident students possess traits and qualities that anyone can develop. This chapter focuses on **flexibility**— the willingness to adapt to changing circumstances.

What is it like to begin a new term in college, or take on a new job, free from self-doubt and certain that you will succeed? How does it feel to enter a class on the first day, believing that good grades are within your reach? What if you had the confidence in your skills to tackle any assignment, without fear of failure? *The fact is that you, or anyone, can achieve this level of confidence.*

Confidence comes from accomplishment, one successfully completed task at a time. Success is not a chance occurrence but is the result of your choices and actions. You can choose your future by using your college's resources and **technology**, by developing your interpersonal skills, and by becoming an active learner.

Chapter 1 will get you started on your journey toward becoming a confident student. Let's begin by working on your ability to be flexible. Do you have the flexibility to replace old study habits with new, more successful, strategies? Read the *Confidence Builder* to get started.

Technology in the workplace consists of appropriate tools for specific tasks, their management, and their use.

CONFIDENCE BUILDER

How Flexible Are You?

Flexibility is one of the key traits of a confident student. Learning to be flexible in your daily activities prepares you to meet life's greater challenges.

Do you hold on to cherished opinions, even in the face of conflicting evidence? Do your first impressions of people remain largely unchanged, even after you get to know them? How do you handle broken relationships, changes in plans, or personal and financial setbacks? If you have difficulty adapting to change, then much of your life—whether at college, at work, or at home—is probably filled with stress. Change, according to many experts, is one of life's greatest sources of stress. People who are inflexible in their beliefs, attitudes, and plans set themselves up for disappointment, discomfort, and distress.

The way to adapt to change is to be flexible. Flexibility is a trait employers often cite as being a valuable personal skill, and it is one you can develop. What are some of the situations at college that call for flexibility? You painstakingly make out a schedule, only to find out that one of your courses is closed. Your roommate is a day person; you are a night person. You spend hours studying for a test, you are motivated and ready to perform, and then your instructor postpones the exam until next week. How can you adapt to day-to-day changes such as these that can make your life miserable if you let them? How can you become more flexible? The following three tips may help.

Watch your attitude. Remember that you are not perfect, and neither is anyone else. Life does not always proceed according to schedule. It isn't the end of the world if things don't go as planned. Learn to shrug instead of vent. Make room in your schedule for unplanned circumstances.

Have a contingency plan. You can't plan for all emergencies or temporary setbacks, but you *can* anticipate some changes. For example, have alternatives in mind when you select courses. Expect that in any situation where people live together, conflicts will arise. Remind yourself to stay calm, talk things over, and be willing to compromise. When you make a schedule, set a goal, or plan for a future event, try to build into your plans some alternatives in case things don't work out.

Keep an open mind. Change has its good points. Change keeps you from getting in a rut. Change also opens up possibilities you may not have previously had a reason to consider. Above all, successfully adapting to change helps you grow and makes it easier for you to accept the next change that comes along.

College is a great place to loosen up rigid ways of thinking and behaving in order to become a more flexible person. The challenges that a college education offers, the diverse learning community, and the opportunity to expand your mind will enable you to meet the even greater challenges that lie ahead.

Follow Up: To explore this topic further, visit *The Confident Student* premium website for an online search activity about the value of flexibility.

Choose Success and Plan for It

• Use honest self-assessment to make the choices that will help you plan for a successful academic future.

College is about the future. College prepares you for the rest of your life and for lifelong learning. This is why your college graduation is called a *commencement*, or beginning. Whether you are a first-time college student or an adult learner, your graduation will mark the beginning of a lifetime of challenges that may require additional learning and the development of new skills. College is also about learning how to interact with people from different backgrounds and cultures. Through this interaction, you will develop the interpersonal and communication skills essential to success in whatever future awaits you.

What makes college such a positive experience is its insistence that you can leave old habits and unproductive behaviors behind and develop new strategies to help you achieve your academic, career, and life goals. Plan now for future success by taking three steps: 1) Use self-assessment to build confidence, 2) define your goals, and 3) think ahead to a major and career. Awareness Check 1.1 that follows will help you practice your self assessment skills.

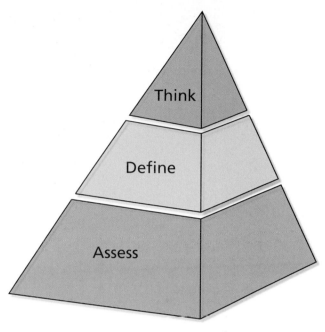

Three Steps to Success

Awareness CHECK 1.1

Are You Ready for College Success?

Check *definitely true* (column A, 3 points), *somewhat true* (column B, 2 points), or *not at all true* (column C, 1 point) to explain how each statement applies to you.

A	B	C	
☐	☐	☐	1. I already think of myself as a confident student.
☐	☐	☐	2. I have selected a major, and I have a career goal in mind.
☐	☐	☐	3. I know what an academic support group is, and I use one.
☐	☐	☐	4. I use email and other technology to enhance learning and study.
☐	☐	☐	5. I embrace diversity and respect others' values that differ from my own.
☐	☐	☐	6. I know what services my college offers and where to find them.
☐	☐	☐	7. I am well informed on campus, local, and world events.
☐	☐	☐	8. I have and use my college catalog and other campus publications.
☐	☐	☐	9. I do not hesitate to ask questions in class or to find out what I need to know.
☐	☐	☐	10. As a student, I am involved in learning and take an active role in class.

A score of 25–30 means you are on your way toward achieving academic success. A score of 15–24 shows some skill strengths and some weaknesses. If your total is 1–14, your confidence will grow as you develop skills and achieve success. Whatever your score, the Skill Finder preceding this chapter or online will help you determine your confidence index as related to the skills covered in The Confident Student.

Use Self-Assessment to Build Confidence

Self-assessment is the process of testing, checking, or evaluating your behavior and accomplishments.

A **self-assessment** is an evaluation of your skills, abilities, experience, values, or other traits or qualities. When you self-assess, you do a mental test or check of your behavior or accomplishments. This textbook encourages self-assessment through the following features:

▼ *Skill Finder*, a self-test printed near the front of your textbook and on *The Confident Student* premium website, will help you assess your strengths and weaknesses as a college student. Take the Skill Finder test if you have not already done so. It will give you a preview of the important topics covered in this book. As you answer the questions, you will discover what you already know about these topics. At the end of your course, you can take the test again to assess what you have learned.

▼ *Awareness Checks* in every chapter are self-assessment tools that help you assess your knowledge about upcoming chapter concepts.

▼ *Your Reflections* near the end of every chapter encourages you to think about or reflect on what you have learned so that you can integrate the new knowledge within your existing mental framework.

▼ *Guided Chapter Review* at the end of each chapter is both a review of the chapter and a self-assessment tool.

Many students enter college feeling insecure because of past failures or difficulties. As a result, they may tend to underestimate the worth of the knowledge and experience that they have accumulated. Many previous experiences bring you to college—not only your academic skills but also jobs you've held, places where you've lived or traveled, your interests, your talents, and even your military experience. Your background provides the framework on which to build new skills and integrate new knowledge. Make your background work for you by continually trying to relate what you are learning to what you already know. Any connection you can make to your prior knowledge will serve as a confidence builder.

You can develop the personal traits that confident students share. Figure 1.1 on page 5 lists fourteen traits of confident students, and each chapter of this book focuses on one of those traits.

Concept Check 1.1

Take a look at Figure 1.1. Do you have a trait or quality that is not listed? If so, what is your trait, and how does it build your confidence?

Define Your Goals

Goal means "outcome" or "objective," a desired end that you will work to achieve.

A **goal** is a desired outcome that you will work to achieve. Goals can be personal, academic, or career related. Some students say they can't set goals because goals are "too restricting" or because "I might decide to do something else." Unfortunately, if you do not set goals, your life may move along according to whim—often someone else's. If you want to stay in charge of your life, set goals, make plans to achieve them, and follow through. A goal is an objective. The plan you make for reaching that goal is a commitment. Commitments give our lives meaning. A goal will keep you focused on the future and will build your confidence by helping you to maintain a positive outlook. Throughout this text, and especially in Chapter 4, *Setting Goals and Solving Problems*, we will discuss goal setting in greater detail.

Think Ahead to a Major or Career

Major refers to an academic discipline, field of study, or certification program such as English, nursing, or electrical engineering.

There is no better way to begin setting goals than to choose a **major**, or field of study. Once you have chosen a major, you can begin to set long-term and short-term goals that will help you complete your program and earn a degree. Of course, you might say, "I'm not ready to select a major," and perhaps you need time to become

FIGURE 1.1

Are You a Confident Student?

Traits of Confident Students	Descriptions	Chapter Featured In
Flexible	You have an open mind and are able to adapt to changing circumstances.	Chapter 1
Self-motivated	You know what you want and will strive to accomplish your goals.	Chapter 2
Intellectual risk taker	You think for yourself, both critically and creatively.	Chapter 3
Enthusiastic	You have a positive attitude, are optimistic, hopeful, and energetic.	Chapter 4
Responsible	You own your actions, accept the consequences, and don't make excuses.	Chapter 5
Self-managed	You have the self-discipline to prioritize tasks and meet obligations.	Chapter 6
Involved	You are an active learner who understands that reading and learning are processes that you can control.	Chapter 7
Focused	You know how to focus your attention on a task and maintain concentration until the job is done.	Chapter 8
Committed	You have pledged your time and effort to learn and will do what it takes to improve your performance.	Chapter 9
Pragmatic	You take a practical approach to studying that involves trying new strategies to see what works.	Chapter 10
Persistent	You never give up, and you stay focused on your goals despite setbacks.	Chapter 11
Empathetic	You are a good communicator who can identify with the situations, feelings, and motives of others.	Chapter 12
Emotionally intelligent	You control your impulses rather than allowing your feelings to control you.	Chapter 13
Future oriented	You look toward the future with the confidence that comes from your successes and achievements.	Chapter 14

www.cengage.com/success/Kanar/Confident7e

adjusted to college life before making this decision. On the other hand, you might already have a major or career goal in mind. In either case, now is the time to think about your future—where you want to live, how much money you will need to support the life you want, and the career choices that will generate your desired level of income.

Selecting a major gives purpose to your college experience and keeps you focused on the future. Your major will prepare you for a career. How is a major different from a career? Remember that a major is a program or course of study in a specific field, leading toward a degree. A **career** is your life's work—your chosen profession or occupation. For example, if your major is psychology, the career you choose might be *social worker*. A major may lead to any number of different careers. To help you think ahead to a major or career, visit your college's career center, where you can explore your options. A career counselor can suggest surveys or assessments you can take to find out which jobs or careers are best for you, based on your interests and skills. Chapters 4 and 14 provide more detailed information about major selection and career goals, but for now, let's talk about your dreams.

Career refers to a profession or occupation and also to the general progress of your working life.

When you were a child, what did you want to be when you grew up: a firefighter, a teacher, a musician, a veterinarian? Has your dream changed now that you are in college? Think about your dream occupation—both then and now—and what it says about you. For example, do you crave excitement, want to travel to distant places, feel a need to express yourself through music or art? Would you prefer to work indoors or outdoors? Do you like doing work at a desk by yourself, or do you prefer interacting with others? Your values and preferences are the keys to who you are, and they can help you open the door to your dream major or career.

As people grow and become aware of real-world limitations, they may abandon their dreams for more realistic goals, yet the dream and reality may coincide. Jay dreamed of becoming a professional golfer but decided instead to pursue a career in golf course management. Rosa had always dreamed of a career in nursing but chose physical therapy when she decided that this career was more suited to her skills and preferences. These students did not give up their dreams; they used their dreams to shape their futures.

As you think ahead to a major or career, here are some tips that may help get you off to a good start:

▼ Chart your academic course. Meet with your advisor, who will help you to come up with an academic plan, select the right courses, and make sure you meet all requirements.

▼ Assess your interests and values to find a major or career that is right for you. A major or career should allow you to take advantage of your strengths and should reflect what you like doing and what is important to you.

▼ Talk to students whose majors you are interested in. Ask them about their courses and what their career plans are. Talk to people who are already working in a career you like. Find out what they do, what their day is like, and how they prepared themselves for that job.

▼ Make sure that you choose a major for the right reasons. The work you do should reflect what you want out of life rather than fulfill what someone else wants for you. Whether you come from a family of lawyers or one of accountants, do not feel that you have to carry on that tradition if it is not something that you would enjoy doing.

▼ Consider a certificate program in a field such as hospitality management, physical therapy, graphic design, etc. Or, if you cannot decide on a major, consider getting an AA (associate of arts) degree that will allow you to take general education courses to apply to a major when you decide what you want to do.

EXERCISE 1.1   Values, Majors, and Careers

A MAJOR OR CAREER CHOICE should reflect your values. To help you think about the connection between values and careers, try this exercise with a partner. Fill out the following chart. In the first column, two common values are listed, followed by spaces for you to list your own values. For each value listed, write a major in the second column that reflects the value. In the third column, list a career or occupation for which the major listed in the second column would prepare you. To help you get started, a portion of the chart is completed for you.

Column I PERSONAL VALUES	Column II MAJORS	Column III CAREERS
1a. creating wealth	1b. business	1c. financial advisor
2a. helping families	2b.	2c. social worker
3a.	3b. criminal justice	3c.
4a.	4b. fine arts	4c.
5a.	5b.	5c. coach of a high school team

Form an Academic Support Group

• Form a network of helpful people who will support your academic and career goals.

In a community of learners, the primary function of each faculty member, administrator, employee, and department is *to help you reach your goals*. Everyone in your college community hopes that you will succeed. Therefore, your college is rich in resources that can guide your progress. For example, people are an important resource. If you have not already done so, form a **support group**: a network of people to whom you can turn for advice, answers to questions, or a boost in confidence.

Support group refers to a network of people you can rely on for advice and help.

Faculty

Your instructors are in the best position to advise you concerning all matters related to their classes. If you are having difficulty in a course, for example, don't postpone getting help or hope that your problem will go away. Make an appointment with your instructor as soon as possible.

Find an instructor with whom you are especially comfortable and turn to this person when you need advice. If your instructor is unable to answer one of your questions or to suggest ways to solve a problem, he or she can direct you to another person or office where help is available.

Advisors and Counselors

Academic advisors and career counselors are professionals who address students' academic and personal needs, such as choosing a major, selecting courses, preparing course schedules, or finding help for a special problem like test anxiety.

Counselors and advisors know your college's rules and requirements. They may provide special services to students with unique needs, such as international students, adult learners, minority students, students with disabilities, and transfer students. Because department names and professional titles differ from campus to campus, check your catalog, campus directory, or college website to learn where the services you need are provided.

Your instructors want you to succeed in their courses. They can answer questions about classroom topics, assignments, and tests, and they can give you sound advice about where to seek extra help if you need it.

Creatas Images(RF)/Jupiter Images

Mentors

Mentor refers to a person who acts as an ally, taking a personal interest in you.

A **mentor** is an ally, a friend, someone who takes a personal and professional interest in you. On many college campuses today, instructors serve as mentors to students. Mentors may offer tips on how to study, take tests, and reduce stress. They may also help students plan their schedules for the following term.

The relationship between student and mentor serves several purposes. It gives the student a contact person on campus to turn to for advice, for help in solving a problem, or for specific suggestions on how to meet course requirements. Mentors and instructors often work together to help students achieve their goals.

Many students complain that the close relationships they enjoyed with faculty in high school are not available in college. Mentoring programs may be one way to fill the gap. Such programs operate differently from campus to campus, but the goal of any mentoring program is the same: to help students choose success. To find out whether there is a mentoring program on your campus, call the admissions office.

EXERCISE 1.2   My Support Group

HAVING A SUPPORT GROUP TO turn to when you need information, the answer to a question, help with a problem, or a boost in confidence makes adjusting to college easier. Write the names, addresses, and phone numbers of several people in your support group on the following chart. Post the chart in a handy place. If you need space for more support group members, go to *The Confident Student* premium website to download additional copies of the chart.

MY SUPPORT GROUP

	Phone number	**Address/office**	**Email address**
Family members			
1.			
2.			

continued

	Phone number	Address/office	Email address
Instructors			
1.			
2.			
Classmates			
1.			
2.			
Advisor, coach, or other person			
1.			
2.			

Extend Your Support Group

Each subject area department—such as English or math—may have special requirements that pertain only to that discipline. Department heads can answer your questions about requirements, course offerings, and the availability of sections. They can also direct you to an instructor's office or mailbox, and they can provide instructors' office phone numbers or email addresses.

Other helpful people include your resident advisor if you live on campus, your coach if you are an athlete, or your club and organization sponsors. All these people share your interests and can help you form networks with others as you engage in campus life.

Don't underestimate the value of making friends with other students. Find a contact person in each class with whom you can exchange personal information in case one of you is absent. Your new friends may become your partners in a study group or the people you rely on when you need a ride or other favor.

Your academic support group might include an advisor, an instructor, a department head or secretary, a coach or club sponsor, and a friend in each class. Their role is a supporting one. They are available when you need them because, in a community of learners, you are not alone.

Computer CONFIDENCE

Tips for Effective Online Communication

The communication skills of reading and writing are among those that your future employers will value most highly. College is a great place to hone your communication skills—not only through classroom participation but also through the use of email, course management systems, and the Internet.

In a college setting, email is useful for sharing notes and materials with classmates, for collaborating with students on other campuses, and for communicating with your instructor. Through most

college websites, you will be able to contact faculty and staff. Some faculty may post information about office hours and assignments online. In fact, some faculty may require you to communicate with them only via email. Your college website may allow you to access your grades, register, and pay fees online. Try these tips for more effective online communication:

- Choose an email address that identifies you and creates a good impression. Your name is the

continued

simplest choice, with some variation such as last name plus initial or your full name. Most colleges also provide personal email addresses for their enrolled students. Avoid the use of cute names such as "Funnygirl" or "FastMax," or reserve them for casual communication with friends. First impressions are important, and choosing a more professional email address shows that you are serious about your work and your goals. Keep your messages brief and to the point. Messages that are too long or wordy waste time—both yours and the reader's.

- Be aware of your reader and adjust your tone accordingly. Is your message business or personal? Your tone will be more casual for a personal message than for a business communication and more formal when writing to an instructor than when writing to a friend.

- Observe rules of *online etiquette* (polite communication). Because online writing is spontaneous—messages and responses can be transmitted instantly—you may have a tendency to write without thinking, which can result in miscommunication. Think before you write, and choose words carefully. Do not put anything in writing that you would not say in person. When in doubt, wait a while before sending a message so that you can review it and make changes as needed. Check *The Confident Student* premium website for more expanded coverage of rules for writing online. For email, *stick to simple typing.* Avoid using features like different fonts. These may not translate well and could cause confusion. For assignments and projects submitted as email attachments, be sure that the software you use is compatible with whatever your instructor uses.

- Check messages regularly and answer in a timely fashion. Especially if you are communicating with an instructor or taking a course online, you wouldn't want to miss an essential piece of information or a deadline.

- Treat important email messages as you would treat an academic assignment. In other words, write a rough draft. Use the "save as draft" or other command (depending on your program) before clicking "send." This will give you time to think about, edit, and revise your message before you send it. Writing a draft and waiting a while to revise and send it may prevent you from saying

something that you will regret—especially if you are angry.

- Although symbols and shorthand are appropriate in text messaging to your friends, they are not appropriate in more formal situations such as emailing an instructor. Your instructors expect you to communicate with them in a professional way—such as you would with an employer—that demonstrates your command of ideas and language. Therefore, use Standard English and spelling when writing to your instructors.

Now apply what you have learned about effective online communication. Begin by asking yourself which one of your courses is giving you the most difficulty. To build your confidence in this course, establish a good relationship with the instructor via email. Write a brief message that identifies you, explains why you are taking the course, and says what is causing your difficulty. Ask your instructor for a suggestion, and then end your message by thanking the instructor for his or her time. Take notes on the lines provided below so that you don't forget anything.

1. Your name, course, and section number:

   _____

   _____

   _____

2. Your major or career goal:

   _____

   _____

   _____

3. Why you are taking the course and what you hope to get out of it:

   _____

   _____

   _____

4. What is giving you trouble in the course:

   _____

   _____

   _____

Embrace Diversity

- Reach out to all students in a spirit of cooperation, understanding, and acceptance.

The composition of the U.S. population has been undergoing rapid change for the last decade. The Bureau of the Census projects that within a few years, minority groups collectively will become the new majority. It is important to remember that the contributions of diverse people have enriched American culture and made us the nation we are today. Because you will live and work in an increasingly diverse society, it is important that you take the opportunities college provides to embrace all students and do your part to break down the barriers that divide people.

Your Diverse Campus

Diversity means variety, pure and simple. Diversity on campus—and in society at large—refers to the variety of races, ethnic groups, cultures, religions, sexual orientations, nationalities, and other constituencies and perspectives that are represented. Colleges have responded to student diversity by offering services and opportunities to meet a variety of needs. Moreover, diversity has many benefits. Exposure to different customs and ways of thinking challenges your ideas and broadens your worldview. Because your campus is a small slice of our larger society, it provides you with an opportunity to hone your interpersonal skills and to develop intercultural communication skills that will prepare you for a career in an increasingly diverse workplace.

Creating a learning environment where all are treated with respect and where all are free to pursue their educational goals is everyone's responsibility. Do your part by being open to ideas and customs that may differ from your own. If you harbor any stereotypical thinking that prevents cross-cultural communication, now is the time to let it go. Look around you at your classmates and instructors. They are individuals—first. Complete Exercise 1.3 to help you explore your feelings and thoughts about diversity.

Embrace diversity by reaching out to others in a spirit of friendship and community. Make all students feel welcome, just as you want to be welcomed. Accept others' differences, listen without being critical, and establish friendships based on shared interests and values. As you form your support group, think of others' differences not as barriers to communication but as bridges to understanding. Let your support group ring with the harmony of different voices.

> **Diversity** means "variety" and refers to the racial, ethnic, cultural, and other differences among people.

> **Concept Check 1.2**
>
> How do you respond to diversity? Try making an effort to meet someone new in each class. What are your similarities and differences? What can you learn from each other?

EXERCISE 1.3   Self-Assessment on Diversity and Identity

WHAT ARE YOUR ATTITUDES TOWARD the different racial, ethnic, cultural, or other groups that make up your campus? What are your thoughts about your own identity? Complete the following self-assessment by answering the questions below in writing. Then be prepared to share your comments in a class discussion.

1. **What is your racial, ethnic, cultural, or other identity, and what makes you proud of your heritage?**

_____

_____

2. **How influential were your family, teachers, and friends in forming your early opinions about members of other racial, ethnic, or cultural groups? What were some of these opinions?**

_____

_____

continued

3. **What advantages or disadvantages do you find in being a member of your specific racial, ethnic, or cultural group? What is one thing you wish others understood or appreciated about you?**

_____

_____

4. **What is one of the things that can make you comfortable or uncomfortable when being in situations that involve people from diverse backgrounds?**

_____

_____

5. **What assumptions or attitudes, either positive or negative, do you think people from different racial, ethnic, cultural, or other groups have about you or the members of your group?**

_____

_____

Diverse Students, Needs, and Services

Your college probably offers a number of programs, services, and interest groups that serve the needs of a diverse student population. On some campuses, women's groups, international student organizations, lesbian and gay men's coalitions, and religion-based student associations provide a place to socialize and conduct special-interest activities.

Although socializing with others like yourself is important, it is equally important to reach out to those who differ. Getting involved in extracurricular activities can help you find new friends who share your interests. Joining a group that appeals to students interested in an art such as dance, drama, or music—or in a career such as engineering or teaching—can serve as a starting point for getting involved in campus life.

Service learning provides another way to meet and interact with people from different cultures and backgrounds. This teaching method integrates classroom activities with community service. If you have difficulty making the first move to meet someone of another culture, service learning may provide the perfect opportunity. Together, you and your classmates will be engaged in helping others and improving your community. Out of this interaction you may forge a friendship, discover common interests, and gain insight into each other's values and viewpoints. If service learning is not an option on your campus, you can still get involved in organizations like Habitat for Humanity, which builds houses for low-income families who could not otherwise afford their own homes, or you can work as a hospital volunteer. Your participation in student government, campus organizations, or community service activities can provide additional opportunities for you to interact with others from diverse backgrounds.

Why should you embrace diversity, and what are the advantages of becoming multiculturally aware? Here are a few reasons:

▼ As your understanding of others' backgrounds and motives increases, you will be more likely to treat them as individuals than as faceless members of a group.

▼ As you interact with people whose beliefs and traditions are different from yours, you will develop the confidence to meet new people and face unfamiliar situations.

▼ You will develop respect for others and be able to put aside false assumptions based on prejudice and stereotypes.

▶ Your campus is a small slice of American life. What you learn about interacting with others here will serve you well in a diverse workplace.

Adult Learners

Adult students, twenty-five and older, make up a significant number of the student body on any campus. Many have stories like this woman's:

> *I am twenty-seven and a divorced mother of two children. I'm continuing my education because I want a better life for my family. I have to work part-time, keep up with my studies, and make time for my kids—all of which is much harder than I ever thought it could be. At night I'm so tired that I'm barely able to get dinner on the table. After helping my boys with their homework and getting them into bed, I'm often too exhausted to study. Time management is my biggest problem. At times I've felt like giving up—especially at first because I felt out of place among all the younger students. But I've made friends and am now in a study group that is helping me become more organized. We meet at my house, which is good for me.*

Adult learners are a welcome group on any campus for several important reasons. First of all, adult learners bring with them knowledge and skills that enrich the college experience for everyone. Second, most people change jobs or careers two or more times during their lives and seek additional skills or training. Moreover, learning does not end at graduation—it is a lifelong process. Despite such current positive views about adult learners, these students often enter college feeling out of place, wondering whether they will be able to catch up and keep up. Adult learners have jobs and families and may feel pressured as they add course requirements to their already full calendars. Embracing diversity means learning from each other's unique experiences and remembering that all students, no matter what their ages, face similar problems of adjustment in college.

Students with Disabilities

Among the many types of students with disabilities that you may encounter on your college campus are individuals with physical disabilities and learning disabilities. Physical disabilities are more apparent and include such things as blindness or paralysis. Learning disabilities are not so easy to recognize and may hinder students' speaking, listening, writing, or other academic skills. Although students with learning disabilities may need help with specific skills and tasks, they are often highly intelligent and creative and can offer a great deal to their learning community. Most students with learning disabilities have developed coping strategies but may still need help with taking notes or getting to and from class; or they may require extra test-taking or writing time—accommodations that all colleges now provide. If you have any kind of disability, take the initiative to find out where on campus these special services are offered, and make your requests known. Instructors will not know what you need unless you ask for it.

Offer students with disabilities your friendship and support. Here are four ways you can help:

1. Aisles between bookshelves in the library may be too narrow to accommodate a wheelchair. A student may need help gaining access to books and other materials.

2. In class discussions, speak slowly enough so that students who find it physically difficult to take notes fast will be able to keep up.

3. When making a presentation, make sure that any handouts or graphics you provide are accessible to the visually impaired.

4. Speak up so that the hearing impaired can participate in discussions.

Remember that students with disabilities like to be as self-sufficient as they can. If you see that a student is struggling with a door or a book bag, do not assume that your help is required. Instead, ask if you can help, and let the student tell you what he or she needs. Try to be open-minded and nonjudgmental about individuals who may look, act, or speak differently as a result of their disabilities.

CRITICAL THINKING

Diversity on Your Campus

Exercise Overview

What is your college doing to embrace diversity? This exercise will help you determine what policies and programs your college has in place to address the needs of a diverse student population.

Exercise Background

Today's campus is more diverse than ever. The percentage of the campus population that each racial, ethnic, or other group comprises varies with both the college and the region of the country in which it is located. How a college responds to diversity can affect a student's comfort level and academic success either positively or negatively.

Exercise Task

Research and answer the following questions by finding relevant printed materials such as your college catalog or student handbook, by interviewing the appropriate people on campus, or by browsing your college's website for official policies or statements about diversity or a code of conduct. Your instructor or a librarian can suggest resources and ways to begin your search. Share your answers orally or in writing, as your instructor directs.

1. Assess the diversity on your campus. What ethnic, racial, international, or other kinds of groups are represented? What percentage of the students, faculty, administration, and staff does each group comprise?
2. What courses that address diversity issues are offered?
3. Is diversity mentioned in your college's mission statement? If so, how?
4. What college policies or procedures are designed to meet the needs of a diverse student population?
5. To what extent does your college promote interaction among students from diverse backgrounds?
6. Do you find any discrepancies between your college's policy on diversity and its actual practice? If so, explain the discrepancies.
7. Based on the facts you have found, what conclusions can you draw about your college's commitment to diversity? For example, how does diversity benefit your campus? Do all students feel welcome? What, if anything, should be done to improve relations among the diverse groups on your campus?

Share your answers in class discussion or in writing, as your instructor directs.

International Students

Even on a campus that embraces diversity, the temptation may be great for international students to restrict their social interaction to those who speak their native language. Many of these students go home to families that also do not speak English. The time that they spend in class may be the only opportunity they have to use English. It is crucial for these students to make friends and interact with native speakers. Therefore, if you are an international student, seek opportunities to practice your English skills. Participate in class discussions. Join clubs or organizations in which you will meet native speakers who share your interests.

If you are new to the United States, you may find that certain expectations of college students may not be consistent with your own values. For example, expectations about punctuality and classroom behavior may differ from what you were accustomed to in your native country. Here are some tips to build your confidence:

▼ In class, you are expected to do your own work. Sharing answers on a test or getting someone else to write your paper is considered cheating. For more information on academic honesty, see Chapter 5.

▼ When working in a group, you are expected to make your own contribution, and grades for group work are often assigned individually.

▼ Your instructors expect you to think for yourself and may even encourage you to challenge their authority. However, some instructors may not take this view. In class discussion, observe how other students respond to the instructor and notice how their comments are received. Then act accordingly.

▼ Being on time to class is not only valued but required. Some instructors punish lateness with grade reductions. Although you may come from a culture that values time and punctuality differently, find out what your instructor expects and adapt to those requirements.

If you are an American student, reach out to the international students in your classes. Take the initiative to collaborate with them in class activities. Make eye contact with them in class discussion. Invite them to join you and your friends at lunch or to join your study group after class.

One of the reasons for attending college is to broaden your perspective by exposing you to new ideas as well as to new people.

David Young-Wolff/Alamy

Students with Diverse Sexual Orientations

Many heterosexuals react negatively toward gays and lesbians because of learned stereotypes that act as barriers to communication and obscure the truth. For one thing, you cannot determine a person's sexual orientation based on his or her outward appearance. Within the lesbian and gay community—as in any community—a variety of values, behaviors, and personality traits are represented. Finally, gay and lesbian students—like most students—just want to make friends, pursue their educational goals, find meaningful work after college, and build lasting relationships. The LGBTA (Lesbian, Gay, Bisexual, and Transgendered Alliance) is active on some campuses and provides a meeting place for these students.

Any student can choose success. No matter what your age or background is and no matter what your academic performance has been, college offers a new beginning. Every chapter in this book contains strategies that will help you build the confidence and skills needed to achieve your goals.

Diversity also refers to ideas as well as to people. One of the reasons for attending college is to broaden your perspective by exposing you to new ideas as well as to new people. How diverse is your circle of friends? Do you have some friends of different races, ethnicities, or cultures? Do some of your friends have religious beliefs or political views that are different from yours? Take Awareness Check 1.2 to assess your friendships.

Awareness CHECK 1.2

Who Are Your Friends?

Listed below are several categories of people. Beside each category, check the column that best expresses your viewpoint. Column A: *I have a friend or an acquaintance in this category.* **Column B:** *I don't have a friend in this category but would welcome one.* **Column C:** *I would not be comfortable having a friend in this category.* **When you have finished, read the analysis that follows.**

A B C

☐ ☐ ☐   1. African American

☐ ☐ ☐   2. Asian or Asian American

☐ ☐ ☐   3. Biracial or multiracial

☐ ☐ ☐   4. European American

☐ ☐ ☐   5. Hispanic or Latin American

☐ ☐ ☐   6. Native American

☐ ☐ ☐   7. Catholic or other Christian

☐ ☐ ☐   8. Muslim

☐ ☐ ☐   9. Jewish

☐ ☐ ☐   10. other religion

continued

☐ ☐ ☐   11. Democrat

☐ ☐ ☐   12. Republican

☐ ☐ ☐   13. Independent

☐ ☐ ☐   14. gay or lesbian

☐ ☐ ☐   15. bisexual

☐ ☐ ☐   16. transgendered

☐ ☐ ☐   17. senior citizen

☐ ☐ ☐   18. people with disabilities

Obviously, there are no right or wrong responses to this list. For any categories that you checked C, ask yourself why you feel the way you do. What can you do to overcome your reservations and broaden your perspective? Share your views in a class discussion.

Be an Active Learner

- Use strategies that will keep your mind active and engaged in the process of learning.

Some students sit passively in a lecture or class discussion, letting their minds wander, not taking notes, and never asking questions. Later, they wonder why they can't remember what the lecture or discussion was about. The key to getting more out of class, and out of your college experience as a whole, is your active engagement in the process. An **active learner** is one who gets involved by taking notes, asking questions, participating in discussions, and joining clubs and organizations—someone who pays attention and knows what is going on in class and on campus. Your active involvement makes you a better informed and more confident student.

> **Active learner**, opposite of *passive learner*, refers to a person who is both aware of and involved in the process of learning.

All of the strategies explained in the chapters of this book promote active learning. This section explains several things that you can do right now to become an active learner: Know where to find help, inform yourself, get involved, and ask questions with confidence.

Know Where to Find Help

It is up to you to seek the help you need, when you need it. For example, if you have a learning disability or a health problem that needs special attention, you should inform your instructors so that they can help you get whatever assistance you might require.

Your campus offers a variety of resources to help you succeed. Although every college is different, you can probably find on your campus the offices and services listed in Figure 1.2. Check your college catalog, campus directory, or website for specific listings.

Inform Yourself

One way to become an active learner is to read your college's publications. Most colleges publish a catalog, newspaper, or student bulletin, and these contain a wealth of information that can keep you informed and involved in campus life.

The *college catalog* lists important dates, deadlines, fee payment schedules, and course offerings by discipline. Your *college newspaper* contains information of interest to the college community, along with articles that report on local, national, and world events from a

FIGURE 1.2

Know Your Way around Campus

OFFICES/CENTERS	SERVICES THEY PROVIDE
Registrar's Office	Records grades, issues transcripts, answers questions about graduation requirements, credits, and other related matters
Career Center	Offers career counseling, career-related interest and skill assessment, job placement services, recruitment programs
Academic Advising and Counseling Office	Provides academic advising and counseling, help with course selection, planning, and scheduling
Financial Aid Office	Handles loan and scholarship applications, work/study grants, campus employment, fees, fines, and payments
Library/Media Center	Provides print and online resources and other media and technology for students' and instructors' use
Tutorial Center	Trains and provides student tutors in a variety of subjects and may or may not charge fees
Learning Lab/Center	Offers materials and programs for independent or course-related work in skill development
Student Health Services	May provide limited or emergency health care or refer students to appropriate agencies
Computer Lab	May allow students to schedule time for online course activities and other tasks

EXERCISE 1.4   Using Your College Catalog

USE YOUR COLLEGE CATALOG (online or hard copy) to find the answers to the following questions, noting the page number where you found each answer. *Hint:* Use the contents and index to help you find the topics each question covers.

1.   **How many credits are required for graduation?**

    _____

2.   **What degrees are offered?**

    _____

3.   **What GPA (grade point average) must you maintain in order to avoid being placed on probation?**

    _____

4.   **Does your college offer a grade of I (incomplete)?**

    _____

continued

5. **What happens if you don't make up an incomplete grade?**

_____

6. **Is class attendance required? Is there an attendance policy stated in the catalog?**

_____

7. **What are the degrees held and colleges attended by one of your instructors?**

_____

8. **Where do you go to get a campus parking permit?**

_____

9. **What courses are all students required to take?**

_____

10. **On what dates are final exams given?**

_____

11. **When does the next registration period begin?**

_____

12. **What are the number and title of a reading course offered?**

_____

13. **How many math courses are all students required to take?**

_____

14. **What are two clubs or organizations you can join?**

_____

15. **What is the college president's name?**

_____

student's perspective. Your student government association may sponsor a _student bulletin_ that informs you of campus activities or a _student handbook_ that summarizes college policies and regulations in plain language. Bulletin boards and kiosks may display flyers advertising various services and upcoming events. By regularly checking your college's publications, you will become more knowledgeable about your campus and its culture.

As an active learner, also pay attention to what is going on in the surrounding community and the world. Keep informed by regularly reading a newspaper and other periodicals. Television news and websites are additional sources of information. Make a point of getting your news from a variety of sources so that you are exposed to a wide range of opinions. Keeping up with current events helps you build background, adding to your knowledge framework.

Get Involved

Active learning takes place in a social setting as well as an academic one. One of the important outcomes of a college education is that it provides opportunities for you to work cooperatively and interact socially with a diverse group of people. Through interaction with others, you may find new interests and develop communication skills and relationships that will help you build an impressive résumé. However, this will happen only if you take the initiative to participate in campus activities, events, and organizations.

A word about *Greek organizations*: As do all other organizations, fraternities and sororities have advantages and disadvantages. They can be strong support groups where you can develop social skills, lasting friendships, and a network of people who can help you make a smooth transition from college to career. On the negative side, Greek organizations can be both exclusive and expensive. Some may have a reputation for excessive drinking and socializing that undermines their members' academic success. Some may require you to participate in activities and events that leave little time for study, and this negative aspect may also apply to many other types of organizations.

Ask Questions with Confidence

Questioning is the hallmark of active learning. By asking questions, you can clear up any misunderstandings you may have about the information presented in class and assigned readings. Unfortunately, most students hesitate to ask questions for many reasons. Some students fear that others will think they are trying to impress the instructor. Others fear that their questions may make them seem uninformed. Still others may be shy and will hold back, hoping that another student will ask their question. All these fears betray a lack of confidence. To overcome your fear of asking questions, remember that your goal is to learn, and learning requires action. In addition to asking questions in classes and lectures, you can contact your instructor through email and during office hours. Also knowing *how* to ask questions will give you the confidence to speak out. Try

EXERCISE 1.5 Campus Tour

TAKE A WALKING TOUR OF your campus. Your college may not have all of the places listed here, but find as many of them as you can and write down their building and office or room numbers. If an office on the following list is not on your campus, write "none" in the space provided. Post this list in a handy place.

Important Campus Locations

Registrar's office _____

Student health service _____

Career center _____

Advisor's office _____

Athletic director's office _____

Learning lab or writing center _____

Financial aid office _____

English or other departmental office _____

the following tips. Four key words, all beginning with *T*, will help you remember them. For additional information on asking the right questions, also see Chapter 3.

▶ **Topic:** Your question should directly relate to the lecture or the topic under discussion. Avoid asking questions that were answered in your assigned reading or in a previous class or lecture. The best way to ensure that your questions are on topic is to attend class regularly and read assigned material.

▶ **Tone:** Ask your question in a respectful tone of voice. This is not the time for sarcasm or inappropriate remarks. A serious question merits a serious answer.

▶ **Timing:** No one likes to be interrupted. Wait for a pause in the lecture or discussion to ask your question. Also, observe your instructor's teaching style. Some instructors prefer you to hold your questions until the end of the lecture, while others may not mind if you ask questions along the way.

▶ **Trust:** Look at the person to whom you are directing the question and listen attentively to the answer, using appropriate body language such as eye contact or a nod of the head to show understanding. This is the *posture of involvement*, and it helps establish trust between you and those to whom you are speaking.

EXERCISE 1.6   Collaborative Activity on Finding Help

APPLY WHAT YOU HAVE LEARNED about the places to find help on campus. Discuss and answer the following questions, doing any research that may be needed. Resources to consider include your college catalog and your college's website, both of which are good sources of information on available courses, programs, and services. Working in a group or with a partner, follow the guidelines for successful collaboration that appear in Figure 1.3 and on the inside back cover. Write your evaluation on your own paper or download the Collaborative Exercise Form from *The Confident Student* premium website.

1. **Adult Learners**

   a. **What special services or programs exist on your campus for adult learners?**

   _____

   b. **Where is the service or program offered (office or other location)?**

   _____

   c. **Give the name of a contact person to ask for information.**

   _____

2. **Women**

   a. **What special services or programs exist on your campus for women?**

   _____

   b. **Where is the service or program offered (office or other location)?**

   _____

   c. **Give the name of a contact person to ask for information.**

   _____

continued

3. Students with Disabilities

    a. What special services or programs exist on your campus for students with learning disabilities and physical disabilities?

    _____

    b. Where are the services or programs offered (office or other location)?

    _____

    c. Give the name of a contact person to ask for information.

    _____

4. Does your campus provide help for students who need to reduce stress? Where is the service offered, and who is a person to contact for information?

_____

5. Does your campus provide help for students who need a tutor? Where is the service offered, and who is a person to contact for information?

_____

Group Evaluation:
Evaluate your discussion. Did everyone contribute? Did you accomplish your task successfully? What additional questions do you have about places on campus to go for help? How will you find answers to your questions?

Special Challenges for Commuters

Active learning takes active involvement. Therefore, if you are a *commuter*, you have some special challenges. Because you do not live on campus, it may be less convenient for you to participate in campus events and organizations, and this may limit your opportunities for social interaction. To become more involved, do the following:

▼ Schedule classes so that you have some free time on campus to participate in an organization or study group.

▼ Arrange with other commuters to share transportation to and from extracurricular activities.

▼ Make the most of class time by volunteering for projects and answering questions.

▼ Form a study group with other commuters and arrange meetings either on or off campus.

▼ Participate in class and small group discussions.

Although it may be less convenient for you to become involved in activities and events than it would be if you lived on or near campus, there are ways for you to take a more active part in campus life. Consider your interests. What are your career aspirations? Is there an activity that you would like to try but have not had an opportunity to pursue? Many clubs and organizations on your campus would be happy to have you as a member. If you join one of these groups, you will meet people who share

FIGURE 1.3

GUIDELINES FOR GROUP DISCUSSION

Each chapter contains a collaborative exercise—an activity intended for partners or a small group. Exercise 1.6 in this chapter is an example. Successful collaboration requires teamwork. Ideally, every member has a role, and everyone participates fully. Before beginning an exercise, decide which members will perform the following roles. Also be aware that some activities may require different roles and responsibilities from those described here. Your instructor may have additional guidelines as well. See also the inside back cover of the text for additional group discussion guidelines.

ROLES	RESPONSIBILITIES
Leader	The leader makes sure everyone understands the assignment's purpose (what you are expected to learn) and task (what you are expected to do). The leader keeps the discussion on target and settles conflicts. Although everyone's responsibility is to stay on task and avoid rambling discussion or socializing, the leader is in charge.
Recorder	Everyone takes notes. The recorder compiles the notes into a final report to present to the whole class, but everyone should be prepared to share in the discussion.
Researcher	The researcher manages whatever resources are needed—textbook, handouts, dictionary, or other materials—and refers to them for answering questions or resolving arguments about facts.
Timekeeper	The timekeeper makes sure the group starts and ends on time, emails or calls group members to remind them of meeting times, follows the discussion, and helps the leader keep things moving so that the task gets completed on time.

A small group is a good place to develop the interpersonal skills that employers expect. Courtesy, professionalism, and respect for others' opinions are hallmarks of successful group interaction. Monopolizing the discussion, interrupting, making personal remarks, and socializing are unproductive behaviors that you should avoid.

your interests, and you may learn even more about an activity you already enjoy. You may also meet people with whom you can share transportation to and from campus activities and events. Your catalog and student handbook contain a list of campus organizations. You could also drop by your student government office and introduce yourself. Someone there can tell you about the many activities and upcoming events in which you can take part. Forming a study group that meets on campus or scheduling some on-campus study time is another way to remain on campus and stay involved.

Guided CHAPTER REVIEW

The following checklist summarizes this chapter's key terms and strategies. After reading the chapter, how confident are you that you can apply the information you have learned? To assess your level of confidence, respond to each statement with one of the following: *very confident* (3 points), *fairly confident* (2 points), *not very confident* (1 point), *not confident* (0 points). Write your number of points in the box beside each statement. Then add your score and read the analysis that follows. When you have finished, take the chapter quiz.

SUMMARY CHECK

How confident are you about applying these strategies?

Points

☐ 1. Assessing your knowledge, behavior, and accomplishments

☐ 2. Defining your goals

☐ 3. Selecting a major or course of study

☐ 4. Forming a network of supportive people

☐ 5. Being able to interact cooperatively with diverse people

☐ 6. Being able to find help on campus

☐ 7. Asking good questions

How confident is your understanding of this chapter's key terms?

☐ 8. technology

☐ 9. self-assessment

☐ 10. goal

☐ 11. major

☐ 12. career

☐ 13. support group

☐ 14. mentor

☐ 15. diversity

☐ 16. active learner

   Total

Add your score. The highest possible score is 48. The closer your score is to 48, the higher your level of confidence. Use your Summary Check results to help you determine which parts of the chapter to review.

YOUR WEBSITE RESOURCES

This chapter's resources include the following items. To access them, go to *The Confident Student* premium website.

- **Video Skillbuilder: Diversity and Exploring Majors**
- **Chapter Exercises**
- **Forms to Download**
- **Chapter Summary of Topics**
- **Review Exercise**
- **Thinking Ahead About Career**
- **Confidence Builder Web Search**
- **Remembering Cultural Differences**
- **Self-Test**

CHAPTER REVIEW Quiz

Answer the following questions from memory. Then return to the chapter to check your answers. As a final activity, complete *Show Your Confidence* at the end of the quiz.

1. What can you do to "choose success"?

   _____

   _____

2. What is a self-assessment and how is it helpful?

   _____

   _____

3. Why is setting goals important?

   _____

   _____

4. What is the difference between a major and a career?

   _____

   _____

5. What is an academic support group and how is it helpful to have one?

   _____

   _____

6. Who are some of the people that would be included in an academic support group?

   _____

   _____

7. What is diversity and why should you embrace it?

   _____

   _____

8. What is one strategy for becoming more flexible in your attitudes?

   _____

   _____

9. What are at least two kinds of information that can be found in your college catalog?

   _____

   _____

10. What is one characteristic of an active learner?

    _____

    _____

SHOW YOUR CONFIDENCE

Go to a place on campus where a lot of students gather. Your cafeteria or student center are two examples. Describe the students and what they are doing. For example, how many racial, ethnic, or cultural groups do you see? Are the students studying, socializing, or engaging in other activities? Are the groups mixed or do students of the same race or ethnicity stick together? Based on these observations, what conclusion can you draw about diversity on your campus? Be prepared to share what you have learned either in writing or in a class discussion.

Your REFLECTIONS: BECOMING A CONFIDENT STUDENT

To reflect means to think seriously. Your reflections are your carefully considered thoughts; for example, you might reflect on something you value or hope to accomplish. Near the end of each chapter, you will have an opportunity to reflect on what you have learned and how you will apply the information. Your reflections can help you set goals, focus your actions, and monitor your progress.

For your first reflection, consider what you have learned from this chapter about becoming a confident student. Use the following questions to stimulate your thinking; then write your reflections. Incorporate in your writing specific information from the chapter.

- Would you describe yourself as *flexible*? Why or why not?
- Figure 1.1, on page 5, lists the traits of confident students. Which traits do you possess?
- What is one thing you will do to become a more flexible person or to develop any other trait listed in Figure 1.1?

_____

_____

_____

_____

_____

_____

_____

_____

_____

_____

_____

_____

_____

_____

_____

2 Motivating Yourself to Learn

Picturenet/Blend Images(RF)/Getty Images

- Describe yourself as a learner: what you already do well and what skills you would like to develop.

- Identify your learning style and your source of motivation.

- Be able to adapt to learning styles and motivating factors that differ from your own.

- Use critical thinking and learning strategies that make studying more efficient and productive.

Confident students are **self-motivated**. They know what they want and will strive to accomplish their goals.

Motivation is the incentive or desire that prompts you to act. For example, a desire for love, companionship, and a family motivates your search for a life partner. A desire for a certain level of income motivates your career choice. Wanting to help others is the incentive for volunteering your services. Why have you come to college? What do you want most out of life? What kind of work would you like to do in the future? Answer those questions and you will find your incentives to study, learn, and succeed.

In other words, the motivation to learn lies within you—it is your responsibility. First, decide what you want. Then become a self-starter, one who is not afraid to ask questions and who takes the initiative to set goals and put plans into action. Being a self-motivated student means that you take **personal responsibility** for your life and its outcomes. You know that with hard work and persistence, achievement is within your grasp.

To help you get motivated and stay motivated, this chapter explains four keys to success in college as illustrated in Figure 1.1.

▼ Assess your strengths and weaknesses.

▼ Discover and use your learning style.

▼ Adapt to others' styles.

▼ Develop critical thinking and learning strategies.

Use these keys to unlock your learning process, free the confident student within you, and open doors for your future.

Before you read about the first key to college success, think about intelligence: What is it, who has it, and can you develop it? For answers to these questions, read the following *Confidence Builder*.

Personal responsibility is a quality of people who take initiative and accept the consequences of their actions.

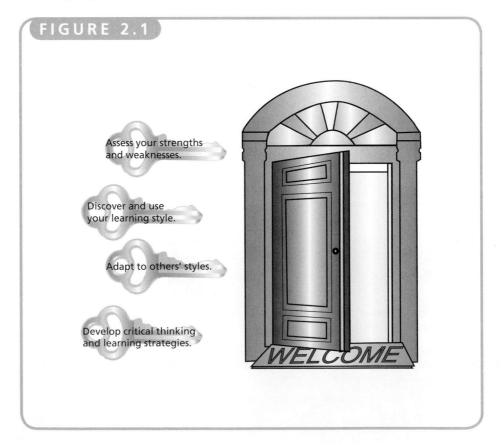

FIGURE 2.1

Assess your strengths and weaknesses.

Discover and use your learning style.

Adapt to others' styles.

Develop critical thinking and learning strategies.

WELCOME

CONFIDENCE BUILDER

Howard Gardner's Multiple Intelligences Theory

Those who study intelligence are divided between two camps: Some believe intelligence is a single ability measured by IQ tests and others think intelligence is multifaceted. Howard Gardner, a professor at Harvard University's Graduate School of Education, belongs to the second camp. Author of *Frames of Mind* (1983) and *Multiple Intelligences: The Theory in Practice* (1993), Gardner argues that we have eight different kinds of intelligence. Everyone possesses these multiple intelligences to some degree, but some people may show greater strength in one or more areas. Gardner also believes that we can encourage the development of our various intelligences and that we can learn to use them to our advantage:

- **Linguistic** intelligence is characterized by skill with words and a sensitivity to their meanings, sounds, and functions. If your linguistic intelligence is high, you probably learn best by reading.
- **Logical-Mathematical** intelligence is characterized by skill with numbers, scientific ability, and formal reasoning. If your logical-mathematical intelligence is high, you probably learn best by taking a problem-solving approach to learning. Outlining or making charts and graphs may be good study techniques for you.
- **Bodily-Kinesthetic** intelligence enables people to use their bodies skillfully and in goal-oriented ways such as playing a sport or dancing. If your bodily intelligence is high, you may be able to learn more effectively by combining studying with some physical activity.
- **Musical** intelligence is characterized by the ability to find meaning in music and other rhythmical sounds and to reproduce them either vocally or with an instrument. If your musical intelligence is high, you may want to choose a career in music or engage in leisure activities that allow you to pursue your musical interests. Although studying to music is a distraction for some, you may find that it aids your concentration.
- **Spatial** intelligence is characterized by the ability to perceive the world accurately and to mentally reorganize or reinterpret those perceptions. For

example, an artist perceives accurately what a bowl of fruit looks like—the colors and sizes of the fruit and how the fruit is arranged. However, the artist's painting of the bowl of fruit is a new interpretation—the artist's mental image of the bowl of fruit—and this image may distort the sizes or change the colors of the fruit. If your spatial intelligence is high, you may learn best by finding ways to visualize or restructure the material you want to learn.

- **Interpersonal** intelligence is characterized by the ability to read people's moods and intentions and to understand their motives. *Empathy* is another characteristic of interpersonal intelligence: the ability to identify with another person's feelings. People who have a high degree of interpersonal intelligence may be said to have "good people skills." If your interpersonal intelligence is high, you may learn best by collaborating with others on projects or by participating in a study group.
- **Intrapersonal** intelligence is characterized by self-knowledge: the ability to read your own emotions, to understand what motivates you, and to use that understanding to shape your behavior. If your intrapersonal intelligence is high, you should be able to make use of all your other intelligences to find the best study methods that will work for you.
- **Naturalistic** intelligence is the ability to perceive the world from an environmental perspective: feeling, sensing, and relating to your environment through its natural features and rhythms. For example, people living in remote cultures become skilled at coping with nature, navigating without maps, and surviving in a hostile climate. For others, this intelligence may reveal itself in curiosity about nature, love of the outdoors, or special ability in the natural sciences. (Gardner added naturalistic intelligence in 1996.)

Gardner's theory of multiple intelligences (MI) is widely accepted among educators, but opinions about the theory's usefulness differ. Many psychologists and educators praise Gardner for raising public

continued

awareness about the various facets of intellectual ability, but others are concerned about the difficulty of testing for such subjective capacities as most of Gardner's intelligences describe. Linguistic and logical-mathematical intelligence can be measured by traditional IQ tests and represented on a numerical scale, 100 being average, for example. However, it is difficult to place a score on musical intelligence, and capacities such as self-knowledge or sensitivity toward the natural world do not respond to traditional testing. Does it matter? In any case, it is important to remember that most employers place great value on verbal and math skills, believing that they are the strongest predictors of success at work. The practical value of Gardner's theory may be that it encourages students to discover and use all of their talents and intellectual capacities to create success in college and in life. What about you? Which of the multiple intelligences above best characterize your strengths?

Follow Up: To explore this topic further, visit *The Confident Student* premium website for an online search activity about multiple intelligence theory.

Assess Your Strengths and Weaknesses

- Describe yourself as a learner: what you already do well and what skills you would like to develop.

Basic skills include reading, writing, and math, among others.

The first of this chapter's keys to success in college is a realistic assessment of your strengths and weaknesses in the **basic skills** of reading, writing, and math. Today, computer skills are also essential. If you do not know what your strengths and weaknesses are in those areas, you may overestimate your skills and take courses for which you are unprepared. Or you may underestimate the value of your experiences outside of college, which can make up for some skill deficiencies. For example, you may have gained knowledge and abilities from reading, working, traveling, or serving in the military that you can apply to your college courses. Knowing what you can and cannot do, and making decisions based on that knowledge, will help you make responsible course selections.

Form a study group with students who have different strengths.

Bob Mahone/The Image Works

Your self-assessment should take into consideration the advice you have received from helpful people at your college. Your academic advisors and instructors are eager for you to be successful. That is why they have invested so much time in testing you, advising you, and perhaps requiring you to take a skill-development course in reading, writing, math, or computer literacy. They also know that a strong foundation in these basic skills is a career asset.

Self-assessment is a key to success in the workplace as well as in college. When confronted with any new learning situation, ask yourself questions such as "What do I already know?" "What skills do I have that I can use?" "What personal qualities apply?" "What additional knowledge, skills, or qualities do I need?" Your answers will provide the self-knowledge you need to make good choices.

For an informal assessment of your strengths and weaknesses in the basic skills, complete Awareness Check 2.1.

Awareness CHECK 2.1

What Are Your Strengths/Weaknesses in Basic Skills?

Check *definitely true* (column A), *somewhat true* (column B), or *not at all true* (column C) to explain how each statement applies to you.

A	B	C	
☐	☐	☐	1. I can read college textbook assignments without difficulty.
☐	☐	☐	2. I can distinguish between main ideas and details.
☐	☐	☐	3. I can determine an author's purpose.
☐	☐	☐	4. I know how to write a well-organized essay.
☐	☐	☐	5. My sentences are clear in meaning and error-free.
☐	☐	☐	6. I have an extensive vocabulary and good spelling skills.
☐	☐	☐	7. I can add, subtract, multiply, and divide with few or no errors.
☐	☐	☐	8. I can easily understand mathematical concepts.
☐	☐	☐	9. I am computer wise and Internet savvy.
☐	☐	☐	10. Assessment tests place my basic skills at college level or beyond.

If you answered definitely true to all ten statements, you may already have a solid foundation in the basic skills, making it easy for you to acquire new knowledge. If you answered somewhat true or not at all true no more than three times, your strengths should enable you to overcome your weaknesses. More than three somewhat true or not at all true answers may suggest basic skill development as a top priority. An advisor can help you select appropriate courses. Basic, or academic, skills are one kind of "intelligence" and the one most often addressed in college courses. However, there are other kinds of intelligence, as this chapter explains. The more you learn about the ways that you learn, the more control you will have over what you learn and the more confident you will grow.

Discover and Use Your Learning Style

- Identify your learning style and your source of motivation.

Discovering and using your learning style is the second key to success in college. Like everything else about you, your learning style is uniquely your own, different from anyone else's. Your **learning style** is your preferred way of learning. Another way to look at learning style is to think of it as the conditions under which you find it easiest and most pleasant to learn and to work. For example, suppose you buy a new piece of software. What would be the easiest, quickest, and most pleasant way for you to learn how to use it? Would you read the manual, follow the instructions in a tutorial program, ask a friend who knows how to use it, or sign up for a course? None of these ways is the *best* way to learn how to use new software, but one of these ways, or a combination of them, may be the best way for *you* to learn.

Your learning style has many components. We will discuss four of them:

1. Your five senses
2. Your body's reactions
3. Your preferred learning environment
4. Your level of motivation

Learning style is a preferred way of learning, but you can also adapt your study methods to take advantage of other learning styles as well.

Visual learners prefer to learn by reading or watching.

Auditory learners like to learn by listening.

Tactile/kinesthetic learners learn best by hands-on or motor activity.

Your Five Senses

Is your learning style primarily visual, auditory, or tactile? **Visual learners** prefer to learn by reading or watching. **Auditory learners** like to learn by listening. **Tactile/kinesthetic learners** learn by doing, by touching or manipulating objects, or by using their hands. Figure 2.2 shows how learning style preferences affect the way you learn

---

EXERCISE 2.1 Learning Style Demonstration

TRY THIS EXPERIMENT FOR A vivid example of the way your learning style affects you.

1. **Fold your hands.**

2. **Look at which thumb and fingers are on top. Are they your left or right?**

3. **Now fold your hands again so that the other thumb and fingers are on top. Does this position feel as comfortable to you?**

4. **Fold your hands your preferred way and notice any difference in feeling.**

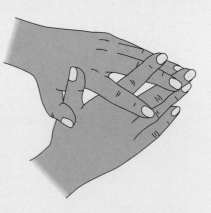

Folding your hands is something you do automatically, and because you always do it your preferred way, you feel comfortable. But when you fold your hands differently, you have to think about what you are doing, and it may take some effort to position your fingers and thumb. You feel uncomfortable because that position is not natural for you. Your learning style is automatic in a similar way. When you are in a classroom environment that matches your learning style, everything feels right. But if the environment does not match your style, you may feel out of place, uncomfortable, and unable to do your best. To combat feelings of discomfort in a classroom environment, understand your learning style. Find ways to adapt your style to fit the environment, and you will be successful. Adapting your style is like learning to live with the wrong thumb on top. At first, it may feel a little strange, but with practice the difference will not be noticeable.

best, the instructional methods you prefer, and some adaptive strategies to try. As you read the chart, remember that it illustrates *preferences*: what each type of learner feels most comfortable doing. The most successful learners are those who take control of the learning situation by adapting to different modes of instruction and by using a combination of learning methods.

Although everyone can learn to adapt to different learning styles, most people have difficulty at first when asked to do something that seems unnatural to them. Imagine the frustration of a visual learner whose instructor gives a lecture without any visual aids. You may have felt a similar frustration in classrooms when the instructor presented material in a sensory mode other than your preferred one. For example, if you are a student who dislikes lecture courses, loses concentration, or has trouble following ideas, maybe you're not an auditory learner. To be successful in a lecture class, you may need to develop strategies that will help you adapt to auditory modes of instruction. For one thing, you could concentrate on developing good note-taking skills and listening techniques, as explained in Chapter 5. To fill in gaps in your notes, compare them with those of someone in the class who does have a strong auditory preference and who is good at taking notes.

Because instructors' teaching styles and methods differ, you must be flexible enough to adapt to whatever instructional mode is being used. To determine your sensory preferences, complete Awareness Check 2.2 on page 34.

Your Body's Reactions

When you are in a classroom or study area, lighting, temperature, and the comfort of the furniture may or may not affect your ability to pay attention or to get your work done. If your body does react strongly to these and other influences such as hunger, tiredness, or mild illness, then you may lose concentration. You should take care of

---

FIGURE 2.2

Understanding Learning Style Preferences

If your style is:	You learn best by:	Your preferred instructional mode is:	To adapt to other styles you can:
Visual	reading, observing, looking at diagrams and other graphics, watching a demonstration	a PowerPoint presentation or lecture/ discussion supplemented with visual aids or handouts	recite from your notes to add an auditory mode to your review
Auditory	listening to others explain, instruct, or discuss	a live or taped presentation or lecture, class discussion in which you can express your ideas and listen to others	take notes to add both tactile and visual modes to listening
Tactile-kinesthetic	engaging in hands-on or physical/motor activity	any activity that allows you to manipulate things or move around; for example, computer-aided instruction appeals to you, as does working in a group	add a visual mode to studying, make diagrams or charts of information you want to learn

Awareness CHECK 2.2

What Are Your Sensory Preferences?

Check all of the statements that seem true of you.

☐ 1. I learn best by reading on my own.

☐ 2. I get the best results from listening to lectures.

☐ 3. I enjoy courses where there is some physical activity involved.

☐ 4. I can learn how to do something by watching a demonstration of how it's done.

☐ 5. Class discussions are helpful to me.

☐ 6. I like to type and to use computers.

☐ 7. Illustrations, charts, and diagrams improve my understanding.

☐ 8. I'd rather listen to the instructor's explanation than do the assigned reading.

☐ 9. I get more out of labs than lectures because of the hands-on approach.

☐ 10. How-to manuals and printed directions are helpful to me.

☐ 11. I like to use podcasts or audio recordings of lessons and exercises.

☐ 12. I'd rather work with machines and equipment than listen to or read explanations.

☐ 13. I can learn to do something if someone shows me how.

☐ 14. I can follow directions best when someone reads them to me.

☐ 15. It's not enough to show me; I have to do it myself.

Statements 1, 4, 7, 10, and 13 are characteristic of visual learners. Statements 2, 5, 8, 11, and 14 are characteristic of auditory learners. Statements 3, 6, 9, 12, and 15 are characteristic of tactile learners. If your checks are spread evenly among two or more categories, you may be equally comfortable using one or more of your sensory modes. But remember that this Awareness Check is only an informal survey. For a formal assessment of your learning style, see an academic or career development counselor, who may be able to give you one of several well-known tests.

these physiological needs before attempting to do anything that demands your full attention. Determining your physiological preferences and building your schedule accordingly is one way to use your learning style to create the conditions under which you will stay most alert.

Like most people, you probably have a peak time of day when you are most alert and energetic. Throughout the day, your concentration, attention, and energy levels fluctuate. In the morning, you might be alert and ready for anything, but by afternoon you might feel sapped of energy. If you are a morning person, then it would make sense to schedule your classes in the morning if you can. But if you are alert and concentrate better in the late afternoon or at night, then schedule as many of your courses as possible in the evening hours. If you anticipate that a certain course will be difficult, make every effort to schedule it at your peak time of day. Then plan to do as much of your studying as possible at this time of day.

If you learn to accept what you cannot change, then you can adapt to situations that don't meet your preferences, knowing that you will have to try harder to pay attention and remain on task. Although you have limited control over your classroom environment, you can set up your study environment to reflect your preferences. See Chapter 8 for a detailed discussion and suggestions about arranging your study environment. Awareness Check 2.3 will help you understand how your body's reactions might affect your ability to learn.

Your Preferred Learning Environment

A learning environment is much more than the place where your class meets. The way the class is structured is also an important part of the learning environment. In what kind of learning environment are you most comfortable? Do you like a traditional classroom, where desks are arranged in rows and the instructor directs activities? Or are you more comfortable in a looser arrangement, where instructor

---

Awareness CHECK 2.3

How Does Your Body React?

Check the statements that best describe you.

☐ 1. I feel most alert in the morning hours.

☐ 2. I don't "come alive" until afternoon or early evening.

☐ 3. I am definitely a night person.

☐ 4. I concentrate and work best in a brightly lit room.

☐ 5. Bright light distracts me; I prefer natural or nonglare lighting.

☐ 6. Overhead lighting is never right; I need an adjustable lamp.

☐ 7. The temperature in a classroom does not usually affect my concentration.

☐ 8. I can't work or concentrate in a room that is too hot or too cold.

☐ 9. I usually get chills when sitting next to a fan, air conditioner, or open window.

☐ 10. If my chair or desk in class is uncomfortable, I am usually able to ignore it and concentrate.

☐ 11. If my chair is not the right height, my back or neck aches.

☐ 12. If I feel a little ill or headachy, I can't think about anything else.

☐ 13. I can ignore feelings of hunger or tiredness long enough to keep my attention on my work.

☐ 14. Mild feelings of illness don't usually distract me from my work.

Your answers to the Awareness Check indicate the following about your body's reactions: the time of day when you are most alert (items 1–3), your lighting preferences (items 4–6), your temperature preferences (items 7–9), your comfort in relation to furnishings in your classroom (items 10–11), the extent to which hunger, tiredness, and illness affect your ability to concentrate in class (items 12–14).

EXERCISE 2.2 Learning Style Application on Classrom Environment

ANSWER THE FOLLOWING QUESTIONS ABOUT your best class and your worst class—*best* meaning the class in which your performance has been most successful and *worst* meaning the class in which your performance has been the least successful. Compare your body's reactions to each classroom environment (questions 1–6). Then determine to what extent your body's reactions affect your learning in each class and what you can do to adapt more effectively (questions 7–8).

1. **What time does the class meet and are you most alert at this time?**

    best class _____

    worst class _____

2. **Is the temperature in the classroom generally comfortable for you?**

    best class _____

    worst class _____

3. **What type of lighting is available in the classroom and do you find the lighting acceptable?**

    best class _____

    worst class _____

4. **Are you generally rested or tired when you go to class?**

    best class _____

    worst class _____

5. **Have you eaten recently before class or do you become hungry during class?**

    best class _____

    worst class _____

6. **Would you describe the seating arrangement and the furniture in the classroom as comfortable or uncomfortable?**

    best class _____

    worst class _____

7. **What relationship do you see between your body's reactions and your performances in your best and worst class?**

    _____

    _____

8. **What can you do to improve your performance in your worst class? What can you do to make your worst class seem more like your best class?**

    _____

    _____

and students sit together in a circle, for example, or where small groups of students sit together at tables?

Perhaps you are a self-directed student who prefers to work alone in a self-paced class or lab. Or you may need a lot of direction and supervision while you learn. You may be a student who learns more from the instructor's lectures and comments than from class discussions. Or you may be a student who doesn't get much out of class unless you have opportunities to share ideas with others in group activities. The following comments illustrate three learning environment preferences. Do you recognize yourself in one of these comments, or do you have yet another preference?

1. **Carol**: The instructors are the ones I've paid my money to hear; they're the experts. I resent it when class time is taken up answering questions that are covered in the reading assignments.

2. **Andy**: I hate this class. All the instructor does is lecture. I learn more from class discussions and listening to different people's opinions.

3. **Grant**: I don't like it when I have to adjust my pace to the rest of the class. I'd rather work independently so I can progress at my own rate, taking as much time as I need.

Carol likes a traditional, teacher-centered classroom. Andy prefers a student-centered environment. Grant, who likes to work alone, prefers individualized instruction.

Most of the time, you will have to adapt to whatever learning environment is available. However, understanding your preferences will enable you to select the kind of classes in which you are most comfortable, if you have a choice. Advisors and other students are good sources of information about the type of learning environment a specific course or instructor provides.

> **Concept Check 2.1**
>
> Do you think some majors or careers might be better suited to one learning style over another? Athletes may be more tactile-kinesthetic, physicians more visual. What about actors or accountants? How will your learning style influence your career choice? What challenges will you face?

EXERCISE 2.3 Learning Style Inventories

Exercise Purpose

Learning style preferences can influence, but not necessarily determine, how well you will do in a course. Knowing how you learn can help you create a study environment and materials that work best for you. This exercise will help you find out more about your learning preferences.

Exercise Background

As you have learned from taking Awareness Checks 2.2 and 2.3, self-assessment is the key to discovering your learning style. These short, informal tests provide a brief example of the kinds of questions asked and behaviors surveyed on more extensive formal and informal inventories. Tests like the following help you identify personality traits or preferences that may influence your life interests and career choices as well as the ways that you learn, interact with others, make decisions, and solve problems.

- **Meyers-Briggs Type Indicator (MBTI)**

- **Kolb Learning Style Inventory**

- **Hogan/Champagne Personal Style Inventory**

- **Keirsey Temperament Sorter**

One or more of these tests may be available to you through your college's career center or counseling department.

continued

Exercise Task

1. Take a learning styles inventory, such as one of those listed previously. Your instructor may suggest one or may direct you to an office on campus where such testing is done. If you prefer, you can also search the Internet for an informal inventory. Many are available free of charge. Try the search phrases *learning styles*, *learning styles inventories*, and *learning styles and testing*. Also see the text website for suggested sites.

2. Compare your results for whatever inventory you take with your results from Awareness Checks 2.2 and 2.3. What is your learning style? What do your results suggest that you do to improve your learning and studying?

3. Write a paragraph in which you explain the results of your search and assessment, and be prepared to share it in class.

Your Level of Motivation

A **motive** is a reason, purpose, or incentive for behavior.

What do you want and how hard are you willing to work for it? How you answer this question depends on your motives. A **motive** is a reason or purpose for your behavior. A motive can be a desire you want to fulfill, a need that has to be met, a reward you seek, or some other incentive. For example, if a student attends class regularly, always comes prepared, asks questions, takes notes, and generally is attentive, the motive behind these actions might be the desire to earn a good grade. If a student shops at discount stores, compares prices to find the best deal on products and services, carpools to conserve gasoline, the motive might be to save money. Motives can be hard to pinpoint, but we can infer them from behavior. **Motivation** is the impulse to act on your incentives and desires. Your level of motivation can vary in intensity and persistence, depending on how much you want something and how hard or long you will work to achieve it. What motivates you?

Motivation is the impulse to act on your incentives and desires.

Psychologists believe that motives are both intrinsic (internal) and extrinsic (external). **Intrinsic motives** originate within the self. Examples are the desire for self-fulfillment, feelings of personal responsibility, and pride in achievement. **Extrinsic motives** are rewards or incentives that are imposed from outside the self. Some examples are grades, money, and recognition from others. People are influenced by both intrinsic and extrinsic motives, but what prompts a person to act in certain ways? Why do some people believe that they can make things happen while others believe that life just happens? Motives are only part of the answer. The real key to understanding motivation is to recognize how much control you believe that you have over the events of your life.

Intrinsic motives are internal rewards or incentives, such as desires or needs.

Extrinsic motives are external rewards or incentives, such as money or recognition from others.

Your Source of Motivation

If you believe that you have the power to shape your life's outcomes through your attitudes and behavior, then your source of motivation is internal: it lies within you. If you believe that chance or fate rules your life or that people more powerful than you determine what happens to you, then your source of motivation is external: it rests in the hands of others.

Internally motivated means "self-motivated," having intrinsic or internal motives for behavior.

Students who are **internally motivated** are also called "self-motivated." They can see a direct connection between their efforts and their grades. These students tend to be positive thinkers who believe that they can do whatever they set out to accomplish.

They are not afraid of change and welcome challenges. When they make a mistake, they can usually trace it to something they did wrong or something they did not understand. These students don't believe in luck or fate. They are in control of their lives. When things go wrong, they try to figure out what they can do to make things right again.

Students who are **externally motivated** are also called "other-motivated." These students see little or no connection between their efforts and their grades. They may believe that instructors award grades on the basis of personal feelings or that their grades result from good or bad luck. These students tend to be negative thinkers who believe that no matter how hard they try to succeed, someone or something is standing in their way. They often fear change and prefer to follow familiar routines. When they make mistakes, they often blame others for being unfair or for not giving them the right information. These students believe that they have little control over their lives. When something goes wrong, they may believe that there is nothing they can do about it.

> **Externally motivated** means "other-motivated," having extrinsic or external motives for behavior.

Does a person have to be either internally or externally motivated? Internal and external motivation represent two extremes of behavior. Although you may tend toward one extreme, your level of motivation may vary depending on the circumstances. For example, do you remember when you got your driver's license? You probably did not need any prodding from anyone. You found the self-motivation to practice your driving skills so that you could get that license. On the other hand, you may have needed a little external motivation in the form of an allowance to make you do household chores.

How internally motivated or externally motivated are you, generally speaking? Think of a straight line. The ends of the line represent extremes of behavior: internal motivation versus external motivation. Points at equal intervals along the line between the two extremes represent different degrees of control a person might feel. Look at Figure 2.3 below. Where would you place yourself on this line? For example, the more in control you feel and the more self-motivated you are, the closer to the internal extreme you will be. The more out of control you feel and the more other-motivated you are, the closer to the external extreme you will be. Can you become more internally motivated? Should you?

Knowing whether you are more internally or externally motivated can help you look for the best incentives to accomplish your goals. It is also important to recognize that most instructors and many employers not only value self-motivation but expect you to find your own rewards and incentives. For example, some instructors do not take attendance. They expect you to have or to find the motivation for coming to class. Similarly, an instructor may not take class time to review before a test, expecting you to do your own review and to be prepared. So if you are the type of student who expects your instructors to remind you that an assignment is due, then you may need to work on becoming more self-motivated. To find out more about what motivates you, take Awareness Check 2.4; then read the explanation that follows.

Research shows that motivation affects achievement. The more self-motivated you are, the greater your chances for success in college. Thinking positively about yourself and your abilities, accepting responsibility for motivating yourself, and doing what is

FIGURE 2.3

Internal and External Motivation: A Continuum

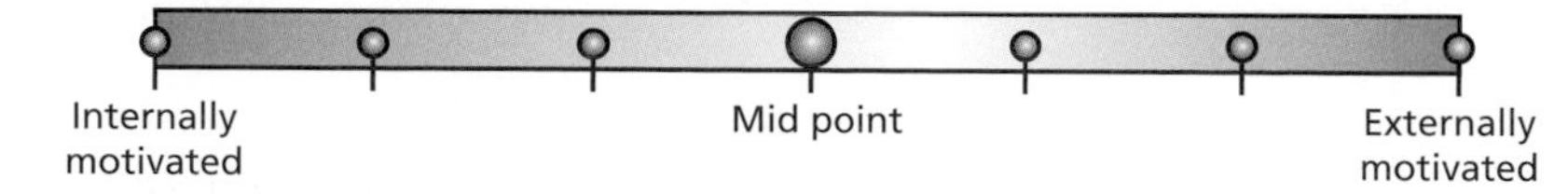

Internally motivated   Mid point   Externally motivated

Awareness CHECK 2.4

What Is Your Source of Motivation?

Yes   No   **Check *yes* if you agree with a statement; check *no* if you disagree.**

☐ ☐ 1. If I can do the work, I can get a good grade in any course, no matter how good or bad the instructor is.

☐ ☐ 2. If the teacher isn't a good speaker or doesn't keep me interested, I probably won't do well in the class.

☐ ☐ 3. I believe that I have the power to control what happens to me.

☐ ☐ 4. I believe that I have very little control over what happens to me.

☐ ☐ 5. When I make a mistake, it's usually my fault.

☐ ☐ 6. When I make a mistake, it's usually because someone didn't make clear to me what I was supposed to do.

☐ ☐ 7. My grades are the result of how much studying I do.

☐ ☐ 8. My grades don't seem to be affected by the amount of studying I do.

☐ ☐ 9. I can adapt easily to a change of plans or events.

☐ ☐ 10. Adapting to change has always been difficult for me. I like things to be as predictable and orderly as possible.

☐ ☐ 11. When I fail a test, it's either because I didn't study or because I didn't understand the material.

☐ ☐ 12. When I fail a test, it's either because the test was unfair or because the instructor didn't cover the material.

☐ ☐ 13. I don't usually need anyone to push me or make me study.

☐ ☐ 14. I can't seem to make myself study.

☐ ☐ 15. I am a self-motivated person.

☐ ☐ 16. I need someone to motivate me.

Look at your answers in both columns. If you checked mostly odd-numbered items in the yes column and mostly even-numbered items in the no column, then you may be internally motivated. If you checked mostly even-numbered items in the yes column and odd-numbered items in the no column, then you may be externally motivated. Based on the text descriptions of students who are internally or externally motivated, which one most accurately describes you?

necessary to succeed will produce results not only in college but also in your job or career and in your personal life. If you need a little prodding to reach your goals but would like to become more self-motivated, follow these suggestions:

1. **Become a positive thinker**. Earlier in this chapter, you assessed your strengths and weaknesses. Focus on your strengths. Remind yourself of all the things you do well and take action to overcome your weaknesses.

2. **Take responsibility for motivating yourself**. Realize that only you can make yourself study. When you study as you should, congratulate yourself and enjoy your good grades. When you don't study, accept the consequences and don't blame others.

3. **Accept the fact that success results from effort**. If you are not getting where you want to go, then apply yourself with more determination and be persistent. The greater your effort and persistence, the more likely you are to get what you want.

4. **Start listening to yourself talk**. Eliminate the nameless "they" from your vocabulary. "*They* made me do it," "*They* keep me from succeeding," and "If only *they* had told me" are comments externally motivated students make when things go wrong. By replacing *they* with *I* in your self-talk, you are taking control of your thoughts and your life.

Your source of motivation is your index of personal responsibility. The more internally motivated you are, the more you believe that you are in control of your life.

Concept Check **2.2**

Listen carefully to a friend talk about a course, an instructor, or a grade. Can you tell whether your friend is internally or externally motivated? What specific words or actions reveal your friend's source of motivation?

One aspect of self-motivation is a willingness to adapt to the learning environment.

Michelle D. Bridwell/PhotoEdit

EXERCISE 2.4 Collaborative Activity on Sources of Motivation

DISCUSS THE FOLLOWING STUDENT BEHAVIORS and excuses with your group members. Follow the guidelines for successful collaboration that appear on the inside back cover. Listed below are four common student behaviors. Each one is followed by a list of excuses for the behavior. (1) Determine whether the behavior is one that you can control. (2) Explain why each excuse listed is valid or not. (3) Determine what the student would have to do to take responsibility for the behavior. Write your evaluation on your own paper or download the Collaborative Exercise Form from *The Confident Student* premium website. Share your work with the rest of the class.

1. **You arrive late for class because:**
   Your alarm didn't go off.
   Your ride didn't come.
   You had to work late the night before.
   You had car trouble.

2. **Studying is difficult for you because:**
   There are too many distractions at home.
   You have a family to take care of.
   The textbooks are difficult or boring.
   You don't know what to study.

continued

3. **You never seem to have enough time because:**
   People are always interrupting you.
   Your instructors assign too much outside work.
   You have too many things to do.
   You often procrastinate.

4. **You often leave homework undone because:**
   You are too tired to do it.
   You can't seem to turn down your friends' offers to socialize.
   You get stuck or don't understand how to do the assignment.
   You put work or family obligations first.

Group Evaluation:

Evaluate your discussion. Did everyone contribute? Did you accomplish your task successfully? What additional questions do you have about sources of motivation? How will you find answers to your questions?

The more externally motivated you are, the more you believe that someone or something outside yourself is controlling the circumstances that affect your life. In other words, the degree to which you *believe* you can control what happens to you largely determines the amount of control you *actually* have.

Adapt to Others' Styles

- Be able to adapt to learning styles and motivating factors that differ from yours.

Everyone has a learning style. In your college's diverse learning community, it is important to acknowledge and accept the different ways in which instructors teach and students learn. Adapting to others' styles is the third key to your success.

When working collaboratively with classmates or when speaking in front of a class, acknowledge others' styles. For example, a person who prefers to work alone may have to be encouraged to participate with group members. Similarly, if you are planning to give an oral presentation, supplement it with visual aids to appeal to the visual learners in class.

You probably won't find it difficult to adapt to your classmates' styles. Many of them are your friends, but you should make an effort to get along with all of your classmates because you will be working with them throughout the term.

The greatest challenge lies in adapting to your instructors' teaching styles. Just as you have a learning style, your instructors have teaching styles. An instructor's teaching style determines, to some extent, the instructional methods he or she prefers to use. Although educational researchers define a number of teaching styles, we will consider only two basic types: *independent* and *interactive*. Each of these styles represents an extreme of behavior. However, many instructors' styles fall somewhere between these extremes. For example, an instructor may use *mixed modes*: a combination of teaching methods such as lecturing, collaborative activities, and group discussion.

The instructor whose style is *independent* is usually formal and businesslike with students and places more importance on individual effort than on group effort. This instructor expects students to assume responsibility for learning, to work independently, and to seek help when needed. Lecturing is the preferred teaching method of this instructor, who will often call on students rather than ask for volunteers. Students often feel competitive in this instructor's class. If you feel most comfortable in lecture courses and like working independently, then you may do your best work with an instructor whose style is independent.

On the other hand, the instructor whose style is *interactive* is usually informal with students and places more importance on group effort than on individual effort. The interactive instructor guides students step by step through tasks and anticipates their needs. Small group activities and large group discussions are this instructor's preferred teaching methods. Rather than call on students, he or she will usually ask for volunteers. Students often feel cooperative in this instructor's class. If you feel more comfortable in classes where students do most of the talking and if you would rather work with others than by yourself, then you may be able to do your best work with an instructor whose teaching style is interactive.

If you do not like or do not get along with one of your instructors, you may be reacting negatively to a teaching style that conflicts with your learning style. However, don't let personal feelings keep you from being successful in the course. Instead, focus on what you can do to meet the instructor's requirements and make an extra effort to adapt to his or her teaching style. By making this effort, you may find that your relationship with your instructor will improve dramatically.

EXERCISE 2.5 Collaborative Activity about Teaching Styles

GET TOGETHER WITH A CLASSMATE who is taking one or more of the same courses you are. Analyze the teaching style of an instructor by completing the checklist that follows. Fill in the name of the course; then check each phrase that describes the instructor. If you analyze more than one instructor's style, complete a checklist for each one. Visit *The Confident Student* premium website to download an additional checklist. Then compare your checklist with your partner's. Do your results agree?

Teaching Style Checklist

Course:_____

- [ ] 1. **Formal, businesslike attitude**
- [ ] 2. **Informal, casual attitude**
- [ ] 3. **Encourages competition among students**
- [ ] 4. **Encourages cooperation among students**
- [ ] 5. **Lectures most of the time**
- [ ] 6. **Holds class discussions most of the time**
- [ ] 7. **Stresses importance of individual effort**
- [ ] 8. **Stresses importance of group effort**
- [ ] 9. **Often uses visual aids**
- [ ] 10. **Rarely uses visual aids**
- [ ] 11. **Calls on students**
- [ ] 12. **Asks for volunteers**
- [ ] 13. **Expects students to ask for help**
- [ ] 14. **Guides students step by step**
- [ ] 15. **Mainly sticks to facts**
- [ ] 16. **Often shares personal experiences**
- [ ] 17. **"Tells" what to do, gives directions**
- [ ] 18. **"Shows" what to do, gives directions**

If you checked mostly odd-numbered items, your instructor's teaching style is independent. If you checked mostly even-numbered items, your instructor's teaching style is interactive. If you checked some even- and some odd-numbered items, your instructor's style may combine modes from both the independent and interactive styles.

In an ideal situation, advisors would match students with instructors who have similar styles. But in the real world, you may not always get the courses and instructors that you want. Also, you usually will not know in advance what an instructor's teaching style is. A good rule of thumb to remember when dealing with instructors is that it is *your* responsibility to adapt to their styles, not the other way around. By learning to adapt to your instructors' styles now, you are preparing for the future. Throughout your career, you will encounter employers, coworkers, and others whose styles differ from yours, and you will be expected to work effectively with all of them.

Develop Critical Thinking and Learning Strategies

- Use critical thinking and learning strategies that make studying more efficient and productive.

Read the following student comments about studying and learning. Do any of them sound like statements you have made? Can you think of another one? Add it to the list in the space provided.

Student A: "My academic skills are OK, but I still don't make the grades I want."

Student B: "I study a lot, but I often study the wrong things."

Student C: "I usually get the main idea but forget the details."

Student D: "I never seem to have enough time for studying."

Student E: "I've found several Internet sources on my research topic, but I don't know how good they are."

Your comment about studying and learning: _____
_____

These statements illustrate common problems that students encounter as they attend classes and study. You can solve these problems by learning to think critically and study efficiently. However, you may have to work hard to overcome your difficulties and may need to devote some time to skills development.

Developing critical thinking and learning strategies is your fourth key to success in college. Knowing how to study helps you apply your knowledge and use your skills so that you can be successful in your courses. For example, if you learn how to listen effectively and take good notes, then you will be able to follow lectures and to record essential information for study and review. If you learn how to manage your time, then you will be able to keep up with assignments and meet deadlines. If you learn how to prepare for and take tests, then you will be able to make the grades you want. If you learn how to evaluate what you read, on the Internet and elsewhere, then you will be able to select appropriate sources when researching a topic.

Learning styles, critical thinking, and learning strategies overlap. *Thinking critically* is the means by which you make sense of the world around you. The learning activities that college students must do require critical thinking. For example, you must be able to make decisions, solve problems, reason logically, use your creativity, and know how to use appropriate learning strategies. Developing critical thinking skills will also make you more employable in the future. Those who can think critically and who know how to gather and use information will get the best jobs and will advance more rapidly in their careers than those who don't. For example, do the following *Critical Thinking* exercise on MI theory and you will gain a better understanding of what critical thinking entails.

CRITICAL THINKING

Applying Gardner's Multiple Intelligences Theory

Exercise Overview

Howard Gardner believes that we have not one intelligence but several. As he defined them, the "intelligences" are *linguistic, logical-mathematical, bodily-kinesthetic, musical, spatial, interpersonal, intrapersonal,* and *naturalistic*. The *Confidence Builder* at the beginning of this chapter summarizes Gardner's theory and the eight intelligences. This exercise will help you apply what you have learned about Gardner's theory as it relates to your life and experience.

Exercise Background

Educators have debated the meaning of intelligence, what it is, the role it plays in learning, and whether it can be developed or improved. Gardner's theory of multiple intelligences impressed educators for two reasons. First, Gardner defined intelligence as multifaceted rather than a single capacity. Second, he theorized that everyone possesses all the intelligences to some degree. These two ideas explained how a student might be strong in math but not so strong in English. More important, the theory gave hope to students that they could develop the skills they were lacking. To educators who accept Gardner's theory, it is not valid to classify students as "intelligent" or "unintelligent." Instead, students are seen to have strengths and weaknesses, with a potential for improvement.

Exercise Task

Choose a partner for this exercise. First, review together the summaries of Gardner's intelligences listed in the *Confidence Builder* on pages 29–30. Also review any notes either of you may have taken if you did the online search on Gardner's theory. Then discuss and answer the following questions. Be prepared to share your answers in a class discussion.

1. Which one of Gardner's intelligences is your strongest? Which one is your weakest? Explain why you think so.
2. Which kind of "intelligence" does it take for someone to excel in sports or another physical activity? Explain your reasons.
3. Which one of the intelligences do you think is most valued in an academic setting, and why do you think so?
4. Think of someone you admire. How would you describe this person's strengths, using Gardner's intelligences?
5. Which one of Gardner's intelligences would you most like to develop and why?

Studying is a kind of concentrated thinking that, at its best, involves more than one of your senses. For example, when you read a textbook chapter and underline portions, you are using your visual and tactile senses. Studying is easier and more efficient when you use what you know about your learning style to create the conditions in which your concentration will be greatest. Figure 2.4 indicates how critical thinking and learning

FIGURE 2.4

Using Critical Thinking and Learning Strategies

CRITICAL THINKING	TASKS TO DO	LEARNING STRATEGIES NEEDED/USED
Making decisions	Decide when to study. Decide what's important. Select courses. Decide what to study.	Set up a schedule. Read for main idea, details, key terms. Know requirements; use resources. Review notes, old tests, assignments.
Solving problems	Solve math problems. Avoid procrastination. Reduce test anxiety.	Record problems and solutions on note cards. Make and follow a schedule. Practice relaxation techniques.
Reasoning	Write a speech. Follow an author's ideas. Compare theories.	Make an outline. Look for patterns of organization. Make a chart or information map.
Knowing how to learn	Learn from reading. Learn from listening.	Locate, understand, interpret information. Use listening and note-taking skills.
Thinking creatively	Compose an original piece of work. Develop a project.	Keep an "idea" journal. Combine ideas in unique ways.

strategies work together to help you complete typical tasks that your instructors might ask you to do.

Chapter 3, Thinking Critically and Creatively, provides a more detailed explanation of critical thinking and how to develop and use your critical thinking skills. The fact is that you have already been using critical thinking for many everyday tasks. For example, choosing courses and making this semester's or quarter's schedule required you to make decisions: What courses should I take? At what times should I schedule them? If a course you had wanted to take was filled or if your work hours conflicted with the class hours, those situations required you to use your problem-solving skills. The exercises in each chapter of this book ask you to apply skills or knowledge that you have gained from the chapter to practical situations that you might encounter either in college, at work, or in your personal life. In other words, when you use what you already know to find out what you don't know, you are thinking critically.

Guided CHAPTER REVIEW

The following checklist summarizes this chapter's key terms and strategies. After reading the chapter, how confident are you about applying the information you have learned? To assess your level of confidence, respond to each statement with one of the following: *very confident* (3 points), *fairly confident* (2 points), *not very confident* (1 point), *not confident* (0 points). Write your number of points in the box beside each statement. Then add your score and read the analysis that follows. When you have finished, take the chapter quiz.

SUMMARY CHECK

How confident are you about applying these strategies?

Points

☐ 1. Determining your strengths and weaknesses in basic skills

☐ 2. Understanding your learning style and using it to your advantage

☐ 3. Knowing what your sensory preferences are

☐ 4. Finding your preferred learning environment

☐ 5. Determining what motivates you

☐ 6. Determining your instructors' teaching styles

☐ 7. Adapting to different teaching styles

☐ 8. Being able to think critically

How confident is your understanding of this chapter's key terms?

☐ 9. personal responsibility

☐ 10. basic skills

☐ 11. multiple intelligences

☐ 12. learning style

☐ 13. visual learners

☐ 14. auditory learners

☐ 15. tactile-kinesthetic learners

☐ 16. motive

☐ 17. motivation

☐ 18. intrinsic motives

☐ 19. extrinsic motives

☐ 20. internally motivated

☐ 21. externally motivated

Total

Add your score. The highest possible score is 63. The closer your score is to 63, the higher your level of confidence. Use your **Summary Check** results to help you determine which parts of the chapter to review.

YOUR WEBSITE RESOURCES

This chapter's resources include the following items. To access them, go to *The Confident Student* premium website.

- Video Skillbuilder: Learning Styles: The VAK
- Chapter Exercises
- Forms to Download
- Chapter Summary of Topics
- Review Exercise
- Thinking Ahead About Career
- Confidence Builder Web search
- Self-Test

CHAPTER REVIEW Quiz

Answer the following questions from memory. Then return to the chapter to check your answers. As a final activity, complete *Show Your Confidence* at the end of the quiz.

1. Why is assessing your basic skill strengths and weaknesses the most important key to college success?

   _____

   _____

2. This chapter identifies four keys to college success. Assessing your strengths and weaknesses is one key. What are the other three?

   _____

   _____

3. Which learning style explained in this chapter is most like your own? Give an example.

   _____

   _____

4. What do your five senses have to do with learning style?

   _____

   _____

5. How can understanding your body's reactions help you in planning a course schedule?

   _____

   _____

6. What are *intrinsic* and *extrinsic motives*? Give examples.

   _____

   _____

7. How do students differ who are internally or externally motivated?

   _____

   _____

8. Why do educators think that students should become more internally motivated?

   _____

   _____

9. What is the connection between self-motivation and personal responsibility?

_____

_____

10. What is one way that the independent and interactive teaching styles differ?

_____

_____

SHOW YOUR CONFIDENCE

Using information from your textbook and from your own experience, construct a chart that compares internally motivated students with externally motivated students. Divide your chart into two columns, label the columns, and list traits for comparison. Be prepared to share your chart in a class discussion.

Your REFLECTIONS: MY PROFILE AS A LEARNER

Reflect on what you have learned from this chapter about **self-motivation**. Let this reflection be a profile of yourself as a learner. Monitor your progress by revisiting your profile throughout the term, making changes as you gain new skills. Use the following questions to stimulate your thinking, and include in your profile specific information from the chapter.

- What have you learned from this chapter's *Awareness Checks* about your basic skills, learning style, and locus of control?
- What does Gardner's MI theory say about you? Which kinds of intelligence best describe you?
- Which of the critical thinking skills or learning strategies listed in Figure 2.4 are strong points for you?

_____

_____

_____

_____

_____

_____

_____

_____

_____

_____

3 Thinking Critically and Creatively

Adam Woolfitt/Robert Harding Picture Library Ltd/Alamy

- Think critically and creatively to meet all of your academic and life challenges.

- Ask questions that demonstrate your ability to think critically and creatively on six different levels.

- Set the stage for learning by determining what you already know or think and what you need to find out.

- Look beyond what is stated to understand what may be implied or unstated.

- Determine whether an informational source is credible by applying standards of evaluation such as reliability, objectivity, and usefulness.

Confident students are **intellectual risk takers**. They think for themselves, both critically and creatively.

Thinking is the mental processing of information that is taken in through the senses. Thinking involves reasoning, imagining, visualizing, inventing, and remembering.

You know what thinking is, right? You do it all the time. However, most of the time information processing—or **thinking**—is taking place below your level of awareness. For example, how do you know how to do anything, such as ride a bicycle, build a fence, arrange the furniture in a room, paint a picture, write an essay for your composition class, or drive a car? If you know how to drive, you do not have to think through each step in the process: "First I start the car, now I put it in gear, next I look in the rearview mirror," and so on. Because you have internalized these steps through practice, you go through them automatically. But if you were teaching someone else to drive a car, you would then have to bring those steps back up to your level of awareness so that you could explain or demonstrate the process of driving to someone else.

As in the driving example above, this chapter asks you to become aware of yourself as a thinker. In the process, you will learn what it means to think critically and creatively and how you can develop your thinking skills. In order to think more critically and creatively, you may need to make some changes as you begin thinking like a college student. Will you take the intellectual risk to give up old thinking habits and replace them with new ones? Read the following *Confidence Builder* for inspiration.

CONFIDENCE BUILDER

Are You Willing to Take Intellectual Risks?

Look at the photograph of Stonehenge that opens this chapter. One of the world's wonders, Stonehenge is a mystery that has inspired and confounded thinkers for centuries. Who built it? How? Why? These questions remain unanswered, though there are plenty of theories.

One man, Wally Wallington, believes that the answer to the question of how Stonehenge was built may be quite simple. Using ordinary tools such as boards, weights, and a garden hose, Wallington is able to move heavy objects. By applying principles of physics known to most builders, Wallington used a fulcrum made of wood, some boards, and counterweights to move an eleven-foot block of concrete to a standing position. He also built an arch out of three huge concrete slabs that weighed about three tons each. This arch is the first structure in a "Stonehenge" replica that Wallington is building on his land just to prove that it can be done. By taking an intellectual risk, Wally Wallington found a creative solution to an age-old mystery.

Frenchman Phillippe Petit is another risk taker who solved a problem by thinking critically and creatively. His special feat involved both physical risk and intellectual risk. The recent film *Man on Wire* documents Petit's high-wire act many stories above Manhattan, between what used to be the world's

tallest buildings: the twin towers of the World Trade Center. At 7:15 a.m. on August 7, 1974, Petit walked a tightrope, suspended 1,350 feet in the air between the towers. This stunt required a 450-pound cable and a 26-foot balancing pole weighing 55 pounds. The stunt was illegal and eventually landed Petit in jail. When asked why he did it, he replied, "There is no why." Petit had a dream for which he was willing to risk his life. How to get his team into the building, how to move heavy equipment up many floors, and how to suspend the cable from one building to another—all while eluding security systems and personnel—required taking intellectual risks as well: What Petit did had never been done.

Both Wally Wallington and Phillippe Petit are men who did not take no for an answer. They refused to believe that anything is impossible, and they teach us that any challenge can be met with critical and creative thinking. Trying a new learning strategy may not be the same as lifting a three-ton slab of concrete or walking a tightrope high above a city street, but it is a challenge, nonetheless, and an intellectual risk worth the challenge.

Follow Up: To explore this topic further, visit *The Confident Student* premium website for an online search activity about critical and creative thinking.

Think for Yourself

- Think critically and creatively to meet all of your academic and life challenges.

How many times has someone said to you, "Think for yourself"? How many times have you thought, "I am thinking for myself," but were you really? Was the opinion you expressed your own, formulated after careful thought and consideration of a variety of viewpoints on the subject? Or did you simply repeat what you have heard or always believed without thinking? Thinking for yourself is different from thinking off the top of your head or stating the first thing that comes to mind or repeating to your instructor what you think your instructor wants to hear. *Thinking for yourself means thinking critically and creatively to form your own opinions.*

What Is Critical Thinking?

Broadly defined, **critical thinking** is *the process of constructing and evaluating meaning.* Specifically, critical thinking is *logical* or *analytical, self-reflective, conscious,* and *purposeful* thinking. Let's look at each part of this definition to demonstrate what you will do when you are thinking critically:

Critical thinking is logical, analytical, self-reflective, conscious, and purposeful reasoning.

- **logical, or analytical:** When you reason through a set of facts and apply your experience to solve a problem, answer a question, or explain an opinion, you are being logical and analytical. For example, let's say you have decided to buy a car and you have only so much money to spend. You have narrowed your choices down to two cars that are about the same price. To aid your decision making, you compare the cars based on several characteristics that are important to you, such as size, comfort, gas mileage, and cost of service. Here is another example: Suppose you earn a failing grade on a test. A less analytical thinker might blame the instructor for being unfair or the course for being difficult, but you put the blame where it belongs—on you. By analyzing your errors to determine their cause, you may discover that your mistakes were the result of poor preparation, carelessness, or a failure to understand the material. Whatever the cause, you now know what you can do to prevent similar errors in the future.

- **self-reflective:** When you attempt to integrate new information with prior knowledge, you are being self-reflective. Using the example above, let's say that the test you failed was an algebra test and that your errors were careless ones, such as failing to reduce a fraction to its lowest terms or leaving off a plus or minus sign. If you are self-reflective, then you will learn from your mistakes. On the next test, you proofread your paper before handing it in so that you can catch and correct any careless errors you may have made. Here is another example. Your psychology professor has assigned a paper. To ensure a good grade, you use the skills you have learned in your composition class to select an appropriate topic and plan your essay. A self-reflective student is one who regularly thinks about what he or she is learning and how to apply it in other contexts.

- **conscious:** Critical thinking is conscious thinking. You know you are doing it; you are aware of yourself in the process of thinking. For example, let's say you are reading an assigned chapter in your biology textbook and halfway down the page, your mind wanders. You suddenly become conscious that you don't know what you have read. Now you have to go back to the beginning, and this time you work at paying attention. Fortunately, this textbook, and the course in which you are using it, will help you develop strategies for focusing and maintaining your attention.

- **purposeful:** When you are thinking critically, you are focused on a particular task such as solving a problem, making an important decision, answering a

Thinking critically takes decisive action.

question, or looking for a piece of information. For example, suppose you need a part-time job to help meet your tuition costs. Should you look for a job on campus or off campus? Can you effectively balance a work and study schedule? Would you be better off seeking a scholarship or student loan? College is your top priority. Above all, you want to stay in school and earn good grades. By letting this purpose drive your decision making, you will be able to consider the pros and cons of your financial alternatives to find the best one.

Here is another way to look at critical thinking. At any given time, there are a lot of thoughts running through your mind. While sitting in a lecture, you may be hearing the words, but you are also aware of two students next to you engaged in a conversation. You may also be thinking ahead to your next class or feeling hungry. When the lecture ends, you gather up your books and realize that you have not taken any notes. This is not critical thinking. Critical thinking is focused. As a critical thinker, you would come to the lecture prepared to take notes. You would fight to maintain your concentration by sitting closer to the speaker, by taking detailed notes, and by reflecting on the speaker's meaning and how it applies to you. Quite simply, critical thinkers *decide* to think.

What Is Creative Thinking?

Creative thinking has some of the qualities of critical thinking but is also inventive and original.

How does **creative thinking** differ from critical thinking? The tool of the critical thinker is *analysis*. The tool of the creative thinker is *invention*. Analysis is the process of logical reasoning. When you think through the steps of a process or consider all sides of an issue or argument, you are using analysis. When you come up with a new solution to an old problem or whenever you use what you know to discover what you don't know, you are using invention. For example, in a writing class, you learn the basic steps for choosing a topic, thinking it through, and writing an essay that has a central idea and supporting details. So far, this engages you in thinking critically. Obviously, you will not be the first person to write about the topic you have chosen. However, your essay will not be exactly like anyone else's. Why? Because you are you. Your experiences and the opinions formed and conclusions drawn from them will be your own invention. Like an original essay, anything you produce—such as a poem, a work of art, or a musical composition—calls for creative thinking. When you think creatively, you may examine what other people have said or done, but you try to find some new angle or twist on the information that puts your stamp on it and makes it yours. For example, *American Idol* contestants often perform songs by popular artists, but rather than imitate those artists, the contestants perform the same songs in original ways that display their unique talents. Similarly, in an academic setting when you are thinking creatively, you will raise questions or add new information to a discussion rather than repeating the same things that others have said.

Creative thinking is *inventive* because it operates outside the bounds of logic, seeking new forms of expression. Like critical thinking, creative thinking is self-reflective, conscious, and purposeful. Critical thinking helps you analyze a topic in depth to find shades of meaning. Creative thinking helps you reorganize information in new patterns or contexts. For example, the information you gather from several sources might enable you to write a research paper that draws an original conclusion from accepted facts. Your analysis of the facts calls for critical thinking. The original conclusion calls for creative thinking. Although critical thinking and creative thinking differ, they also overlap in some ways, as illustrated in Figure 3.1.

A valuable question you might ask to start the creative thinking process is "What if?" This question takes you beyond what you know to imagine what could be. For example, what if you could avoid procrastination? What if you could fight your distractions and control your concentration? What if you took charge of your learning by designing your own study system that incorporated strategies known to increase comprehension and improve retention? Imagine what you could achieve. Now take *Awareness Check* 3.1 to assess your critical and creative thinking skills.

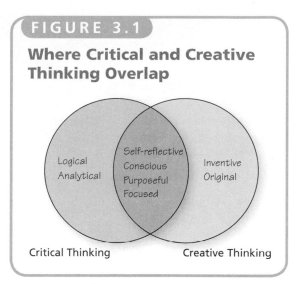

FIGURE 3.1

Where Critical and Creative Thinking Overlap

Logical Analytical

Self-reflective Conscious Purposeful Focused

Inventive Original

Critical Thinking   Creative Thinking

AWARENESS CHECK 3.1

Are You a Critical and Creative Thinker?

Choose one of the following as your response to each statement:
Strongly agree **(4 points),** ***somewhat agree*** **(3 points),** ***neither agree nor disagree*** **(2 points),** ***somewhat disagree*** **(1 point),** ***strongly disagree*** **(0 points). Write your number of points in the box beside each statement. When you are finished, add your score.**

Points

1. I have felt the difference between doing something without thinking and really trying to think about and understand what I am doing.

2. When I am doing an assignment, I am often conscious of the fact that I am either "getting it" or not.

3. I try to determine the purpose of an assignment and what I am supposed to learn from it.

4. Before making a decision, I consider as many alternatives as I can.

5. Some people would describe me as a critical thinker.

6. I have ideas or am able to do things that some would call "creative."

7. I am able to apply the skills I've learned in one course to help me complete assignments in another course.

8. I am self-reflective in that I try to relate what I am learning to my experience or my prior knowledge.

9. When I make a mistake, I am able to figure out what I did wrong and how to correct it.

10. Although I may be guided by the opinions of others, I like to think for myself.

Total

Add your score. If your total is 35–40, your critical and creative thinking skills are already helping you to meet your academic and life challenges. If your total is 25–34, you have some thinking skill strengths on which to build new skills. If your total is 0–19, you have much to gain by developing your thinking skills. Whatever your level of skill, this chapter will help you become a more critical and creative thinker.

The Thinker, François Auguste René Rodin.

An **argument** is a debate or discussion in which different points of view may be examined and either supported or rejected.

An **inductive argument** proceeds from specific instances or observations to a general conclusion.

You Can Improve Your Thinking

Yes, you can improve the way you think. You have already started on the road to improvement just by reading this chapter. No doubt, you recognized yourself in some of the examples given in the previous two sections and you now realize that you have been thinking critically and creatively all along. The difference is that now you are becoming aware of what is going on in your mind as you read, as you listen to a lecture, as you complete an assignment, and even as you struggle to solve problems and make decisions outside of class. Perhaps you have never thought of yourself as a thinker. When you arrived on campus that first day, what were you thinking? Were your thoughts positive and confident or were they filled with self-doubt? Did you think, "I don't belong here"? Did you think, "I know I can make it here"? As you become aware of yourself as a thinker, you begin to pay attention to your inner voice and are able to counteract negative thoughts with positive ones. You can also examine your beliefs or opinions to discover the experiences or knowledge that helped you form your ideas. Armed with this understanding, you will be able to defend your point of view when others challenge you. As a thinker, you will be able to recognize, respond to, and construct good arguments, which is essential to your success in college.

You probably think of an argument as a disagreement, and on one level it is. However, an **argument** such as one you might make in a research paper or a presentation is a discussion in which you state your point of view and back it up with evidence, both from your own experience and from different sources. A good argument anticipates the objections others might have and attempts to answer them. Arguments are about issues. In a history class, the argument may be about the causes and effects of a war or other world-changing event. In a psychology class, the argument may be about the usefulness of different theories that describe normal versus abnormal behavior. In an environmental science class, the argument may be about protecting the environment versus encouraging economic growth. In every course you take, try to determine what the important issues and arguments are.

Recognize Inductive and Deductive Arguments

Not only is argument commonplace in academic life, you can also find examples in everyday life. Political debates are an important factor in every presidential election. The candidates are presented with issues and are given time to express their viewpoints. The winner of the debate is the person whose argument is the most convincing to voters. Another example can be found on the editorial page of your local newspaper. Commentators take opposing positions on various issues of national concern, such as whether to nationalize health care, pass more gun legislation, or close the border between the United States and Mexico. The type of formal argument with which you are probably most familiar is the courtroom debate where lawyers for the plaintiff and defendant face off against each other and argue the issues of the case. Television shows such as *Law and Order* have popularized this form of argument.

A formal argument such as a political debate, a trial, or even the thesis of a research paper may be one of two types: inductive or deductive. An **inductive argument** reasons through specific facts or observations to arrive at a general principle or draw a broad conclusion. Think of the homicide detective who follows specific clues and collects pieces of evidence such as the fingerprints on a gun that will lead to the perpetrator of a crime. Like the detective, you might search through a stack of graded tests (the evidence), looking for clues that will tell you what to study for your midterm exam. As another example, perhaps you made good grades in your high school biology course. You enjoyed that course and you reason, inductively, that biology would be a good major for you. However, a biology major consists of many other courses, some of which you may not like at all. Also, your choice of a major should reflect your strengths and career aspirations and not be based only on whether you like one course in a discipline. In other words, not all conclusions drawn inductively are good conclusions. An inductive argument can be weak or strong, depending on the facts that support it, how the facts are connected, and whether the conclusion follows from the facts.

Unlike an inductive argument, a **deductive argument** reasons from a broad generalization or stated principle to draw a conclusion about one specific instance. For example, to solve an equation, you must follow algebraic rules to work through the steps that will lead to a solution. If you apply the right rules and if you do each step correctly, your answer will be correct. Mistakes in applying the rules will result in an incorrect answer. A deductive argument is convincing only if the underlying principles on which it is based are sound. Here is another example of deduction: A child goes missing and the mother is accused of murder. Although the mother says she is innocent, the press reports that she shows no concern for the missing child. It is widely believed that a mother in this situation would be visibly grief stricken (generalization). Therefore, most people who have heard about the case have concluded that the mother is guilty (specific instance). However, people express grief in different ways, and under the law an accused person is presumed innocent until proven guilty. A conclusion arrived at by deduction is valid only if you can demonstrate that the generalizations on which it is based are true. To help you differentiate between inductive and deductive reasoning, see Figure 3.2.

A **deductive argument** proceeds from a broad generalization to draw a conclusion about a specific instance.

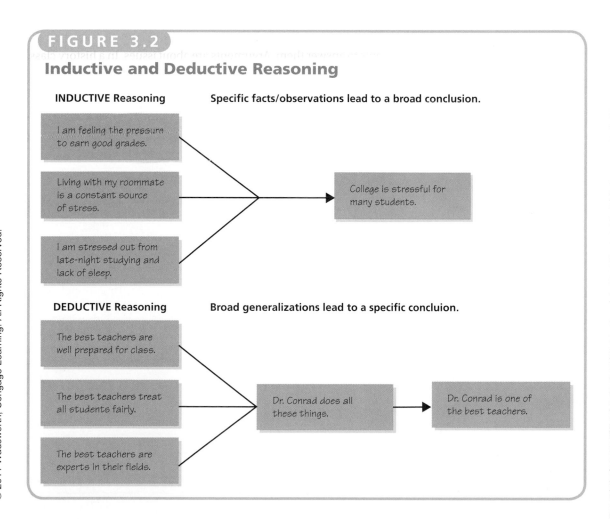

FIGURE 3.2

Inductive and Deductive Reasoning

INDUCTIVE Reasoning   Specific facts/observations lead to a broad conclusion.

I am feeling the pressure to earn good grades.

Living with my roommate is a constant source of stress.

I am stressed out from late-night studying and lack of sleep.

College is stressful for many students.

DEDUCTIVE Reasoning   Broad generalizations lead to a specific concluion.

The best teachers are well prepared for class.

The best teachers treat all students fairly.

The best teachers are experts in their fields.

Dr. Conrad does all these things.

Dr. Conrad is one of the best teachers.

As mentioned before, the strength of an inductive or deductive argument depends on the accuracy of the facts that support it and the soundness of the reasoning on which it is based. False reasoning can weaken an argument, as you will learn in the next section.

Spot False Reasoning

A **fallacy** is an error in reasoning that interferes with the validity, or soundness, of an argument.

Another way to improve your thinking is to recognize the common fallacies that interfere with sound reasoning. A **fallacy** is an error in logic, or false reasoning. Most fallacies can be sorted into two categories: those that ignore issues and those that oversimplify issues. A fallacy that ignores an issue distracts your attention from the argument as a whole. For example, politicians running for election often attack each other's character instead of debating the issues that are important to voters. It's easier to attack your opponent than to explain your position on an issue, especially if you know that your position will be unpopular with voters. Some fallacies are unintentional, the result of sloppy reasoning. However, some people intentionally use false reasoning when they think it will give them an advantage. For example, politicians will make emotional appeals to voters when their arguments are weak or the facts do not support their claims. Democrats accuse Republicans of trying to "poison our water and air by opposing environmental regulations," and Republicans accuse Democrats

FIGURE 3.3

Fallacies That Ignore Issues

Fallacy	Definition	Example	Reasoning Error
Argument to the Person*	An attack on the person instead of the argument	Calling someone a racist when race has nothing to do with the issue	Emotional words detract from the argument.
Argument to the People**	An appeal to people's emotions instead of to reason	Predicting dire consequences of an action without offering facts to support your claim	Predictions do not mean anything without facts to back them up.
Begging the Question	Stating an opinion as if it were a fact	A city council member saying "Orlando is a beautiful city, as anyone can see."	Beauty is a matter of opinion.
Circular Reasoning	Restating a claim as part of the evidence	Saying that the roads are crowded because there are too many cars on the roads	Why are the roads crowded? Why are there too many cars? The conditions are not explained.
Non Sequitur	A conclusion that does not follow from the facts given	Concluding that someone who is a good teacher would also be a good department chair	Being a good teacher does not necessarily make one a good leader.
Red Herring	Changing the subject; distracting readers from the issue	Answering "I'm for family values" to the question "What is your stand on gun control?"	Family values and gun control are two different issues.

*Argument to the person is also called *argumentum ad hominem*.

**Argument to the people is also called *argumentum ad populem*.

From Kanar, *The Confident Writer*, Fifth Edition. © 2009 Heinle/Arts & Sciences, a part of Cengage Learning, Inc. Reproduced by permission. www.cengage.com/permissions.

of attempting to "destroy the economy through overregulation of businesses." Neither claim is true, but emotional appeals seldom are.

Now let's consider two examples of false reasoning that are closer to home. A student who earns a poor grade on an assignment says, "I can't make a decent grade in this course because the instructor doesn't like me." This argument keeps the student from facing the real issue: What was wrong with the assignment? What did the student do or not do that resulted in a poor grade? Here is another example: A student misses several assignments in an algebra class and receives a midterm warning. The student says, "Either I do my algebra homework or my essays for the writing class, but I can't do both." Actually, the student can do both, as many students do. By acknowledging only two alternatives, the student limits the possibilities for success. Can you spot the fallacies in your own reasoning as well as those in other people's arguments? See Figures 3.3 and 3.4 for examples of various kinds of fallacies; then complete Exercise 3.1.

Besides understanding arguments and recognizing false reasoning, you can do even more to think for yourself. The rest of this chapter explains four more strategies for thinking critically and creatively: *Ask the right questions, prepare yourself for learning, make inferences,* and *evaluate information and sources.* Together, the first letters of the key words form the acronym A PIE. Use the acronym and Figure 3.5 to help you recall the four strategies. The figure is also a visual outline of the next four sections. To learn more about acronyms and how to use them as memory cues, see Chapter 8.

FIGURE 3.4

Fallacies That Oversimplify Issues

Fallacy	Definition	Example	Reasoning Error
Bandwagon	An argument based on the idea that "everybody does it" or wants it	A teenager saying "Why can't I stay out past 10:00 P.M.? All my friends do."	The teenager's parents make the rules, not friends or their parents.
Either-or	Reducing an issue to only two sides	Reducing the abortion issue to pro-choice or pro-life	There are other possible positions to take on this issue.
Faulty Analogy	An inappropriate or inaccurate comparison	A parent saying, "When I was your age I walked five miles to school in the snow, so why do you need a car?"	The conditions that existed when the parent was young are not the same as today's conditions.
Post Hoc (Faulty Cause and Effect)	Believing that because one event follows another, the first event must be the cause of the other	Someone saying, "I left my window open last night, so now I have a cold."	Leaving the window open does not cause a cold; germs do.
Hasty Generalization	A conclusion drawn from insufficient evidence at hand	Concluding that blind dates are a waste of time based on one bad experience	One bad experience on a blind date does not prove that all blind dates are bad.

From Kanar, *The Confident Writer*, Fifth Edition. © 2009 Heinle/Arts & Sciences, a part of Cengage Learning, Inc. Reproduced by permission. www.cengage.com/permissions.

EXERCISE 3.1   Your Fallacies Are Showing

CAN YOU SPOT THE FALLACY in each statement below? Read the statement. Then, using Figures 3.3 and 3.4 as a guide, determine which fallacy the statement contains and write it on the line beneath the statement. Be prepared to explain your answers in a class discussion.

1. **Everybody knows that you can't get drunk on only one drink.**

   _____

2. **The most reckless drivers on the road today are young women.**

   _____

3. **I don't watch disaster movies; I saw one once and didn't like it.**

   _____

4. **You're either with us or against us.**

   _____

5. **We need the undocumented immigrants in this country because they are willing to do the jobs that Americans won't do.**

   _____

6. **You and I are the same size, so that shirt will look as good on me as it does on you.**

   _____

7. **Ron is failing biology, but his work hours have changed, so he should do better in the course.**

   _____

8. **Everyone else has signed this petition, so you should sign it too.**

   _____

9. **The instructor wanted to know why Lenore was late for class, and Lenore said, "I have the assignment."**

   _____

10. **We need to make health care available to everyone so that everyone will have access to health care.**

    _____

11. **I knew it would rain today because I left my umbrella at home.**

    _____

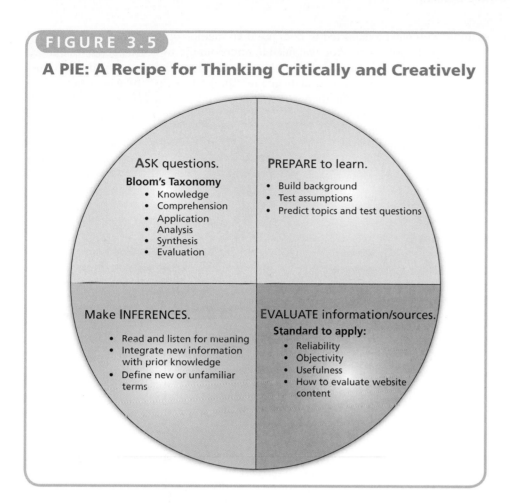

FIGURE 3.5

A PIE: A Recipe for Thinking Critically and Creatively

ASK questions.

Bloom's Taxonomy
- Knowledge
- Comprehension
- Application
- Analysis
- Synthesis
- Evaluation

PREPARE to learn.
- Build background
- Test assumptions
- Predict topics and test questions

Make **I**NFERENCES.
- Read and listen for meaning
- Integrate new information with prior knowledge
- Define new or unfamiliar terms

EVALUATE information/sources.

Standard to apply:
- Reliability
- Objectivity
- Usefulness
- How to evaluate website content

Ask the Right Questions

- Ask questions that demonstrate your ability to think critically and creatively on six different levels.

It is in our nature as human beings to ask questions because this is one of the primary ways we learn. One of the first questions a young child asks is "Why?" Yet so many college students seem to have lost their curiosity. Why do college students seem afraid to ask questions? Perhaps they think their questions are insignificant or they fear being ridiculed by their peers. Whatever the reason, when instructors ask, "Do you have any questions?" they are often met with silence. Questions open discussions. Questions clarify misunderstandings, promote self-discovery, and initiate the process of knowledge acquisition. Questions start you off on a journey that could lead you to some interesting places. Don't be afraid to ask questions. If you need a model for asking good questions that get to the heart of issues and help you explore ideas critically and creatively, Bloom's Taxonomy is your guide.

Bloom's Taxonomy is a classification of six levels of thinking and learning, as explained in *Taxonomy of Educational Objectives, Handbook 1: Cognitive Domain*, published in 1959 by the David McKay Company. Benjamin S. Bloom was an American educational psychologist and professor at the University of Chicago. Bloom died in 1999, and his legacy, the *Taxonomy*, continues to influence educators today.

Bloom identified six levels of learning, each more demanding than the previous one. He believed that you must master each level before proceeding to the next. Many instructors develop test questions based on Bloom's levels. In a history course, for

Bloom's Taxonomy is a classification of six levels of thinking and learning, ranked from lowest to highest.

example, you will be expected to do more than memorize names of key people and dates of important events. You will need to understand how those people influenced the thinking of future generations and how those events changed the course of history. In Bloom's terms, if you recall the name "Charles Darwin" and you associate him with the theory of evolution, then you are thinking at the *knowledge* level. If you are able to explain in your own words the broad principles of the theory of evolution, then you are thinking at the *comprehension* level. To *apply* the idea of evolution to your own life, you might think about the way your taste in music has evolved from liking one kind of music to appreciating music in all its forms. Then, what are some other theories about the origin of humans and other living things? How do these theories compare to Darwin's theory? What are the strengths and weaknesses of the theories? These questions are at the level of *analysis*. Can you see that with each level of thinking or questioning you begin to explore a topic in greater depth? Therefore, it is to your advantage to know more about Bloom's Taxonomy, because it will help you think more critically to analyze information and what it means, instead of relying on memorization as your primary learning strategy. Here are some of the things an understanding of Bloom's levels will help you do:

▼ Ask more meaningful questions in class that demonstrate your ability to think deeply about a topic.

▼ Anticipate what kinds of questions an instructor might ask on a test and their level of difficulty.

▼ Analyze your mistakes so that you know what level of thinking was required and are able to determine why you missed a question.

▼ Monitor your own thinking so that you know which level you are operating at and can try to move to the next level.

So what are Bloom's levels of thinking? First, look at Figure 3.6, which lists the levels on a staircase, ranking them from lowest to highest. Starting from the bottom of the staircase, the first three levels comprise the lower-order thinking skills, which are the foundation of learning. As you move up the staircase, the next three levels are the higher-order thinking skills that require more in-depth thinking. With this visual image of Bloom's levels in mind, now read the explanation of each one.

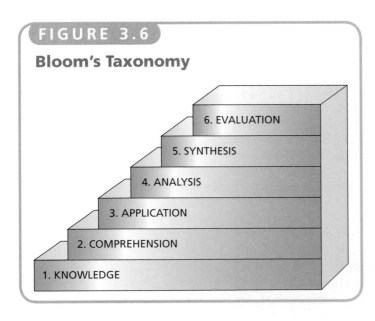

FIGURE 3.6

Bloom's Taxonomy

6. EVALUATION
5. SYNTHESIS
4. ANALYSIS
3. APPLICATION
2. COMPREHENSION
1. KNOWLEDGE

1. **Knowledge** is the most basic level of thinking and learning. At this level, you are able to remember something without necessarily understanding it. This is the level at which you memorized the alphabet, the multiplication tables, and the U.S. capital cities when you were young. Test questions at the knowledge level might ask you to define a term, list items, or recall names, dates, or places. Can you see why you might miss a question that asks you to do more with the information than these simple tasks? If you simply memorize a list of items, you will not be prepared for a test question that asks you to explain what the items mean or apply them to another context. Similarly, when you ask for simple information in class—such as a date when an event occurred or the name of an author—you are questioning at the knowledge level.

2. **Comprehension** requires that you both remember and *understand* the information. To check how well you understand some information you have been studying, try to put it in your own words as if you were explaining

it to a friend. You cannot explain what you do not understand. Test questions at the comprehension level might contain the direction words *describe, discuss, interpret,* or *summarize.* Suppose you are learning about prime numbers in your algebra class. You recall the term "prime number," but you are not sure that you understand what it means. A comprehension question you might ask the instructor is "Can you give an example of a prime number?" or "What are the properties of a prime number?"

3. **Application** is the practical level of thinking. How can you use the information? How can you apply, or relate, it to your own life and needs? For example, you learn in a composition class that a paragraph should have a topic sentence. But can you write a topic sentence for a paragraph of your own? Can you find the topic sentence in a paragraph of an article or a textbook chapter? If you can, then you are thinking at the application level. Test questions that ask you to apply your knowledge might contain direction words such as *calculate, demonstrate, illustrate, examine,* or *relate.* To ask an application question in any class, you would ask how a theory or principle you have learned could be applied in daily life.

4. **Analysis** is the process of breaking down a complex idea into its components, or parts, so that they can be more easily understood. For example, when you follow the steps of a procedure to do an experiment in your biology lab, you are using analysis. When you explain to your algebra instructor how you arrived at the solution to an equation, you are thinking at the analysis level. Finding the meaning in a poem calls for analysis. Test questions at the analysis level may contain the direction words *analyze, arrange, classify, explain, compare,* or *differentiate.* When a student in your class states his or her position on an issue and you ask, "Why do you think that way?" or "How do you know?" you are questioning the student at Bloom's fourth level.

5. **Synthesis** is the level of thinking that requires you to make connections, see relationships among different things, and be creative. Drawing conclusions from stated facts, relating what you have just learned to what you already know, and pulling ideas together from several sources to write a research paper in which you draw an original conclusion are all examples of synthesis. Test questions at the synthesis level might ask you to *combine, design, formulate, plan,* or *compose.* The question *"What if . . .?"* is a synthesis question because it asks you to imagine something other than what is known. For example, in a biology lab, you might be doing an experiment that combines different chemicals in a growth medium for a plant, to see what happens. The question you start with might be this: "What if I add this chemical and change the amount of water?"

6. **Evaluation** is an estimation of worth, a judgment call. How are you doing in your courses so far? Are the study strategies you are using working? Are you making progress toward the goals you have set? If not, what can you do to redirect your efforts and get back on track? That is evaluation in a nutshell. Test questions that call for an evaluation might ask you to *assess, measure, rank, judge, evaluate,* or *explain advantages and disadvantages* in order to assess worth. In a psychology class, you might ask this question: "How useful are Freud's theories in the everyday practice of psychology?" Your question calls for a value judgment.

FIGURE 3.7

Asking Questions on Bloom's Six Levels of Thinking

Level	Questions About Topic Sentences	What the Questions Show
Knowledge	What is a topic sentence?	This question asks for a definition.
Comprehension	If a paragraph doesn't have a topic sentence, does it still have a main idea?	This question shows that you understand that a topic sentence states a main idea.
Application	How can I write a topic sentence for my own paragraph?	This question asks for a process and shows that you are trying to apply what you have learned.
Analysis	How is the topic sentence related to the other sentences in a paragraph?	This question shows that you are making connections; you understand that the other sentences in a paragraph must also have purposes.
Synthesis	Where would I find the main idea of an entire essay or a textbook chapter?	This question shows that you have drawn a conclusion: If a paragraph has a main idea, then so does a longer piece of writing composed of many paragraphs.
Evaluation	Which one of my own topic sentences is better?	This question shows that you have made a judgment about your writing.

Bloom's levels of thinking are simply meant as a guide to show you *how* to think more critically and creatively. The levels are tools you can use to bring more depth into your studying and to help you ask more useful questions in class discussion so that you can get the information you need. As previously mentioned, Bloom's Taxonomy is widely accepted in the academic world. It has been the subject of many articles and studies. Some have tried to improve on it with modifications of their own. However, Bloom's original categories set the standard. Now look at Figure 3.7, which demonstrates how to ask questions on six levels. The questions are about topic sentences, a subject you will cover in a writing class. You can also use Bloom's levels for predicting what kinds of questions might be asked on a test, as you will learn in the next section.

CRITICAL THINKING

Applying Bloom's Levels of Thinking

Exercise Overview

The purpose of this exercise is to increase your understanding of Bloom's levels of thinking and learning and to give you some practice working with the different levels.

Exercise Background

Most students study at the knowledge level, memorizing facts without understanding what they mean or why they are important. Yet most instructors ask very few test questions at this basic level. Instead,

continued

you are expected to demonstrate that you understand the material and are able to apply what you have learned. Most test questions, and many of your assignments, require you to operate at Bloom's higher levels of thinking: analysis, synthesis, and evaluation. Have you ever wondered why an assignment is so difficult? Could it be because the assignment is asking you to do more than recall a simple fact?

Exercise Task

Resources for this task include the explanations of Bloom's levels on pages 61–64 and Figure 3.7. To help you think critically about the material in one of your courses, write six questions on a topic of your choice that you could ask in a class discussion. Write one question for each of Bloom's levels. As an example, suppose your topic is learning styles from Chapter 2 of this book. A *knowledge* question might be "What are the three learning styles?" All this question asks you to do is recall three terms: visual, auditory, and tactile-kinesthetic. But if your question is "Name and explain the three learning styles," then *comprehension* is also required. A question that calls for *analysis* might be "How can you adapt your learning style to an instructor's teaching style?" Be prepared to share your questions in a class discussion if asked to do so.

Your Questions

1. Knowledge:

   _____

2. Comprehension:

   _____

3. Application:

   _____

4. Analysis:

   _____

5. Synthesis:

   _____

6. Evaluation:

   _____

Prepare to Learn

- Set the stage for learning by determining what you already know or think and what you still need to find out.

Decisive action is an essential part of learning. In other words, before any learning takes place, you must first decide to learn. Sounds obvious, doesn't it? However, you might be surprised to know how many students sit down to study without any preparation. They just open the book and start reading, or they begin working the first algebra problem in an assignment, and so on. When they get to the end, they stop. As will be stressed many times in the following chapters, there are important things you need to do before, during, and after study for maximum learning and retention. This section is about three critical thinking skills you can use to prepare yourself for learning *before* studying, listening to a lecture, or going to class.

▼ Build background.

▼ Test your assumptions.

▼ Predict topics and test questions.

Build Background

Every course you take follows a sequential development of skill from basic concepts to the more complex applications of those concepts. You will see this most clearly in an algebra course, where each chapter of the textbook depends on your understanding what was explained in previous chapters. If you miss a few days of class, you can really get behind because you lose one or more steps in a sequence of skills that are being taught. A writing class might begin with a basic skill such as choosing a topic and gradually move on to more complex issues such as choosing an organizational pattern for an essay. If you have had the experience of feeling "lost" in a course because you have been absent for a few days, then you can relate to this discussion. The first step in building background for learning is to recognize that your courses follow a sequence.

Your best guide to the sequence of skill in any course is your syllabus. Additional background-building tools are your class and lecture notes, your textbook, and returned tests and assignments. Review is also an important part of the background-building process. Now here are four things you can do to build background for your next class in any course.

1. **Check your syllabus**: Briefly review the topics and assignments covered at the last class meeting. Then read what is scheduled for the next class. Can you see a sequence forming? If not, look back over the topics listed for the past several classes until you can see where the class has been and where it is going.

2. **Review your notes** from the previous class or lecture, any graded test or assignment that was returned to you at the last class meeting, and the chapter that was covered. What connections can you make between these materials and the chapter or topics assigned for your next class meeting? Do the topics build on each other? Are new topics introduced?

3. **Think about the new topic** that will be covered at the next class meeting. What do you already know about this topic, either from your own experience or from reading the assigned material? This is the background that you will bring to class. This is the framework on which you will attach any new information you learn.

4. **Write down one or more questions** that you would like to have answered in class. Your questions can come from your reading, your notes, or an assignment. Use Bloom's levels of thinking to help you construct good questions.

Testing assumptions is another way to prepare yourself for learning. The next section explains how you can use this skill.

Test Your Assumptions

An **assumption** is an idea or belief taken for granted based on knowledge or experience.

An **assumption** is an idea or belief that is taken for granted or accepted without thinking. Assumptions are based on what we know or have experienced. Everyone has certain assumptions about family, education, government—any aspect of life—and people's assumptions differ. For example, most people agree that some sort of health-care reform is needed. Those who favor nationalized health care subsidized by government funding assume that under such a system costs for services would be lower and that more people would be able to afford health care as a result. Those opposed to nationalized health care assume that lower costs would mean lower payments for services, which would result in a decline in the quality of service. They may also assume that their taxes would be increased to pay for the program. What do those on either side of this issue stand to gain or lose? What evidence supports their assumptions? Are there other points of view?

These are the kinds of questions critical thinkers ask. To think critically, you must test your own assumptions—and others' assumptions—to determine what is known, believed, or taken for granted about a given topic or issue. For example, what assumptions did you have about your courses, instructors, and college life before your first day on campus? Did you assume that college courses would be difficult, interesting, useful, or what? Did you assume that college instructors would be more or less friendly and helpful than your high school teachers? What assumptions did you have about your roommate, about the friends you might meet, or about living on your own? How accurate were these assumptions, and did you learn anything that changed your mind? Keep an open mind and be willing to change your assumptions based on new evidence or experiences. Before you read an assignment or listen to a lecture, build background by asking, "What do I already know about the topic?" and then test your assumptions by asking, "What opinions have I already formed about the topic?" Then, after reading or listening, determine whether your assumptions were correct; and, if they were not, what can you now add to your existing framework of knowledge? What new assumptions have you formed?

Assumptions can be compelling. Your beliefs, the ideas you take for granted, shape your thoughts and actions. As you gain knowledge, skill, and experience, some of your assumptions may change. This is natural and part of the maturing process.

EXERCISE 3.2 Learning Style Activity about Assumptions

IT IS IMPORTANT TO RECOGNIZE and think about the assumptions that you bring to everyday interactions with people as well as to the subjects you study. To test some of your assumptions about other people, look at the group in the following photograph and then answer the questions.

Marty Heitner/The Image Works

continued

1. **Who are these people? What assumptions can you make based on their clothing or on other details in the photograph?**

    _____

    _____

2. **Where are they, and what do they seem to be doing? What details in the photograph help you make your assumptions?**

    _____

    _____

3. **Based on their expressions, what do these people seem to be thinking or feeling?**

    _____

    _____

4. **How do your assumptions about the people in the photograph relate to your own experiences?**

    _____

    _____

5. **Compare and discuss answers to questions 1–4 with a classmate. Did your assumptions differ? After your discussion, did any of your assumptions about the photograph change?**

    _____

    _____

6. **The photograph adds a visual element to this exercise. Did the photograph make the exercise more or less interesting for you, based on your learning style? Explain your answer.**

    _____

    _____

Predict Topics and Test Questions

Predict means to anticipate or foresee an outcome.

To **predict** means to anticipate what comes next or see ahead to an outcome. Predictions are based on prior knowledge and assumptions. Because you believe that certain things are true, you expect or believe that certain things will happen. If you believe, for example, that you are good at math, then you can predict that you will do well in a math course. If you have a favorite author who has just published a new book, you can predict that you will probably like it. Your prediction is based on the assumption that the new book will be similar to others by this author that you have read and enjoyed.

Being able to predict outcomes is an important aspect of critical and creative thinking. Predictions are often the result of asking yourself questions and looking for answers. When you wake up in the morning, you may wonder, "What will the weather be like today? What should I wear?" You look out the window at a sunny, cloudless sky. You step outside and it is breezy and cool enough for a sweater. You remember that yesterday's weather started out cool, but by noon the temperature had risen to eighty degrees. Predicting that today's weather will be the same, you dress in layers so that you can remove some of your clothing as the temperature warms. By lunchtime, however, clouds have begun to form. Friends tell you that rain is on the way. You run out to your car to grab an umbrella from the trunk. In doing so, you have acted on the prediction that it will rain. Based on new information—the clouds and your friends' comments— you now think rain is a likely outcome.

Before listening to a lecture or reading an assignment, anticipate topics and purposes by asking and answering questions such as these: "What will the lecture cover?" "What am I expected to learn?" Remember that any course may begin at a basic level of skill (Bloom's levels of *knowledge*, *comprehension*, and *application*) and may work up to a more advanced level of skill (Bloom's levels of *analysis*, *synthesis*, and *evaluation*) by the end of the term. You can keep up with the course by reviewing after each class and anticipating what comes next. This will help you decide what to study. It will also place assignments in perspective: They build background for the next topic that will be covered. Anticipating what comes next also helps you stay focused in a lecture. Most lectures begin with a brief statement of the topic and an overview of the major points that will be covered. Jot these down, leaving space between so that you can listen for them as they come up in the lecture. At the end of each class, many instructors give a preview of what will happen at the next class meeting. Listen for these statements so that you will know what to expect and be prepared.

To predict what an instructor might ask on a test, ask and answer questions like these: "What have we covered since the last test?" "Which topics has the instructor emphasized in class?" "On which assignments did the instructor spend the most time?" In addition, follow these steps to predict test questions.

1. Check your syllabus for a brief overview of the topics that have been covered since the last test.

2. Check your class and lecture notes for topics or concepts that your instructor identified as important.

3. Examine old tests, especially questions you missed, and make sure you know the answers now.

4. Review the questions at the end of each assigned chapter. Which concepts or topics did the authors think were important enough to feature in these sections? Chapter summaries and questions are good predictors of what might be on a test.

5. Determine which of Bloom's levels the questions from previous tests address. Are you asked to define a term (level 1: *knowledge*), summarize or explain the steps in a process (level 2: comprehension), write the solution to a problem (level 3: *application*), express your opinion (level 4: *analysis*), explain the results of a lab experiment (level 5: *synthesis*), or make a judgment about the worth or value of something you have learned (level 6: *evaluation*). Knowing what level of understanding your instructor expects will not only help you anticipate test questions but will also help you determine the level at which you should be thinking about the material as you study.

See also Chapter 11 for more extensive information on how and what to study for tests and the types of questions that might be asked.

EXERCISE 3.3 Collaborative Activity on Predicting Test Questions

SELECT CHAPTER 1 OR 2 of *The Confident Student.* Think critically about the chapter to predict what questions might appear on a test. Each group member may have different assumptions about what is important. By sharing your information gathered from notes and other sources, you should be able to determine the kinds of questions your instructor might ask. Based on your discussion, write three test questions that address what your group decides are some important chapter concepts. Your questions can be true/false, multiple choice, short answer, or essay. In addition, identify which one of Bloom's levels of thinking each question addresses. Then share your questions in a class discussion.

Make Inferences

- Look beyond what is stated, to understand what may be implied or unstated.

Much of what you learn in college courses comes from reading textbooks and listening to lectures. Reading and listening are active processes that require concentration and critical thinking. To fully engage your mind, read or listen for two levels of meaning. The *literal level* consists of stated information. The *implied level* is the suggested meaning—the unstated ideas or a viewpoint that you get by making inferences from what is stated. An **inference** is an informed guess about an author's or speaker's meaning. Some of your inferences will be more informed than others and will be based on the prior knowledge or experience that you bring to the topic and on how well you understand the stated information. Figure 3.8 shows how making inferences extends to many skill areas and activities. Now read the following poem and make some inferences about the author's meaning.

An **inference** is an informed guess or conclusion drawn from stated information, based on prior knowledge and experience.

On Reading a
Favorite Poem
Carol C. Kanar

Deep in the Maine woods,
On a starless September night,
Lights flicker, then go out.
Miles from any incandescence,
I sit in a thicket of fear,
Black, thorough,
And mourn the sudden loss of sight
As if it were not temporary.
The mind adjusts, takes its measure
Of eternity.
My book lies open in the dark;
I read by lights I cannot see.

On a literal level, the author states facts of time, place, and event. Something happens on a September evening in the Maine woods that causes the lights to go out. On an implied level, what inferences can you make from these facts and the other stated information in the poem? Because the night is "starless," you can infer that it is cloudy, perhaps even stormy. A downed utility line could explain why the lights have gone out. "Deep in the Maine woods" may suggest that the poem's speaker is isolated, far from neighbors or a town. What experience do you bring to the poem? Have you ever been in the woods on a starless night? Have you ever spent time in Maine during September when frontal storms pass through and power outages are common? Why does the author mention the "loss of sight" and "eternity"? What do these ideas suggest to you?

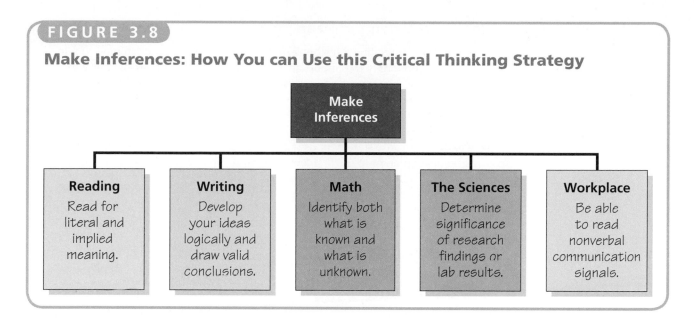

FIGURE 3.8

Make Inferences: How You can Use this Critical Thinking Strategy

Make Inferences

Reading	**Writing**	**Math**	**The Sciences**	**Workplace**
Read for literal and implied meaning.	Develop your ideas logically and draw valid conclusions.	Identify both what is known and what is unknown.	Determine significance of research findings or lab results.	Be able to read nonverbal communication signals.

What does the title have to do with the rest of the poem? A poem's literal and implied meaning may support more than one interpretation.

Your personal experience not only affects the inferences you make from poetry, but also influences how you read textbooks. If you have some prior knowledge about a subject, understanding may come easier. New material and unfamiliar concepts make greater demands on you as a reader. Reading on two levels of meaning will help you think critically about your assignments and make good inferences. At the literal level, pay attention to what an author *says*. For example, when you read a chapter in an algebra textbook, determine what rules or steps are involved in solving a certain kind of problem. When you read the introduction to any textbook chapter, look for a statement of purpose: What does the author want you to learn from the chapter? At the implied level, try to figure out what an author *means* by making inferences. Ask questions such as "Why is this material important?" and "How can I use this information?" For example, you read the rules for solving an equation that has two unknowns, *x* and *y*. You look at the example problem in the textbook and trace the steps. You watch the instructor solve a problem on the chalkboard. So far, you are learning at the literal level by reading and by direct observation. Later that day, you do the problems your instructor assigned for homework. These are not the same problems that you saw in the textbook and in class, but you recognize that they are similar in type. Therefore, you infer that the same rules will apply. If you have trouble working the problems, you can refer to the textbook example as a reminder and then practice applying the rules and steps to similar kinds of problems in the chapter. When you read a chapter in a psychology textbook, read about experiments on two levels. At the literal level, determine who conducted the experiment, why, what data were collected, and what happened. At the critical level, determine the experiment's significance. What did it prove, and why is it an important piece of research? No matter what you are studying, the more facts you have and the more related experience you can bring to the subject, the more valid your inferences will be.

The following three steps will help you process information on two levels so that you can make meaningful inferences about what you learn.

1. Read and listen for meaning.

2. Integrate new information with prior knowledge.

3. Define new or unfamiliar terms.

Concept Check 3.1

Making inferences also applies to situations outside your studies. For example, can you tell when someone is being honest with you? What facial expression, gesture, tone of voice, or manner of speaking might suggest that someone is not telling the truth?

Read and Listen for Meaning

Whether you are reading a textbook or an online document or listening to a lecture, your goal is to identify the important ideas and understand their meaning. In a nutshell, these are the strategies to use: Identify the author's or speaker's purpose; find the central idea; then read or listen for the examples and other details that support the central idea.

Purpose means "aim" or "goal."

A **purpose** is an aim or a goal—what you are expected to learn, understand, or be able to do. A purpose statement usually comes early in a lecture, near the beginning of a textbook chapter, or in the first few paragraphs of an article. But even if the purpose is not stated, you can infer it from the title and introduction. Suppose you are assigned to read "Chemical Reactions," a chapter in your chemistry textbook. The introduction states, "This chapter explains the main types of chemical reactions." From the title and this sentence, you can infer that the author wants you to know everything about chemical reactions: what a chemical reaction is, what the main types of chemical reactions are, and why they are important. Use this information to guide your reading by looking for a definition of *chemical reaction* and the names and properties of the main types. An author's or speaker's purpose guides the choice of examples and other details. By determining a purpose for reading or listening, you are on your way toward finding the most important ideas.

Many students say, "I can't tell which ideas are the most important in a lecture or a textbook chapter." The ideas that you need to identify are the central idea and the details that support it. The **central idea**, or main idea, is the author's or speaker's opinion about a topic. The **supporting details** are the examples, facts, reasons, or other stated information on which the author's opinion is based. In other words, the central idea tells you *what* a lecture or chapter is about. The details answer the questions *why*, *how*, *when*, *where*, and *what if*? Suppose you are listening to a lecture on reducing test anxiety. After a brief introduction, the speaker says, "Because test anxiety is a learned response, you can unlearn it by identifying and overcoming its causes." If you correctly identify this statement as the central idea, then you can ask yourself several questions that will help you listen for the details: How is test anxiety "learned"? What causes test anxiety? How can a person overcome it?

Central idea (also called the *main idea*) refers to an author's or speaker's stated or implied viewpoint on a topic.

Supporting details consist of facts, reasons, examples, or other stated information that supports a central idea.

In some printed materials, the central idea may be unstated, or implied. However, you can infer the central idea from the title, the introduction, or the first few paragraphs

---

EXERCISE 3.4   Collaborative Activity about Making Inferences

APPLY WHAT YOU HAVE LEARNED so far about making inferences by completing this exercise with group members. Follow the guidelines for group discussion that appear on the inside back cover. Read the following paragraph and determine whether you can make the inferences that follow it. Discuss each inference, arrive at a consensus, and then check *yes* or *no* for each statement. Finally, evaluate your work.

> Susan is not doing well in her composition course. She missed the first two days of class because she was dropping and adding other courses. She missed the introduction to the course and the instructor's description of the course requirements. Her instructor gave her a syllabus, but she didn't read it. As a result, she was not prepared for the first grammar test, and she earned a D on it. She decided that the instructor was too demanding, and she tried to get into another section. Unfortunately, the drop-add period was over. Susan's advisor convinced her to stay in the course and suggested that she make an appointment with the instructor to see what she can do to catch up. The advisor believes that if Susan begins right now to take a serious interest in the course, do the assignments, and keep up with the syllabus, she can still do well in the course because it is early in the semester.

continued

Yes	No	
☐	☐	1. **Susan will fail the course.**
☐	☐	2. **The instructor is too demanding.**
☐	☐	3. **If Susan had read the syllabus, she might have known that a test was scheduled.**
☐	☐	4. **The instructor may be willing to let Susan make up what she missed on the first two days of class.**
☐	☐	5. **It is important to attend the first few days of class.**

Group Evaluation:

Evaluate your discussion. Did everyone contribute? Did you accomplish your task successfully? What additional questions do you have about making inferences from facts? How will you find answers to your questions? Write your evaluation on your own paper or download the group exercise form from *The Confident Student* premium website.

and the last paragraph. Taken together, these parts of an article or chapter contain key details that will help you figure out what the central idea is. Chapters 7, 9, and 10 explain in more detail how to read and study from textbooks and other printed materials. Chapter 5 explains strategies for listening to lectures and taking notes on the important ideas.

Integrate New Information with Prior Knowledge

As you learn new information, you will quickly forget it unless you integrate it with prior knowledge. This is why making inferences is so important. Try to understand the significance of each new skill or concept you learn. Determine how you will use the information; then put your knowledge into action. For example, in a writing class you learn to develop an essay by stating your central idea and supporting it with specific details and examples. Why not use that skill to write papers for your other courses or to develop a speech, activities that also benefit from a clearly stated central idea and well-chosen examples? Using skills in new contexts expands your knowledge base.

No matter what you learn in a course, find ways to apply your knowledge. Determine how new information is testing your assumptions and challenging your beliefs. One goal of learning is to make positive changes in your life. Self-reflect regularly to examine how your college experience is changing you.

Define New or Unfamiliar Terms

Most academic disciplines use special terminology to describe theories, concepts, and principles. You may have encountered the terms *id, ego,* and *superego* in a psychology course; *photosynthesis* in a biology course; and *integer, binomial,* and *polynomial* in a math course. In order to understand the information presented in each course, make an effort to learn the meaning of the key terms related to each discipline. Use your dictionary and textbook glossaries. While reading or listening to a lecture, keep a separate notepad or index cards handy for listing unfamiliar words that you can look up later.

The best way to develop your vocabulary is by reading. The more you read, the more you are exposed to new words and ideas that will increase your store of knowledge.

Concept Check 3.2

Pinpoint one skill that you have read about in this chapter that you could apply at work or in your other courses. Why is this skill important, and what will it help you accomplish?

Evaluate Information and Sources

- Determine whether an informational source is credible by applying standards of evaluation such as reliability, objectivity, and usefulness.

Evaluate means to determine worth or value, to make judgments.

To **evaluate** means to determine worth or value. To evaluate also means "to judge," that is, to make decisions about whether something is right or wrong, good or bad, fair or unfair. If you decide to withdraw from a course, you must evaluate that decision on the basis of whether doing so will be good or bad for you. On the one hand, withdrawing from a course may have a negative effect on your grade point average. But a positive effect might be that it would leave you more time to devote to your remaining courses. Evaluating your progress in a course means monitoring your progress for improvement. What skills have you mastered since the beginning of the term, and what effect has the application of these skills had on your grades?

Making evaluations is a critical thinking strategy you use in other areas of your life besides college. Deciding whether to take a job, quit a job, marry, divorce, or buy a home all depend on making judgments about these important decisions. At work, you may be asked to judge which machines, tools, or procedures produce the desired outcomes.

An evaluation is a *measurement* of worth. "How much will this help or hurt me?" and "How important is this to me?" are questions you can ask when making evaluations. To make evaluations, you need a standard to go by. To evaluate the worth of continuing a relationship that has proved unsatisfying, your standards might be the expectations you have for a good relationship. To evaluate the purchase of a car, your standards might include the car's safety, dependability, and affordability. There are many criteria, or standards, by which you can make sound evaluations. As a college student, you can evaluate what you learn by applying three basic standards: *reliability*,

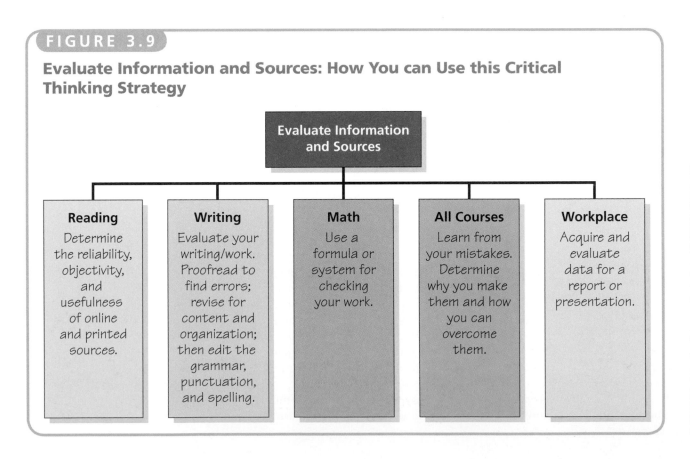

FIGURE 3.9

Evaluate Information and Sources: How You can Use this Critical Thinking Strategy

Evaluate Information and Sources

Reading
Determine the reliability, objectivity, and usefulness of online and printed sources.

Writing
Evaluate your writing/work. Proofread to find errors; revise for content and organization; then edit the grammar, punctuation, and spelling.

Math
Use a formula or system for checking your work.

All Courses
Learn from your mistakes. Determine why you make them and how you can overcome them.

Workplace
Acquire and evaluate data for a report or presentation.

objectivity, and *usefulness*. Figure 3.9 shows how making evaluations extends to several skill areas and activities.

Reliability

To evaluate a source for **reliability**, determine its credibility and trustworthiness by finding answers to three questions:

▼ Who says so?

▼ What are his or her credentials?

▼ How does he or she know?

> **Reliability** means dependability, credibility, and trustworthiness.

As you read, research, and listen to lectures, remember that primary sources are more reliable than secondary sources. A *primary source* is a firsthand or direct source of information. A *secondary source* is an interpretation of a primary source. For example, if the president of the United States addresses the nation on television, the text of his speech is a primary source. If a newscaster summarizes what the president said, the summary is a secondary source. A newspaper account of the president's speech is also a secondary source unless the newspaper reprints the entire text of the speech. Have you ever listened to a reporter's summary of a speech and wondered whether that reporter had heard the same speech you heard? A secondary source is only as reliable as the person who interprets the primary source.

When you are researching a topic, you may have difficulty determining whether a source is primary or secondary. Look at the bibliographies at the ends of books and articles. If the same titles and authors appear over and over again, chances are good that they represent either primary sources or reliable secondary sources of information. If you are just beginning to do research, your instructor or a librarian can help you select sources and evaluate their reliability.

Another way to evaluate reliability is to check an author's background or credentials. Suppose you are interested in learning about global warming. A paper written by a respected scientist with expertise in climatology or publications from organizations such as NASA and the National Weather Service would be reliable sources of information. On the other hand, a political activist's blog, the publications of an environmental group, or the commentary of someone who is well known in his or her own field but who has no scientific expertise in global warming might be interesting to read but neither reliable nor objective. Instructors try to select textbooks that are reliable sources of information, written by experts in their fields. A textbook's title page may list the author's college or other affiliation.

Objectivity

To evaluate a written or oral presentation for **objectivity**, determine how evenhanded, unemotional, and free from bias it is by asking and answering three questions:

▼ What is the author's or speaker's purpose?

▼ Are all sides of the issue presented or acknowledged?

▼ Is the language free of slanted or manipulative words and phrases?

> **Objectivity** means "evenhandedness," expressing opinions that are unclouded by emotion or bias.

If an author's or speaker's purpose is to inform, then you should expect factual details and reasoned opinions. You should also expect fair treatment of differing viewpoints and language that is free of words and phrases designed to provoke emotional reactions that could cloud your judgment. Although most authors and commentators—including textbook authors and college lecturers—would probably say that they are objective, some may have a motive, viewpoint, or bias that influences their choice of words or examples.

An author or speaker who has something to gain by a change in readers' beliefs or behaviors will not be as objective as one who has nothing to gain. Those whose purpose is to persuade may write forcefully in favor of one viewpoint. If they try to persuade fairly, they will acknowledge other viewpoints. Those who attempt to persuade unfairly are likely to distort facts, leave out facts, state opinions as if they were facts, and use manipulative language. Usually they have something to gain by appealing to your emotions or changing your beliefs or behavior. Advertisers want your money. The proponents of various interest groups want your support. Politicians want your vote. Where self-interest is high, objectivity is low.

Can you spot the manipulative language in these two examples?

- An animal rights activist says, "We must stop the needless torture of animals in medical experiments that serve only to provide researchers on college campuses with lucrative grants."
- A medical researcher says, "No one in our profession sets out to hurt animals, but some pain and even death may be necessary if, through our experiments, we can effect cures that will prevent the loss of human life."

In the first example, the activist tries to manipulate your feelings by suggesting that research is an excuse to get grant money, that animals in experiments are always tortured, and that the experiments are needless. In the second example, the researcher denies that anyone in his or her profession would deliberately cause an animal pain. At the same time, the researcher suggests that some animal pain or death is acceptable if it will save human lives. In this example, the researcher manipulates your thinking so that you must make a choice: your life or an animal's life.

Manipulative language is characterized by simple arguments that seek to explain complex issues. Read the next two examples.

Concept Check 3.3

Some students complain that their instructors are not objective in the classroom. How can you determine the objectivity of your instructors? The following questions are a simple test. Does the instructor treat all students in the class fairly? Are students encouraged to form their own opinions? Do students who disagree with the instructor receive the same treatment as those who do agree? Does the instructor discourage name-calling or other behavior that stifles free and open discussion?

PASSAGE A

It is becoming impossible to find good candidates willing to run for public office. A politician's life is an open book. The would-be candidate for office must dodge photographers and news reporters lurking in the bushes around his house, eavesdropping on his conversations in restaurants, and spying on him through binoculars when he thinks he has escaped from their prying eyes. If a person has ever taken a drink, smoked a marijuana cigarette, had a meaningless affair, or cheated on an exam, his chances of winning an election are compromised. The press has gone too far. Everyone, even a political candidate, is entitled to a private life.

PASSAGE B

As soon as someone runs for election, it is understood that she gives up her right to privacy. Indeed, the U.S. Constitution guarantees no one a right to privacy. We the public have a right to know what to expect from those who seek office. Cheating on one's husband or on an exam is not the issue. The real issue is whether we can trust a person who has a history of dishonesty or poor judgment. We want our elected officials to be responsible people. Therefore, the press performs a valuable public service by exposing candidates' indiscretions.

Both passages oversimplify the issues their proponents raise. Both authors manipulate your thinking by appealing to your emotions instead of to your reasoning. The author of the first passage blames the press for making people afraid to run for office. The author of the second passage praises the press for exposing the weaknesses of potential candidates. The first author wants you to identify with the candidate whose privacy has been violated. The second author appeals to your right as a citizen to know as much as you can about a candidate. Are members of the press scandalmongers or public servants? Neither passage offers convincing evidence to support its author's viewpoint. Complete Exercise 3.5 now to practice identifying manipulative language.

EXERCISE 3.5   Identifying Manipulative Language

IDENTIFY WORDS OR PHRASES IN passages A and B on page 76 that appeal to readers' emotions and manipulate their feelings.

Passage A: _____

_____

_____

_____

_____

_____

_____

Passage B: _____

_____

_____

_____

_____

_____

_____

Usefulness

To evaluate the usefulness of what you are learning, consider what you have already gained from it. Has it improved your understanding of the subject? Have you gained a skill or knowledge you can use now or in the future? Can you relate the knowledge or skill to your course objectives? Has the information made you more interested in the topic it covers? If you answered *no* to all of these questions, then try to figure out what is missing and what you might need to learn next.

How to Evaluate Website Content

How do you evaluate a website for usefulness? For that matter, how can you tell if the information provided on a website is reliable or objective? Evaluating online resources is especially difficult, because on the Internet, anything goes. Anyone can post information on a website, and much of the information available on any given topic is not very useful or reliable. Figure 3.10 on page 78 lists tips for evaluating online sources. Also, do not hesitate to ask your instructor or a librarian if you have any doubt about a website or the information it provides. In addition, complete Exercise 3.6 which follows.

FIGURE 3.10

Tips for Evaluating Online Sources

Standards to Apply	Questions to Ask
AUTHORITY	Who is the author, editor, host, or web master? What are the source's credentials? (author's degrees, publications) What bias is revealed? (affiliations with known groups/companies)
COVERAGE	Is coverage thorough, detailed? Is the information specific? Is it balanced, presenting more than one side or argument?
DOMAINS	What is the address (URL)? Is it affiliated, unaffiliated, or unrestricted? (affiliated: *.edu, .gov;* unaffiliated: *.net;* unrestricted: *.info*) *Caution:* Affiliated sites tend to be trustworthy, but others may be questionable.
CURRENCY	When was the information last updated (posting date)? Is it updated regularly?
LINKS	Is the site linked to other sites? Can the site be accessed from a variety of other sites (an indication of usefulness)? Are the links of the same quality as the site?
DOCUMENTATION and STYLE	Is the information on a site attributed to a source? How much information comes from primary or secondary sources? (Primary sources are more reliable.) Is the style appropriate; free of slang, jargon, and errors?

EXERCISE 3.6 Computer Application on Usefulness of Websites

LOOKING AHEAD TO THE FOLLOWING chapters of *The Confident Student*, choose one topic that you would like to pursue further, such as time management, concentration, memory—anything that interests you. Research your topic on the Internet. Find two different websites that deal with this topic and explain which one seems most useful, based on the tips for evaluating online sources listed in Figure 3.10 above. Be prepared to discuss in class the topic you chose, a brief summary of the information found on the websites you selected, and your evaluation of these websites.

Search Tips: Be specific. If your search word is *memory*, you will get hundreds of websites. Limit your search to what you want to know about memory. *Improving memory* or *combating forgetting* would be better choices. To refine your search, Watkins and Corry, in *E-Learning Companion, A Student's Guide to Online Sources*, give this advice: "Many search engines allow you to limit your search to websites that provide specific types of information or files (such as news, shopping, pictures, and audio). Use these features to reduce your search time; buttons provided on the search engine webpage can access them."

Guided CHAPTER REVIEW

The following checklist summarizes this chapter's key terms and strategies. After reading the chapter, how confident are you that you can apply the information you have learned? To assess your level of confidence, respond to each statement with one of the following: *very confident* (3 points), *fairly confident* (2 points), *not very confident* (1 point), *not confident* (0 points). Write your number of points in the box beside each statement. Then add your score and read the analysis that follows. When you have finished, take the chapter quiz.

SUMMARY CHECK

How confident are you about applying these strategies?

Points

☐ 1. Thinking critically and creatively to meet your academic and life goals

☐ 2. Recognizing inductive and deductive arguments

☐ 3. Understanding and applying Bloom's levels of thinking and learning

☐ 4. Building background for reading and lectures

☐ 5. Making assumptions and recognizing others' assumptions

☐ 6. Predicting topics and test questions

☐ 7. Making inferences from your reading and other sources

☐ 8. Using the standards of reliability, objectivity, and usefulness to evaluate information from print and online sources

How confident are you about this chapter's key terms?

☐ 9. thinking

☐ 10. critical thinking

☐ 11. creative thinking

☐ 12. argument

☐ 13. inductive argument

☐ 14. deductive argument

☐ 15. fallacy

☐ 16. Bloom's Taxonomy

☐ 17. assumption

☐ 18. predict

☐ 19. inference

☐ 20. purpose

☐ 21. central idea

☐ 22. supporting details

☐ 23. evaluate

☐ 24. reliability

☐ 25. objectivity

Total

Add your score. The highest possible score is 75. The closer your score is to 75, the higher your level of confidence. Use your Summary Check results to help you determine which parts of the chapter to review.

YOUR WEBSITE RESOURCES

This chapter's website resources include the following items. To access them, go to *The Confident Student* premium website.

- **Video Skillbuilder: Critical Thinking: What Is Critical Thinking?**
- **Video Skillbuilder: Critical Thinking in Action: Career Planning**
- **Chapter Exercises**
- **Forms to Download**

- **Chapter Summary of Topics**
- **Review Exercise**
- **Thinking Ahead About Career**
- **Confidence Builder Web Search**
- **Self-Test**

CHAPTER REVIEW Quiz

Answer the following questions from memory. Then return to the chapter to check your answers. As a final activity, complete *Show Your Confidence* at the end of the quiz.

1. How does this chapter define "critical thinking"?

_____

_____

2. How does creative thinking differ from critical thinking?

_____

_____

3. What are inductive and deductive reasoning?

_____

_____

4. What is Bloom's Taxonomy? Explain any two of Bloom's levels.

_____

_____

5. What is an assumption? As an example, list one of your assumptions about studying.

_____

_____

6. What does the acronym A Pie stand for, and what is its purpose?

_____

_____

7. How can you build background for reading?

_____

_____

8. Which is a more reliable source of information and why: the transcript of a politician's speech or a reporter's analysis of the speech?

_____

_____

9. Which standard of evaluation means fairness or evenhandedness?

_____

_____

10. If you were given an assignment to read, how would you determine its usefulness?

_____

_____

SHOW YOUR CONFIDENCE

Breaking old study habits is hard. It may be more comfortable to keep doing the same old thing, even if it isn't working, than to try something new. College is the perfect environment for taking intellectual risks. So if you haven't been getting much out of your studying lately, a change in environment or method may help. Try one of the following: Find a better study place, study with a partner instead of on your own, or pay a visit to your instructor and ask for advice. Then be prepared to share your strategy and its outcome either in writing or in class discussion.

Your REFLECTIONS: HOW DO YOU THINK?

Reflect on what you have learned from this chapter about thinking critically and creatively. Use the following questions to stimulate your thinking; then write your reflections. Include in your writing specific information from the chapter.

- Based on your answers to Awareness Check 3.1, are you a critical and creative thinker? Why or why not?
- Reflecting on this chapter's strategies for thinking critically and creatively, which strategy appeals to you most and why?
- What is one intellectual risk you have taken this term?

_____

_____

_____

_____

_____

_____

_____

4 Setting Goals and Solving Problems

Enigma/Alamy

This chapter encourages you to:

- Determine what is important to you, and set goals that reflect your values.

- Identify different types of goals, and know how to set goals that will help you achieve academic and career success.

- Learn the six characteristics of reachable goals that will make your dreams attainable.

- Make a commitment to reach your goals by writing and following an action plan.

- Use the COPE strategy for making decisions and for thinking through problems to find workable solutions.

Confident students are **enthusiastic**. They have a positive attitude and are optimistic, hopeful, and energetic.

What do you want from college? What would you like to be doing five years from now? What grade do you want on your next test, and how will you ensure your success? These questions address goals, or outcomes. Goals have a direct relationship to your **values**, the principles or ideals that you think are important. Values shape your opinions and influence your behavior. For example, if you value learning and achievement, then you can't go to class whenever you feel like it, look over your notes the night before a test, avoid choosing a major until making a decision becomes critical, and still hope to succeed. Success is a matter of desire, intention, and effort. In other words, wanting is not enough; it takes decisive action to reach a goal. Figure 4.1 below illustrates that goals are rooted in values, and your behavior determines whether you will succeed in reaching your goals.

Successful people are self-managed: They set goals, meet problems head-on, and work to find solutions—all while maintaining a positive attitude. How are your attitude and **self-management** skills? Do you have a positive outlook? Do you feel in control of your life and its circumstances? The following *Confidence Builder* will help you develop the optimism you need to take charge of your life and set attainable goals.

Values are the underlying principles or ideals that influence opinions and behavior.

Self-management is the personal quality of self-discipline or self-control. Self-motivated people are also self-managed people.

Your values are the soil that generates your goals. Nourish your goals with the right behavior, and they will flourish.

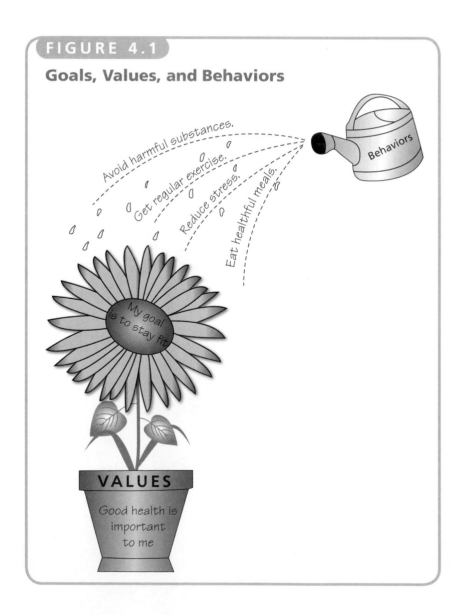

FIGURE 4.1

Goals, Values, and Behaviors

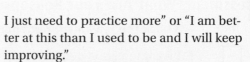

CONFIDENCE BUILDER

How to Develop a Positive Attitude

Changing your attitude is the first step toward solving many problems you will face in college. A negative attitude may be a habit that you have developed—a characteristic response to problem solving that has prevented you from being successful in the past. Negative attitudes also affect self-esteem, destroying your confidence and creating an illusion of helplessness. But positive attitudes build confidence and self-esteem, enabling you to take control and find the motivation to do the work necessary to achieve your goals.

As Shakespeare said, "There is nothing good nor bad, but thinking makes it so." Choosing to regard a problem as a challenge casts it in a positive light, focusing your attention on the actions you can take to find solutions. Here are five more steps you can take to develop a more positive attitude.

Visualize yourself being successful. Once you have set a goal, picture in your mind what you will have or will be able to do once you reach it. Keep that picture in your mind whenever you feel negative or are concerned about mastering a skill. For example, some golf instructors advocate using visualization during practice. Golfers picture themselves making a perfect swing, then repeat the process during a game.

Control your inner voice. You talk silently to yourself all the time. If your self-talk is mainly negative and derogatory, you are programming yourself for failure. Listen for those times during studying or test taking when you say to yourself, "I can't do this" or "I'm no good at this," and counteract those negative thoughts with positive ones: "I *can* do this;

I just need to practice more" or "I am better at this than I used to be and I will keep improving."

Reward yourself for doing well. When you know you have done your best or when you have accomplished a short-term goal that will help you reach a long-term goal, treat yourself to a movie, a new paperback novel, or lunch with a good friend. Be sparing with these rewards and save them for when you really deserve them. What you choose as a reward doesn't matter as long as it acts as a positive reinforcement for good behavior.

Be a positive listener and speaker. If you have trouble screening your own words for negative remarks that you need to change into positive ones, listen carefully to others. When a friend says, "I'm not going to pass algebra," explore this problem with him or her. Ask your friend to think of possible solutions. Make positive suggestions such as: "Why don't you get a tutor to help you with the concepts you don't understand?" Being a positive listener and speaker may help you think more positively about your own challenges as well.

Be persistent. *Persistence* means continuing in spite of obstacles. Do not give up at the first setback or sign of failure. Keep trying to reach your goals. Be optimistic, seek help, and try again. Persistence will pay off, and the confidence you feel will be the reward for your effort.

Follow Up: To explore this topic further, visit *The Confident Student* premium website for an online search activity related to attitudes.

Define Your Values

- Determine what is important to you, and set goals that reflect your values.

What is important to you? How you answer this question is a direct reflection of your values. Similarly, what you want out of college also reflects your values. Values are intangibles like *a good life*, *a satisfying relationship*, or *a rewarding career*. Your values influence your goals and shape your actions. What do you value? Why are you in college? *Awareness Check* 4.1 will help you think critically about your values.

Here are some other reasons for attending college that you may or may not have considered.

Awareness CHECK 4.1

Goal Assessment: What Are Your Reasons for Attending College?

Yes   No   **Check the reasons for attending college that match your own.**

☐ ☐   1. I want to earn a degree, but I haven't yet chosen a major.

☐ ☐   2. My friends are in college and I want to be with them.

☐ ☐   3. My parents want me to get a college education.

☐ ☐   4. I want to prepare myself for an interesting career.

☐ ☐   5. I have an athletic scholarship, veteran's benefits, or some other source of funding.

☐ ☐   6. I want to make a lot of money.

☐ ☐   7. I want to improve my skills so that I can change jobs or careers.

☐ ☐   8. I want to broaden my knowledge.

☐ ☐   9. I wasn't able to go to college when I was younger; now I want that experience.

☐ ☐   10. Improving my education will help me advance to a higher-level position at work.

A goal should be something that you desire and that you will be motivated enough to reach. Your answers to the Awareness Check provide the key for understanding how your reasons for attending college can motivate you to reach your goals. If you checked only item 2 or item 3, for example, then you may have difficulty motivating yourself to do well because your reasons for attending college are based more on others' expectations than on your own. You need to decide what you want out of college. If you checked only item 7 or item 10, then you have a more specific goal in mind and are probably already working to accomplish it. You may need to find additional motivation only if you encounter a setback. If you checked only item 1 or item 4, then you have a practical reason for being in college, but you have not chosen a career or major. As soon as you do that, course selection will be easier because you will be motivated by a clearer sense of direction. If you checked only item 6, then you may have set an unrealistic goal. A college education, although it does prepare you for a career, does not guarantee that you will make lots of money. Motivation is easier to find when your goals are realistic and you believe you can achieve them.

Perhaps you checked several items. Checks beside items 7, 8, 9, and 10, for example, could mean that you are seeking a college education to broaden your understanding and to provide access to a better job. If you checked items 1, 4, and 5, then you may be a student who wants a degree and has the funding to get it, but you are still exploring the possibilities of what you might do with your education. A visit to your college's career center might help you decide on a major or set a career goal that will keep you motivated.

▼ **Exposure to new ideas:** In the courses you take, you will be exposed to new ideas, beliefs, and ways of looking at the world. At times, you will be excited by what you are learning; at other times, you will be frustrated by opinions and values that challenge your own.

▼ **Opportunities for enrichment:** A college education can enrich your life by sharpening your ability to think, by teaching you new ways to approach problem solving and decision making, and by helping you to develop a flexible and open mind.

▼ **Development of new skills and interests:** In your college courses, you may learn new skills and develop new interests. Through membership in campus organizations, you may apply your talents or discover new ones.

▼ **Personal growth:** As you gain knowledge, experience, and skill, you will also gain the confidence that comes from accomplishment.

Most students are in college because they seek the skills and knowledge that will make them employable. Although some enter college with a career in mind, many are undecided. Some students, like Ellen, change their minds. Ellen had always wanted to be a nurse, even though she knew little about what the job entailed. After completing her required courses, she was accepted into her college's nursing program. Ellen's math and science skills were strong, and she enjoyed taking her anatomy and physiology course as well as the other courses in her program. But when one of her courses required her to spend time in a local hospital tending to the needs of the sick, she realized immediately that nursing was not what she wanted to do for the rest of her life. She was suited neither to working in a hospital environment nor to the stress that accompanies a career in nursing. At first, Ellen was at a loss. She had invested her time and money in a career that she no longer wanted to pursue. To change her major could add a year or more to her graduation time; nevertheless, that is what she decided to do. Ellen is now the financial manager of an electronics corporation. She can't imagine having a more rewarding career, and she believes that changing her major from nursing to marketing was the right decision for her.

Sonda Dawes/The Image Works

Through service learning you can practice setting and reaching goals while helping others to reach theirs.

Ellen's story illustrates how personal, academic, and career goals can overlap. Ellen's career goal was to become a nurse; her academic goal was to complete her degree in nursing. Ellen had hoped to find satisfaction in her work, so her personal goal was to have a career doing something she liked. At the time, she thought she would enjoy being a nurse. As she learned more about her chosen career, however, Ellen's personal goal of job satisfaction was not being met. This led to her decision to change her career goal. She decided that she wanted a management-level position within a large corporation. As a result, her academic goals changed as well. Her new goals were to change her major to marketing and to complete the courses required for her degree.

Ethics are community standards of behavior based on generally accepted values and ideas of right and wrong.

What about values and ethics? Did they play a role in Ellen's goal setting? *Values* include your judgments about what is right and wrong. They are your standards of behavior and include reliability, respect, responsibility, fairness, caring, and citizenship. **Ethics**, on the other hand, are community standards of behavior, based on generally accepted values. Cheating in college is unethical because the college community expects students to earn their grades. Making personal calls at work or taking office supplies to use at home are unethical practices because someone else has to pay for the calls and the supplies. Employers expect you not to steal from them. Would it have been ethical for Ellen to pursue a nursing career, feeling as she did? No, because the medical community expects its workers to be dedicated. How could Ellen be dedicated to a job she didn't like? Ellen's values shaped her decision to change majors. She did not want to pursue a career in which she might not be able to live up to her employer's and patients' expectations.

Character means moral or ethical strength, or reputation.

Personal values and ethical choices are not only an important part of goal setting; they also influence every aspect of your life. They make up what is called **character**. Character is an asset in college, at work, and in all your relations with others. Figure 4.2 lists values that build character. You can build your character by incorporating these values into your life and by considering them as you set goals.

FIGURE 4.2

Core Ethical Values

Trustworthiness	Be honest and reliable. Don't deceive, cheat, or betray a trust. Be loyal to family, friends, and country. Strive to do what is right.
Respect	Be courteous, considerate, and polite. Show respect for others' differences. Don't threaten or abuse others. Settle disputes peacefully.
Responsibility	Be self-disciplined and self-controlled. Think before you act, and accept the consequences of your behavior. Have high expectations for yourself, do your best, and be persistent.
Fairness	Treat everyone fairly. Listen to others and keep an open mind. Neither make nor accept excuses for bad behavior, and don't take advantage of others.
Caring	Kindness, sharing, compassion, and empathy should be hallmarks of your character. Be gracious, forgiving, and willing to help those in need.
Citizenship	Stay informed and get involved. Take part in community affairs and service learning projects. Obey laws, follow the rules, and show respect for authority. Vote.

© 2009 Josephson Institute. The definitions of the Six Pillars of Character are reprinted with permission. www.CharacterCounts.org

EXERCISE 4.1 Discovering Your Values

Exercise Purpose:
This exercise will help you clarify your values in four major areas.

Exercise Background:
What are your core values? What values shape your choices and decisions? We form our values while growing up, and we continue to refine them throughout life. Family, education, religious training, and other influences shape our values.

Exercise Task:
For each personal influence listed, answer the following questions using your own paper.

Personal Influences:
Family

Education

A major event

A person whom you admire

Reflective Questions:

1. **What is the influence, and how has it affected your life?**

_____

_____

2. **What lesson did you learn, or what understanding did you reach?**

_____

_____

3. **What value grew out of this influence?**

_____

_____

4. **Why is this value important to you?**

_____

_____

5. **What is another major influence in your life, and what value has it shaped?**

_____

_____

Differentiate Between Long-Term and Short-Term Goal

- Identify different types of goals, and know how to set goals that will help you achieve academic and career success.

A goal is an outcome, an objective, a desired result. Goal setting is an active step that you take toward managing your life. Without goals, you are the victim of chance, a person to whom things happen rather than one who makes things happen. A goal can be any outcome you want, but the more specific it is, the better, and if you write it down, you own it.

If your goal is vague, or unclear, you run the risk of not being able to determine what actions to take. As a result, you will have difficulty writing an action plan. State your goal as an action or a result that can be measured. It may be helpful to identify your goal as personal, academic, or career/work related. Figure 4.3 lists types of goals followed by specific goal statements. Some goals take longer to reach than others. Completing one goal may conclude one of several steps that bring you closer to accomplishing a more far-reaching outcome. When you state a goal or write an action plan, differentiate between your long-term goals and your short-term goals.

Long term and *short term* as applied to goal setting are time markers. For example, graduation from college can be viewed as a **long-term goal** because it will take years to accomplish. Choosing a major or program of study, completing each course, and meeting all other graduation requirements are tasks of shorter duration and can be viewed as the **short-term goals** that will bring you nearer to graduation. Because long term and short term are relative ideas, it is more pragmatic to think of outcomes and the steps required to reach them. For example, if graduation from college is the outcome (long-term goal), then the completion of each class is a step (short-term goal) toward graduation. If earning a 3.5 grade point average this semester or quarter is the outcome (long-term goal), then completing each assignment or test with a grade of 3.0 or better is a step (short-term goal) toward the final grade you want. Graduation from college, a long-term goal, could itself be viewed as a short-term goal when seen in relation to a total life plan from your first job to starting a family, planning for your kids' college education, and retiring. In other words, each goal you set should have a realistic

Long-term goals can take from several years to a lifetime to achieve. These goals represent major life outcomes.

Short-term goals are the intermediate steps between setting a long-term goal and achieving it. *Long term* and *short term* are relative ideas whose meanings may change depending on the context in which they are used.

FIGURE 4.3

Three Types of Goals

GOAL TYPE	GOAL STATEMENT
PERSONAL	• I will lose ten pounds over the next four months. • I will improve my fitness by exercising for twenty minutes at least three days a week this term. • To develop a more positive attitude about studying, I will practice countering negative thoughts with positive ones before tackling an assignment.
ACADEMIC	• I will choose a major by the end of this term. • I will study two hours for every hour spent in class. • I will review my notes for each class every day.
CAREER/WORK RELATED	• I will find out where and when a job fair is being held in my area and make plans to go. • I will visit the college career center and take an interest inventory within the next two weeks. • I will begin keeping a record of my accomplishments so that I can build my résumé.

FIGURE 4.4

Long-Term and Short-Term Goals

LONG-TERM GOALS	SHORT-TERM GOALS
Graduate from college	I will choose a major in the first year of college. I will complete my required courses first. I will keep track of deadlines and pay fees on time.
Complete my algebra course with an A	I will find a study partner and set up a study schedule within the first two weeks of class. I will take notes in class and review my notes after class. I will do all the problems in a chapter, assigned or not.
Get my financial affairs in order	I will prepare a monthly budget this week. I will pay all bills as soon as they come in. I will use my credit card only for emergencies, and I will not carry a balance.

time frame. Break down each goal into a longer-term outcome to be reached and the shorter-term steps you will take to get there. Figure 4.4 lists long-term and short-term goals and shows their relative relationship.

Now that we have outlined short-term and long-term goals, complete Exercises 4.2 and 4.3 to help you identify your short- and long-term goals related to your own life and your college career.

EXERCISE 4.2 Self-Management and Goal Setting

BY SETTING GOALS, YOU CAN manage your life instead of letting life manage you. This exercise will help you think through a desired outcome and break it down into long-term and short-term goals. If you need more space, write your responses on a sheet of paper.

1. **What is one thing in your life that you want very much?**

   _____

2. **What values underlie this desire?**

   _____

3. **Write a long-term goal statement that incorporates your answer to question 1. See Figures 4.3 and 4.4 for examples of goal statements.**

   _____

4. **Break down your long-term goal into three or more short-term goals and write your goal statements.**

   _____

   _____

   _____

EXERCISE 4.3 Goal Setting and Major Selection

THIS EXERCISE WILL HELP YOU with major selection. If you already have a major, write it in the appropriate space. If you are undecided, select a tentative or working major.

1. **What is your major or tentative major?**

   _____

2. **Search your college catalog for information on your major; then briefly summarize the requirements for completion and the amount of time it will take.**

   _____

   _____

3. **Completing the requirements for your major is your long-term goal. Now list three short-term goals to achieve as you work toward the long-term goal.**

   _____

   _____

   _____

4. **What personal value is reflected in your choice of a major?**

   _____

   _____

   _____

Set Reachable Goals

- Learn the six characteristics of reachable goals that will make your dreams attainable.

A goal should be reachable—an outcome that you can reasonably expect to achieve. A realistic assessment of your strengths and weaknesses, your level of motivation, and your values will help you set goals that are attainable. Figure 4.5 illustrates the six characteristics of reachable goals that are explained in this section.

A reachable goal is realistic. It is based on your abilities, interests, needs, and desires. For example, when choosing a career goal, you should consider your skills and interests. If you dislike math and dread balancing your checkbook every month, then accounting may not be a realistic career goal for you. If you like to write, have always done well in English courses, and enjoy working with others to make reports and presentations, then a career as a technical writer might be a realistic goal for you. Your college may have a career center or provide career counseling that will help you evaluate your interests so that you can consider the jobs, professions, or public services best suited to your abilities and preferences. Career counseling can help you determine your chances for employment in specific fields. You might learn that jobs are scarce in a field you have been considering. Or you might discover a new field of interest that offers many employment opportunities.

A reachable goal is believable and possible. You must believe that you *can* reach your goal and that it is possible to reach it within a reasonable length of time. Suppose you want to buy a new computer. After doing some comparison shopping, you find that the price is more than you expected, so you decide to wait. You set a goal to save the money. Knowing how much money you need and how much you can afford to set aside each month, you determine that it will take five months to save the money. Each month, you deposit the amount you have designated. Your goal is believable because you can afford the extra savings. Your goal is possible because you think five months is a reasonable amount of time. Your long-term goal is to save enough money to make your purchase. Each deposit you make represents the achievement of a short-term goal needed to reach the long-term goal.

A reachable goal is measurable. Establish a time frame and a foreseeable outcome. For example, if your goal is "to make a lot of money," decide how you are going to do it, when you are going to do it, and how much is "a lot." Have a foreseeable outcome at the end of which you can say, "I have reached my goal." If you set a goal to graduate from college four years from now, determine which courses to take and plan your schedule so that you can earn a sufficient number of credits each semester or quarter.

A reachable goal is flexible. Rarely do you set a goal and follow it through to completion without any problems. In working toward your college degree, for example, you may fail or withdraw from one or more courses or you may change majors and lose credits that you have to make up. These are temporary setbacks that may interrupt your progress but need not keep you from reaching your goal. Reassess your action plan; then revise it or make a new plan. Although it may take you longer to reach your goal, it is time well spent if you are doing what you want to do. To help you think through some of your goals, complete Exercise 4.4 with a partner.

A reachable goal is controllable. Use self-management: Set goals you can control and determine your own time frame for completing them. No one can, or should, set goals for you. Suppose you need to study for an important exam and you know from past experience that you need at least three days to prepare yourself. Your study partner says, "We can ace this test with a four-hour study session the night before." That strategy may work for your study partner, but will it work for you? If your goal is to make a good grade, set up your own study schedule and stick to it. Only you can determine how much time you will need to prepare for a test.

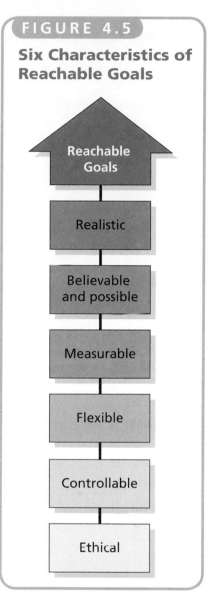

FIGURE 4.5

Six Characteristics of Reachable Goals

Reachable Goals

Realistic

Believable and possible

Measurable

Flexible

Controllable

Ethical

EXERCISE 4.4   **Collaborative Activity on Reachable Goals**

WORKING WITH A PARTNER, DISCUSS the personal or academic goals that you would each like to achieve over the next few months to a year. Then choose one goal that you both share, and determine whether it meets the six characteristics of reachable goals.

1. **Write your goal statement.**

    _____

    _____

2. **What skills and interests do you possess that make this a *realistic* goal?**

    _____

    _____

continued

3. What makes your goal *believable* and *possible*?

   _____

   _____

4. Is your goal *measurable*? For example, how long will it take you to reach your goal? What check-points can you build into your plan?

   _____

   _____

5. What makes your goal *flexible*? What will you do if you experience a setback?

   _____

   _____

6. Is your goal *controllable*? Can you manage time limits and conditions? Explain your answer.

   _____

   _____

7. Is your goal *ethical*? Explain how.

   _____

   _____

A reachable goal is ethical. Is it fair to all concerned? The steps you take to reach your goal should not in any way cause you to violate rules, take advantage of others, or compromise your values. Suppose you are enrolled in a reading class that requires you to spend at least two hours a week in a learning lab practicing the skills you have learned in class. The reading class is required as a prerequisite for a composition course that is also required. You have set a short-term goal of completing the course with a grade no lower than B. On your way to the lab, a friend says, "Let's cut today. We work on our own in lab anyway. If we sign in and leave, no one will know." You know this is probably true because the lab is monitored by a technician who sends a copy of the sign-in sheet to the instructor.

What are the ethics involved in this situation? If you cut the class, you are engaging in unethical conduct for three reasons. First, you are breaking a rule. Second, you are taking advantage of your instructor by signing in and leading him or her to believe that you were present. Third, if honesty is one of your values, then you are compromising it. On the practical side, cutting lab doesn't help you reach your goal. Avoiding practice time prevents your mastery of the skills and may lead to a poor grade. Is it possible to engage in unethical behavior and still reach your goals? In the short term, maybe. But in the long run, unethical conduct catches up with you. Because ethical behavior improves your chances of reaching your goals, it makes sense to say that a reachable goal is also an ethical one.

Concept Check 4.1

You have read that an ethical goal is fair to all concerned. What does "ethical" mean to you? What examples of ethical behavior or decisions have you seen either among people you know or people in the public eye?

Write Your Action Plan

- Make a commitment to reach your goals by writing and following an action plan.

A goal is the first link in a chain of events that are connected by cause and effect. For example, this semester, Eric has had some health problems that have caused him to fall behind in one of his courses. Although he has tried to make up the work, he has missed too many classes and has been unable to catch up. As a result, his grade has suffered. However, Eric does not regard this as a setback from which he cannot recover. Instead, he has written an **action plan** that includes a schedule for next term, allowing him to carry a lighter work load and leaving some free time between classes for studying on campus. This schedule should result in a high grade point average that will offset the previous term's poor performance.

Action plan refers to a written plan that establishes a time frame and lists steps for accomplishing a goal.

Writing an action plan is the same as making a commitment. Like Eric's action plan, your plan will commit you to a course of action that should meet with success—if you follow the plan. In any plan, some setbacks are bound to occur. With a positive attitude, you can take setbacks in stride and revise your action plan to overcome difficulties and get back on track.

Suppose your goal in an algebra course is to pass with a grade of A or B. From reading the course syllabus, you learn that homework counts for 25 percent of the grade, unit tests count for 50 percent, and the final exam counts for 25 percent. A missed assignment lowers your homework grade by several points. The homework grade is an easy 25 percent to make because there are proofs in algebra that you can use before handing in your work to determine whether your answers are correct. Unit tests are more difficult, but your instructor will allow you to drop your lowest test score before averaging the grade. Also, you are allowed to retake one more unit test in addition to the one you drop. The final exam is very important because 25 percent of the grade can make or break your average. What is your action plan for reaching the goal of earning an A in the course? An action plan lists short-term goals, or steps, that will help you reach your long-term goal. To pass the algebra course, you could write the action plan shown in Figure 4.6. Exercise 4.5 below also provides a schematic/template for creating your own action plans.

EXERCISE 4.5 · Computer Activity on Developing an Action Plan

WRITE AN ACTION PLAN FOR achieving a long-term goal. Choose a personal, academic, or career goal that is important to you. For example, you could focus on a course as in Figure 4.6 or you could use your major from Exercise 4.3, the goal you selected for Exercise 4.4, or any other goal. If you like to work on the computer, you can type your action plan as a table or in some other format that you design. As an alternative, you can download a blank action plan form like the one in Figure 4.6 from *The Confident Student* premium website. Whatever template you choose, the following guidelines will help you determine what to include in your action plan.

1. **State your long-term goal and be specific.**

2. **Explain how your goal meets the six characteristics of reachable goals.**

3. **Write three or more short-term goal statements that explain specifically what you will do and how these goals will help you reach the long-term goal.**

4. **Explain how and when you will evaluate your action plan.**

FIGURE 4.6

Action Plan for Passing Algebra 1

1. **My long-term goal:** I want to pass Algebra I with a grade of A or B.

2. **How my goal meets the six characteristics of reachable goals:**

Characteristics	My Explanations
a. Realistic	I like math and my basic math skills are good.
b. Believable and possible	I have made good grades in math classes before, and common sense tells me that I can succeed in this course.
c. Measurable	I have the entire term to reach my goal, and I can monitor my progress using the unit tests and midterm exam as checkpoints.
d. Flexible	I know the course will be difficult, but I can adjust to any setbacks.
e. Controllable	I can control my results through self-motivation and effort.
f. Ethical	I am willing to do the work and do not expect the instructor to give me a grade that I don't earn.

3. **My short-term goals:** I will do the following to achieve a grade of A or B in the course.
   a. Attend class regularly.
   b. Do all required work and extra problems for practice.
   c. Make and follow a study schedule that allows me to review daily, weekly, and just before a test.
   d. Chart my grades on homework and tests. If I lose points or miss problems, I will correct my mistakes before moving on.
   e. Keep up with the work and seek help if I have problems.

4. **How I will evaluate my action plan:** I will review my plan every Friday to check my progress. If I am falling behind in algebra, or if I am having trouble following my plan, I will determine what is wrong and get help if I need it.

Think Through Decisions and Problems

• Use the COPE strategy for making decisions and for thinking through problems to find workable solutions.

In order to reach short- and long-term goals, you will need to make important decisions and solve various problems along the way. Decision making and problem solving are two critical thinking skills that you will use now and throughout your life. This section introduces strategies that will help you make better decisions and solve problems more effectively.

Decision making and problem solving are linked. Both require you to consider several **options** or alternatives before making a choice or taking an action. Some people have trouble making decisions, either because they see too many options or they don't know what the options are. Decision by indecision may result. Think of a problem as a **challenge**—a call to action that requires the full use of your abilities and resources. You might say, "If I do nothing, everything will work out." Unfortunately, problems don't go away. Without your intervention, they will become more difficult to solve. Face decisions and problems squarely, and you will soon be back on track and moving toward your goals.

As a college student, you will make one of your most important decisions when you choose a major. Your major determines your course selection and your career path. Some students enter college knowing exactly what they want to do. Others prefer to take a few introductory courses before deciding on a major. In the first case, keep an open

Options are choices, alternatives.

A **challenge** is a problem or situation that requires you to take appropriate action.

mind so that you don't limit your opportunities. In the second case, don't wait too long to make a decision. Choosing a major puts you in control of your future. You can set goals for completing your education based on the requirements of your major, and you can begin to seriously consider career options.

How do you go about making this important decision? A good place to begin is with your interests and your accomplishments so far. What subjects appeal to you? What skills do you have? In what courses have you always done your best work? What do you like to do in your leisure time? Answering these questions may help you pinpoint some possible majors or careers that might be a good fit for you. Check your college catalog for a list of majors. Go through the list and check off the ones that appeal to you. Then carefully consider the majors you have checked, and try to narrow the list to one or two majors to explore in depth. The following section explains a problem-solving method that you can apply to major selection and other challenges. For more information on choosing majors, see Chapter 14.

Apply the COPE Strategy

To think through a problem and reach a solution requires a consistent method, or strategy. For example, scientists follow protocols to conduct lab experiments. Physicians rule out serious conditions first when diagnosing an illness. The COPE strategy illustrated in Figure 4.7 and explained in this section is a series of steps that you can follow to solve academic, personal, and work-related problems. COPE stands for Challenge, Option, Plan, Evaluation.

STEP 1: Identify your challenge or problem.

Some people view a problem as an obstacle or a setback. This is negative thinking. To approach a problem in a more positive way, think of it as a challenge—difficult but solvable. State your challenge in writing. Seeing it in print will make it real for you. Answer the following questions in your statement:

▼ What is the problem?

▼ How is it hurting you?

▼ What do you want to do?

© 2011 Wadsworth, Cengage Learning. All Rights Reserved.

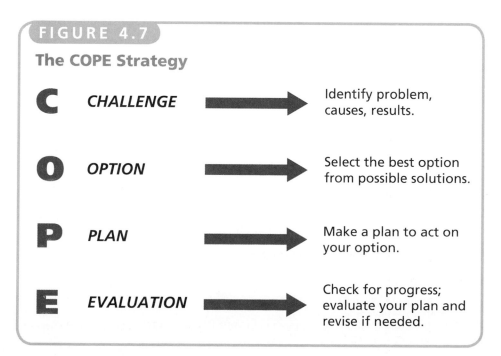

FIGURE 4.7

The COPE Strategy

C *CHALLENGE* ➤ Identify problem, causes, results.

O *OPTION* ➤ Select the best option from possible solutions.

P *PLAN* ➤ Make a plan to act on your option.

E *EVALUATION* ➤ Check for progress; evaluate your plan and revise if needed.

Concept Check **4.2**

Think about the last time you were faced with a problem or had to make an important decision. How did you go about it? Did you use a plan or follow a system that has worked for you before? Did you ask for help, or did you do nothing? What happened, and were you happy with the result?

Suppose you don't have a major. You may not see this as a problem yet, but it can have some negative consequences, as Chris explains:

Not having a major makes me feel as if I have no direction, no basis on which to select courses. I worry that I am wasting my time and money. As a result, I am losing focus, and my grades are beginning to suffer. I have several interests and career ideas and would like to choose a major and begin making plans for my future, but I don't know where to begin.

The following example is a challenge statement that Chris wrote as a response to Step 1 of COPE. The three parts of the statement are identified in parentheses:

I have not chosen a major (the problem), *and this is causing me to lose focus and my grades to suffer* (how it hurts). *I want to learn more about possible majors and find one that is a good fit for me* (what Chris wants).

STEP 2: Select as a solution the best option from alternative solutions that occur to you.

Most problems can be solved in a number of ways. Some alternatives may be better than others. When faced with a challenge, it helps to first determine what the alternatives are, to next note the advantages and disadvantages of each, and then to choose the best option. Keep in mind that the solution you choose may not work. Be ready to try your next best option if necessary. It may help to list your options along with their advantages and disadvantages. Reread the challenge statement following Step 1. By thinking about the problem and talking about it with others, Chris identified several options for learning more about majors and careers. As a response to Step 2 of COPE, this student made the diagram shown in Figure 4.8 on page 99.

All three options have value. Like Chris, you might decide to begin your search by going to the career center first. A survey of your interests and values is a good starting point for choosing a major. Chances are good that you will be happiest and most successful taking courses and pursuing a career in a field that allows you to do what you enjoy doing. Remember that it is more important to choose a major that interests you than to select one that will lead to a specific career. The fact is that most majors, apart from the specialized skills that they teach, also teach you general skills such as thinking critically and using technology that you can apply to a wide variety of jobs and careers. Also, some on-the-job training is a fact of life, no matter what career you choose. What most employers are looking for is someone who has strong communication skills, knows how to learn, and is flexible, confident, and willing to work hard to succeed.

STEP 3: Write an action plan and follow it to meet your challenge.

Suppose that, like Chris, you want to find a major that is a good fit for you. Your plan should address two questions: "What actions will I take?" and "How much time should I allow for my plan to work?" Setting a time limit keeps you from wasting time in the long run. If you are not making progress toward your goal within a reasonable length of time, then you either need to set a new goal or make a new plan. Writing your action plan is the commitment you will make to solve your problem or to meet your challenge.

Say you decide to talk to a recent graduate about your search for a major. To set a time limit for completing the task, you make an appointment with the grad. Then, as your response to Step 3 of COPE, you write as your action plan the following list of questions.

- What field did you major in, and what influenced your choice?
- How did you get your current job or position?
- If I want a career in your field, does it matter what my major is?
- What skills are essential for success in your job?
- What personal qualities do employers in your field expect?

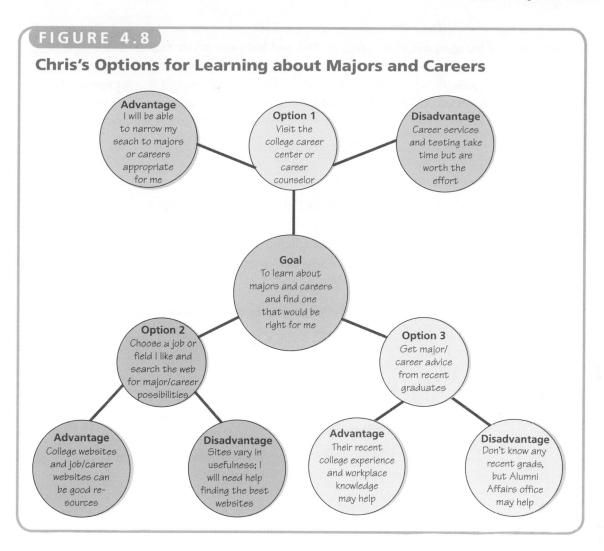

FIGURE 4.8

Chris's Options for Learning about Majors and Careers

Advantage
I will be able to narrow my seach to majors or careers appropriate for me

Option 1
Visit the college career center or career counselor

Disadvantage
Career services and testing take time but are worth the effort

Goal
To learn about majors and careers and find one that would be right for me

Option 2
Choose a job or field I like and search the web for major/career possibilities

Option 3
Get major/ career advice from recent graduates

Advantage
College websites and job/career websites can be good re-sources

Disadvantage
Sites vary in usefulness; I will need help finding the best websites

Advantage
Their recent college experience and workplace knowledge may help

Disadvantage
Don't know any recent grads, but Alumni Affairs office may help

After interviewing a recent graduate and completing Exercise 4.6, are you any closer to making a decision about a major? If not, continue your research. Periodically, you need to evaluate the progress you are making, which is Step 4 of COPE.

EXERCISE 4.6   Thinking Through a Major

CHOOSING A MAJOR REQUIRES A balance between critical and creative thinking. This exercise will help you do both.

1. **To think critically or analytically, start with a list of majors offered at your college. To find a list of majors, check your college catalog or website. Check the ones that interest you most. Make a list of those majors and add to the list any others you might want to consider. Think about each one, gradually narrowing your list to three choices. Now select one as your *trial major* and write it on the following line:**

_____

_____

continued

2. **To think creatively, you are going to use your intuition. This will help you avoid information overload, the feeling of helplessness that comes from having too many options to consider. Close your eyes and visualize yourself doing something that you really enjoy. What courses would let you pursue that interest? What job or career can you think of that would allow you to do what you enjoy most? What major immediately comes to mind? This is your** *dream major.* **Write it on the following line:**

_____

_____

Are your trial major and your dream major the same? If so, this will be your *tentative major.* **If your trial major and dream major are different, select the one that appeals to you most, and that will be your tentative major. Your choice will remain tentative until you are certain that it is right for you. Until then, continue to explore your options, because you can always change your mind. Write your tentative major on the following line.**

_____

_____

STEP 4: Evaluate your plan by asking questions to assess your progress.

Remember that many problems we encounter have developed over time; therefore, it will take time to solve them. If you have clearly defined your goal or the solution you want and have made a plan to achieve it within a reasonable length of time, then you can evaluate your progress by asking questions like these:

▸ Is my plan working?

▸ How close am I to reaching a solution?

▸ What am I doing that is helping or not helping?

▸ What more can I do?

If you are having trouble answering these questions, then you may need to make a new plan or redefine your goal.

Suppose your efforts to find a major that suits you have worked. You have made a selection, so that challenge has been met. Now you can begin to pursue your major by setting long-term and short-term goals. On the other hand, if you were not successful in choosing a major, continue exploring options until you succeed. Using what you have learned about decision making and problem solving, work with Exercise 4.7 and the Critical Thinking box that follows to practice and apply your skills.

EXERCISE 4.7 Applying the COPE Strategy

MARIE IS A POOR PROBLEM SOLVER. Read about her challenge and think about what she should do.

I have a big problem this term: my French class. I'm flunking and I don't know why. I've stopped going to class because it was depressing me to sit there feeling stupid. Now I can forget about how much I hate it, and I can sleep late on Friday mornings too. I'm angry at the college for having so many requirements for students to fulfill. I'm disgusted at my French instructor, who refuses to speak any English in class. How can I learn if I can't understand what's going on? I passed Spanish in high school, so I know this problem is not mine. It must be their crazy new method of teaching languages. Maybe I should take beginning Spanish again. At least I know I could pass!

continued

1. **What is Marie's challenge?**

   _____

   _____

2. **Is Marie self-motivated (intrinsic) or other-motivated (extrinsic)?**

   _____

   _____

3. **What new behaviors could Marie adopt to help her meet her challenge?**

   _____

   _____

4. **Write a short action plan for Marie to follow this week.**

   _____

   _____

CRITICAL THINKING

Applying Your Problem-Solving Skills

Exercise Overview

Goal setting and problem solving are linked. Once you have identified a problem, you can choose a strategy for solving it. Your plan can include long-term and short-term goals that will help you reach your desired outcome.

Exercise Background

As a college student, you face pressures from many sources. Living with roommates, keeping up with assignments, and managing your finances can be stressful. As an adult learner, you may be juggling family, college, and work obligations. The expectations you place on yourself are often the hardest challenges to meet. Acknowledging these pressures and facing problems head-on will help you set realistic goals.

Exercise Task

The following scenarios illustrate common problems that students face. Read the scenarios and then choose one to discuss with a partner. Using the COPE method, or the goal-setting strategies explained in this chapter, or a combination of each, write out your solution to the student's problem.

continued

1. My roommate sleeps in the afternoon and stays up all night studying, which interferes with my sleep. My roommate also has friends over when I am trying to study. Their loud talking and music or TV programs distract me. I'm tired all the time and can't get much work done.

2. I am always low on cash, and I sometimes skip meals because I don't have enough money to pay for food. Tuition and books plus an unexpected medical expense have really depleted my savings. I am worried that I will have to drop out of college and go to work to save the money I need to complete my education. I would hate to do this because my grades are good despite my financial woes, and I don't want to interrupt my momentum.

3. No matter what I do, I can't seem to make it to my 7:00 a.m. writing class. I like this class and the instructor, I want to improve my writing skills, and I need to make a good grade in this class. Why am I having so much trouble getting up in the morning? I set my alarm, but when it goes off, sometimes I say to myself, "I'll just doze for five more minutes." The next thing I know, 30 minutes have passed and I can't get ready in time to make it to class. I wish I knew what to do. I don't have this problem in my other classes that meet later in the morning.

4. I am a divorced father of two. My salary as a claims adjuster supports me and pays child support. I share custody of the kids with my ex-wife, and they spend most weekends with me. Although I like having the kids around, weekends are my only time to study. I attend community college part-time. My goal is to transfer to a four-year college and pursue a law degree, something I've always wanted to do. With my hectic schedule, I wonder if I'll ever make it.

Guided CHAPTER REVIEW

The following checklist summarizes this chapter's key terms and strategies. After reading the chapter, how confident are you that you can apply the information you have learned? To assess your level of confidence, respond to each statement with one of the following: *very confident* (3 points), *fairly confident* (2 points), *not very confident* (1 point), *not confident* (0 points). Write your number of points in the box beside each statement. Then add your score and read the analysis that follows. When you have finished, take the chapter quiz.

SUMMARY CHECK

How confident are you about applying these strategies?

Points

☐ 1. Determining what your values are

☐ 2. Setting long-term and short-term goals to achieve a desired end

☐ 3. Choosing goals that meet the six characteristics of reachable goals

☐ 4. Using the COPE strategy to solve a problem or make a decision

☐ 5. Writing an action plan to reach a goal or to solve a problem

How confident is your understanding of this chapter's key terms?

☐ 6. values

☐ 7. ethics

☐ 8. self-management

☐ 9. character

☐ 10. long-term goals

☐ 11. short-term goals

☐ 12. action plan

☐ 13. options

☐ 14. challenges

Total

Add your score. The highest possible score is 42. The closer your score is to 42, the higher your level of confidence. Use your Summary Check results to help you determine which parts of the chapter to review.

YOUR WEBSITE RESOURCES

This chapter's website resources include the following items. To access them, go to *The Confident Student* premium website.

- **Video Skillbuilder: Motivation and Goal Setting: Staying Motivated as an Adult Learner**
- **Video Skillbuilder: Motivation and Goal Setting: Staying Motivated and Making a Contribution**
- **Chapter Exercises**

- **Forms to Download**
- **Chapter Summary of Topics**
- **Thinking Ahead About Career**
- **Confidence Builder Web Search**
- **Self-Test**

CHAPTER REVIEW Quiz

Answer the following questions from memory. Then return to the chapter to check your answers. As a final activity, complete *Show Your Confidence* at the end of the quiz.

1. What is the relationship between knowing your values and setting goals?

2. What is the difference between a long-term goal and a short-term goal?

3. What are the three categories of goals mentioned in this chapter?

4. What are any two of the six characteristics of reachable goals? Briefly explain the characteristics you choose.

5. What does "self-management" mean?

6. What is one thing you can do to develop a more positive attitude?

7. What is an action plan?

8. Why is it important to put an action plan into writing?

9. What is the COPE strategy, and what do the letters stand for?

10. How are goal setting and problem solving linked?

SHOW YOUR CONFIDENCE

Think about something you wanted to obtain or achieve in the past but were unsuccessful. What kept you from reaching your goal? What have you learned from this chapter that will keep you from making the same mistake again? Be prepared to share what you have learned either in writing or in class discussion.

Your REFLECTIONS: YOUR VALUES AND GOALS

Reflect on what you have learned from this chapter about values and goals. Use the following questions to stimulate your thinking; then write your reflections. Include in your writing specific information from the chapter.

- Describe one of your best accomplishments. How did you achieve it, and was goal setting part of the process?
- Read the values listed in Figure 4.2. Which one of the values is most important to you and why?
- What is one skill or attitude explained in this chapter that you would like to develop, and what can you begin doing today to make that happen?

_____

_____

_____

_____

_____

_____

_____

_____

_____

_____

_____

_____

_____

5 Sharpening Your Classroom Skills

Bob Krist/Terra/Corbis

Confident students are **responsible**. They own their actions, accept the consequences, and don't make excuses.

Learning is often a solitary process. You are sitting alone in front of a computer or at your desk late at night, studying. Or you might be taking a quick look at your notes before an exam. Assigned reading may consume much of your study time. However, the learning you do in class is often collaborative. Class discussion and group activities make up a significant portion of the work in many courses. In other courses, you may spend most of your time listening to lectures and taking notes. A successful day in class requires all your attention, some intellectual risk, and a lot of confidence. Being prepared for class also helps.

How prepared are you? Do you think you are getting as much out of class as you should? Do you participate in class with enthusiasm, or do you sit in the back of the room, hoping that the instructor will ignore you? How are you at listening? Do you know how to take notes, and do you know what notes to take? This chapter explains four strategies that will help you get more out of class and enjoy it more as well: *Prepare for class, become an active listener, commit to using a note-taking system*, and *engage in learning with others*. Use the acronym PACE to help you recall the strategies. Each letter of PACE is also the first letter of a key word that will serve as a memory aid. See Figure 5.1 below for a visual explanation of PACE.

You can now begin to sharpen your classroom skills. Set the PACE for responsible achievement by reading this chapter's *Confidence Builder* on academic honesty. How you deal with this issue can advance or undermine your efforts in the college classroom.

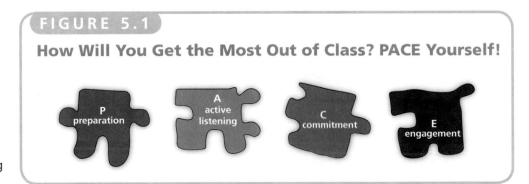

FIGURE 5.1

How Will You Get the Most Out of Class? PACE Yourself!

Plagiarism is the use of someone else's ideas and word choices without giving proper credit to the source.

CONFIDENCE BUILDER

Academic Honesty and You

Cheating and plagiarism are issues for students and instructors on every college campus. What is plagiarism, what constitutes cheating, and what do these issues have to do with you? **Plagiarism** is, literally, stealing someone else's ideas and writings and passing them off as your own. If you hand in a paper taken from the Internet, you are guilty of plagiarism. If you quote material from an article or book without crediting the source, that is plagiarism. Plagiarism is one kind of cheating. Here are some others:

- Copying someone else's answers to an assignment
- Sharing answers or information when you have been assigned to do your own work
- Taking a "cheat sheet" to an exam
- Looking at someone's paper during an exam
- Getting the questions on an exam from students in another section of the course
- Having someone else write a paper or do an assignment for you
- Having someone else take an exam in your place

continued

Plagiarism and other kinds of cheating are not hard to understand. Students are under pressure to earn good grades that will enable them to meet program requirements, to maintain scholarships, to participate on sports teams, to become certified in a field, and so on. Some cheating may not be intentional; instead, it can at times result from not knowing how to document sources or from taking incomplete notes. Some students may "borrow" ideas from others because they lack confidence in their own ideas. Even so, these are excuses for cheating that by no means justify the behavior.

Students may be tempted to cheat because the Internet offers thousands of sites that provide critical commentary, essay services, research papers, and other resources for the academically dishonest. However, your instructors are well aware of these sites. An instructor can take a phrase from a suspicious essay, do an advanced Google search, and have the source in seconds. Although the Internet makes it easy for someone to cheat, it is just as easy for an instructor to catch the cheater.

You have probably heard the old saying "cheaters never prosper," but is this true? Don't you know students who cheated and got away with it? As a student, are you better off cheating if you are guaranteed a good grade, or do you benefit more from being academically honest even if it results in failure? These are questions you will have to answer for yourself. Do cheaters prosper? Maybe in the short run some of them do, but those who make ethical choices are better off in the long run. If you are academically honest, you own your work. You learn what you are really capable of on your own, and you can use that knowledge to grow in skill, accomplishment, self-respect, and confidence.

What are your college's policies regarding plagiarism and academic honesty? To find answers, check your college's catalog or website.

Follow Up: To explore this topic further, visit *The Confident Student* premium website for an online search activity on academic honesty.

Prepare for Class

- Know what to expect from class, and know what is expected of you.

Confident students are responsible. They know what to expect from class because they attend regularly and keep up with assignments. They know what instructors require of them and they strive to meet those expectations. The more prepared you are, the more able you are to take an active role in class. Take the first step toward becoming more actively involved in your own learning process by evaluating your current performance in the classroom with *Awareness Check* 5.1.

Remember that the first letter of PACE stands for *preparation*. Your first strategy for success in any course is to come to class prepared to do the work, whether it involves participating in a group activity or taking a test. Although the following tips may seem obvious, many students sabotage their learning by ignoring them.

Attend Regularly and Be Punctual. Absenteeism has always been a problem in college. Students who cut classes cite many reasons: boredom, dislike of the course or instructor, time constraints, tiredness, and off-campus jobs. Students whose classes meet in a large lecture hall may think that their absence won't be noticed or that they can get the notes from friends. Because many instructors post lectures online, class attendance may seem unnecessary. The reality is that absence hurts you in three important ways.

▼ *Loss of understanding*: Cutting classes can be habit-forming. The first couple of times you do it, you may not notice any ill effects. However, with repeated cuts, you begin understanding less and less. When you finally do decide to show up, the class will have passed you by, and it may be too late to pull up your grade.

Awareness CHECK 5.1

Are You Prepared for Classes and Lectures?

Points

To explain how closely each statement applies to you, choose one of the following as your response: *always* (4 points), *usually* (3 points), *occasionally* (2 points), *rarely* (1 point). Write your number of points in the box beside each statement. When you are finished, add your score.

- [ ]   1. I attend class regularly, and I am absent only in case of emergency.
- [ ]   2. I make a point of arriving to a class or a lecture on time and staying until the end.
- [ ]   3. I use my syllabus to review requirements and keep up with assignments.
- [ ]   4. I begin studying for a test as soon as it is announced.
- [ ]   5. I do not forget to bring my book and other materials to class.
- [ ]   6. I always complete assigned work and hand it in on time.
- [ ]   7. I usually know what the instructor expects me to do.
- [ ]   8. I can pick out the important ideas in a lecture.
- [ ]   9. I can easily ignore distractions when I am listening to a lecture.
- [ ] 10. Even if I don't agree with an opinion that is expressed or don't understand everything that is said, this situation doesn't interfere with my ability to listen and learn.

Total   *Add your score. If your total is 35–40, you have a solid foundation of classroom preparation and listening skills. If your total is 30–34, you have some strengths but also some weaknesses. If your total is 25–29, practicing this chapter's strategies will improve your classroom performance. If your score is 10–24, you may have had difficulty in the past with meeting course requirements. It is never too late to make a new start. Whatever your level of skill, if you apply this chapter's strategies, you should see improvement not only in your grades but also in your level of confidence.*

▼ *Skipped steps in a sequence*: Second, in many courses—and especially in math courses—the material is presented sequentially: Each day's lesson builds upon previous lessons. Basic concepts and foundational skills are taught early in the course, and the level is raised gradually over the entire term. Cutting class cuts you out of the information loop.

▼ *Missed opportunities for learning*: An essential part of any course is the interaction you have with other students as you work cooperatively to solve problems and apply concepts. Concepts from assigned reading that may be difficult to understand are examined more fully through class discussion and planned activities. Students who have been absent often ask, "Did I miss anything?" Students who plan to be absent often ask, "Will we be doing anything important?" The answer to both questions is yes.

Punctuality is the quality of being on time.

Punctuality is as important as attendance. Emergencies will happen, and once in a while you may have to be late, but if you make lateness a habit, here's what can happen. Instructors usually state objectives during the first few moments of class. During the last few minutes, the instructor concludes the lesson and may announce a test or make a change in an assignment. Whether you arrive late or leave early, you miss something. Chronic lateness sends the message that you are irresponsible and not in control of your time and your life. Also, arriving late and leaving early are distracting, disruptive, and discourteous.

Punctuality is also a time-management issue. Be aware of the problems that can result from scheduling classes without leaving enough time to get from one to the next—on time. If your classes are in separate buildings or if you have a long walk between classes or if you need a restroom break, arriving on time may be difficult. If you know that you have trouble getting started in the morning, avoid scheduling early morning classes when possible.

Some students argue that since they are paying for the course, they have a right to attend or not. Don't make this faulty assumption. Your tuition buys you a place at the table. It does not buy you the right to behave any way you choose. You are bound by college policy, the instructor's requirements, and rules of etiquette. Since you do pay for every moment you spend in class, why not get your money's worth? Come every day, arrive on time, and stay until the end.

Watch Your Etiquette. Enter class quietly, find your seat quickly, and arrange your materials with a minimum of fuss. Turn your cell phone off and your mind on. The classroom, like the workplace, is not a casual setting. Here you do not prop up your feet, kick back, and relax. Let your posture show that you are engaged, involved, attentive, and interested—even if you are not. It's the polite thing to do. Be respectful of your classmates and instructor. Raise your hand and wait for acknowledgment instead of blurting out a comment or question. Take part in the class. Dozing at your desk, studying for another class, working on an assignment that should have been completed yesterday, socializing with friends, or texting with them are activities that show disrespect for the serious work in which the class is engaged.

Text messaging deserves special attention because it is so widespread. Students text their friends wherever they are, without thinking about the consequences. Texting is an annoyance and a distraction to your instructors, who may deal with this behavior in various unpleasant ways such as confiscating your BlackBerry or other device for the duration of the class or deducting points from your grade for texting. But perhaps more important is the fact that for every moment you spend texting in class, your attention is being distracted. You may think that you are "multitasking" when you are texting while listening to a lecture, but this is like an alcoholic who thinks he or she can have "just one drink." It doesn't work. Moreover, you cannot engage fully with others in class activities if you are absorbed in texting. Observing the rules of classroom **etiquette** means thinking about what you do and how it affects others.

Use Your Syllabus and Course Website. The course **syllabus** helps you keep up with assignments and tests, tells you what topics were covered if you were absent, and summarizes the instructor's requirements. Nowadays, many courses and professors also have their own websites where they review assignments, post the syllabus, and reflect on events related to the course. Check course and professor websites often to keep important course and assignment information fresh in your mind. Bring your syllabus to class every day or view it online. Then, if the instructor makes a change or postpones a test, you can note the change directly on the syllabus. Your syllabus is a confidence builder because it gives you a plan to follow.

Bring Textbooks and Other Supplies to Class Every Day. Instructors often call attention to information in the textbook, or they may ask you to do an exercise from the textbook in class. Some instructors lecture on material contained in the book, especially if the material is complicated or needs supplementing. If you bring your textbook to class, you will be able to follow along and mark important passages. A pencil, pen, and notebook should also be among the supplies you bring to class every day. Being prepared with the necessary supplies is your responsibility. You cause disruption when you attempt to borrow supplies or share a textbook.

Etiquette means good manners, polite behavior, and rules of conduct that make people feel comfortable being together.

Syllabus refers to the document that lists general course requirements and specific assignments.

Concept Check 5.1

Predicting topics and test questions is a critical thinking strategy covered at length in Chapter 3. You apply this strategy when you try to anticipate the next day's assignment.

Do the Assignments. Assignments provide the practice you need to acquire new skills. They help reinforce ideas and concepts discussed in class. Most important, doing the assignments provides you with background information that will help you make sense of future assignments. Also, you may lose points on tests if you are not able to answer questions that come directly from your assignments.

Anticipate the Next Lesson. Follow two simple steps to anticipate what will be covered in class each day.

1. **Review the previous day's work.** Read your notes from the last class. Review the previous chapter and the assignment, if any. The next class is likely to expand on this information. Reviewing the work from the previous class helps you retain the information and prepare for the next class.

2. **Preview the next day's assignments.** Review your syllabus to determine what will be covered and how it relates to what was covered in the previous class. Formulate some questions in your mind about the topic. Ask yourself "What do I already know?" Also, skim assigned chapters before reading them to preview content and to determine whether new words or terms are introduced; then look up the terms and definitions to familiarize yourself with them before doing the reading. Considering past assignments, try to predict what the instructor's approach to the material will be—whether lecture, discussion, or group work—and prepare for class accordingly. Previewing helps you relate new information to your prior knowledge, placing it in a meaningful context.

If you attend class regularly, are punctual, use your syllabus, bring your textbook and other supplies to class, do the assignments, and anticipate the next lesson, you will always know what to expect from your classes, you won't feel lost, and you will be in the proper frame of mind to listen attentively. In addition, use a daily planner or make a "to do" list of things you need to do to prepare for class. Then, before you go to bed, check off each item as you organize your materials for the next day's classes. What you put on your list is up to you. The purpose of daily planning is to help you make a habit of preparing for class. Also see Chapter 6 to learn how you can use daily lists as a time-management tool.

EXERCISE 5.1   Appropriate Student Behavior

Students and instructors often disagree on what students' responsibilities are. They may also disagree on what behaviors are inappropriate in the classroom and what the penalties for these behaviors should be. Read the list and then do the following:

1. **Explain why you think each behavior either *is* or *is not* a serious problem.**

2. **Choose one of the behaviors that you think is serious, and explain what you would do to discourage it if you were an instructor and what penalty you think would be fair. Then share your opinions in a class discussion.**

Student Behaviors

- **Repeated absence or lateness:**

  _____

- **Leaving a cell phone turned on:**

  _____

continued

- **Texting during a lecture or discussion:**

- **Failure to bring the textbook or other required materials:**

- **Not handing in assignments when they are due:**

- **Dozing in class or other inappropriate behavior:**

- **Cheating on an exam:**

Become an Active Listener

- Increase listening efficiency through concentration and application of appropriate strategies.

Remember that the second letter of PACE stands for **active listening**. Your second strategy for classroom success is to become an active listener. Because lecture discussion is the preferred style of many college instructors, you will probably spend most of your class time listening. You might say, "I'm a good listener; I hear what people say and I understand their words." However, active listening differs from simple hearing. Active listening requires more than hearing the words and knowing what they mean. Listening actively is a decisive act in which visual and tactile-kinesthetic senses may also be involved. When you are listening to a lecture—as opposed to merely hearing the words—you are focusing your attention on the speaker and the message, watching for cues, taking notes, and making a conscious effort to ignore other stimuli that compete for your attention. For example, active listening is different from watching television or listening to music. Active listening is purposeful and requires concentration and critical thinking. On the other hand, watching television or listening to music are passive activities that do not require your full attention. Instead, you can let your mind wander, converse with a friend, or engage in some other activity and still enjoy your television program or hear music playing in the background.

Student listeners fall into two categories: passive and active. **Passive listeners** do more hearing than listening. They are aware that the instructor is speaking, but they aren't making sense of what he or she is saying. Passive listening is characteristic of students who are externally motivated. For example, passive listeners may expect instructors to motivate them and to interest them in the topic. On the other hand, **active listeners** pay attention to what they hear and try to make sense of it. Active listening is characteristic of students who are internally motivated. For example, active listeners are self-motivated, and they expect to find their own reasons for being interested in a lecture topic. Figure 5.2 compares the traits of active and passive listeners. Which kind of listener are you?

Active listening is involved listening in which your vision, hearing, posture, and mind each play a role.

Passive listeners are uninvolved, inattentive, and detached from the process.

Active listeners practice the strategies that keep them focused and involved.

FIGURE 5.2

Traits of Passive and Active Listeners

Passive Listeners	Active Listeners
Expect a lecture to be dull	Expect to find something in the lecture that interests them
Assume that information in a lecture will not be useful or pertain to their lives	Assume that information in a lecture will be useful—if not now, then later
Look for weaknesses in the speaker's style instead of listening to what the speaker says	May notice weaknesses in the speaker's style but pay attention to what the speaker says
Listen only for ideas that interest them	Listen for main ideas and the details that support them
Give in to daydreaming and become distracted	Resist daydreaming and ignore distractions
Tune out when they disagree with the speaker	Keep listening even when they disagree with the speaker
Tune out difficult or technical information; do not ask questions	Try to understand difficult or technical information; ask questions as needed
May doze in lectures if tired	Fight to stay awake if tired
Do not take good notes	Take well-organized notes

Pedro Coll/Photolibrary

Active listeners are involved, attentive, and engaged in learning.

To get more out of lectures, become an active listener. Follow these five steps:

1. **Decide to listen**. By deciding to listen, you are strengthening your commitment to learn. Also, by deciding to listen, you are taking an active role instead of sitting back passively, expecting to receive information without effort.

2. **Listen with a positive frame of mind**. Expect to find something in the lecture that will interest you. Assume that you will learn something useful, that you will expand your knowledge, and that you will increase your understanding of the subject.

3. **Assume the posture of involvement**. Sit straight but comfortably and make eye contact with the speaker. Concentrate on what is being said. Your effort to understand and follow the lecture will show in your expression, making you look interested even if you are not. Body orientation, expression, and gestures such as nodding when you agree or displaying a questioning look when you don't understand are cues that help the speaker determine whether the message is getting across. Your involvement will pay off. By trying to appear interested even when you are not, you may actually become interested. At that point, your engagement in learning begins.

4. **Take notes**. Taking notes also helps you concentrate on the lecture. Taking notes activates your tactile-kinesthetic sense, as explained in Chapter 2, so that you are more likely to retain the information, especially if you review your notes soon after the lecture. Take notes consistently when listening to lectures and choose a note-taking system that works for you. (More is said about note-taking later in the chapter.)

5. **Decide what is important**. Listen for repeated terms or ideas. Speakers use repetition to emphasize important points. Watch for gestures and facial expressions that may also be used for emphasis. Listen for signal words or phrases. See Figure 5.3 for a list of signal words and phrases and explanations of what they mean.

Listening for signal words helps you listen for ideas. For example, if an English instructor says, "You can use seven different organizational patterns to arrange the details in a paragraph," then you could number from one to seven on your paper,

---

FIGURE 5.3

Signal Words and Phrases

1. To indicate that another main idea or example follows:

also	furthermore	another
in addition	moreover	

2. To add emphasis:

most important	above all	of primary concern
remember that	a key idea	most significant
pay attention to	the main idea	

3. To indicate that an example follows:

for example	to illustrate	such as
for instance	specifically	

4. To indicate that a conclusion follows:

therefore	in conclusion	finally
consequently	to conclude	so

5. To indicate an exception to a stated fact:

however	although	but
nevertheless	though	except

6. To indicate causes or effects:

because	due to	consequently
since	reason	result
for	cause	effect

7. To indicate that categories or divisions will be named or explained:

types	parts	groups
kinds	characteristics	categories

8. To indicate a sequence:

steps	numbers (1, 2, 3, . . .)
stages	first, second, etc.

9. To indicate that items are being compared:

similar	different	equally
like	in contrast	on the other hand
advantages	disadvantages	contrary to

EXERCISE 5.2   Collaborative Activity on Listening

FORM A GROUP WITH FOUR or five students. Using the traits listed in Figure 5.2 as a guide, prepare a short demonstration on listening behavior. Let one person in the group be the lecturer. Let other group members demonstrate passive or active listening habits. The group member acting as the lecturer should be able to explain to the class which group members were good listeners and which were not. Practice your demonstration. Your instructor may call on one or more of the groups to present in class.

---

skipping lines between, and listen for the seven patterns and the instructor's explanations. If you get to the fifth pattern and realize that you don't have anything written down for the fourth one, then you know you have missed something in the lecture. At this point, you should ask a question.

As a final point, treat class discussions as you would lectures: Listen actively and take notes. Lots of good information comes out of class discussions. Instructors often use discussion to help students apply concepts. Something that you may not have understood from your reading may be clarified during a class discussion. For more information on how to listen effectively, see Chapter 12.

Commit to a Note-Taking System

• Try different note-taking systems; then choose your best system.

A **commitment** is a pledge or vow to take an action. Your commitment to a note-taking system is your pledge that you will use this system to do your best.

Remember that the third letter of PACE stands for **commitment**. The third strategy for classroom success is commit to using a system for taking good notes. There is no *best* way to take notes. The note-taking systems explained in this chapter have helped many students record and retain information presented in lectures. Experiment with the systems, find the style of note-taking that consistently gives you good results, and commit to using it. For information on how to take notes from textbooks, see Chapters 7 and 8. Now complete *Awareness Check* 5.2 before you continue reading.

Awareness CHECK 5.2

How Effective Are Your Note-Taking Skills?

To see where you need improvement, evaluate your lecture notes from a recent class. Read them over and answer *yes* or *no* to the following questions.

Yes   No

1. Did you date your notes and number the pages?
2. Did you write the course name or number on your notes?
3. Did you write down the topic of the lecture?
4. Did you use 8½" x 11" paper to keep in a loose-leaf binder?
5. Did you take notes with a ballpoint pen?
6. Are your notes easy to read?

continued

7. Is this set of notes in the same notebook as all your other notes for this class?

8. Are your notes organized into an informal outline or other logical format?

9. Are you able to distinguish the speaker's main ideas from the examples that illustrate them?

10. As you read your notes, are you able to reconstruct in your mind what the lecture was about?

If you answered no to any of these questions—particularly the last two—then your note-taking skills may need improvement. Try the guidelines that follow for improving your note-taking.

Guidelines for Lecture Notes

▼ Keep track of your notes by heading your paper with the *date, name of course*, and *lecture topic*. Number pages consecutively. Later, when you study, you'll be able to match up class notes and textbook notes or assignments on the same topic.

▼ Use standard-sized paper—8½ × 11-inch—that will fit into most notebooks or folders. Small sheets of paper won't hold enough writing and may get lost or out of order.

▼ Keep the notes for one class separated from the notes for other classes. Use separate notebooks for each class, or use dividers to distinguish different sections in one notebook. Some students like to use spiral notebooks. Many instructors recommend the use of a loose-leaf three-ring binder to keep lecture notes, textbook notes, and handouts organized and available for study. Pages can be inserted, removed, or reorganized as needed.

▼ Use a ballpoint pen for taking notes. Ink from felt-tip pens blurs and soaks through the paper, spotting the sheets underneath. Pencil smears and fades over time. Many students prefer to use blue or black ink because other colors, such as red or green, are hard on the eyes.

▼ It is generally recommended that you write rather than print your notes, because you can write faster than you can print. On the other hand, if your handwriting is illegible or difficult to read because of decorative flourishes, then you may want to print for clarity.

▼ As an alternative to handwriting, another option is to take notes on a laptop. Some students with disabilities may prefer to use keyboarding if handwriting will slow them down. Before choosing this option, make sure that a power outlet is available in the various classrooms on your campus.

▼ To speed up your note-taking, use standard abbreviations and make up some of your own for words or phrases that you use often. Make a key for your abbreviations so you won't forget what they mean. See Figure 5.4 for a list of some common abbreviations. For even greater speed while taking notes, omit the periods from abbreviations.

▼ Copy into your notes anything that is written on the board or projected on a screen. Test questions often come from material that is presented in these ways.

That said, it is important to note that most professors post their lecture PowerPoint presentations on the course website so that students don't have to copy everything down. Some professors also provide PowerPoint slide handouts with write-on lines next to each slide for ease of student note-taking.

FIGURE 5.4

Commonly used Abbreviations and Symbols

1. equal: =
2. with: w/
3. without: w/o
4. number: #
5. therefore: \
6. and: +
7. and so forth: etc.
8. for example: e.g.
9. against: vs.
10. government: gov't.
11. introduction: intro.
12. information: info.
13. department: dept.
14. advantage: adv.
15. organization: org.
16. maximum: max.
17. individual: ind.
18. compare: cf.
19. association: assoc.
20. politics: pol.

Taking notes during a lecture involves your visual, aural, and tactile/kinesthetic senses that open multiple pathways to the brain.

Patrick Ward/CORBIS

- Take organized notes. Use a system such as one of those suggested later in this chapter, or devise your own. Make main ideas stand out from the examples that support them. Do not write lecturers' words verbatim. Summarize ideas in your own words so that they will be easier for you to remember.
- As soon as possible after class, review your notes to fill in gaps while the information is still fresh in your mind. The purpose of taking notes is to help you remember information. If you take notes but don't look at them until you are ready to study for a test, you will have to relearn the information. To retain information in your long-term memory, review it frequently.
- To fill in gaps, compare notes with a classmate or question the instructor if you missed something.

The Informal Outline/Key Words System

Ideas that are organized in a logical pattern are easier to remember than isolated facts and examples that don't seem to relate to one another. Try this simple, two-part system to improve your note-taking.

Draw a line down your paper so that you have a 2½-inch column on the right and a 6-inch column on the left. Take notes in the 6-inch column, using an informal outline. Make main ideas stand out by indenting and numbering the details and examples listed under them. Skip lines between main ideas so that you can fill in examples afterwards or add an example if the lecturer returns to one of these ideas later on. After the lecture, write key words in the right margin that will help you recall information from your notes.

Figure 5.5 on page 120 shows a student's lecture notes on the topic, "Studying on the Right Side of the Brain." The student has used the informal outline/key words system. On the left side of the page, the student has outlined the lecture given in class. Later, on the right side of the page, in the margin, the student has written key words or abbreviations that show at a glance what the lecture covered.

When you use this system, wait to write in the key words until you are reviewing your notes.

The Cornell Method*

Developed by Dr. Walter Pauk of Cornell University, the Cornell method is a classic note-taking system that has worked for many students. One version of the system involves five steps: *record, reduce, recite, reflect*, and *review*.

Begin by dividing an 8½ × 11-inch sheet of notebook paper into three sections, as shown in Figure 5.6 on page 121. Then follow these steps for taking notes from a lecture:

1. **Record** facts and ideas in the wide column. After the lecture, fill in any gaps and neaten up your handwriting, if necessary, so that you will be able to read your notes when you review them later.

2. **Reduce**, or condense, the facts and ideas you recorded in the right column into questions, key words, or brief definitions of terms that you can list in the left column. Keep these notations brief and to the point. Their purpose is to help you recall the more expanded ideas you listed in the right column.

3. **Recite** from the information listed in the left—or recall—column of your notes. First, cover up the right column and recite from the key words or questions you listed in the left column. As you recite each key word or question, try to recall and recite in your own words the whole fact or idea from which it was reduced. To check yourself, uncover the wide column and read your notes. Reciting from your notes makes use of both your visual and auditory senses.

4. **Reflect** on what you have learned from the lecture by applying the facts and ideas to real-life situations. Determine why the facts are significant, how you can use them, and how they expand or modify your prior knowledge. Think critically and creatively about ways you can use the information. Finally, summarize your notes in the space at the bottom of your paper. You can summarize what you have written on each page of notes, or you can summarize the whole lecture at the end of the last page. Doing both a page summary and a whole-lecture summary is even better.

5. **Review** and recite from your notes immediately and periodically. A good way to begin a study session, especially if you have trouble getting started, is to review your notes. Reviewing reminds you of what you have learned and sets the scene for new information to be gained from the next assignment. Reviewing also helps you see connections between new information and prior knowledge.

Now, clarify these steps in your mind by examining the student's lecture notes shown in Figure 5.7 on page 122.

Concept Check 5.2

A note-taking system that is compatible with your learning style may include drawings, diagrams, symbols, and abbreviations that are meaningful to you.

* Walter Pauk, *How to Study in College*, Eighth Edition, Copyright © 2005 by Houghton Mifflin Company. Reprinted by permission of Houghton Mifflin Company/Cengage Learning.

FIGURE 5.5

The Informal Outline/Key Words System

Study Skills 1620		Sept. 18
Studying on the Right Side of the Brain		
Visual thinking		
1.	Use graphic techniques like diagrams, maps, etc. to organize information into a meaningful pattern.	def.
2.	Visual learners need to make verbal information "visual" or they will have a hard time remembering it.	reason for using "visuals"
Fantasy		
1.	The ability to create and use mental images is another kind of visual thinking.	def.
2.	To understand the stages in an organism's life cycle, imagine you are the organism going through the stages.	ex. of fantasy
Hands-on experience		
1.	Get involved in a direct experience of what you are learning.	def.
2.	Do lab experiments, take field trips, role play, look at or touch objects as they are described. Go through the steps of a process.	hands-on activities
Music		
1.	Common belief: music distracts while studying.	
2.	Music can accelerate learning.	effect of music on learning
3.	Studies show retention improved when students read to music.	
4.	Instrumentals that match the feeling or mood of the information to be remembered are the best type of music.	

FIGURE 5.6

The Cornell Method: Setting up the Paper

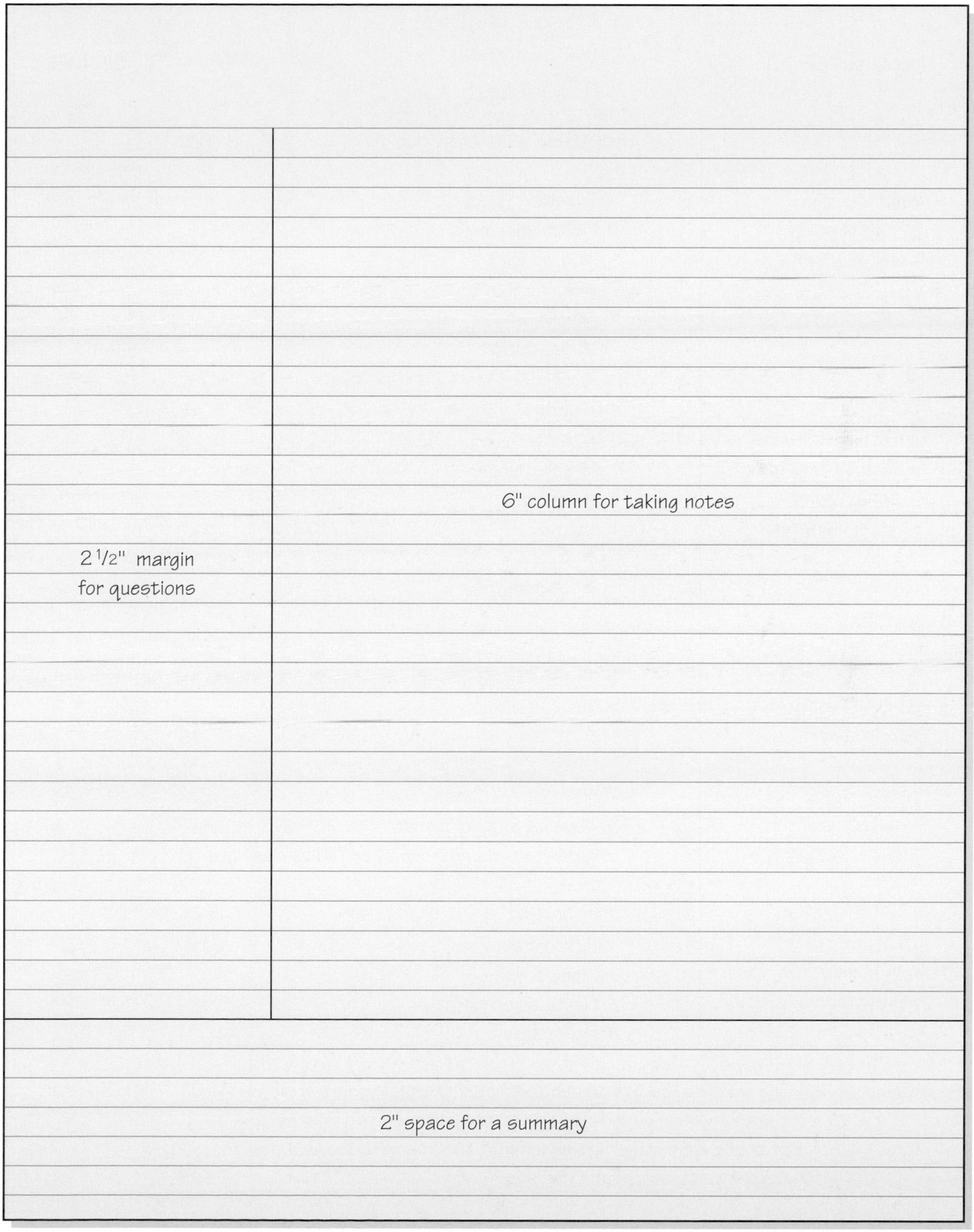

6" column for taking notes

2 1/2" margin
for questions

2" space for a summary

FIGURE 5.7

The Cornell Method: One Student's Notes

Intro. to Literature 2010   Sept. 18

	The Five Elements of Fiction
	1. Plot
How does the	a. Events
plot of the	b. Plot development
story develop?	* conflict
	* complications
	* climax
	* resolution
	2. Characters
What is the	a. Dynamic
difference between	* well-rounded
a dynamic and a	* motives
static character?	b. Static
	* flat
	* stereotype
	3. Setting
When and where	a. Time
does the story	b. Place
take place?	
How is the	4. Theme
theme of the	a. Meaning or significance
story revealed?	b. Revealed through interaction of five elements
	5. Point of view
What are the	a. First person
four points	b. Omniscient
of view?	c. Limited omniscient
	d. Dramatic

The writer uses five elements of fiction—plot, characters, setting, theme, and point of view—to develop the story. Through the interaction of these elements, the meaning of the story is revealed and the reader can understand its significance.

The Idea Cluster

What if you are not a linear thinker? What if a 1-2-3 order of information does not appeal to you because you don't think that way and instructors don't always stick to their lecture outlines? You may prefer a more visual style of note-taking. Try making an **idea cluster**, also called a *concept map*. Start a few inches from the top of the page and write the speaker's first main idea in a circle near the middle of the page. If the speaker gives an example, draw an arrow to another circle in which you write the example. If the speaker presents another main idea, start a new cluster. Figure 5.8 shows an example of an idea cluster. This system will help you visualize the information you want to remember. An advantage of clustering is that if the speaker leaves one idea and returns to it later, it is easy to draw another arrow from the circle and add the new information.

An **idea cluster** is a visual form of note-taking. Major details and examples branch out from a central circle that represents the main idea.

Note-Taking Systems and Learning Style

As explained in Chapter 2, you will not always have your choices of courses and instructors. Although you have a preferred way of learning, you need to be flexible enough to adapt to whatever teaching modes your instructors use so that you are not at a disadvantage, no matter what the situation. One of the advantages of listening and taking notes during a lecture is that through the combined visual, auditory, and tactile-kinesthetic modes, several of your senses are engaged. However, you have a choice of

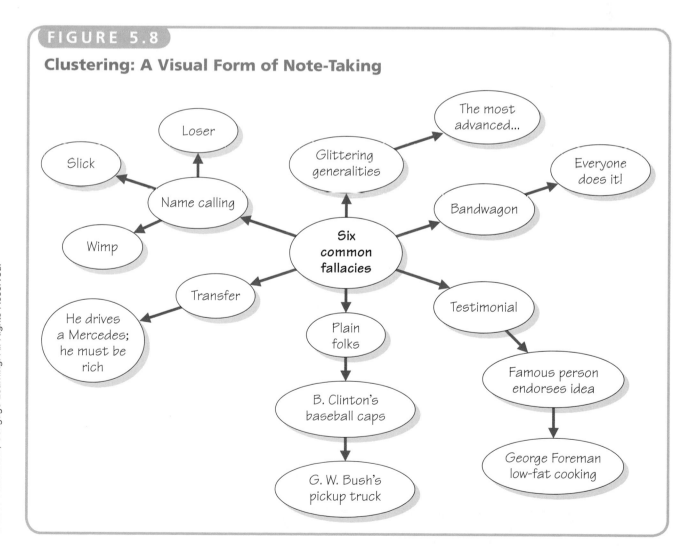

FIGURE 5.8

Clustering: A Visual Form of Note-Taking

EXERCISE 5.3 Learning Styles Application on Taking Notes

PRACTICE NOTE-TAKING WITH A classmate. During the next class meeting, both of you should take notes, using your preferred method. After class, compare your notes. Do your notes cover the same information? Are your note-taking styles similar or different? Whose notes are neater, better organized, and more thorough? What have you learned from this exercise that will help you improve your note-taking skills?

note-taking systems and study techniques to use. If you are a visual learner, you may get more out of clustering. If you are an auditory learner, then reciting from your notes is natural for you. Whether you prefer studying alone or with a group, sharing notes is a good way to check whether you are missing anything from a lecture. If your learning style is more tactile-kinesthetic, reciting from your notes while waiting in line or while sitting outside may appeal to you. For some people, a change of pace or scenery aids concentration, while for others it is a distraction. The best thing about trying out different note-taking systems and different ways of reviewing your notes is that you will discover what works best for you.

Computer CONFIDENCE

Organize Your Notes on Your Laptop or PC

Taking notes in class and while you're reading is an important first step toward understanding new material. But the next step is even more important: organizing your notes into a format from which you can study effectively. That's where your laptop or PC can make a big difference. Whichever note-taking style you prefer—the informal outline/key words system, the Cornell method, clustering, or a system of your own—organizing your notes electronically offers several advantages over handwriting:

1. It's easy to move whole blocks of words around to rearrange information into a format that makes sense to you.
2. It's easy to add new ideas to your notes as you go along or to combine class and textbook notes to give yourself the most complete coverage of the information.
3. The actual process of typing your notes on a keyboard improves your memory by engaging your tactile and visual senses.
4. If you miss something, or if you want to go through your notes to find a certain topic, you can do a search for specific words or phrases.

Many word processing programs offer easy-to-use outlining features that automatically provide an outline format into which you can type your notes. Or you can create your own outlines by following these simple steps:

1. Open a separate file for each of your courses. Create a name for the file.
2. Try to get to the computer soon after each class, while the lecture is still fresh in your mind. Enter the date and topic of each lecture at the top of a new page.
3. Review your class notes. No matter what note-taking system you're using, this is a good time to focus on the main ideas or key questions. Then type your notes, using a system. For example, use the boldface function to make main ideas stand out, use tabs to indent details, and set special margins for key words or questions.
4. At this point, you may wish to add comments, insert notes from your reading, or move sections of your outline around. To create a formal outline, insert Roman numerals and uppercase letters to mark major divisions, and move each

continued

line so that it aligns correctly. Then insert Arabic numerals and lowercase letters in front of the details and also align them.

5. Print out the final version. Double-space the printed copy so that you will have room to insert additional notes.

Other options for note-taking include using voice-recognition software that allows you to dictate your notes. A laptop computer is convenient to use between classes to enter a few ideas while on the run until you have time to sit down and review the lecture and organize your notes.

Engage in Learning with Others

• Develop the skills that will help you speak, present, and participate more confidently and effectively in group settings.

Remember that the fourth letter of PACE stands for *engagement*.

Engagement, in this sense, means active involvement plus commitment. An engaged student is completely occupied, or caught up, in what is going on in class. An engaged student is committed to learn—and to support and encourage others as well. Students engaged in learning interact in various ways: through class discussion, making oral presentations, and working cooperatively on projects or in group activities. Even though lecturing is still the primary mode of instruction in many courses at least some of the time and in some courses most of the time, your active participation will be required. If you are reluctant to express your opinions in class or to contribute your share in group activities, the strategies explained in the next two sections will build your confidence.

Engagement means active involvement. Students who are engaged in learning are busy, occupied, and committed to their goals.

Participate Actively and Confidently

Chapter 1 introduces the idea of active learning. Chapter 4 encourages you to write action plans to achieve your goals. This chapter promotes active listening and involvement in class. Throughout *The Confident Student*, you will see an emphasis on active processes to enhance learning. If you sit back passively in your class or group, letting others take the risks and do the work, you are not really involved. You may be taking in some information, but you aren't *doing* anything to promote learning and retention. *The key to active learning is participation.*

Do you try to avoid sharing your thoughts aloud in class? Do you often feel you have something to contribute but refrain from speaking up? If so, you are not alone. Many students would rather listen than engage in class discussion for several reasons. Some are afraid that their ideas will not be well received. Some students who are confident about what they think are reserved by nature. Still others are from cultures in which students are not expected to speak out or share their opinions. However, class discussion is a normal and expected part of academic work in the United States. So if you are uncomfortable with participating in class, now is the time to get over those feelings. It may not be easy at first, but each time you enter the conversation it will become easier. Start by asking a question when you have one. This will break the ice. Then you can move on to expressing your opinion during a discussion or offering an answer to a question.

To become more active during class discussion, listen attentively, take notes, and make eye contact with whoever is speaking, whether it is the instructor or a student. Ask questions if appropriate and express your opinion when you have something to contribute. Avoid distracting behaviors such as socializing. Good classroom etiquette requires that you treat your classes with the same seriousness as you would a job. Be professional at work; be academic in class.

Small group work also calls for a serious attitude and polite behavior. The group is not a social gathering; it has a task to perform. Clearly define the task and your role within the group—leader, recorder, timekeeper, and so on. Understand what part of the work is your responsibility and stay on task. In addition, follow these guidelines for successful work within groups:

1. Allow each person to contribute to the discussion; take turns and don't interrupt.

2. Question facts, argue the details, but do not take part in personal attacks.

3. When it is your time to share, be precise and to the point, and do not monopolize the discussion.

4. If you are the group leader, keep the discussion focused, encourage everyone to contribute, and summarize the group's conclusions at the end of the discussion.

5. Do your part to keep the group on task. Do not let the discussion degenerate into a social exchange.

Participation in class and group work helps you build interpersonal skills and also keeps you actively involved in the learning process. By becoming engaged in learning, you become a part of something larger—people working together to reach common goals.

EXERCISE 5.4   Learning Styles Application on Classroom Behavior

HOW INVOLVED OR ENGAGED ARE you in your classes? Read about three members of a sociology class and see if you find yourself mirrored in their profiles. Then answer the questions that follow.

> Bob always sits at the back of the classroom so that he can nap quietly if he has stayed out late the night before. He rarely makes a comment or asks a question. If he doesn't understand something the instructor says, he forgets about it. He's sure that he'll figure the problem out when he does the reading just before the final exam. He would probably forget about it anyway before the exam rolled around.
>
> Sam can't wait to get to class. He has done all the reading, and he has millions of questions to ask. Sam's voice is always the first one heard. His hand is raised many times each class hour, whether there's a lecture or a discussion. Often frustrated, Sam does not listen to either his peers or his instructor. If he did listen, he'd realize that many of his questions had already been addressed. Sometimes Sam is so interested in getting his point across that he interrupts his classmates' remarks or he attacks them for challenging his views.
>
> Carmen loves sociology class. She enjoys listening to the lecture, but she also enjoys the give-and-take of class discussions. At first, she was hesitant to speak out, but once she became convinced that she could learn a great deal from the questions and comments of her peers, she tried participating. When she leads a discussion, Carmen makes sure that everyone has a chance to contribute, keeps the discussion focused, and summarizes the discussion at its close.

1. **List three negative behaviors that Bob exhibits in class.**

   _____

   _____

   _____

continued

2. **How could Bob change his behavior so that he could participate more fully in class?**

_____

_____

_____

3. **Why is Sam's behavior negative? How could he change his behavior to participate in a more positive way?**

_____

_____

_____

4. **How does Carmen play an active role in class?**

_____

_____

_____

5. **Why is Carmen a good discussion leader?**

_____

_____

_____

6. **Where do you place each students' source of motivation (internal or external), and why?**

_____

_____

_____

Become an Effective Presenter

Being able to speak in front of a group or to make an effective oral presentation is a valued skill. President Obama was elected, in part, because of his speaking skills. A speech course is a general education or liberal arts requirement at many colleges and universities because oral communication is an important academic and career skill. In a speech class, you learn how to plan, organize, and make speeches. You also learn how to cope with _stage fright_, the fear of speaking or performing in front of an audience, and the stress that results from that fear. If you have not yet had an opportunity to take a public speaking course, then the following suggestions may help you prepare yourself for making an oral presentation and also speaking in class. In Chapter 12, you will learn more about public speaking and reducing stage fright.

Suppose your literature instructor asks you to give an oral interpretation of a poem you were assigned to read. Or maybe your biology instructor asks you to report to the class about the results of an experiment you performed in the lab. In each case, you would first decide what your *purpose* is. For example, the purpose of your interpretation of a poem might be to explain what you think the writer's theme is. In your report about your lab results, your purpose would be to tell what conclusion you reached as a result of your experiment.

Once your purpose is clear, you can *plan* and *organize* your speech. Outline your main idea and the details that support it. Recite from your outline several times until you know what you want to say. Try your speech out on a friend or family member and ask for suggestions about how to improve your delivery or how to explain your ideas more clearly. If you think you might forget something, summarize your main idea and details on 3×5-inch cards. The notes will jog your memory, and holding the cards will give you something to do with your hands.

In general, a good plan to follow in preparing an oral presentation is to use a three-part development:

1. **Introduction:** A good introduction gets the audience's attention and makes them want to listen to what you have to say about your topic. State your thesis (opinion) and purpose in the introduction, and give your listeners a preview of your main points.

2. **Body:** The body is the main part of your presentation in which you will support your thesis with the evidence you have gathered from your own experience or from research. An article from a book or periodical, an interview with an expert on your topic, and information gathered from websites are possible sources for you to consider. Your instructor or librarian can help you find credible sources, or use the evaluative strategies explained in Chapter 3. Support your presentation with media such as PowerPoint (or other digital slide programs) or graphic materials, but only if these materials significantly enhance your presentation.

3. **Conclusion:** Tell your listeners why the information you have just given them is important and how they can use it. Review or summarize your thesis, evidence, and purpose.

See Figure 5.9 for a summary of the three parts of a presentation and what to include in each part plus some additional suggestions.

It is normal to feel some nervousness before giving a presentation. Preparation is the best antidote to stage fright. Practice your presentation in front of a roommate or friends until you feel comfortable with it. Before the presentation, take a few deep breaths to relax yourself and clear your mind. To prevent dry mouth, put some lip balm on your lips. To control shakiness, hold your note cards. Most important, focus on your message and your audience instead of your own feelings.

Remember that your audience is on your side. They are interested in what you have to say. You can make it easy for them to pay attention by making eye contact, speaking loudly enough to be heard in the back of the room, and speaking distinctly. Also, watch your pace, because speaking too fast or too slowly is distracting and interferes with the flow of ideas. Making oral presentations is like any other skill: The more practice you have, the more you will improve.

FIGURE 5.9

What to Include in Your Oral Presentation

Three Parts	What to Include in Each Part
INTRODUCTION	• Start with an attention-getting quote, question, or story. • Build background for your topic to arouse interest. • State your thesis and purpose. • Preview main points for your listeners.
BODY	• Use evidence such as facts, reasons, or examples to support your thesis. • Include information gathered from sources such as books, articles, websites, and interviews to add credibility. • Support your presentation with media such as PowerPoint or Keynote slides, graphics, and so on.
CONCLUSION	• Restate your thesis and purpose. • Review your main points. • Relate the significance of your information to your listeners' lives.

CRITICAL THINKING

Presenting a Skill to the Class

Exercise Overview

One test of knowledge or skill is this: Can you teach it to someone else? This exercise will not only give you practice in preparing and making a short oral presentation, but it will also help you review one of the topics covered in your textbook. In addition, you will test your knowledge by teaching your classmates something you have learned.

Exercise Background

Speaking is an often-neglected skill. Students who have stage fright may avoid taking a speech course unless it is required, depriving themselves of the opportunity to develop and practice this skill. Being able to speak with confidence or to make a well-organized presentation is an asset in the workplace. Planning an effective speech or presentation involves both critical and creative thinking.

Exercise Task

Working with a partner or a group of three or four students, plan and make a brief presentation to the class on a topic of your choice from Chapters 1 through 4 of *The Confident Student*. Your purpose is to teach your classmates a skill or to help them gain greater understanding of a concept. Develop an introduction, body, and conclusion for your presentation. You also have the option of supplementing your presentation with media, information from another source, or a brief skit or demonstration.

Guided CHAPTER REVIEW

The following checklist summarizes this chapter's key terms and strategies. After reading the chapter, how confident are you that you can apply the information you have learned? To assess your level of confidence, respond to each statement with one of the following: *very confident* (3 points), *fairly confident* (2 points), *not very confident* (1 point), *not confident* (0 points). Write your number of points in the box beside each statement. Then add your score and read the analysis that follows. When you have finished, take the chapter quiz.

SUMMARY CHECK

How confident are you about applying these strategies?

Points

☐ 1. Being well prepared for class

☐ 2. Listening actively

☐ 3. Trying out different note-taking systems and choosing your best system

☐ 4. Becoming engaged in learning through effective participation

☐ 5. Working cooperatively in a group

☐ 6. Speaking and presenting in class

☐ 7. Choosing academic honesty over plagiarism and other forms of cheating

How confident is your understanding of this chapter's key terms?

☐ 8. plagiarism

☐ 9. punctuality

☐ 10. etiquette

☐ 11. syllabus

☐ 12. active listening

☐ 13. passive listeners

☐ 14. active listeners

☐ 15. commitment

☐ 16. idea cluster

☐ 17. engagement

Total

Add your score. The highest possible score is 51. The closer your score is to 51, the higher your level of confidence. Use your Summary Check results to help you determine which parts of the chapter to review.

YOUR WEBSITE RESOURCES

This chapter's website resources include the following items. To access them, go to *The Confident Student* premium website.

- **Video Skillbuilder: Taking Notes to Improve Your Grades**
- **Chapter Exercises**
- **Forms to Download**

- **Chapter Summary of Topics**
- **Thinking Ahead About Career**
- **Confidence Builder Web Search**
- **Self-Test**

CHAPTER REVIEW Quiz

Answer the following questions from memory. Then return to the chapter to check your answers. As a final activity, complete *Show Your Confidence* at the end of the quiz.

1. What is *plagiarism*? Give an example.

_____

_____

2. Your textbook explains several ways that absence from class can hurt you. What is one of these ways?

_____

_____

3. What is one example of poor classroom etiquette that you have noticed?

_____

_____

4. What is the difference between an active listener and a passive listener?

_____

_____

5. How does listening differ from hearing?

_____

_____

6. This chapter explains three note-taking systems. Which one do you prefer, and why?

_____

_____

7. Describe any two of the steps of the Cornell note-taking system.

_____

_____

8. Of this chapter's guidelines for taking notes, which one seems most important to you?

_____

_____

9. What does it mean to be "engaged" in learning?

_____

_____

10. What are the three parts of an effective presentation?

_____

_____

SHOW YOUR CONFIDENCE

Choose a course in which you are doing well. Rate yourself on attendance, punctuality, and keeping up with assignments in that course. To what extent have these three behaviors contributed to your performance? What have you learned from your preparation for this class that you can apply to your other classes? Be prepared to share what you have learned either in writing or in class discussion.

YOUR REFLECTIONS: IMPROVING CLASSROOM PERFORMANCE

Reflect on what you have learned from this chapter about classroom skills that can improve your performance. Use the following questions to stimulate your thinking; then write your reflections. Include in your writing specific information from the chapter.

- PACE stands for this chapter's four strategies for sharpening your classroom skills. Which of the PACE strategies is your strongest? Which one could use improvement? Explain your answer.
- How has your preparation for classes either led to or prevented your success in one or more of your courses?
- What is one strategy explained in this chapter that you think every student can benefit from trying?

_____

_____

_____

_____

_____

_____

_____

_____

_____

_____

_____

_____

_____

_____

_____

_____

_____

_____

6 Making the Most of Your Time

Alex Kraus/vario images/vario images GmbH & Co.KG/Alamy

This chapter encourages you to:

- Set goals that will help you meet responsibilities and keep your life in balance.

- Construct schedules for more efficient time management that sets the stage for achievement.

- Meet the time-management challenges you may face as a community college student, commuter, or student athlete.

- Beat procrastination by identifying its causes and by learning how to avoid it.

Confident students are **self-managed**. They have the self-discipline to prioritize tasks and meet obligations.

You already know about time and how it affects every aspect of your life. Classes begin and end at certain times, employers expect you to be at work on time, children must be fed, the dog has to go out, the car needs to be serviced, and so on. You may have appointments, meetings, or special events to attend at fixed dates and times. You also have to make time for study, sleep, and a few moments to yourself among other things.

As a college student, you are undoubtedly aware that studying is a top priority. However, you may have trouble settling down to study when so many other responsibilities compete for your time. Like many others before you, you may wish that there were more than twenty-four hours in a day. You may also be tempted to play the procrastination game when an assignment is long or seems difficult.

Resource means "asset." Resources include time, money, and materials that can be managed effectively for specific purposes.

Time is a manageable **resource**, and this chapter is filled with strategies that will put you in control of your time. Now read the following *Confidence Builder* to learn your first strategy for making the most of your time.

CONFIDENCE BUILDER

"I work better under pressure" and Other Myths

What is time anyway? Time is a human invention. The calendar is our creation. Before we divided history into decades, years into months, and days into hours, there was only the vast reach of undivided time. People from different cultures may have different concepts of time. As people age, time—even more than money—may be what they value most. Right now you may be feeling a little pressed for time.

Don't let time get the best of you. Instead, get the best from time by prioritizing tasks, by setting goals for their completion, and by following a schedule to get things done. But before you begin, let's dispose of a few common myths about time management that may be holding you back from accomplishing what you have the skill and ability to do.

- *I work better under pressure.* This myth is an excuse for putting off work that needs to be done. You may think you work better under pressure, but who knows what more you might accomplish if you would set aside enough time to do your work in a systematic way instead of waiting until the last minute.
- *Making schedules takes more time than it is worth.* You may think you will get more done if you just plunge in and do the work, but this is

rarely the case. Scheduling actually saves time because it provides an organizational framework that helps you balance study time with other responsibilities.

- *Too much time management will destroy my spontaneity.* Too often, being "spontaneous" means doing what you want to do first and doing what you need to do in the time remaining. As a result, the work doesn't get done. It is better to be organized than spontaneous when it comes to studying. Also, there is no such thing as too much time management. The way you manage your time is either effective or ineffective.
- *My time is beyond my control.* It is true that class times and working hours may be beyond your control. It is also true that other obligations may be set at certain hours that are nonnegotiable. However, you can find ways to work around these fixed times to plan the rest of your time. No matter how many things you have to do, you can probably do them more efficiently.

Follow Up: To explore this topic further, visit *The Confident Student* premium website for an online search activity about time management.

How to GRAB Time

• Set goals that will help you meet responsibilities and keep your life in balance.

To take control of your time, you must be aggressive, especially if you are a chronic procrastinator—someone who consistently puts off doing difficult, boring, or time-consuming tasks. Unless you live alone, you may have to fight for study time. Talk honestly with family members about your goals. Ask for their suggestions. Make it clear that their support, cooperation, and encouragement will increase your chances for success. Talk plainly to roommates about your and their study needs, and arrange your schedule accordingly. Above all, be candid with yourself about your own time-management issues. Time will slip away from you unless you GRAB it and hold tight (see Figure 6.1).

Goal

To GRAB study time, set a goal. What do you want to do? Would you like to set aside a block of time each day for completing your assignments? Would you like to have Tuesday and Thursday evenings free for study? Do you want to set aside one afternoon a week in the library to write drafts of essays for your composition class? The goal is up to you; it should be a reachable goal, one you can reasonably expect to achieve. The time limit you set should be one you can live with. For more information on how to set reachable goals, see Chapter 4.

Responsibilities

Determine your responsibilities. To manage time, you must first determine what your responsibilities are. Do you live alone? If not, then you have responsibilities toward those with whom you live. Do you work? If so, then you have obligations toward your boss and coworkers. As a student, you have course requirements to meet. All of these responsibilities—which may include child rearing, cooking, cleaning, working, and studying—somehow have to be met. Sharing household tasks with family members will leave you more time for study. By considering your roommate's needs, you can work out a study schedule that is mutually agreeable. Your employer may be willing to adjust your hours to accommodate your course schedule. Enlist the aid of family members, roommates, your boss—whoever is in a position to help you reach your goals. With a little effort, you can manage your time so that you can meet all your responsibilities.

Analysis

Analyze where your time goes; then you may be able to find a more efficient way to use your time. What are the fixed times in a typical day for you? **Fixed times** include the hours you spend working, attending classes, and traveling to and from each activity.

Concept Check 6.1

Define *time* as you see it: What is time? Why do people seem to have so little of it? What would you do if you had more time?

Fixed times are times you cannot change, such as work hours or class times.

FIGURE 6.1

How to Grab Some Time

G	GOAL	Set a goal.
R	RESPONSIBILITIES	Determine your responsibilities.
A	ANALYSIS	Analyze where your time goes.
B	BALANCE	Balance work, class, study, and leisure time.

These are the time slots that may be difficult or impossible to change. For example, if you are an athlete, then your fixed times will include practice and participation in games or events. If you are a parent, then your fixed times may include driving children to and from school and to other regularly scheduled activities. If you are working full-time and attending college part-time, then your fixed times include the hours you spend in classes and at work. For many students, regular exercise warrants a fixed time in their schedules. **Flexible times** include the hours you spend doing things such as sleeping, eating, watching television, and studying. You can choose when you do these activities and how much time you spend on each.

Flexible times are the hours of a day that you can control, such as when to sleep or eat.

Balance

Balance your time through scheduling. A **schedule** is a structure that you impose on the events of a day, a week, a semester, or a quarter—or any other block of time you choose. A schedule is a plan for getting things done. Think of a schedule as your commitment to complete certain tasks at certain times so that you make steady progress toward your goals.

Schedule means "timetable," "plan," or "program" of events or activities.

Managing your time will allow you to balance work and leisure so that you meet your responsibilities and still have time for yourself. To bring work, classes, study time, and leisure into balance, first determine how much time you usually spend on these activities. When you have a clear picture of the fixed and flexible times in your day, then you will be able to set more realistic goals and create schedules you can live with. Now complete *Awareness Check* 6.1 to assess your use of time.

Awareness CHECK 6.1

Where Does Your Time Go?

Estimate the number of hours you spend each week on the following activities. When you are finished, subtract your total hours from 168, the number of hours in a week. How much time is left? How can you use this time to reach your goals?

Activity	Hours per Week
1. Attending classes	_____
2. Working	_____
3. Sleeping	_____
4. Dressing, showering, etc.	_____
5. Traveling to and from work, college, etc.	_____
6. Studying	_____
7. Eating	_____
8. Watching television	_____
9. Engaging in leisure activities	_____
10. Caring for family	_____
11. Cleaning and doing laundry	_____

continued

12. Socializing   _____

13. Attending athletic practice   _____

14. Surfing the Internet   _____

15. Other   _____

Total =   _____

168 Hours minus Total =   _____

Now answer the following questions:

1. On which activity do you spend the least amount of time?

   _____

2. On which activity do you spend the most time?

   _____

3. Is the amount of time that you spend studying producing the grades you want?

   _____

4. Overall, are you satisfied with the way you spend your time? Why or why not?

   _____

5. If you could make some changes, what would they be?

   _____

After completing the Awareness Check, *you may find that you have some surplus time during the week. You might use this time for: scheduling additional study hours as needed; setting aside a block of regular, consistent study time; or completing a task or activity you did not think you had time to do. Schedules can make your life easier, not harder, because they help you organize your time.*

How to Schedule Your Time

- Construct schedules for more efficient time management that sets the stage for achievement.

Schedules put you in control of your time and your life. Your schedule is the result of the inward decisions you make to control events instead of letting external circumstances control you. **Semester or quarter calendars, weekly schedules,** and **daily lists** are three time-honored plans that have helped thousands of students become better time managers. Build confidence in your ability to manage your time by trying out each of these plans.

The Semester or Quarter Calendar

A calendar for the current term allows you to see at a glance what you need to accomplish each month in order to complete your course requirements. A semester

Semester or quarter calendars provide an overview of an entire term at a glance.

Weekly schedules help you manage your assignments and other obligations one week at a time.

Daily lists help you prioritize tasks on a daily basis.

is about sixteen weeks long, a quarter about ten weeks long. If your college is on a semester system, you probably attend different classes on alternate days: Mondays, Wednesdays, and Fridays or Tuesdays and Thursdays. On the quarter system, however, you may attend some classes every day. The system your college uses will determine what your calendar will look like and how you will be able to schedule the rest of your time around your classes. To make a complete semester or quarter calendar, you need the following three items:

1. *Your college calendar*, which is printed in the college catalog or posted on your college's website.

2. A *syllabus*, or instructor's outline, for each course.

3. A *personal calendar*—one you either buy or make yourself—that contains squares big enough for you to record information.

Use your semester or quarter calendar as a quick reference to remind you of upcoming tests and the due dates of assignments. Keep the calendar on your desk, on a wall above your desk, or on a bulletin board where you will see it every day when you sit down to study. Always have two months visible so that by the last week of the current month, you will also be aware of what's ahead in the next month. Follow these steps to make your calendar:

1. Enter the following information in the appropriate squares: when classes begin and end, holidays, registration, exam times, and any other important dates or deadlines. Your college's catalog or website may contain most of this information.

2. Review the instructor's syllabus that you received for each course. The syllabus, or course information sheet, may list test dates and major assignments such as essays, research papers, or projects that are due throughout the term. Some instructors do not plan very far ahead. They may wait to announce test dates several days beforehand. If that is the case, you will want to update your calendar as you receive this information.

3. Enter any other information, event, or activity you want to include. For example, if you plan to attend sports events or concerts, fill in those dates on the calendar. If you take part in any regularly scheduled activities such as sports practice and club or organization meetings, add them to your calendar.

4. Be sure to leave enough space in each square. You may have to list more than one item under each date.

Figure 6.2 shows one month from a student's calendar for a typical semester. Be creative with your calendar. Make planning your semester or quarter an enjoyable activity. Either purchase a calendar that you find attractive or make your own. Use different colored inks or marking pens for each kind of information you enter. You can also create your calendar on the computer. There are many websites that offer applications for creating daily, weekly, and monthly calendars, such as the calendar functions within Yahoo email and Google.com. You can enter your information online and then print out hard copies of your daily, weekly, and monthly schedules. Above all, choose a "hard copy" or electronic calendar preparation system that you think will work best for you.

Your Weekly Schedule

The main purpose of the weekly schedule is to help you plan your study time. By scheduling your study time and making a commitment to stick to your schedule, you will

FIGURE 6.2

One Month in a Student's Semester

October						
Sunday	Monday	Tuesday	Wednesday	Thursday	Friday	Saturday
	1	2	3	4	5 Comp. essay due	6
7 2 p.m.–4 p.m. Charity walk/run	8 Dentist appt. 4:00 p.m.	9 Hum. paper due	10 Concert 8:00 p.m.	11	12 Comp. 1 midterm 10:00 a.m.	13
14	15 Alg 1 midterm 8:00 a.m.	16	17 Psych. midterm 7:00 p.m.	18	19 Hum. midterm 10:00 a.m.	20
21	22	23	24	25	26	27 Homecoming
28	29	30	31			

be giving studying the same importance that you give to working or attending classes. Without a schedule, you may begin to study only when you have nothing else to do, at the last minute before a test, or late at night when you are tired. If you are a procrastinator, a weekly schedule may provide the extra motivation you need to get your work done. Your schedule is your commitment to learn. Figure 6.3 shows an example of a student's weekly schedule.

This student, Otis, has fixed times for classes and church attendance. He has flexible times for his other regular activities. In the time remaining, he has allotted the same block of time each day for studying. He has made a commitment to treat studying like a job. If Otis sticks to his schedule, then, over time, studying will become a habit for him. When he sits down to study at his regular time, he will be able to get to work quickly and to give his assignments maximum concentration. During some weeks, Otis may need additional time to study for a test or to complete an especially lengthy assignment. On these occasions, he can use some of his "free" hours for more studying. What if Otis decides to take a part-time job? Then he will have to modify his fixed, flexible, and free times. Otis's schedule puts him in control of his time and his life.

FIGURE 6.3

Otis's Weekly Schedule

	Sunday	Monday	Tuesday	Wednesday	Thursday	Friday	Saturday
6:00 – 7:00	Sleep	Run, Dress, Eat	→→→→				Sleep
7:00 – 8:00	Sleep	← Transportation to class →					Sleep
8:00 – 9:00	Sleep	Algebra class	Study in library	Algebra class	Study in library	Algebra class	Eat, Run
9:00 – 10:00	Run, Dress	Comp. 1	French 1	Comp. 1	French 1	Comp. 1	Study
10:00 – 11:00	Eat, Trans. to church	Biology class	Biology lab	Biology class	French lab	Biology class	Study
11:00 – 12:00	Church	Lunch/ Trans.	↓	Lunch/ Trans.	↓	Lunch/ Trans.	Lunch
12:00 – 1:00	Trans. church to home	Home		Home		Home	
1:00 – 2:00	Lunch	Study	Study	Study	Study	Study	
2:00 – 3:00	Clean apartment						
3:00 – 4:00	Free	Laundry, other chores →					Leisure
4:00 – 5:00	Free						or study
5:00 – 6:00	Free						May go
6:00 – 7:00	Dinner						out later
7:00 – 8:00							
8:00 – 9:00	Study or						
9:00 – 10:00	Watch TV						
10:00 – 11:00							
11:00 – 12:00							
12:00 – 1:00	Sleep						

As you experiment with making schedules, keep in mind that for maximum performance, most instructors recommend at least two hours of study time for every hour spent in class. For a class that meets three times a week, this would mean six hours of studying per week. So if you are taking five three-hour courses and you want to do your best, you will need to schedule thirty hours a week of study time. If you are a working student, you may have difficulty finding that much time to study. To reach your goals, you may be forced to either take fewer courses or to reduce your working hours.

If the ratio of study time to class time seems high, remember that it takes a lot of time and effort to acquire new knowledge and to learn skills. However, you may spend less time studying subjects that are easy for you than you spend studying difficult ones.

A Daily List

Keep a daily list of things to do and appointments to keep. Nearly everyone makes lists: grocery lists, appointment lists, errand lists. As a student, you need to make lists too—when to return library books, specific study tasks you must complete, counseling appointments, and so on. Consult your lists frequently and check off items as you complete them. A list is a motivational aid that reminds you to stay on track. Each item you complete and check off brings you closer to achieving your day's goals, boosting your confidence. Exercises 6.1 and 6.2 will help you with making schedules.

Some people make lists on little scraps of paper. Others use fancy note pads, small spiral-bound notebooks, daily planners, or appointment books that they buy in bookstores or office supply stores. (If you buy a daily planner or appointment book, be sure to get one with squares that are big enough to hold several items or one that includes a separate notepad.) Whatever you use for making your daily lists, make sure it is a convenient size, and keep it handy.

As we explained above, there are many online programs and computer applications that allow you to keep track of important dates and appointments and set up your calendar in a variety of formats. When you turn on your computer, for example, the calendar function can tell you the day's date and list your schedule for the day. You can also set up your computer or handheld electronic device (like a Blackberry phone) to beep as a reminder that you have an appointment.

EXERCISE 6.1 Computer Application on Making Your Calendar

DEVELOP A SEMESTER OR QUARTER calendar. Your calendar is a highly individual matter. You can buy a wall calendar, a desk calendar, or a pocket calendar—whatever works best for you. Another option is to make copies of the template in Figure 6.4, page 142, for each month in your semester or quarter; or you can download copies of this template from *The Confident Student* premium website. If you prefer to work online, you can make a calendar using a Microsoft Word table, or through a web-based program like Yahoo or Google (find the tab or clickable button labeled "Calendar"). Whatever you decide to use for your calendar, enter the following information on it:

1. **When classes begin and end, holidays, final exam dates**

2. **The registration date for the next semester or quarter**

3. **Test dates and dates when major assignments are due**

4. **Dates of activities or events that you want to participate in or attend**

5. **Any other dates or deadlines you want to remember**

FIGURE 6.4

Calendar Template

	Sunday	Monday	Tuesday	Wednesday	Thursday	Friday	Saturday

EXERCISE 6.2   Computer Application on Making a Weekly Schedule

MAKE A WEEKLY SCHEDULE. See Figure 6.5 on the next page for the template that accompanies this exercise, or download copies of the template from *The Confident Student* premium website. If you prefer to use the computer, make a table as your schedule template. To fill in your schedule, follow these directions:

1. **Fill in your fixed-time activities. These are the things you must do at scheduled times—for example, working and attending classes.**

2. **Fill in your flexible-time activities. These are the things you need or want to do that you can schedule at your own discretion.**

3. **Fill in a regular time each day for study.**

4. **The squares remaining are your free time. Remember to schedule time for exercise or other leisure activity.**

5. **Fill in every square. If new obligations or appointments arise, you can adjust your schedule to accommodate them.**

FIGURE 6.5

Weekly Schedule Template

	Sunday	Monday	Tuesday	Wednesday	Thursday	Friday	Saturday
6:00 – 7:00							
7:00 – 8:00							
8:00 – 9:00							
9:00 – 10:00							
10:00 – 11:00							
11:00 – 12:00							
12:00 – 1:00							
1:00 – 2:00							
2:00 – 3:00							
3:00 – 4:00							
4:00 – 5:00							
5:00 – 6:00							
6:00 – 7:00							
7:00 – 8:00							
8:00 – 9:00							
9:00 – 10:00							
10:00 – 11:00							
11:00 – 12:00							
12:00 – 1:00							

FIGURE 6.6

A List for One Day

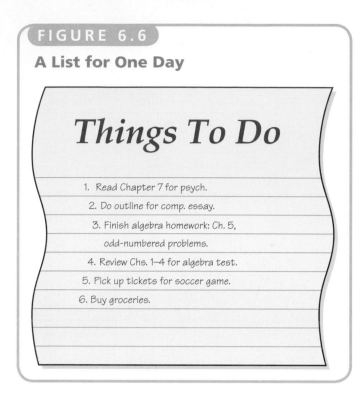

Things To Do

1. Read Chapter 7 for psych.
2. Do outline for comp. essay.
3. Finish algebra homework: Ch. 5,
   odd-numbered problems.
4. Review Chs. 1–4 for algebra test.
5. Pick up tickets for soccer game.
6. Buy groceries.

Keeping a daily list can be a quick and easy way to start planning your time effectively. Your daily lists should include whatever you want to do or whatever you need to remember that you might otherwise forget. Figure 6.6 shows a student's list for one day.

Time Management and Learning Style

Chapter 2 explains that your body's reactions affect your learning style. For example, you probably have an optimum time of day when your concentration seems to be at its peak and you are most productive. But being a morning person or a night person isn't just a preference, nor do you have a choice about it.

You have a biological clock that regulates your internal rhythms, telling you when to eat, when to sleep, and when to get up and get moving. The time of day when your temperature is highest is what determines whether you are an "early bird" or a "night owl." Since you can't control fluctuations in your body's temperature, you may as well take advantage of them. Do important activities that require critical thinking and concentration during your optimum time of day. Try to schedule your classes—especially ones that you expect to be

EXERCISE 6.3 Awareness Check Recap

REVIEW YOUR RESPONSES TO *Awareness Check* 6.1 on pages 136–137. Notice how many hours per week you estimated that you spend on each of the activities listed. For one week, keep track of the *actual* hours you spend on those activities. Write down the actual amounts of time as you spend them (*not* later that day, or you could easily end up estimating your time again). At the end of the week, write your original time estimates and the exact hours you spent on the following lines; then complete the lists and answer the question.

Activity	Estimated Time	Actual Time
1. **Attending classes**	_____	_____
2. **Working**	_____	_____
3. **Sleeping**	_____	_____
4. **Dressing, showering, etc.**	_____	_____
5. **Traveling to and from work, college, etc.**	_____	_____
6. **Studying**	_____	_____
7. **Eating**	_____	_____
8. **Watching television**	_____	_____
9. **Engaging in leisure activities**	_____	_____
10. **Caring for family**	_____	_____

continued

11. **Cleaning and doing laundry**   _____   _____

12. **Socializing**   _____   _____

13. **Attending athletic practice**   _____   _____

14. **Surfing the Internet**   _____   _____

15. **Other**   _____   _____

1. **List the activities in which you spent more time than you had estimated.**

    _____

    _____

2. **List the activities in which you spent less time than you had estimated.**

    _____

    _____

3. **How can you use this new information to revise your weekly schedule?**

    _____

    _____

EXERCISE 6.4   Collaborative Activity on Using Schedules

APPLY WHAT YOU HAVE LEARNED about schedules by doing this exercise with group members. Follow the *Guidelines for Group Discussion* listed on the inside back cover. Discuss the following questions and write your answers on the lines provided. Then write your evaluation on your own paper or download the group exercise form from *The Confident Student* premium website.

1. **What are your experiences with making and following schedules? Which group members have used schedules and which have not?**

    _____

    _____

2. **What are the advantages and disadvantages of making daily, weekly, and semester or quarter schedules?**

    _____

    _____

3. **Which type of schedule do you find most useful, and why?**

    _____

    _____

continued

4. **Discuss a specific problem you have had with time management. How could you use schedules to overcome this problem?**

_____

_____

Group Evaluation:
Evaluate your discussion. Did everyone contribute? Did you accomplish your task successfully? What additional questions do you have about making and following schedules? How will you find answers to your questions?

difficult—at the time of day when you are most alert. If you have to take a class at a time when you know you will be working at a disadvantage, try these suggestions:

▼ When you feel yourself getting drowsy, take a few deep breaths.

▼ Change your position every few minutes: Cross and uncross your legs, sit up straight, and make other adjustments in the way you are sitting.

▼ Eat a snack such as a handful of raisins or a piece of fruit before you go to class. This will raise your blood-sugar level and your body temperature, making you feel more alert.

▼ Take deep, rhythmic breaths to get more oxygen into your bloodstream.

Try these suggestions whenever you must study at a time when you are tired. In addition, when you are at home, prop up your feet to increase the blood flow to your brain.

Make Time for Reading

One of the big differences between high school and college is the amount of reading assigned. You may be frustrated by the number of pages per week that each instructor assigns. A common complaint you will hear from college students of all ages is "Each of my instructors must think his or her class is the only one I have." Nevertheless, the reading has to be done. Are there any shortcuts? No. Reading takes time. The more difficult the reading, the more time it takes. However, you can learn to read more efficiently. Try these strategies:

▼ Determine the time you will need for reading.

▼ Schedule your reading time.

▼ Develop active reading habits and study skills so that you do not waste time.

To calculate your reading time, follow the steps given in Figure 6.7 on page 147. For example, suppose you have been assigned a fifty-page chapter from your biology text.

EXERCISE 6.5 Learning Style Essay

WRITE A SHORT ESSAY IN which you explain how your present schedule of classes and study times either do or do not conflict with your learning style and personal habits. Consider which classes require the most work, which assignments need greater concentration, your optimum time of day, and whether your schedule permits you to eat regularly and to get enough rest. What are your schedule's strengths and weaknesses? How can you improve your schedule next semester or quarter? Give your essay a title.

FIGURE 6.7

Calculate Your Reading Time

1. Choose three consecutive textbook pages that contain mostly print.

2. Time yourself on the reading of these three pages.

3. Jot down your starting time in minutes and seconds. When you have read three pages, jot down the time and subtract your starting time to get the total reading time. Divide the total time by 3 to get the time that it takes you to read one page.

4. To get the time needed to complete a reading assignment, multiply the number of pages by your time per page. Divide by 60 to get the number of hours and minutes it will take you to finish your reading.

Example: You have twenty pages to read. How long will it take you?

Here are the results of your initial calculation:

Starting time: 3:00
Finishing time: 3:18

Subtract starting time from finishing time:

$$3:18$$
$$-3:00$$

$$0:18 \div 3 = 6 \text{ minutes per page}$$

Multiply the number of minutes per page times the number of pages in the assignment and divide by 60:

$$6 \times 20 = 120 \div 60 = 2 \text{ hours (time needed to read twenty pages)}$$

The assignment is due at the next class meeting. You have determined that it takes you two hours to read twenty-five pages from this book. Sometime between now and the next class meeting, you should schedule four hours of reading time for biology.

Active reading habits include underlining, making notes in the margins of your textbooks, outlining, and other activities such as using a reading system and organizing information for study—strategies explained in Chapters 7 and 8. These strategies lead to concentrated review and may eliminate the need for rereading entire chapters. In fact, rereading is an inefficient way to study and one you should avoid. If you take the time to read, mark your text, and make notes, you may be able to shorten your review time. If you think that you have missed something, you can always reread just those sections of a chapter that contain the information you need.

Challenges for Community College Students and Others

- Meet the time-management challenges you may face as a community college student, commuter, or student athlete.

If you are a community college student—or anyone who commutes to campus—building travel time into your schedule may be a challenge. The time you spend traveling to and from campus or from campus to work to home leaves less time for studying and other activities. You may also need to transport your children to and from school. Because it is easy to underestimate the time it takes you to get from place to place, give special consideration to travel time as you plan your schedule and select courses.

Adding college courses and study time to an already busy schedule is another challenge. You may be tempted to meet it by scheduling all your classes on one or two days. Although this may seem like a good idea at the time, you may encounter one or more common problems. Suppose you schedule all your classes on the same day. If you are absent one day, then you will miss *all* your classes for the whole week. Also, papers, tests, and other assignments for those classes will always be due on the same day. Instead of having a paper due on Monday, several math problems due on Wednesday, and a test on Thursday or Friday, you will have to turn in the paper and the problems and take the test all in one day. Spreading your classes over two days is not much better; you may still have several assignment deadlines or tests on the same day.

What happens at the end of the one or two days when you attend class? For one thing, you are probably exhausted and have so many other things to do that you don't or can't take time to review your notes from each class or begin doing the assignments. Also, you may postpone the work until the night before your classes meet, leaving you only enough time to do a portion of the work. You may even skip one or two assignments, thinking you'll catch up later. This almost never happens. One- or two-day schedules often lead to scheduling classes back to back, which may seem like another good way to save time. Unfortunately, when you attend one class right after another, you don't have time to absorb and process the information covered in the previous class. You set yourself up for *information overload*, a condition in which the material explained in one class gets confused with that covered in another.

Ideal schedules are those that spread classes and study times over the whole week and alternate class periods with free periods. During your free periods, you can either review notes from your previous class or do some last-minute review for a test you must take in the next class. Because you have free time between classes, you must remain on campus. This puts you in a good position to form a study group that you'll meet with at a regular time or to set up a standing appointment with a tutor if you are having difficulty in one of your classes. You may find that by scheduling classes over the whole week, you are actually *saving* time. This can happen because it's easier to schedule study time around one or two classes a day and still meet your other obligations than it is to try to pack in some study time after having attended four or five classes. However, if you absolutely have to attend classes on a two-day schedule because of work or other obligations, at least try to schedule a free hour between classes

Time-Management Tips for Student Athletes

College takes a physical and mental toll on student athletes. The hours spent practicing, weight training, competing, and traveling to and from sports events leave student athletes physically exhausted. As a result, they are often too tired to participate fully in classes, remain attentive during lectures, or study with maximum concentration. Exhaustion may also lead to poor eating and sleeping habits, which sap students' energy, making study even more difficult.

In addition to the physical toll, student athletes may also pay a mental toll. For one thing, these students are under pressure to earn good grades on which their scholarships and their eligibility to play depend. Also, negative stereotyping in the form of taunts and lowered expectations on the part of some instructors and classmates may lead to depression and a loss of self-esteem in all but the most confident students.

What we all need to remember is that every student has strengths and weaknesses, and on any college sports team, as wide a range of abilities will be represented as in any other area of campus life. Nevertheless, the student athlete who *is* underprepared for college work carries a double burden: the need to develop academic skills and the need to resist being dragged down by others' negative attitudes toward him or her.

If you are a student athlete, follow these time-management tips to meet your physical and mental challenges so that you can be successful in your sport and in your academic program. If you are not an athlete, pass these tips on to a friend who is and be supportive of his or her efforts to succeed.

- Use daily lists, weekly schedules, and semester or quarter calendars to manage your time. Remember that if you don't manage time, time will manage you.
- Although it may be too late to do anything about this term's classes, you can plan ahead for next term. Keep track of where your time goes and when you are most alert, and use this information to build your ideal schedule next term.
- Put studying first. You can't maintain eligibility without grades, so schedule regular study time. If your coach requires you to attend group study sessions, great! If not, form your own study group. Be sure to include one or more nonathletes in your group so that different perspectives are represented. Schedule a meeting time for your study group and follow through on your schedule.
- Arrange your schedule so that you have regular mealtimes and get adequate rest. If you don't, exhaustion will overtake you.
- If you have weaknesses in any basic skills (reading, writing, mathematics), take any required courses in these subjects as soon as possible. Schedule regular meetings with a tutor, if necessary. It's more efficient to take care of basic skills *now* than to risk getting more and more behind. As you build skill, your grades will improve, and with improved performance comes confidence.
- Use *all* your time. Write information for studying on 3 × 5-inch note cards that you can carry with you everywhere. While waiting in lines, between classes—anywhere you have extra time that you might otherwise waste—review your notes. In other words, be efficient in your use of time.
- Other people's negative attitudes and stereotypical thinking may be difficult to overcome, but you can control how you respond to them. Let nothing stand in the way of your own success. Arrange your schedule so that you are able to do the studying and skill building needed to ensure successful classroom performance. Scheduling time for adequate rest and proper nutrition will keep you alert and ready to participate in class. Be punctual and prepared, and you may change a few minds about the seriousness of student athletes.

Procrastination is a behavior characterized by the needless avoidance of obligations and by putting off tasks.

Student athletes, community college students—all students, in fact—should avoid procrastination. The following section explains how.

How to Avoid Procrastination

- Beat *procrastination by* identifying its causes and by learning how to avoid it.

Procrastination means needlessly postponing tasks until some future time. Although procrastinating once in a while may not hurt you, if you delay studying and put off doing important assignments too often, you will sabotage your efforts to succeed. Complete *Awareness Check* 6.2 on the next page to gauge your tendency to put off tasks.

Why Do People Procrastinate?

Ana has to write a research paper for her composition course. The paper is due in six weeks. She thinks she has plenty of time, so for the first two weeks, she doesn't even think about the project. That leaves her only a month in which to choose a topic, do her research in the library, make an outline, and

If you budget your studying time wisely, you will have more time for leisure activities.

David Stuart/Getty Images

AWARENESS CHECK 6.2

Are You a Procrastinator?

Choose one of the following as your response to each statement: *always* (4 points), *usually* (3 points), *sometimes* (2 points), *rarely* (1 point). Write your number of points in the box beside each

Points **statement. When you are finished, add your score.**

1. If I know that an assignment will be difficult, I will put off doing it.

2. If an assignment is going to take a lot of time, I will procrastinate.

3. I will put off studying if I don't like the subject or the course.

4. I can't start studying until I am in the mood to do it.

5. Writing papers is hard for me, so it takes me a lot of time to get started.

6. I often wait until the last minute to study for a test.

7. Being too hungry or too tired is reason enough for me to delay studying.

8. If I have a slight cold or am not feeling my best, I won't study.

9. I forget all about studying if an opportunity arises to socialize.

10. Because studying is boring, I don't do it as much as I should or when I should.

Total

For this survey, the lower your score, the better. If your score is 35–40, procrastination is a major problem in your life and you will benefit from identifying and eliminating its causes. If your score is 30–34, procrastination is a definite obstacle to overcome. If your score is 25–29, you may be managing your time in some areas, but procrastination is keeping you from reaching some of your goals. If your score is 10–24, you may be able to avoid procrastination some or much of the time. Whatever your score, applying this chapter's strategies will help you gain better control of your time.

write the paper. It takes her another week to select a topic, but when she gets to the library, she finds that several of the books she wants have been checked out. By the time Ana chooses another topic and compiles her research materials, she has only one week left to complete the paper. She *does* hand it in on time, but she knows it's not her best effort. She doesn't like to write anyway and is not expecting to receive a very good grade. "Next time," she swears, "I'll get started sooner." But next time Ana will probably procrastinate again because that is her pattern of behavior. She doesn't like to do difficult or lengthy assignments and will put them off until the last minute. Like many students, Ana procrastinates for one of four common reasons. Perhaps you also procrastinate for one of these reasons:

▼ Your tasks seem difficult or time consuming.

▼ You have trouble getting started.

▼ You lack motivation to do the work.

▼ You are afraid of failing.

Putting off difficult or time-consuming assignments makes them even harder to do when you actually get started and further ensures that you won't be able to do your best because you will not have enough time. However, a task may be less difficult than you think if you break it down into segments that you can handle during short periods of time. If you have trouble getting started on an assignment, or if you waste a lot of time before sitting down to study, then you may be using **avoidance tactics**. Why are you avoiding what you have to do? Perhaps you aren't interested in the subject, or perhaps you'd simply prefer to be doing something else. You may be insufficiently motivated to perform the work. You may not see a direct connection between the assignment and your goals or your overall grade in the course. Or you may be afraid of failure. If you believe that you will not get a good grade no matter what you do, you may delay getting started on an assignment. Complete *Awareness Check* 6.3 for more insight into why you procrastinate.

> **Avoidance tactics** are habitual behaviors we've developed over time to keep from doing difficult or unpleasant things.

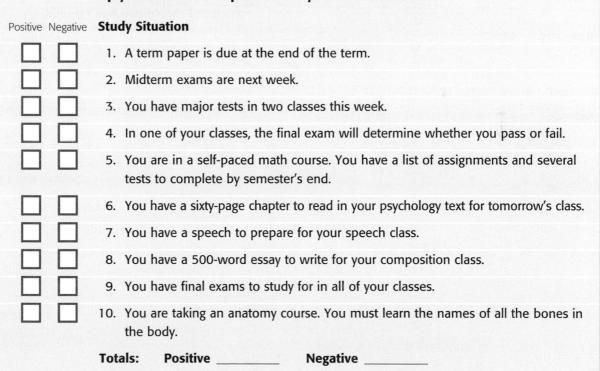

Awareness CHECK 6.3

What Is Your Attitude Toward Studying?

Read all of the following study situations and imagine that they apply to you. Put a check in the column that best describes how you feel about each one; then add up your checks. An explanation of your results follows.

Positive	Negative	**Study Situation**
☐	☐	1. A term paper is due at the end of the term.
☐	☐	2. Midterm exams are next week.
☐	☐	3. You have major tests in two classes this week.
☐	☐	4. In one of your classes, the final exam will determine whether you pass or fail.
☐	☐	5. You are in a self-paced math course. You have a list of assignments and several tests to complete by semester's end.
☐	☐	6. You have a sixty-page chapter to read in your psychology text for tomorrow's class.
☐	☐	7. You have a speech to prepare for your speech class.
☐	☐	8. You have a 500-word essay to write for your composition class.
☐	☐	9. You have final exams to study for in all of your classes.
☐	☐	10. You are taking an anatomy course. You must learn the names of all the bones in the body.

Totals: **Positive** _____ **Negative** _____

All of these study situations represent tasks that are difficult or time consuming. Look at your checks in each column. In general, based on this exercise, what do you think about difficult or lengthy assignments? Specifically, if you checked negative for items 1 and 8, perhaps writing is difficult for you and you avoid getting started

continued

for that reason. If you checked negative for items 2, 3, 4, and 9, perhaps you avoid studying for tests because you have test anxiety or are afraid that you will fail. See Chapter 11 for some suggestions to ease test anxiety. If you checked negative for item 5, maybe the self-paced learning situation seems overwhelming and you need the structure of a classroom setting, where the instructor sets the pace for you. If you checked negative for item 6, it could be that the length of a reading assignment affects the way you approach it. Perhaps you'd be more motivated to start sooner if you divided the reading assignment into smaller segments with breaks in between. If you checked negative for item 7, perhaps you don't like giving speeches, can't think of what to say, or are afraid you will get nervous and do a poor job. The sooner you start writing your speech and the more time you give yourself to practice it, the more confident you will feel about your ability to do a good job. Chapter 12 explains how to improve your speaking skills. If you checked negative for item 10, perhaps you avoid starting assignments like this one because the number of items you have to learn and remember seems like more than you can handle. One of the memory techniques suggested in Chapter 8 may make it easier for you to get started.

Tips to Beat Procrastination

Concept Check 6.2

Procrastination has more to do with your attitude and emotions than with the availability of time. If you learn to manage your attitude and emotions, you can work around your time constraints to beat procrastination.

To avoid procrastination, change your behavior. If you procrastinate when assignments are too difficult or too long, or if you have trouble getting started or lack the motivation to do the work, then instead of focusing on your feelings about the assignment, focus on the advantages of completing it on time. If you get started right away, you will have the advantage of enough time to do your best. You may even complete the assignment with time left over to do something else. However, if you wait too long to begin, then you won't be able to do your best, or you may not finish at all. Fear of failure is sometimes the result of not knowing what to do. If you are not sure about what is expected of you, then you may not know how to begin the assignment. To help you overcome the fear of failure and get started, try using these tips that have worked for many students:

1. Break a large assignment or project into smaller units of work that you can complete in one sitting.

2. Plan rewards for yourself for completing each part of the assignment. Take a break, call a friend, or do something else you enjoy.

3. Schedule enough time for completing a long assignment. Set a goal to spend a certain amount of time working each day until the assignment is finished.

4. Get organized. Your attitude toward studying will improve if you have an orderly work area with everything you need at your fingertips—books, pens and pencils, paper—so that you will be ready to begin the moment you sit down.

5. If you put off assignments because you don't know where to start or aren't sure how to do the work, find out what you need to know. Make an appointment with your instructor. Explain the difficulty you are having and ask for advice. If you have started the assignment, show your instructor where you are having trouble. Or talk to someone in the class. If you missed a lecture or have gaps in your notes, a classmate might be able to fill you in.

6. Assume an attitude of confidence, and you will *be* confident. Instead of thinking, "This is too difficult" or "I'll never finish this," think, "I can do this if I get started right now" or "There's a lot of work to do, but if I do a little bit at a time, I'll be finished before I know it."

Learning to manage time and avoiding procrastination requires some effort. Do not be discouraged if your first efforts are unsuccessful. Try to pinpoint your reasons for procrastinating. Identify your avoidance tactics and try to eliminate them. Experiment with schedules until you come up with a plan that works for you. With determination, you will take control of your time and your life—and you will reach your goals.

Manage Your Study Environment

What is the connection between where you study and avoiding procrastination? You are more likely to get down to business if you have an appropriate time and place for study. Your study environment should be as quiet and distraction-free as you can make it. If you are a resident student, you probably do most of your studying in your room or in the library. If you are a commuter, chances are you do the majority of your studying at home. In either case, you probably have to fight distractions, and the best way to do that is to schedule your study time when and where you are least likely to be disturbed.

If you are a commuter, set up a study area in a quiet part of your home. Your study place doesn't have to be elaborate; a desk or small table in your bedroom or in a guest room will do. Avoid studying in bed, because you will probably fall asleep. Avoid places in high-traffic areas such as the kitchen or family room. Not only will you be distracted, but your family may also conclude that your studying is not serious business and that you won't mind being interrupted. Having a study area away from the family and the noise of the TV and children's play—a place where you do nothing but study—sends a subtle message that you are treating studying like a job and do not want to be distracted.

Let your family know that you need quiet time to do your work. Schedule a regular time for studying at home and make studying a routine. Soon your family will get used to the idea that when you are in your study place, you are unavailable except in an emergency. If you can plan your study time for when your children are asleep or when no one else is at home, so much the better.

To help fight procrastination, outfit your study place with everything you might need to get the job done: pens, pencils, paper, a dictionary, a good desk lamp, and whatever other supplies you will need. When you come in from class, go immediately to your study place and unload your books. Then they will already be there waiting for you when you are ready to study.

If you are a resident student, set up a study area in your part of the room. Put your desk against a wall—away from the door, if possible—and keep the door closed while you are studying. Then you won't be tempted away from your books by whatever is going on outside your room or in the hallway. Like the commuter, you should avoid studying in bed. Like the commuter's family, your roommate and friends across the hall are your temporary "family" and therefore a source of distractions. Early in the term, work out mutually agreeable study times with your roommate. For example, one of you might study while the other is in class. On the other hand, you may want to schedule some of your studying so that you can work together or both study at the same time. For more information on how to choose or create your best study environment, see Chapter 8.

A well-equipped, distraction free study area is your best hedge against procrastination.

Comstock Images (RF)/Jupiter Images

CRITICAL THINKING No Excuses

Exercise Overview

Procrastinating only now and then won't hurt you. But if it becomes chronic, you are in for trouble. Most people can find excuses for putting off doing their work, and students are no exception. This exercise will help you reflect on your own excuses so that you can recognize them as avoidance tactics to be overcome.

Exercise Background

Most instructors who have taught for a while think they have heard it all. It takes a very clever student to come up with a unique excuse for not being prepared for a test, not completing an assignment, or not handing in a paper when it is due. As you read the following two lists of excuses, see how many you have heard or used yourself.

Exercise Task

Listed next are two questions instructors often have to ask, followed by the excuses students make. Read all of the excuses with a partner. Be able to explain why each excuse is invalid and what students can do to beat procrastination.

"Why were you not prepared for today's exam?"

1. I didn't know what to study.
2. I didn't know we were having a test.
3. I forgot.
4. I was too tired.
5. I didn't understand the material.
6. I knew I wouldn't make a good grade.

"Why haven't you done today's assignment?"

1. I wasn't here when it was assigned.
2. It was too difficult.
3. I didn't know how to do it.
4. I had to go to work.
5. My computer crashed.
6. I lost it.

Guided CHAPTER REVIEW

The following checklist summarizes this chapter's key terms and strategies. After reading the chapter, how confident are you that you can apply what you have learned to manage your time more effectively? To assess your level of confidence, respond to each statement with one of the following: *very confident* (3 points), *fairly confident* (2 points), *not very confident* (1 point), *not confident* (0 points). Write your number of points in the box beside each statement. Then add your score and read the analysis that follows. When you have finished, take the chapter quiz.

SUMMARY CHECK

How confident are you about applying these strategies?

Points

1. Using the GRAB strategy for managing time

2. Scheduling time for completion of tasks

3. Making adjustments to your schedule based on learning style

4. Determining the amount of time to spend on assigned reading

5. Determining what causes procrastination and knowing how to avoid it

6. Studying at a consistent time in an appropriate environment

7. Managing your time well enough to be able to pass on tips to others

How confident is your understanding of this chapter's key terms?

8. resource

9. fixed times

10. flexible times

11. schedule

12. semester or quarter calendars

13. weekly schedules

14. daily lists

15. procrastination

16. avoidance tactics

Total

Add your score. The highest possible score is 48. The closer your score is to 48, the higher your level of confidence. Use your *Summary Check* results to help you determine which parts of the chapter to review.

YOUR WEBSITE RESOURCES

This chapter's resources include the following items. To access them, go to *The Confident Student* premium website.

- **Video Skillbuilder: Time Management**
- **Chapter Exercises**
- **Forms to Download**
- **Chapter Summary of Topics**
- **Thinking Ahead About Career**
- **Confidence Builder Web Search**
- **Self-Test**

CHAPTER REVIEW Quiz

Answer the following questions from memory. Then return to the chapter to check your answers. As a final activity, complete *Show Your Confidence* at the end of the quiz.

1. What is the GRAB strategy's purpose?

   _____

   _____

2. What are the four steps of GRAB?

   _____

   _____

3. What is the relationship between setting goals and managing time?

   _____

   _____

4. What is one type of schedule mentioned in this chapter and its purpose?

   _____

   _____

5. What is the difference between *fixed times* and *flexible times* as they relate to making schedules?

   _____

   _____

6. What is one block of time that students often forget to consider when scheduling a week's activities?

   _____

   _____

7. What is the definition of *procrastination*?

   _____

   _____

8. What is one common cause of procrastination?

   _____

   _____

9. What are two of the tips this chapter suggests for beating procrastination?

   _____

   _____

10. What are at least two characteristics of a good study environment?

   _____

   _____

SHOW YOUR CONFIDENCE

To complete your chapter review, interview a second- or third-year student who seems to be a good time manager. Ask this student to share with you one or more tips for effective time management. Then be prepared to pass on what you have learned either in writing or in a class discussion.

Your REFLECTIONS: BUILD CONFIDENCE THROUGH SELF-MANAGEMENT

Reflect on the trait of self-management and how it affects your performance as a student. Use the following questions and what you have learned from this chapter to stimulate your thinking; then write your reflections.

- How would you describe a self-managed person?
- In what way are you or are you not a self-managed student?
- What does self-management have to do with time management?

_____

_____

_____

_____

_____

_____

_____

_____

_____

_____

_____

_____

_____

_____

_____

_____

_____

7 Becoming an Active Reader

Tim Pannell (RF)/Corbis

This chapter encourages you to:

- Learn how you can break passive reading habits to become an active reader.

- Understand the process of reading and how you can take control of it.

- Use strategies that will help you read for ideas.

- Use marking systems and summarizing to get more out of reading your textbooks.

Confident students are **involved**. They are active learners who understand that reading and learning are processes they can control.

R eading is a lifelong skill and a key to success in college and career. Reading for your college courses may include textbook assignments, articles from journals and periodicals, and information gathered from books and websites. Reading is essential for success in any career where processing information from correspondence, email messages, manuals, and graphics is a daily occurrence. By practicing active reading habits in your personal life, you can improve your understanding of everything from the fine print on contracts and insurance policies to the latest best-selling novel.

Reading is also a necessary part of any study system. You can gain essential information from your textbooks by knowing what to underline, using a textbook marking system, and writing summaries. Finally, reading is a source of pleasure and enlightenment that can enrich and expand your inner life.

Did you know that in college you will spend most of your study time reading assigned material? Are you currently allowing yourself enough time for reading? The following *Confidence Builder* explains how to calculate your reading rate so that you can set goals for reading and use your study time more efficiently.

CONFIDENCE BUILDER

How to Calculate Your Reading Rate

You may have read accounts of people who can "read" 1,700 words per minute, and you may have wished you could read that fast. Speed-reading is a controversial issue. Although you may want to increase your reading rate in order to save time or improve your chances of answering all the items on a timed reading test, you may lose comprehension as you gain reading speed if you try to read *too* fast.

Let *efficient reading*, not speed-reading, be your goal. To read efficiently, vary your reading rate with the *type of material* and your *purpose* for reading. For example, you can skim a news or magazine article that you read for personal interest, but when you read textbooks and other materials to gain and retain knowledge, you must read slowly and carefully for maximum comprehension.

Do you read everything at the same rate? If you do, then you are not reading as efficiently as you could. Use this formula to calculate your reading rate; then experiment with adjusting your rate to the type of material and your purpose for reading it.

$$\frac{\text{No. of words in passage}}{\text{Reading time}} = \frac{\text{Reading rate in words}}{\text{per minute (wpm)}}$$

To estimate the number of words in a passage, find the average number of words per line and multiply that number by the number of lines in the whole passage (if the passage is less than one page) or by the number of lines on one page (if the passage is several pages). Then use a stopwatch, digital watch, or clock with a second hand to time yourself in minutes and seconds as you read. Finally, round off to the nearest minute to use the formula.

Knowing that your reading rate for difficult or unfamiliar material is naturally going to be slower than your rate for less complex kinds of information can help you plan your study time. Suppose you are taking a biology course and have been assigned a 60-page chapter to read for the next class meeting. First, time yourself to determine how many minutes it will take you to read one page. Then multiply your time by 60 (the number of pages in your assignment) to get your total time in minutes. Divide this total by 60 to determine how many hours and minutes you will need to schedule for reading the assigned chapter. If it will take you three hours to read 60 pages, then you may want to break up the time into three one-hour segments so that you stay focused. To read efficiently, adjust your reading rate and schedule your reading time to meet the demands of any reading task.

Follow Up: To explore this topic further, visit *The Confident Student* premium website for an online search activity related to reading.

Active Versus Passive Reading

• Learn how you can break passive reading habits to become an active reader.

As explained in Chapter 1, active learning is the key to academic achievement. Students who are active learners are involved, self-motivated, and willing to take intellectual risks. As explained in Chapter 5, active learners are active listeners. Just as listening requires your decisive action, so does reading. Are you an active reader? To find out, complete *Awareness Check* 7.1.

Awareness CHECK 7.1

Are You an Active Reader?

To determine how actively you read now, check all of the following statements that apply to you.

☐ 1. I usually read straight through a textbook chapter from beginning to end without stopping.

☐ 2. I stop frequently to reread difficult parts or to check my comprehension by asking myself questions about what I have read.

☐ 3. If I don't understand something I have read, I wait to hear the instructor's explanation in class.

☐ 4. When I hit a rough spot, I make a note to remind myself to ask about it in class.

☐ 5. I usually have trouble deciding what is important in a chapter; often I'm not sure what the main idea is.

☐ 6. I can usually find the author's main idea, and I rarely have trouble determining what is important.

☐ 7. I often have a hard time relating textbook information to my life or to the course as a whole.

☐ 8. I can often see a connection between something I've read in a chapter and my life or the course.

☐ 9. I rarely underline, mark, highlight, or write notes in my textbooks.

☐ 10. I usually mark, underline, highlight, or write notes in my textbooks.

☐ 11. I have difficulty deciding what to mark or underline.

☐ 12. I can usually tell what to mark or underline.

☐ 13. I have to be interested in what I am reading to get anything out of it.

☐ 14. Even if a subject covered in a textbook doesn't interest me, I can still determine what I should learn and remember from it.

☐ 15. I think I should be able to read a passage once and remember the information covered in it.

☐ 16. I know that I may have to read a passage several times before the information sinks in.

☐ 17. When I read documents on the Internet, I can't tell which ones are reliable sources and which ones are not.

☐ 18. I am able to evaluate the reliability of Internet documents and sources.

If you checked mostly even-numbered statements, you are probably already an active reader. If you checked mostly odd-numbered statements, you may be a passive reader who would benefit from developing active reading strategies.

Active readers are aware of and are in control of their reading process. They use active learning strategies.

Passive readers are not aware of their reading process. They read inattentively and usually do not make use of active learning strategies.

Interact, as applied to the reading process, means to engage your mind with the writer's through questioning and other active strategies.

Readers fall into two categories: active readers and passive readers. **Active readers** control their interest level and concentration. They read with a purpose: They know what information to look for and why. Active readers constantly question what they read. They relate the author's ideas to their own experience and prior knowledge. On the other hand, **passive readers** are not in control of their reading. They lose interest easily and give in to distractions. They read the same way they watch television programs and movies, expecting others to engage them and keep their attention. A common passive reading experience is to "wake up" in the middle of a paragraph, wondering what you have just read. Active readers control the process of reading; passive readers are unaware that reading *is* a process they can control.

The key to active reading is to **interact** with the text, to engage your mind with the author's. Taking notes, marking the text, questioning, thinking about the author's ideas, even talking them over with a friend—these are all ways to interact with the text. Passive readers do none of these things. They open the book to the assigned chapter and read from the first word to the last without really thinking about the author's ideas. As a result, they can't decide what is important, don't know what to review, and soon forget what they have read. Consequently, passive readers often feel "lost" in class. The

---

FIGURE 7.1

Active and Passive Readers

ACTIVE READERS:

- have a positive attitude toward reading
- read for ideas
- ask questions to guide their reading and thinking
- manage their reading process
- schedule time for reading
- have a purpose for reading

PASSIVE READERS:

- have a negative attitude toward reading
- read only words
- read without thinking or questioning
- are unaware that reading is a process they can manage
- read only if they have time
- read because "it is assigned"

- know how to keep their interest and motivation high
- control their concentration
- use study systems and memory strategies
- underline and annotate textbooks
- make graphic organizers to use as study guides
- relate what they read to prior knowledge and experience
- review by reading notes and other materials
- seek help as needed
- know what is going on in class due to active reading

- expect the author to interest and motivate them
- are easily distracted
- resist using study systems and memory strategies
- do not use marking systems
- think making graphic organizers is too much work
- see no connection between college reading and life or work
- review by re-reading entire chapters
- resist asking for help
- often feel lost in class due to passive reading

chart in Figure 7.1 on page 162 compares active and passive readers. Becoming an active reader takes self-motivation, a commitment to try proven strategies, the desire to succeed, and the persistence to make it happen.

The Reading and Study Connection

• Understand the process of reading and how you can take control of it.

Do you remember that in Chapter 3 we defined *critical* and *creative thinking*, in part, as *conscious* processes? Remember that we discussed the importance of becoming aware of yourself as a thinker? Well, there is a word for that kind of awareness: **metacognition**. This term describes both a process and a field of study that investigates the act of thinking or reading or learning and what is going on in the minds of people who are engaged in these activities. The connection between reading and studying is that they are both processes that you can control by the choices you make and the actions you take. This is what you can do to take control of your learning:

Metacognition is the awareness of yourself in the process of thinking and the actions you take to control the process.

▼ Set reachable goals for completing reading and study tasks.

▼ Be realistic about your strengths and weaknesses: recognize that some subjects will be harder for you than others and plan accordingly.

▼ Know how you learn best—your learning style.

▼ Study at times and in places that help you focus.

▼ Find ways to motivate yourself.

▼ Monitor your progress: Keep track of your grades, learn from your mistakes, and consistently try to do better.

▼ Evaluate your results.

▼ Get help when you need it.

Earlier in this chapter, you took an *Awareness Check*, as you do in every chapter. Can you now see how these exercises serve a metacognitive purpose? They raise your awareness of what you already know and help you build background for what you are about to learn, putting you in charge of your learning. Another way to take control is to choose an appropriate strategy to complete a task. For example, to become an active reader, try these strategies:

▼ **Set a realistic reading goal.** Don't try to read 60 pages all at once. Break up the assignment into two or three sessions—for whatever amount of time you think you can maintain optimum concentration. If you feel your concentration slipping before your time is up, stop, take a break, and then refocus your attention.

▼ **Read with a purpose.** Know what you are expected to get out of the assignment. Perhaps you will be tested on the material or asked to summarize the information, or perhaps you have several questions in mind that you expect the assignment to answer. Having specific information to look for may help you keep your attention focused on your reading and should give you a reason to talk yourself out of any boredom or lack of interest.

▼ **Read with a pen or highlighter** so you can mark parts of the chapter that answer your questions, suggest possible test questions, explain concepts, or expand on topics covered in class lectures. If you are reading from a library book or other source that you cannot mark, take notes on index cards or in a notebook, making sure to label your cards with the source's title, page number, website address (URL), or any other identifying information you may need later. How to mark textbooks is explained later in this chapter.

EXERCISE 7.1 Learning Styles Application on Reading and Studying

WRITE AN EVALUATION OF YOURSELF as an active or passive reader. Describe your study system for reading a textbook chapter or other assigned reading material. Be specific. What type of learning style is dominant in the way you read? For example, would you rather read on your own, forming your own opinions, or would you prefer to read and then discuss the assignment with others? If possible, describe the study system you used most recently for an assigned reading in one of your classes and any difficulties you had. Also, take into consideration your results from *Awareness Check* 7.1 as you complete this exercise.

▼ **Review and recite from your notes or markings.** Reviewing helps reinforce the information you have learned so that it stays in your memory. Reciting from notes or textbook markings provides another pathway into your memory via your auditory sense. Reciting is especially helpful for those who have an auditory learning preference, but anyone can benefit from it.

The more active you become in taking control of your reading process, the less likely you will be to lapse into passive reading habits. As an active reader, you are *doing something* throughout the process, whether it is marking the text, stopping to think about what you have read, rereading difficult passages, asking questions and looking for answers, or reciting from your notes and markings. These activities aid in the transfer of information from your short-term memory to your long-term memory. For more on how the memory process works and is enhanced by the way you study, see Chapter 8. See also Chapter 9 to learn how using a reading system such as SQ3R can give you even more control over your reading process.

Skimming and Scanning

Skimming is a quick reading to get a general idea or overall impression of what is covered. Skimming is a "big picture" strategy.

Scanning is a quick reading to find a specific fact or piece of information. Scanning is a "detail" strategy.

Not all reading is alike. Active readers use different strategies for different purposes. **Skimming** and **scanning** are two strategies that you will use often. When you *skim* a chapter, you quickly glance through it to get a general idea of what it covers—the topic, author's purpose, and key ideas. Skimming the introduction, headings, and summary will give you the big picture and may also help you determine how difficult the reading will be and how much time you should plan to spend on it. Skimming is different from reading in depth. Skimming the chapter first will help you anticipate what is to come when you read the chapter in depth and begin to think critically about the author's ideas.

Like skimming, *scanning* is also rapid reading, but for a different purpose. When you scan, you are searching for a specific fact or detail. Let's say you have already read a chapter and are now doing an assigned exercise. You might scan the chapter to find a specific fact or definition of a term that will help you answer a question.

Skimming and scanning are two reading strategies that you probably already use. For example, when you look up a number in the telephone book or a word in a dictionary, you don't read every word on the page. Instead, you scan over the page until you find the desired information. When you pick up a newspaper, you probably don't read every word on the front page. Instead, you skim an article or two, reading just their titles and first and last paragraphs to see if one of them is worth reading all the way through. Can you think of other times when you might use skimming or scanning? See Figure 7.2 for suggestions.

When English Is Your Second Language

If you are a nonnative speaker of English, then you probably have already discovered that reading English can be challenging. English has many inconsistencies in spelling and grammar. The common expressions that native speakers of English take for granted can be perplexing to nonnative speakers. For example, if someone "gets your goat," no animal is involved. The expression means "to annoy." Remember that as an active reader, it is your responsibility to seek help if you need it. You can manage reading assignments if you use the following strategies:

FIGURE 7.2

When to Skim or Scan

Skim for these Purposes	Scan for these Purposes
• To get a general idea of what a book or a chapter covers	• To find the answer to a question
• To preview the day's big stories without having to read the entire newspaper	• To find a specific fact such as a name or a date
• To determine what a midterm exam will cover by glancing through previous tests	• To find a piece of information listed on a chart or other graphic
• To read through a chapter introduction to find the author's purpose	• To find a specific topic in an index, table of contents, or reference book
• To preview several articles to find one that contains the information you need	• To find a piece of information that you previously read on a website

1. **Find or start a study group.** As explained in Chapter 1, studying with others can help you fill in gaps in your own understanding of assigned material. This can be a great help if English is your second language. Make sure your study group includes one or more native speakers.

2. **Ask Questions.** During the process of reading an assigned chapter, you may encounter words or ideas you don't understand. Mark the passages in your textbook and ask your instructor or study partners for an explanation.

3. **Talk through the material** with a study partner, preferably one whose native language is English. Talking about what you read will help you discover your areas of strength and weakness.

4. **Read** often and read a variety of material. The best way to build your vocabulary and become familiar with English usage and expressions is to read. Start with newspapers and magazines and gradually work up to full-length books on subjects that interest you. Then talk with others about what you are reading.

5. **Use your dictionary.** All students, both native and nonnative English speakers should keep a dictionary close by while reading. The dictionary may not always help, because words have multiple meanings and you must be able to choose the one that fits the context of what you are reading. So if you still have questions, mark the sentence or passage to remind yourself to ask your instructor or study group about it.

6. **Take an ESL (English as a Second Language) course** if your college encourages or requires you to do so. Some nonnative speakers object to taking these courses for two reasons: the time involved and the fact that they may carry no credit. If you need help with your language skills, get it now because it will save you time in the long run.

Discussing your reading with other students and friends will improve your comprehension and fluency.

INSADCO Photography/Alamy

Improve Your Reading Comprehension

• Use strategies that will help you read for ideas.

Reading involves more than word recognition. Reading is about comprehending, or understanding, an author's ideas as they develop from sentence to sentence. Many things can interrupt the flow of ideas and cause your comprehension to break down: Distractions, unfamiliar terms, and difficulty of the material are a few "interrupters" that you have probably experienced. What you may not know is that several common misconceptions about reading can also interfere with your ability to understand, learn from, and remember what you read. Accepting the realities about reading is your first step toward improving your comprehension. Figure 7.3 lists some common myths about reading that many students believe—and the realities that shatter the myths.

Now that you have put aside the myths about reading and are facing the realities, you are ready to take the second step toward better reading comprehension: Read for ideas.

Read for Ideas

Ideas develop from words to sentences, then to paragraphs, and on to larger units of meaning such as multiparagraph essays, articles, and textbook chapters. The sentences in a paragraph are related: They all support one main idea. The paragraphs in a longer passage are similarly related: They all support the one central idea of the entire passage. This is why the main idea of a multiparagraph passage such as a textbook chapter or newspaper article is often called the *central idea*, to distinguish it from the main idea of each paragraph.

FIGURE 7.3

Myths and Realities about Reading

Myths about Reading	The Realities
You should be able to read a chapter once and remember the important points.	One reading is not enough. Several readings combined with frequent review may be necessary to prevent forgetting.
Reading skill is like musical talent: Either you have it or you don't.	Good readers are made, not born. With practice, anyone can become a better reader.
You should read all types of material at about the same speed.	Comprehension, not speed, is the goal. Adjust your reading speed to the type of material and its level of difficulty.
You can skip tables and diagrams because they are explained in the text.	You should always read graphic materials because they condense, summarize, or illustrate complex ideas, making them easier to understand.
The best way to read a textbook chapter is to start at the first page and read until you are finished.	If you read without stopping, you are not giving yourself time to think about the ideas. Break a chapter into smaller segments and read actively: Think, question, and reflect.
Marking and underlining are not necessary and take too much time.	If you mark or underline the important ideas, then you will know what to review later on, which saves time.
Reading will not be an important factor in my career.	Most employers value reading as a necessary skill for doing any job well.

In a textbook chapter, the title and introductory paragraphs usually provide strong clues to the chapter's central idea. In fact, the central idea of a longer passage is often stated near the beginning. Therefore, you can use the title and introduction to create a context for reading. For example, the title of this chapter, *Becoming an Active Reader*, and the introductory paragraphs make clear that the central idea is that several strategies can help you become an active reader. Both the title and the introductory paragraphs should raise two questions in your mind: "What is an active reader?" and "What are the strategies?" Using these as guide questions, you can read the chapter to find the answers. Each paragraph within a chapter provides important information that is essential to your understanding of the entire chapter's central idea.

To improve your reading, begin by learning how to find a paragraph's main idea. A paragraph can be anywhere from one to several sentences long, and it may contain three types of sentences:

1. The *topic sentence* is a direct statement of the author's main idea.

2. The *support sentences* contain major or minor details that develop, or explain, the main idea.

3. The *concluding sentence* may restate the main idea, introduce a new but related idea, make an inference, end the paragraph with another detail, or provide a transition to the next paragraph.

For examples of these three kinds of sentences, read the next paragraph and the explanation that follows it.

> *Adjusting to college can be difficult for students because of the pressures they face from family, instructors, and friends.* → Topic sentence: Main Idea
>
> *Family members, for example, may expect a student to add studying and attending classes to his or her other responsibilities. They may resent being asked to take on more chores or spend time alone while the student studies. A student who faces this kind of pressure from family may have difficulty reaching desired goals. Another pressure students face is from instructors. From the student's point of view, each instructor acts as if the student has no other courses to take. Add to this the need to get to every class on time, attend class regularly, and keep up with all assignments. Friends can also make a student's adjustment difficult. For one thing, they may pressure a student to put off studying to engage in leisure-time activities. Friends who are not attending college feel threatened and, without meaning to, may do or say things that can make a student wonder if college is worth it.* → Support sentences: Details
>
> *To overcome these pressures, a college student must have a strong desire to succeed.* → Concluding sentence

The first sentence of this paragraph is the *topic sentence*, which states the author's main idea: Pressures from family, instructors, and friends can make students' adjustment to college difficult. The last sentence of the paragraph is the *concluding sentence*. In between are the *support sentences*, which give examples of three kinds of pressures and explain how these pressures can make it difficult for a student to adjust to college. The concluding sentence then introduces a new but related idea: Students can overcome these pressures.

Find the Main Idea

In a paragraph, an author may express the main idea in one of two ways: (1) by stating it directly in a topic sentence, as in the example paragraph about pressures students face, or (2) by implying it through the choice of details and the use of key words.

Now read another paragraph about students' pressures:

> *Some parents insist that a student carry a full-time load and maintain an A or B average while also working part-time and sharing household tasks. A student who has too many things to do may not be able to do any one of them very well. Another pressure*

students face is from instructors' expectations. Instructors expect students to arrive on time, attend class regularly, and keep up with all assignments. They also expect students to participate in class, ask questions, and do extra work or get help outside of class if they are having trouble meeting course objectives. Friends, too, can make a student's adjustment difficult. For one thing, they may pressure a student to put off studying in order to party or to engage in some other leisure-time activity. Friends who choose not to attend college may try to make a student feel guilty for leaving them behind. To overcome these pressures, a college student must have a strong desire to succeed.

This paragraph has no topic sentence, but several clues can help you infer the author's main idea. From the third sentence, which begins with "Another pressure," you can infer that the first two sentences explain one kind of pressure and that now you are reading about another kind. The sixth sentence, which begins with "Friends, too," introduces a third pressure students face. In the last sentence, the phrase "these pressures" is the strongest clue that the paragraph is about the effects of the three kinds of pressure.

When a paragraph has no topic sentence, the author's main idea is implied by the details in the supporting sentences. Once you identify the idea, opinion, or topic that all the details support, you should be able to state the author's main idea in your own words.

To find the author's main idea, read a paragraph carefully and then follow these steps:

1. Look for the topic sentence. It can be anywhere in the paragraph, but it is often the first sentence. The topic sentence is the most general sentence in the paragraph. It combines the author's topic and opinion, and it summarizes *all* the information presented in the support sentences. The topic sentence expresses the author's main idea.

2. If the main idea is not stated in a topic sentence, identify the topic by inferring it from the details. Ask yourself, "What subject do all the sentences in the paragraph support?" Look for signal words—such as *for one thing, another,* and *for example*—that introduce major details.

3. Determine the author's opinion about the topic. In general, what does the author say to expand your knowledge about the topic? Does the author *explain how* to do something? Does the author *compare two things*? Does the author *explain why* something exists or *give reasons* as to why something happens in a certain way? Does the author *argue for or against* one point of view? By identifying the author's opinion, you may be able to infer the main idea.

Concept Check **7.1**

You may get more out of your reading by discussing the author's ideas with members of a study group. Everyone brings different knowledge and experience to reading. Through discussion, you may gain deeper understanding and broaden your perspective.

Identify Supporting Details

By itself, the main idea is only a statement of fact or opinion that means little without evidence to support it. An author's evidence may include three types of details.

▸ Facts

▸ Reasons

▸ Examples

Facts can be verified. They include such things as dates, names, places, and events.

Facts. A **fact** is a direct observation, quotation, statistic, date, number, report of an event, or expert testimony that can be verified. For example, if a movie critic says there are 12 shootings within the first seven minutes of a new action film, you can verify this information by seeing the movie and counting the shootings that occur within the first seven minutes.

The author of the following paragraph supports the main idea with facts:

> In the Twilight *series, Stephenie Meyer has written a timeless love story that appeals to young girls—and their mothers. Based roughly on Shakespeare's* Romeo and Juliet, *the series consists of four novels.* Twilight *is about two lovers, Edward and Bella, whose families disapprove of their relationship, and for good reason: Edward is a vampire.* New Moon, *the second book, introduces Jacob, a rival for Bella's affection— Jacob is a werewolf. In* Eclipse, *Jacob and Edward fight both to protect Bella from evil forces and to win her love. In* Breaking Dawn, *Bella chooses—well, you'll have to read the book to find out. But unlike Shakespeare's play, this story has a happy ending.*

EXERCISE 7.2　What Is the Main Idea?

FIND THE MAIN IDEA in each paragraph. If the main idea is stated, underline it. If the main idea is implied, write a sentence that expresses it.

> 1. During the 1960s, several prominent African American authors wrote fiction and nonfiction works about lives of poverty and disenfranchisement. One of them, Claude Brown, died in February 2002. While still a student at Howard University, Brown wrote his novel, Manchild in the Promised Land, about growing up in the streets of Harlem. Brown, once a gang member himself, became an advocate for those trapped in the cycle of poverty, drugs, violence, and death.

_____

_____

> 2. What is binge drinking? The NIAAA Advisory Council defines binge drinking as having several drinks in quick succession—five for males, four for females. The Council defines a "drink" as 12 ounces of beer, 5 ounces of wine, or 1.5 ounces of distilled spirits. To help people understand the magnitude of the problem, the Center for Science in the Public Interest reported in 2005 that 44 percent of students at four-year colleges are binge drinkers. In fact, most of the alcohol consumed by college students is the result of binge drinking. To discourage binge drinking, college administrators have tried everything from limiting the availability of alcohol to banning it at athletic events, but without much success. Obviously, binge drinking is a serious problem on college campuses, compromising students' achievement and putting their health and lives at risk.

_____

_____

> 3. In 2001, Surgeon General David Satcher issued some disturbing findings in Women and Smoking: A Report of the Surgeon General. Satcher reported a 600-percent increase since 1950 in smoking-related deaths among women. The Centers for Disease Control and Prevention (CDC) reported that from 2000 to 2004, 174,000 women per year died from smoking-related illnesses. Moreover, findings from a 2007 CDC survey showed that among women 18 years of age or older, one in six are smokers.

_____

_____

The author's main idea, stated in the first sentence, is that Meyer has written a timeless love story in the *Twilight* novels. The supporting evidence includes the titles of the novels and brief details about characters and plot. Book titles, characters' names, and an author's number of works can all be determined by checking your library's reference works on books and authors. To research an author on the Internet, simply type the author's name as a keyword.

Reasons are details that answer the question "Why?" Either facts or opinions can be given as reasons.

Reasons. Authors use **reasons** to support a main idea when their purpose is to explain *why* something happens, *why* something is important, *why* one thing is better than another, or *why* they feel or think as they do. Think of reasons as the *causes* that are responsible for producing certain effects, results, or outcomes. For example, a sportswriter may use reasons to explain why a basketball team lost an important game that it was favored to win. Or a political commentator might write an article explaining reasons for a presidential candidate's popularity among a certain group of voters.

In the following paragraph, reasons support the author's main idea:

> *One of the most important goals that a college student can aim for is an expanded vocabulary. One reason this goal is so important is that an expanded vocabulary can improve students' writing. With sufficient words and definitions at their command, students will have less difficulty writing what they mean. Also, increased vocabulary improves reading, which leads to greater comprehension. A third reason for improving vocabulary is the confidence students feel when they use words accurately. Students are less afraid to speak out in class discussions or to give reports and speeches when they know they are not going to mispronounce or misuse words. Increasing vocabulary is a worthwhile goal for students who also want to improve their speaking, reading, and writing.*

The main idea of this paragraph is that an expanded vocabulary is an important goal that students should try to reach. The main idea is stated in a topic sentence, which is the first sentence of the paragraph. The author supports the main idea with reasons that explain why students should increase their vocabularies.

1. An expanded vocabulary improves writing.

2. An increased vocabulary improves reading comprehension.

3. An improved vocabulary results in confidence.

The *signal phrases* "one reason" and "third reason" help you locate the major details. The second reason follows the signal word *also*.

Examples are illustrations used to describe or explain. "Red" is one *example* of a color.

Examples. An **example** is a situation, instance, or even a person that authors use to illustrate, support, or clarify a main idea. Authors may use one extended example or several short ones. Or they may support a main idea with an example, then use facts or reasons as additional evidence. Some use examples as minor details to explain and clarify major details.

Notice how the author of the next paragraph uses examples.

Can you distinguish among facts, reasons, and examples? Select a newspaper article that interests you. As you read it, try to find one or two examples of each of the three types of details.

> *Have you ever stopped to wonder why Monday is called "Monday"? The days of the week have roots in ancient Roman and Norse mythology. These origins are obvious in some of our names for the days. For example, Sunday—or "Sun's Day," as it was once called—and Monday (or "Moon's Day") were named for the sun and moon, respectively. Saturday was named for the planet Saturn. The other four days originally took their names from the planets, which were themselves named for Roman gods. For example, Tuesday was called* Dies Martis *("Mars Day") to honor Mars, the god of war. The Roman names for the planets Mercury, Jupiter, and Venus gave us Wednesday, Thursday, and Friday. The ancient Germanic people later honored their own gods by renaming Tuesday, Wednesday, Thursday, and Friday. For example, Tiw (god of war) replaced Mars and became "Tiw's Day," or Tuesday. Woden, god of wisdom, was the source for Wednesday. Thursday was renamed for Thor, god of thunder. Frigg, goddess*

> *of love, gave her name to Friday, replacing Venus, the Roman goddess of love. Each language has its own names for the weekdays, but you can see the ancient Roman and Norse roots in those names. For example, Sunday in today's German is* Sonntag, *and Monday in Spanish is* lunes—*which comes from* luna, *the Spanish word for "moon."*

In the first sentence of this paragraph, the authors state the idea that our names for the days of the week come from ancient Roman and Norse mythology. Examples then follow that trace the origin of each day's name.

Make Inferences from Reading

As explained in Chapter 3, an *inference* is an idea that is implied, not stated. When the author's main idea is unstated, try to infer it from the details that are given. You might make many inferences from an author's main idea and details, but most can be classified into one of two categories. **Personal inferences** are those you can make by relating ideas you have read to what you know or have experienced. **Textual inferences** are educated guesses or conclusions drawn about an author's meaning based on stated

Personal inferences are educated guesses based on personal experience or common knowledge.

Textual inferences are conclusions drawn from stated information.

EXERCISE 7.3 Details, Details

READ EACH PASSAGE AND DETERMINE whether the details are mainly facts, reasons, or examples. Then check the appropriate box.

1. *A balance sheet consists of three parts: assets, liabilities, and net worth. Your **assets** include everything you own that has monetary value. Your **liabilities** are your debts—amounts you owe to others. Your **net worth** is the dollar amount left when what is owed is subtracted from the dollar value of what is owned—that is, if all the assets were sold at the listed values and all debts were paid in full.*

From Garman, *Personal Finance*, Ninth Edition. © 2008 South-Western, a part of Cengage Learning, Inc. Reproduced by permission. www.cengage.com/permissions.

☐ **Facts**   ☐ **Reasons**   ☐ **Examples**

2. *Memo to All Employees*
From J. Todd, Manager

It is with deep regret that I inform you of the passing of one whose life set an example for all of us. Spot was the mainstay of Curtis Nursery and Landscaping. The first to arrive and the last to leave, he greeted everyone warmly. He was a friend to all and discriminated against none. Who among us has not sought Spot's company when in need of a little cheering up? Spot has never been one to miss a day at work. This morning, we knew something was wrong when he was not waiting for us in the back of the truck. Instead, we found him in his favorite place under the house, where he had died peacefully during the night. A gentleman among dalmatians, he will be missed.

☐ **Facts**   ☐ **Reasons**   ☐ **Examples**

3. *A job with the United States government provides security, a stable income, and a sense of purpose. Moreover, career opportunities have never been better, according to the U.S. Department of Labor, which predicts that 53 percent of federal employees will reach retirement age over the next few years. What this means is that about 900,000 new job openings will be available for those seeking government jobs.*

☐ **Facts**   ☐ **Reasons**   ☐ **Examples**

details. The ability to make inferences is a critical thinking skill. Let's now explore personal and textual inferences in greater detail.

Personal Inferences. You probably make personal inferences about every day's events, because your experience tells you what to expect or what seems likely. Here are some examples of personal inferences:

▶ Suppose you are absent from several classes and the next time you attend, the classroom is empty. You wait ten minutes and still no one shows up. You conclude that class must not be meeting for some reason that was announced during your absence.

▶ When you visit your favorite website, you know the information will be accurate and up to date because every time you have visited the site in the past, the information you have gained has proven to be reliable.

▶ The manager of the company where you are employed needs someone to work overtime. You assume she will ask you because she knows you need the extra money and because you have helped out before.

Earlier in this chapter, you found the main idea and details in a paragraph about the pressures students face from instructors, family, and friends. Now read a paragraph about another common source of pressure:

> *Stress is one pressure you bring on yourself when you go to class unprepared or when you don't manage your time effectively. Poor preparation results in inattention and that "lost" feeling. When you haven't read the assignment, you can't enter into the class discussion. If you haven't studied for a test, you are not likely to do well. In either situation, knowing your performance is not at its best creates stress. Being unprepared is almost always the result of poor time management. If you are like many students, you have more to do than you can possibly get done, unless you schedule your time. Time management also involves setting priorities. You have to decide which is more important: seeing that new movie with a friend tonight or getting those algebra problems done for tomorrow's class. If you consistently put off doing things you need to do so that you can do what you want to do, the stress will eventually catch up with you. Make a decision now to improve your time management and to become better prepared for class, and you will have taken the first step toward reducing some of your stress.*

One student who read this paragraph said, "Boy, that's me; I can always find something else to do besides algebra." This student related a detail from the paragraph to his own experience: "It's not that I don't want to do the work or that I don't realize I'm undermining my chances for success in the course. It's just that algebra is so hard. I know I'm going to get frustrated, so I dread getting started. As a result, I wait until the last minute, and doing that stresses me out." Relating the idea that stress can be self-induced to what she had read about internal and external sources of motivation, another student said, "Since this kind of stress is the result of your own behavior, you can get rid of it by changing your behavior. In a way, this is easier to deal with than the stress that comes from the pressures you get from family, instructors, and friends. Those pressures are external, so they're harder to control." These are all excellent examples of making personal inferences.

Textual Inferences. What you read in your college textbooks will be more meaningful for you if you relate it to your experience with and your knowledge of the author's subject. Just as you can make personal inferences about what you read, you can make textual inferences about what an author writes. A valid inference is one that can be supported by an author's main idea and details.

Read the following paragraph.

> *Styles in cars, dress, furniture, and architecture come and go. Some styles become outdated or may disappear. Others never really go away but reassert themselves, with*

some changes, over many years. A fad *is a style of short duration. A* fashion *is a more lasting style. Both fads and fashions are engaged in by large groups of people. Fads of the past forty years include the hula hoop, hot pants, love beads, disco dancing, automobile "tail fins", the Rubik's Cube, and Nintendo. You may be thinking, "I've never heard of some of these fads," and for good reason: They have come and gone. Fashions stay with us. Miniskirts—once considered a fad—have enjoyed several revivals. Columns, a feature of ancient Greek architecture, have never gone out of style. You see them on public buildings and private homes—wherever a "classic" look is desired. Because fashions are more lasting than fads, they tend to be more socially acceptable. What is the difference between a fashionable person and a faddist? One is selective about which trends and behaviors to embrace, developing his or her own personal style. The other is swept along by each new fad that enjoys a brief popularity and seems to have no recognizable style.*

According to this paragraph, both fads and fashions are forms of collective behavior, but they differ in duration. You can use this information to make inferences about other behaviors. For example, if you are in your twenties, your parents can probably remember when tattoos were considered vulgar. In the nineties, tattoos became a fad among the young, probably as a result of their prevalence among rock musicians. Now tattoos have gone mainstream, with everyone from soccer moms to celebrities sporting them. At this point, tattoos may be more fashion than fad. This is an example of making a textual inference.

EXERCISE 7.4 Collaborative Activity on Reading for Ideas

APPLY WHAT YOU HAVE LEARNED about the main idea, details, and inferences by completing this exercise with group members. Follow the guidelines for group discussion that appear on the inside back cover. Read each paragraph. Then discuss the main idea, identify the details, and read the inferences that are listed. If you think most readers would make these inferences, check *yes*. If not, check *no*. In either case, explain your answer. Record your conclusions on the lines provided. Next, evaluate your work. Then write your evaluation on your own paper or visit *The Confident Student* premium website to download the group evaluation form.

If you want to expand your vocabulary, there are two methods you might want to try. The first method involves making note cards and using them for recitation and review of words that you want to learn. Prepare each note card by writing the word on one side of the card and its definition on the other side. Recite to learn by pronouncing the word and saying its definition. Then turn the card over and check yourself. Do this with each card until you can recite all the definitions from memory. Review the words by repeating these steps once a week, or as often as needed, to keep the words in your memory. The second method for learning words involves keeping a word list as you read. As you are reading an assigned chapter in one of your textbooks, jot down in a notebook any unfamiliar words you encounter. Look at these words and write the definitions that fit the contexts in which the words appear. The next time you read a chapter from the same textbook, keep your word list handy. You can add to the list or use it to review definitions of your words when they appear in new contexts. These two methods have worked for many students.

Main Idea: If you want to expand your vocabulary, there are two methods you might want to try.

Details:

a. _____

_____

_____

continued

b. _____

_____

_____

Inferences:

	Yes	No
a. These vocabulary-building methods may work for you.	☐	☐

Explain your answer: _____

_____

_____

	Yes	No
b. Using one of these two methods is the only way to expand your vocabulary.	☐	☐

Explain your answer: _____

_____

_____

Group Evaluation:
Evaluate your discussion. Did everyone contribute? Did you accomplish your task successfully? What additional questions do you have about the main idea, details, and inferences? How will you find answers to your questions?

Look for Organizational Patterns

Not only is it necessary to identify an author's important ideas, it is also essential to understand how those ideas connect. Common organizational patterns link a central idea and details. If you can spot the pattern early in your reading, you can use it as a guide to predict what will follow. Key words may suggest how ideas are organized. For example, if the author's main idea is that memory is a three-stage process, then the key words *three-stage process* should alert you to the **process** pattern of organization. Read for the explanation of each stage and how it works.

You can learn to recognize six other common organizational patterns that help you follow an author's ideas:

1. If two things are being compared, the pattern is **comparison and contrast**. Read to find similarities and differences.

2. If an author explains *why* something happens, the pattern is **cause and effect**. Read to find reasons and results.

3. If an author groups items into categories, the pattern is **classification**. Determine the number of categories and identify the characteristics of each category.

4. If an author supports a main idea by giving examples, the pattern is **example**. Read to find key introductory phrases such as *for example* and *for instance*. These phrases alert you that an example follows.

5. If an author's details follow a certain order, the pattern is **sequence**. Read to find numbers in a sequence or events that are explained according to time periods. A sequence is often part of a process, especially when the stages of a process occur in a certain order or at specific times. Processes explain *how* things happen. Sequences explain *when* things happen.

6. If an author provides an extended meaning of a word or a concept, the pattern is **definition**. Read to find phrases such as *the meaning is, can be defined as*, and *to define*. These phrases alert you that a definition follows.

An author who brings together more than one organizational pattern in a single explanation is using **mixed patterns**. For example, someone might use classification to describe the kinds of students who attend a certain college and then use comparison and contrast to describe the similarities and differences among them. Identifying organizational patterns requires slow and careful reading. Look for key words that provide clues to an author's pattern.

> **Concept Check 7.3**
>
> Speakers as well as writers use common organizational patterns to connect their ideas. Can you see how listening for an organizational pattern in a lecture might help you follow the speaker's train of thought with greater understanding?

EXERCISE 7.5 Looking for Patterns in Your Reading

THE FOLLOWING STATEMENTS MIGHT BE the topic sentences of paragraphs in a textbook or an article. Each sentence gives you a clear idea of what might follow, and each sentence suggests how the details in a paragraph are organized. Read each statement to predict the author's organizational pattern. Write the letter of your answer in the space provided.

A. cause and effect   C. sequence   E. classification   G. process
B. example   D. comparison and contrast   F. definition

1. _____ Both Grant and Lee were civil war generals, but that is where their similarities end.

2. _____ The Cornell method is a widely used note-taking system.

3. _____ According to Freud's theory, the personality has three components: the id, the ego, and the superego.

4. _____ Computer-managed inventory control systems have proven beneficial to small businesses for a number of reasons.

5. _____ When it comes to managing your money, you need to be aware of the advantages and disadvantages of using credit cards.

6. _____ Emily Bronte's *Wuthering Heights* is an early example of the romance novel.

7. _____ Some of the great films of the 1930s fall into the following categories: musicals, gangster films, and horror films.

8. _____ What is the *autonomic nervous system*?

9. _____ The next section traces the history of rock and roll from its roots in rhythm and blues.

10. _____ To make an electrical circuit, follow these steps—and be careful.

Use a Textbook Marking System

• Use marking systems and summarizing to get more out of reading your textbooks.

Marking your textbooks by *underlining* or *highlighting* and by *annotating* (making notes) improves your concentration for two reasons: It focuses your attention on the task of reading, and it provides a tactile/kinesthetic pathway to the brain. You must think critically about what you read so that you can make decisions about what to underline, highlight, or annotate. When done well, marking your textbook saves time by providing you with specific information to review so that you do not have to reread a whole chapter in order to study for a test. Whether you underline or highlight is a matter of personal preference. Highlighting pens come in a variety of colors, and the type of ink they contain may vary. Experiment with highlighters to find one that won't bleed through your pages. Underlining is best done with a fine-line ballpoint pen or felt-tip marker. Again, choose one that doesn't bleed through. A pencil may not be as good a choice for underlining. A sharp point may tear the paper; also, pencil smudges and fades and doesn't show up nearly as well as ink.

Marking your textbook is an essential part of any study system because it improves your acquisition and retention of information. In the next paragraph, a student (Alex) describes the system he worked out for underlining and marking his textbook.

> I read one section at a time. After I read the section, I draw brackets, [ ], around the main idea and put a star beside it in the margin. I underline the major details, and I put a number in a circle next to each detail. That way, I can see how many details there are when I review the section for a test. If a word I don't know is defined in a section, I underline it and write "def." in the margin. If I have to look up a word that is not defined, I circle it and write my definition in the margin. Also, I don't underline everything in a sentence. I just underline key words. Before I did this, I used to underline too much; then I would end up having to reread almost the whole chapter when I reviewed, instead of studying just the important parts.

Alex makes a good point: Underlining too much is not useful (nor is underlining too little). The purpose of marking textbooks is to make the important ideas stand out and to provide memory cues. Then you can determine what you need to study in depth and what you can skip when you review. Here is what one of Alex's underlined passages

DRESSING FOR SUCCESS

Dress conservatively for an interview. →

The most effective strategy for <u>making a good impression</u> is to <u>pay careful attention to your dress, grooming, and posture.</u> Dress in a manner that flatters your appearance while conforming to the office norm. The employment interview is not the place for a fashion statement. You want the interviewer to remember what you had to say and not what you wore. Although different positions, different companies, different industries, and different parts of the country and world have different norms, in general [they] <u>prefer well-tailored, clean, conservative clothing for the interview</u>.

Be well-groomed; blend in. →

For most business interviews, <u>men</u> should dress in a <u>blue or gray suit and a white or pale blue shirt with a subtle tie, dark socks, and black shoes.</u> <u>Women</u> should dress in a <u>blue or gray tailored suit with a light-colored blouse</u> and <u>medium-height heels.</u> Avoid excessive or distracting jewelry, heavy perfumes or after-shave lotions, and elaborate hairstyles. <u>Impeccable grooming</u> is <u>a must</u>, including clothing clean and free of wrinkles, shoes shined, teeth brushed, and hair neatly styled and combed.

Avoid anything excessive: perfume, elaborate hairstyles. →

<u>Blend in</u>; you will have plenty of opportunity to express your individual style once you've been hired.

Scott Ober, *Contemporary Business Communications,* Sixth Edition. Copyright © 2008 by Houghton Mifflin Company. Reprinted by permission of South-Western College/Cengage Learning.

looks like. Notice how he has annotated the passage in the margins.

Try these guidelines for effective textbook marking. Then, like Alex, develop a system that works for you and use it consistently.

What to Mark in Textbooks

Deciding what to mark is the same as deciding what is important. *Definitions of terms* are important. Even if they are already italicized or printed in boldface, mark them anyway if you do not already know them. *Examples* used to illustrate theories are important; so are *experiments*, including who conducted them, what happened, and what they proved. *Names*, *dates*, and *historical events* are important. *Principles*, *rules*, and *characteristics* are additional examples of the kinds of information that may be important within the context of what you are reading.

Marking your textbook keeps your attention focused.

How to Mark Your Textbooks

1. It is usually better to read before you underline and to read one section at a time. You may not be able to tell what is important until you have read a whole section to see how the ideas relate to each other.

2. In the margin, write key words or symbols that will serve as memory cues to call your attention to special terms, names, dates, and other important information.

3. Use your own words when you make notes in your textbook. Putting the author's ideas into your own words will help you test your understanding, and you will be more likely to retain them.

4. Choose some symbols to indicate certain kinds of information, and use your symbols consistently. Here are some common symbols students use. You probably already use some of them.

   def. = definition

   ex. = example

   T   = possible test item

   *   = an important point

   1., 2., 3., etc. = used when sequence matters

5. Underline or highlight key words and phrases.

Review for a test or prepare for class by reciting from what you have marked or annotated in the margin. Use your underlining and marking to identify processes or concepts you can illustrate using charts or diagrams for easy review and recall.

Summarize Information from Textbooks

Most textbook chapters have a summary at the end that condenses the chapter's main ideas. Reading the summary before you read the entire chapter builds background for the reading by focusing your attention on the ideas that the author thinks are important. Also, reading the summary is part of the survey step of the SQ3R reading system, as explained in Chapter 9. Just as reading a summary is a helpful study strategy, so is writing your own summary.

CRITICAL THINKING

Evaluate Textbook Marking

Exercise Overview

This exercise will help you think critically about what and how to underline and annotate in textbooks.

Exercise Background

Deciding what or how much to underline is difficult for many students. Basically, you should underline only as much as necessary to clearly identify the important ideas. Look for the same three things that you would include in a summary: the main idea, the major details, and the information's significance. Special terms and definitions should also be marked or annotated in the margin.

Exercise Task

Examples A and B show the same passage as marked by two different students. Evaluate each student's markings for their usefulness. Determine which student has successfully applied the suggestions for marking textbooks as explained in this chapter. Briefly explain in writing which passage is the best example of how to mark your textbook.

Example A

Behavioral Stress Responses. Clues about people's physical and emotional stress reactions come from changes in how they look, act, or talk. Strained facial expressions, a shaky voice, tremors, and jumpiness are common behavioral stress responses. Posture can also convey information about stress, a fact well known to skilled interviewers.

Stress shows in your face, voice, actions, posture.

Even more obvious behavioral stress responses appear as people attempt to escape or avoid stressors. Some people quit their jobs, drop out of school, turn to alcohol, or even attempt suicide. Unfortunately, as discussed in Chapter 5, learning escape and avoidance tactics deprive people of the opportunity to learn more adaptive ways of coping with stressful environments, including college (M. L. Cooper et al., 1992). Aggression is another common behavioral response to stressors. All too often, this response is directed at members of one's own family (Polusny & Follette, 1995). For instance, in the wake of hurricanes and other natural disasters, it is not uncommon to see dramatic increases in the rate of domestic-violence reports in the devastated area (Rotton, 1990).

Cooper et al.: avoidance tactics keep you from dealing with stress.

Aggression often directed at family.

Example B

Behavioral Stress Responses. Clues about people's physical and emotional stress reactions come from changes in how they look, act, or talk. Strained facial expressions, a shaky voice, tremors, and jumpiness are common behavioral

continued

stress responses. Posture can also convey information about stress, a fact well known to skilled interviewers.

Avoidance tactics   <u>Even more obvious behavioral stress responses appear as people attempt to escape or avoid stressors. Some people quit their jobs, drop out of school, turn to alcohol, or even attempt suicide. Unfortunately, as discussed in Chapter 5, learning escape and avoidance tactics deprive people of the opportunity to learn more adaptive ways of coping with stressful environments, including college (M. L. Cooper et al., 1992).</u> <u>Aggression</u> is another common behavioral response to stressors. All too often, this response is directed at members of one's own

Polusny, Follette, family (Polusny & Follette, 1995). For instance, in the wake of hurricanes and

Rotton   other natural disasters, it is not uncommon to see dramatic increases in the rate of <u>domestic-violence reports</u> in the devastated area (Rotton, 1990).

Excerpt from Douglas A. Bernstein and Peggy W. Nash, *Essentials of Psychology,* Fourth Edition. Copyright © 2007 by Houghton Mifflin Company. Reprinted by permission of Wadsworth/Cengage Learning.

By now, you know that writing engages your tactile/kinesthetic sense. Also, writing a summary tests both your comprehension and your critical thinking. Summarizing information requires that you understand it well enough to explain it in your own words, in a condensed version. Your summaries make good study guides that you can review along with your other notes and materials as part of your preparation for a test. A summary of a passage or body of information includes three things:

▶ The main idea

▶ The major supporting details

▶ Why the information is significant

Although the summary should be stated in your own words, it should maintain the author's meaning. A good summary will be shorter than the original but no less complex. The following paragraph summarizes "Dressing for Success" on page 176.

> *To make a good impression in an interview, be well groomed and wear an appropriate outfit. Clean, conservative clothes are best. For both men and women, this means a well-tailored blue or gray suit. The idea is to blend in, not stand out.*

If you compare this summary with the original passage about how to dress for an interview, you will see that the summary states the main idea, condenses the major details, and explains why the information is significant: to make a good impression.

EXERCISE 7.6   Collaborative Activity on Summarizing

WORKING WITH A PARTNER, SELECT some information to summarize from this chapter or from another chapter of *The Confident Student.* For example, you could summarize the COPE problem-solving strategy from Chapter 4 or the types of schedules from Chapter 6. Discuss the information, decide what is important, and then write your summary. Share your finished product with the class.

Guided CHAPTER REVIEW

The following checklist summarizes this chapter's key terms and strategies. After reading the chapter, how confident are you that you can apply the information you have learned? To assess your level of confidence, respond to each statement with one of the following: *very confident* (3 points), *fairly confident* (2 points), *not very confident* (1 point), *not confident* (0 points). Write your number of points in the box beside each statement. Then add your score and read the analysis that follows. When you have finished, take the chapter quiz.

SUMMARY CHECK

How confident are you about applying these strategies?

Points

☐ 1. Reading actively rather than passively

☐ 2. Knowing when to skim or scan

☐ 3. Finding a main idea

☐ 4. Identifying supporting details

☐ 5. Making personal and textual inferences

☐ 6. Recognizing organizational patterns

☐ 7. Marking and underlining textbooks

☐ 8. Writing a summary

How confident is your understanding of this chapter's key terms?

☐ 9. active readers

☐ 10. passive readers

☐ 11. interact

☐ 12. metacognition

☐ 13. skimming

☐ 14. scanning

☐ 15. facts

☐ 16. reasons

☐ 17. examples

☐ 18. personal inferences

☐ 19. textual inferences

Total

Add your score. The highest possible score is 57. The closer your score is to 57, the higher your level of confidence. Use your *Summary Check* results to help you determine which parts of the chapter to review.

YOUR WEBSITE RESOURCES

This chapter's resources include the following items. To access them, go to *The Confident Student* premium website.

- **Video Clip: Metacognition: Helping Students Become Strategic Learners**
- **Chapter Exercises**
- **Forms to Download**

- **Chapter Summary of Topics**
- **Thinking Ahead About Career**
- **Confidence Builder Web Search**
- **Self-Test**

CHAPTER REVIEW Quiz

Answer the following questions from memory. Then return to the chapter to check your answers. As a final activity, complete *Show Your Confidence* at the end of the quiz.

1. In your own words, what is an active reader?

2. How do active readers differ from passive readers?

3. What is skimming? Give an example.

4. What is scanning? Give an example.

5. What is one myth about reading that you used to believe, and what is the reality that you now believe?

6. What is the difference between a main idea and a detail?

7. What is one of the organizational patterns explained in this chapter that you have used in your own conversation or writing and have also recognized in your reading?

8. Why is it important to underline, highlight, or annotate information in your textbook?

9. What kinds of information do you usually underline or mark when reading assigned textbook chapters?

_____

_____

10. What will you do to become a more active reader? List one strategy that you will try.

_____

_____

SHOW YOUR CONFIDENCE

One way to improve your reading is to read. It may sound simple, but like any other skill, reading gets better with practice. You might be tempted to say, "It takes all the reading I can do just to finish my assignments," but is that really true? You can always make time to check the newspaper, read an article from a favorite magazine, or read the latest novel that everyone is talking about—even if you read only a few pages a night before going to sleep. These extracurricular reading activities keep your mind active and make you a more informed person. What have you read lately that you would recommend to a friend? What is one thing you will try to read this week just for fun? Be prepared to share your answers to these questions either in writing or in class discussion.

Your REFLECTIONS: ACTIVE VERSUS PASSIVE READERS

Reflect on what you have learned from this chapter about active reading. Use the following questions to stimulate your thinking; then write your reflections. Include in your writing specific information from the chapter.

- What role does reading play in your life? What kinds of reading do you do?
- Review the traits of active and passive readers listed in Figure 7.1 near the beginning of this chapter. Which traits of active readers do you have? Which ones do you need to develop?
- Has the way that you mark textbooks changed as a result of reading this chapter? Explain your answer.

_____

_____

_____

_____

_____

_____

_____

_____

_____

_____

_____

_____

_____

_____

_____

_____

_____

_____

_____

_____

_____

_____

_____

_____

_____

_____

_____

_____

_____

_____

_____

_____

_____

_____

8 Controlling Attention and Memory

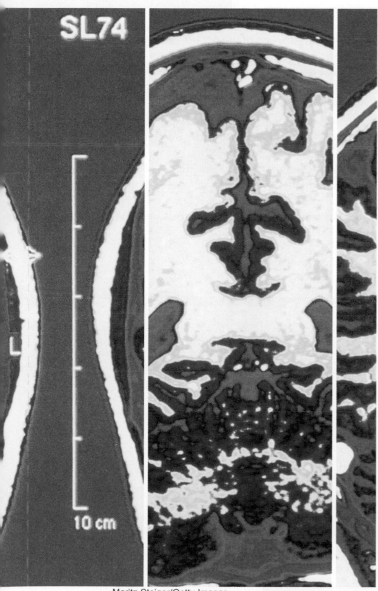

SL74

10 cm

Moritz Steiger/Getty Images

This chapter encourages you to:

- Practice strategies that will help you control your attention and make your mind more receptive to learning.

- Adopt the attitude and study habits that focus attention and aid retention.

- Understand how your memory works to process information efficiently and to minimize forgetting.

- Use common memory techniques to focus your study and enhance learning.

Confident students are **focused**. They know how to focus their attention on a task and maintain concentration until the job is done.

What was your first-grade teacher's name? What is one thing you remember from the last class you attended? What did you have for breakfast this morning? What were you thinking about before you began reading these questions? What is on your mind right now? You are building memories moment to moment. What you choose to focus on shapes your experience. In fact, your memories *are* your experience.

Some events leave an indelible impression on your memory no matter what you do. For example, do you remember where you were on September 11, 2001? You probably do because the Sept. 11 attacks on America were dramatic and traumatic events. On the other hand, you probably don't remember your first-grade teacher's name—unless this teacher made an impression on you. If someone told you that you could remember whatever you wanted and for as long as you wanted, would you believe it? Attention is the key. Attention and memory are linked. You can't remember what you don't pay attention to in the first place.

Sometimes when a relationship breaks up, one of the people involved will say, "we live in two different worlds." What this means, of course, is not that they live on different planets but that they have different world views, different realities. They pay attention to different things. Take Tiger Woods, the famous golfer, or Meryl Streep, a great actor. How are they able to do what they do? They are totally committed to their goals, and most of their attention is focused on maintaining and improving their talents.

Now you're probably wondering what this has to do with you, a college student. The answer is that if you want to succeed in college, strengthen your memory, and get better grades, you have to start paying attention to the right things. Before we discuss the how, the why, and the what of attention and memory, let's take a minute for you to relax and clear your mind. The *Confidence Builder* that follows explains a simple technique for relieving stress and overcoming some of the distractions that compete for your attention.

CONFIDENCE BUILDER

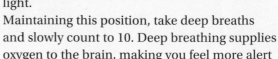

Relax to Concentrate

Have you ever sat down at your desk with every intention of studying, only to find that you can't concentrate or you don't know where to start? Have you ever gone into a test thinking that you are well-prepared and then your mind goes blank? Do you sometimes start to read an assigned chapter that you know will be long and difficult, but then you postpone the reading because you can't seem to make yourself do it? Does knowing that you should be doing your work cause you to feel nervous or a little agitated? These are all signs of stress. All of these situations are telling you that it is time to relax and take control. Relaxation techniques can be helpful in relieving stress and clearing the mind so that you can regain your focus. Here are a few simple steps you can follow to get relaxed. Best of all, you

can do this at your desk or at a table—anytime, anywhere.

1. Sit up straight but comfortably with your feet on the floor. Relax your shoulders and unclench your jaw.
2. Place your elbows on the desktop, lower your head, and close your eyes. Now gently cup the palms of your hands over your eyes. Your fingertips should be resting against the top of your forehead or just above to keep out the light.
3. Maintaining this position, take deep breaths and slowly count to 10. Deep breathing supplies oxygen to the brain, making you feel more alert so that you can think clearly.

continued

4. As you breathe deeply and count to 10, empty your mind of negative thoughts. As thoughts or outside noise begin to compete for your attention, keep concentrating on your breathing and counting. Count past 10, if necessary.
5. When you are feeling relaxed, lower your hands and open your eyes.
6. You should feel comfortable, calm, and ready to take on a test, do an assignment, or perform another mental task.

This technique works because you can't feel relaxed and stressed at the same time. As you concentrate on becoming relaxed, you forget about your distractions. When you return to your studying or other task, your mind is in a more receptive state to absorb the information. If this desktop relaxation technique does not work for you the first time, try it again later. With practice, you will be able to relax yourself. Most important, you can do this in class if you are taking a test, your memory fails, or you begin feeling stressed. Just close your eyes, breathe, and count as directed above. When you are feeling calm again, return to the test. Chances are, the information that was blocked will come back to you. You need not feel self-conscious about using this relaxation method during a test. Other students will think that you are resting your eyes—if they notice at all.

Follow Up: To explore this topic further, visit *The Confident Student* premium website for an online search activity about relaxation techniques.

Control Your Attention

- Practice strategies that will help you control your attention and make your mind more receptive to learning.

Some people have the ability to concentrate for hours at a time. Others can lose concentration at the least distraction. Have you ever noticed that when you are doing something you really like, concentrating is easy? On the other hand, when you are bored or you don't like what you are doing, paying attention may be harder to do. Concentration is intentional. First, you have to decide to pay attention. Staying focused is a matter of not responding to distractions, and it is easier for some people than it is for others. Admittedly, there are some limitations on the ability to concentrate. People with attention deficit disorder (ADD and ADHD) and other disabilities may find it difficult to focus on one thing for any length of time. However, research into these and other attention/memory disorders is ongoing, and there are some promising new pharmaceutical remedies being developed—as well as nonmedical ones. The beneficial effects of meditation on concentration is one example. Limitations aside, most people can gain greater control over their attention and memory processes than they think.

What exactly is **concentration**? Let's start with a few examples. You're sitting in the campus dining hall, eating your lunch. You're not thinking about anything in particular. You are aware of the tastes and smells of the food, the buzz of conversation, and the hardness of the chair on which you are sitting. Occasionally a burst of laughter grabs your attention, or you might snap into alertness if you hear your name being mentioned, but these distractions are fleeting. The busyness of the dining hall settles into a comfortable blur as you relax and enjoy your lunch. Now think about what happens if you are sitting in the same dining hall but you are waiting for your friend to come and have lunch with you. All your attention is focused on looking for your friend. You scan the crowd, glance repeatedly toward the entrance to the dining hall, looking for that one face in the crowd. Concentration is *selective attention*, the process of focusing your attention on some things while ignoring others. We will have more to say about selective attention later in this chapter.

Concentration is *selective attention*, the process of focusing your attention on specific information while ignoring distractions.

We are all susceptible to distractions that can grab our attention if we let them. To take control, start by monitoring your thoughts and feelings whenever you are trying to concentrate. For example, suppose you are reading an assigned textbook chapter. You are concentrating on every word when suddenly you become aware of noise outside, or you feel a draft, or a passage you have just read triggers an emotion that takes your mind away from your reading and onto something else. You have allowed a distraction to take over, but you can regain control by ignoring or eliminating the distraction and by refocusing your attention. You may have to practice this process many times before you can concentrate without becoming distracted. Each time you feel yourself drifting off or losing control, refocus and try to maintain concentration for longer and longer periods of time. (See the illustration on the left about self-monitoring and staying "on task.")

Many factors affect concentration, including the way you study, the environment in which you study, the things that distract you, and how you deal with your distractions. What causes you to lose concentration? Complete *Awareness Check* 8.1 to find out.

Self-Monitoring Cheat Sheet
On Task/Off Task cartoon from *Beyond Behavior Modification: A Cognitive-Behavioral Approach to Behavior Management in the School,* Third Edition (p. 345), by J. S. Kaplan and J. Carter, 1995, Austin, TX: PRO-ED. Copyright 1995 by PRO-ED, Inc. Reprinted with permission.

AWARENESS CHECK 8.1

Where Is Your Attention Going?

Choose one of the following as your response to each statement: *always* (4 points), *usually* (3 points), *occasionally* (2 points), *rarely* (1 point). Write your number of points in the box beside each statement. When you are finished, add your score.

Points

1. I have felt myself losing concentration and then have tried to get it back again.

2. It is easy for me to find something of interest in my assigned reading.

3. I am able to concentrate on listening and taking notes at the same time.

4. Even when I know that an assignment is likely to be difficult, I have no trouble getting started and I am able to maintain my concentration.

5. I may not like the instructor or the class, but I can still keep my interest going.

6. I know what kinds of stimuli (noise, hunger, friends wanting to socialize) distract me when I am trying to study.

7. I am able to relax and control my stress so that it is not a distraction.

8. I can tell when my attention is fading and what I need to do to take control again.

9. I have found a good place to study where I can concentrate with few distractions.

10. I understand that it is my responsibility to determine what my distractions are and to eliminate or reduce them.

continued

Total

Add your score. If your total is 35–40, you may already have control of your concentration. If your total is 29–34, you have some control but could strengthen concentration. If your total is 10–28, you have much to gain by developing concentration. Whatever your level of skill, this chapter's strategies will help you improve the way you concentrate and process information.

Eliminate Distractions

Distractions can have internal or external causes. **Internal distractions** originate within you. They include feelings of hunger, tiredness, and discomfort that you can control. **External distractions** originate outside you. They include noise, temperature, and interruptions. You may not be able to eliminate all external distractions, but you can change the way you respond to them so that they don't keep you from concentrating. Exercise 8.1 will help you identify your distractions.

Internal distractions originate inside you; hunger and feelings of stress are two examples.

External distractions originate outside you; noise and inappropriate lighting are two examples.

EXERCISE 8.1 | **Identify Your Distractions**

Do you often feel distracted and lose concentration when you study? Are your distractions internal or external? To find out, read the following lists of common distractions and check all those that trouble you. Then write a paragraph in which you answer these questions: (1) What is your most common and troubling distraction? (2) What have you tried to do to ignore or eliminate the distraction?

INTERNAL DISTRACTIONS

☐ Hunger

☐ Tiredness

☐ Illness

☐ Thinking about work or personal problems

☐ Worrying about grades or other academic issues

☐ Stress

☐ Physical discomfort

☐ Not knowing how to do an assignment

☐ Negative feelings about courses or instructors

☐ Lack of interest or motivation

☐ Other internal distraction? _____

_____

_____

EXTERNAL DISTRACTIONS

☐ People talking to each other

☐ Cell phone ringing

☐ Music or television playing

☐ Noise or activity going on outside

☐ Lighting too bright or too dim

☐ Temperature too high or too low

☐ Lack of proper materials

☐ Party or other activity that you want to take part in

☐ Friends or family members asking you to do something

☐ Spending too much time on the Internet

☐ Other external distraction? _____

_____

_____

You can eliminate some internal distractions if you anticipate your needs. For example, study when you have eaten and are rested. Study in a comfortable place. Make sure you understand how to do an assignment before you begin. If you are not feeling well, postpone studying until you feel better. Worrying about grades, dwelling on job-related or personal problems, and having negative feelings about courses and instructors may cause stress and distracting thoughts. When you have distracting or negative thoughts, stop studying for a moment and remind yourself of what you are trying to accomplish. Focus your attention on completing the task. If you lack interest in what you are studying or if you don't have the motivation to do the work, studying with a partner might help. Choose someone who *is* interested and motivated. Studying will be more enjoyable, and the time will seem to pass quickly.

You can eliminate most external distractions by creating a study place where *you* may be able to control the lighting, temperature, noise level, and the availability of materials needed for study. Say *no* to friends who distract you from studying by tempting you with invitations to go out and have fun. If you save the fun as a reward for studying, you'll have a better time. Exercise 8.2 will help you think of more ways to deal with distractions.

EXERCISE 8.2 Collaborative Activity about Distractions

THE PURPOSE OF THIS EXERCISE is for you and the members of your group to gain experience identifying internal and external distractions and ways to eliminate them. Follow the guidelines for group discussion that appear on the inside back cover of this text. Your tasks are as follows: Read and discuss the following scenario about a student who has trouble concentrating. Then answer the questions on the lines provided. Write your evaluation on your own paper or go to *The Confident Student* premium website to download the evaluation form.

> Yesterday afternoon I had some time between classes, so I went to the library, found a comfortable couch in the reading section, and began reading a chapter in my psychology book. Two students came in, sat on the couch next to me, and began talking about their dates from the night before. Their evenings sounded pretty funny. I didn't mean to eavesdrop, but I was sitting right there! Suddenly I realized I was shivering. Why had I forgotten to bring a sweater? Not only was I cold, but the light also cast a glare on my book. I moved to a warm spot near the window where the sun was coming in and decided to take notes for the upcoming test. I looked all through my backpack for the pen I was sure I had packed. By the time I had borrowed a pen and sat down to take notes, it was time for my next class. I like psychology. Why was I unable to complete my reading assignment? I felt as though I was struggling with an unknown language.

1. **What is the first distraction the student encounters? Is it an internal or external distraction?**

   _____

   _____

2. **What should the student have done immediately?**

   _____

   _____

3. **What are the student's other distractions? Are they internal or external?**

   _____

   _____

continued

4.   Why is the student unable to complete the reading assignment?

_____

_____

5.   What behavioral changes would help the student eliminate distractions?

_____

_____

Group Evaluation:

What have you learned about internal and external distractions? Do you think some distractions cannot be eliminated? Why or why not? Did your group complete its tasks successfully? What improvements can you suggest? What additional questions do you have about concentration? How will you find answers to your questions?

When Life Intervenes: Quick Tips to Combat Distractions

It's easy to avoid some of the things that make it hard for you to concentrate. If you're hungry, eat. If you're cold, put on a sweater. But what do you do when life presents a challenge that is not so easily solved? A sick child at home, an aging parent who needs your care, the trauma of personal illness or hardship, a death in the family—any one of these can consume your attention and make it hard for you to concentrate on your studies. Here are a few tips to help you cope when life intervenes.

▸ **Be proactive.** Study regularly and stay up to date with assignments so that when a crisis is over, you will be able to get back on track quickly.

▸ **Anticipate problems.** When possible, make arrangements with your instructors to make up tests or assignments that you know you will have to miss.

▸ **Stay in touch with your study group.** During a family emergency or other hard time, ask study partners to share notes with you and keep you informed of class activities.

▸ **Call on family members or a close friend** to help with child care, provide parent care, or simply give emotional support when life's challenges become distracting.

▸ **Be optimistic.** It may be hard to maintain a positive outlook when you are distracted by an illness or other emergency, but try to shift your focus to the future. Plan what you will do when the emergency passes.

▸ **Be realistic.** Good times don't last forever, but neither do bad times.

Your Study Place: Six Characteristics

Do you do most of your studying at home, in the library, or in some other place? Where you study is not as important as whether you are able to concentrate on studying when you are there. If you have a lot of distractions at home—small children who need attention, other family members who make demands on your time, or noise from the television or ringing phones—you may find it more pleasant and productive to study on campus. But many students find they can't concentrate in the library or at other places on campus, so they set aside a place to study at home.

If you prefer to do most of your studying at home, use your learning style to help you create a home study place that meets your needs. Manage your time so that you do most of your studying when your concentration is greatest. To adapt your study place to your learning style, try these suggestions:

▶ **Visual learners.** Make your place visually appealing. Display calendars, lists, and study aids where you can see and use them.

▶ **Auditory learners.** Record lectures and class discussion if there is no prohibition against doing so. Listen to these recordings at home and take notes from them. You may be able to check out recorded lectures from your college library for use at home. You can also record your own notes and other material to use for recitation and review.

▶ **Tactile learners.** If you have a personal computer, use a word processing program to make your own study guides. As we discussed in Chapter 6, create an online or "hard copy" calendar on which you can record important dates and assignments. Using a computer will also activate your visual sense.

You don't have to spend a lot of money to set up an efficient and convenient workplace in your house, apartment, or residence hall. Consider the following six characteristics of a good study environment when you plan your study place: location, lighting, temperature, furniture, supplies, and motivational aids.

1. **Location.** You need a study place where you feel comfortable and where you are likely to have few distractions. Ideally, you should do all your studying in the same place, and you should not use your study place for anything but studying. For example, if you get sleepy while studying, don't nap at your desk. Leave your study area and return after you have rested. Studying in bed is not a great idea because it will encourage you to nap, and it may even make you feel more stressed when you are trying to sleep. If you get hungry, don't eat at your desk. Take a break, have something to eat, and then return to finish studying. Then studying will become a habitual response triggered by your study place, and you will be able to maintain concentration.

   A spare room in your house can become a workplace where you can close the door and shut out distractions. If space is limited, use a corner of your bedroom as a study area. If you share space with someone—in a residence hall, for example—arrange your desks on opposite sides of the room to create the illusion of privacy. Plan your time so that each of you can study when you are most alert, in a room free of noise and distracting activity.

2. **Lighting.** Too much studying in too little light causes eyestrain. Keeping your eyes focused for too long on the pages of your textbook or on a computer screen, especially in poor light, can make you feel tired and tense. Study in a well-lighted place and look up from your work occasionally. Rest your eyes by closing them or by looking off in the distance without focusing on anything.

To prevent eyestrain during long study sessions, rest your eyes by periodically looking off into the distance.

Karim Shamsi-Basha/The Image Works

Overhead lighting should illuminate your whole study area without casting glare or creating shadows. Or use a lamp that can handle a 250-watt bulb and position it close to your work so that you are not reading or writing in glare or shadows. Two lamps, one on each side of your desk, will achieve the same effect if you put a 150-watt bulb in each. Make the best use of whatever lamps are available by placing them properly and by choosing the right bulbs.

3. **Temperature.** Your body is a gauge that registers changes in climate and temperature. Extreme changes affect your ability to concentrate because they cause you to focus your attention on your body's discomfort instead of on your task. Optimum temperatures for most people are between 68 and 72 degrees Fahrenheit. In your study area, you may be able to control the temperature and keep it at the level at which you feel most energetic.

Temperatures in public buildings may vary greatly from room to room, and they are usually controlled automatically. If one of your classrooms stays uncomfortably cold, take a sweater or light jacket to that class. You are probably aware of the hot and cold spots on your campus, so if you prefer to study there, find a comfortable place and dress accordingly.

4. **Furniture.** You'll need a desk or sturdy table big enough to hold a computer (if you have one), with space left over for reading a book, writing a paper, or studying from notes. If you can afford to buy a new desk, get one with drawers for storing paper, pens, and other supplies.

Choose a comfortable chair that provides adequate support for your back and is neither too low nor too high for the table or desk you are using. Studies have shown that many employees who work at computers all day suffer from chronic pain in their necks, arms, and backs. Such discomfort is the result of sitting in one position for long periods of time in a chair that doesn't provide enough support. Your arms or neck may become sore if your elbows and wrists are not supported as you type or if your computer screen is not at eye level. If you cannot buy or do not own a chair that provides enough back support, experiment with placing a pillow behind your lower back and adjusting it for comfort. Figure 8.1 on page 194 illustrates an ergonomically correct seating posture: one that provides proper back support and distance from keyboard and computer screen.

Whenever you have been sitting at your desk for a while and are beginning to feel tired or uncomfortable, try this exercise. Look up from your writing or away from your computer screen. Look to the right or left without focusing your eyes on anything in particular. Lower your shoulders and let your arms hang limp at your sides. Shake your hands. Push back from your desk and stretch your legs. If you still feel tired or stiff, take a short walk before returning to your work.

5. **Supplies.** Keep your supplies handy and replenished. Whatever you need—including textbooks—make sure your supplies are available so that you don't have to interrupt your studying to look for them.

A cardboard file box provides convenient and inexpensive storage for your papers, returned tests, and materials from previous courses that you want to keep for future reference. You can buy a file box at your campus bookstore or office supply store.

> **Concept Check 8.1**
>
> Where do you do most of your studying? Does your study place meet the requirements of a good study environment as explained in this chapter? How would you describe your ideal study place?

© 2011 Wadsworth, Cengage Learning. All Rights Reserved.

FIGURE 8.1

Sitting Comfortably

The science of ergonomics studies the conditions under which people work most comfortably and efficiently. The design of some office furniture is based on information about the way the human body is structured and best supported.

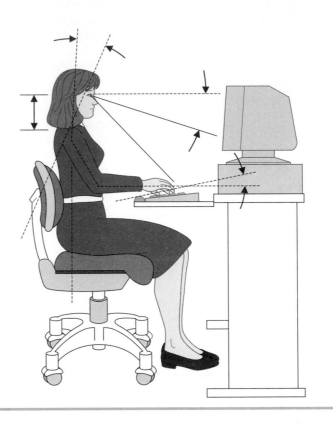

6. **Motivational Aids.** Personalize your study environment. Be creative. Make it *your* place. Tack a calendar on a bulletin board or the wall above your desk. Check off the days as you progress through the term. Keep a record of your grades. This will help you see whether your studying is paying off, and it will signal when you need to make an extra effort. Tack up papers and tests on which you earned good grades. When you are feeling discouraged, look at the evidence of your success.

   If studying away from home or the residence hall is a better option for you, your college library may be a good choice. Find a quiet area that meets your lighting and temperature requirements. Also, visit the library at different times of the day to find a time when it is most distraction-free.

   Make studying in your place a habit so that it becomes your trigger for concentrated effort. Research has shown that studying at the same time every day reinforces the habit. Although your present schedule may not permit a set study time, this is a goal you can work toward.

   An added advantage of finding or creating your best study environment is that you can transfer what you have learned in the process to your workplace environment. The same conditions will apply: location, lighting, temperature, furniture, supplies within reach, and motivational aids. You might not have control of all these conditions, but you may be able to make some changes in the environment that help you increase your productivity. Are you taking advantage of your learning style to help you find your best study environment? Exercise 8.3 may give you some ideas.

EXERCISE 8.3 Learning Styles Application on Your Study Place

YOUR BODY'S REACTIONS AND YOUR preferred learning environment are aspects of your learning style that affect both concentration and your choice of a study place. To review these aspects of learning style, complete the following items.

1. **Based on the items you checked in Exercise 8.1 on page 189, are your distractions mostly internal or external?**

_____

_____

2. **What seems to be your greatest distraction, and why?**

_____

_____

3. **What relationship do you see between your source of motivation and the distractions you checked in Exercise 8.1? Remember that the more internally motivated you are, the more self-motivated you are. The more externally motivated you are, the more you depend on others to motivate you.**

_____

_____

4. **What is your preferred learning environment? Do you prefer working alone or with others, and why?**

_____

_____

5. **Taking into consideration your learning environment preference and your body's reactions to hunger, tiredness, temperature, and lighting, describe your ideal study place and explain what you will do to achieve it.**

_____

_____

Attitude, Active Learning, and Attention

• Adopt the attitude and study habits that focus attention and aid retention.

You may wonder what attitude has to do with attention. Step 4 of the desktop relaxation technique explained in the *Confidence Builder* on pages 186–187 instructed you to breathe deeply and "empty your mind of negative thoughts," and for a good reason. If you open your textbook and begin thinking, "This is hard, I hate this course, I'll never get through this, I can't concentrate," you are programming yourself for failure. Negative thinking is an internal distraction that places the focus on your feelings instead of on the material you are trying to study. To take control of your attention, think positively about the goals you have set, where you want to go in life, and how the successful completion of each assignment brings you one step closer to achieving what you want. A positive attitude will make you receptive to learning. The use of active learning strategies will help you remember what you learn.

In previous chapters, we have emphasized the importance of active learning. Now let's expand on that concept. If you sit passively in class, only half aware of what is going on and letting yourself be distracted by noise, students talking, or random thoughts unrelated to the subject, you will not learn anything. Because you are not involved, you will easily become bored and you may leave class feeling that it has been a waste of time. Chances are good that your grades will be less than exceptional. "But I can't help the way I feel," you say. "I can't control what goes on around me," you say. Active learning isn't about controlling what goes on around you. It is about controlling what goes on inside your mind. You can make choices about what to study and where to study, and you can choose different strategies for learning different things. For example, taking notes while listening to a lecture and observing the speaker's gestures and expressions opens three pathways for the information to be processed in your brain. Listening opens an aural pathway, observing opens a visual pathway, and taking notes opens a tactile-kinesthetic pathway. The more of your senses that are engaged, the more likely it is that you will remember what you learn. Here are a few active learning strategies for you to try:

▼ Use the RMO system. RMO stands for *read, mark, organize*. Read one section at a time and underline important ideas. When you are finished, review your underlining and make a graphic organizer (such as a chart or diagram) that you can use as a study guide for additional review. Chapter 10 explains how to make graphic organizers.

▼ Read with a pen in hand. Make marginal notes: Write definitions, brief examples, or two-line summaries. Then review your notes.

▼ Read with a dictionary. Don't skip over words whose meanings you don't understand. First reread the sentence and the ones just before and after it. You may be able to figure out the meaning based on the context in which the word appears. If that fails, turn to your dictionary.

▼ Monitor your thinking while studying. You may find yourself disagreeing with something you read. Instead of giving in to these thoughts, remember that your first priority is to *understand* the author's ideas and the evidence on which they are based. You can disagree later.

▼ Study with a partner or group. Compare notes. Quiz each other. Restate concepts in your own words.

Most people cannot concentrate for more than an hour without becoming distracted. Take short breaks away from your study area to refresh your mind and body. In addition, try these tips for improving concentration and memory function: Break lengthy assignments into smaller units that you can complete in one sitting. Instead of reading a 60-page chapter all at once, read 20 pages in three separate sessions. Study difficult subjects first, before you get tired. If you can afford to buy your own new textbooks, do so. Although buying used books will save you money, someone else's underlining is distracting and may not accurately identify the most important ideas. If you start with a clean page, you will have to do your own thinking, which is always a good idea.

EXERCISE 8.4 Attitude, Behavior, and Concentration

ATTITUDE AND BEHAVIOR AFFECT CONCENTRATION. Your attitude and behavior in a class are related to the degree of responsibility you take for your academic performance. Select as a target a course in which you would like to do better. Complete the analysis that follows; then decide what you can do to adjust your attitude and improve your performance.

continued

1. What is the name of the course in which you would like to improve your grades?

_____

_____

2. Is there anything about the course that you don't like or that you think is difficult?

_____

_____

3. What are your distractions in this class?

_____

_____

4. Are the distractions internal or external?

_____

_____

5. What is your attitude toward this class? Check *yes* or *no* beside the following statements.

	YES	NO
I enjoy coming to this class.	☐	☐
I like the instructor's teaching style.	☐	☐
I feel confident in this class.	☐	☐
I am not afraid to ask questions in this class.	☐	☐
I am learning something in this course.	☐	☐
I see a relationship between this course and my goals.	☐	☐
I am interested in the subject taught in this course.	☐	☐

6. On your own paper, write an action plan to improve your performance in the course. Select a behavior or attitude that you want to change; then explain what you will do. Try out your plan long enough to receive at least two test or assignment grades. If you are satisfied with the results, continue with your plan. If not, evaluate your plan and make whatever changes are needed.

Manage the Stages of Memory

- Understand how your memory works to process information efficiently and to minimize forgetting.

Becoming aware of and being able to manage the way your mind processes information can ensure lifelong learning. A college degree does not represent knowledge gained or skills learned once and for all. Instead, a degree merely represents where you stand academically at a given time. Throughout life, you will face tasks, problems, and decisions that require you to apply your knowledge in new ways and to develop new skills.

© 2011 Wadsworth, Cengage Learning. All Rights Reserved.

Do you find it easier to remember some things than others? Why is it that once you learn how to ride a bicycle, you never forget? Even if you go 10 years without riding and your skills are rusty, you can still get on the bike and ride. Yet when you read a chapter for your psychology class, you may not remember most of it the next day. As an introduction to the rest of this chapter, *Awareness Check* 8.2 will help you start thinking about what you are able to remember and why.

AWARENESS CHECK 8.2

What Is in Your Memory?

Information comes into your brain through your senses, so the memories stored there have some connection to what you have seen, heard, smelled, tasted, or touched. Some memories are more powerful than others. As you read each question, think about the information you are asked to recall. Write your answers on the lines provided. Then ask yourself, "Why do I remember this?"

1. What is your zip code? _____

2. Does the Statue of Liberty hold the torch in her right or left hand? _____

3. What are the steps to follow when pumping gas? _____

   _____

   _____

4. What is five times nine? _____

5. What is the capital of your home state? _____

6. On a vertically hanging traffic signal, which is on top: the red or the green light?

   _____

7. In an electrical outlet, which slot is longer, the one on the right or the left?

   _____

   _____

8. How do you parallel park a car?

   _____

   _____

9. What are the names of three U.S. presidents?

   _____

   _____

10. How do you perform an exercise such as a sit-up or bicep curl? (Choose an exercise.)

    _____

    _____

continued

Items 1, 4, 5, and 9 call for verbal information, which comes from books and other printed sources. Items 2, 6, and 7 call for visual information—things we recall because we've seen them and paid attention to them. Items 3, 8, and 10 call for physical or motor information—things we've learned by doing or by manipulating objects. We tend to remember best the information that we use often. Your zip code and the position of traffic lights are examples. We also remember things that made a great impression on us. If seeing the Statue of Liberty was a powerful experience for you, then you may recall which one of her hands holds the torch. What kind of information is easiest for you to remember: verbal, visual, or physical/motor information?

The next few sections of this chapter will help you understand how your memory works so that you can improve the way you learn. As you read, keep in mind three simple truths about memory:

▶ It is normal to forget.

▶ You can't remember what you don't understand.

▶ Memory is a process that can be strengthened and managed.

The Three Rs of Memory

When you were a child, your teacher explained the multiplication tables and wrote them on the chalkboard. While you were listening to the teacher and looking at the board, you were processing information about the tables through your senses of sight and sound. Then, to help you learn the tables, your teacher asked you to write them out on paper, and that activity engaged your sense of touch. You also recited the tables aloud. Those practices in the classroom helped you to *record* and *retain* the tables in your memory. Finally, the teacher told you to practice your tables at home because you would be asked to *recall* them on a test. If your practice and memory techniques have served you well, then you have retained the tables and can recall them even now. What is memory and how does it work?

Memory is a mental process that enables you to recall past experience. Without this process, you could not learn and grow in knowledge, skill, or wisdom. Without memory, you would have to learn to drive all over again every time you got in your car. Without memory, you would repeat the same mistakes over and over, never learning from them, never profiting from your experience. In a nutshell, here is how your memory works: Your memory is literally open to the world through your senses. Everything registers on your memory—sounds, feelings, words, images, everything—but only for a moment, and then it is gone. So if you're sitting in class and don't pay attention and don't take notes, guess what? You won't remember anything.

Three steps—we'll call them the *three Rs of memory*—can help you take control of the memory process and direct it toward something productive such as getting ready for your midterm exams. The three steps are *record, retain,* and *recall.* (Researchers also refer to these steps as *encoding, storage,* and *retrieval.*) As illustrated in Figure 8.2, you **record** information by paying attention to it so that you can hold it in your memory long enough to write it down or use it in some way before you forget it. Looking up a phone number and trying to remember it long enough to dial it is one example. However, you can **retain** information and keep it in your memory for longer and longer periods of time if you reinforce it through use, review, or another strategy. Phone numbers that you use often will stay in your memory. On the other hand, you have probably forgotten some phone numbers that you no longer use. For example, can you remember the first phone number you had as a child? Let's say you are going to be tested on some information you have covered in class. If you have studied and reviewed the information sufficiently to store it in your memory, then you will be able to **recall** or retrieve it for

Memory is the mental process that enables you to retain and recall past experience.

Record means to select and focus on something you want to remember.

Retain means to store information or keep it in your memory for later use.

Recall means to retrieve, recognize, or remember stored information.

© 2011 Wadsworth, Cengage Learning. All Rights Reserved.

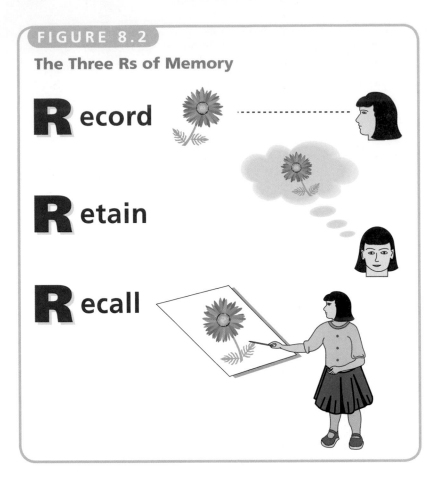

FIGURE 8.2

The Three Rs of Memory

Record

Retain

Recall

Sensory memory takes in data from the senses and registers it fleetingly.

Selective attention is a process that enables you to focus your attention on certain things, ignoring others. When you concentrate, you apply selective attention.

Short-term memory, also called "working memory," has a limited capacity and retains information—such as the name of someone you just met—for less than a minute.

the test. Now let's put the three Rs in perspective by examining how they operate through the three stages of memory: *sensory memory, short-term memory,* and *long-term memory.*

Sensory Memory: Input and Attention

As mentioned before, your five senses—sight, hearing, taste, smell, and touch—are the media through which you experience the world. Your **sensory memory** translates information from the senses into mental images or impressions. Your mind takes in all this information and, through a process called **selective attention**, sorts the important from the insignificant.

You've felt this process at work whenever you've been so caught up in watching a television program that you didn't hear someone speak to you. Your mind screened out the interfering sound of the person's voice. Had you lost interest in the show, your attention would have shifted to something else.

In class, when you are listening to a lecture, your task is to concentrate on the speaker's words and take notes on the important ideas. Although everything the speaker says registers on your sensory memory, you may have to work at paying attention to the speaker's ideas and ignoring external stimuli such as a conversation between two students who are sitting next to you.

Everything registers fleetingly on your sensory memory. By concentrating on a certain idea or image—like the phone number you looked up—you can transfer the information to your short-term memory, where you can retain it for about 30 seconds.

Short-Term Memory: Record

You can hold information in your **short-term memory** for up to one or two minutes. For example, you meet someone at a party. He tells you his name, and you strike up a conversation. A few minutes later, you see a friend whom you want to introduce to the person you just met, but you can't remember his name. Or you're reading an article and you stop to look up the meaning of a word. Several paragraphs later, the word comes up again, but you can't remember the definition, so you have to look it up again. Have you ever had an opinion or the answer to a question that you wanted to bring up in class discussion but by the time you can get a word in you have forgotten what you wanted to say? You probably remember situations like these, but you can do something about them. You will remember names, phone numbers, definitions, and other

---

EXERCISE 8.5 | Computer Application on Technology and Studying

WITHOUT A DOUBT, TECHNOLOGY HAS changed students' college experience for the better. For example, previous generations did not enjoy the benefits of the Internet as a research tool, the convenience of online courses, or the ease and speed of communication made possible by email, text messaging, and cell phone use. But technology can also be a distraction if overused or used inappropriately. Discuss with class members how technology has helped or hindered your performance as a student. Come up with a list of guidelines for using technology in appropriate ways and for avoiding its distractions.

bits of information longer if you recite them or write them down. These actions open sensory pathways into your short-term or "working" memory where you can record the information long enough to use it. Therefore, if you have something important to add to a discussion, jot it down so you won't forget.

Research has shown that short-term memory has a limited capacity. You can hold only about five to nine numbers at a time in your short-term memory. Seven is average for most people. Most phone numbers have seven digits; most zip codes have five digits. You might have difficulty remembering your nine-digit driver's license number or a sixteen-digit credit card number unless you break the number up into "chunks," or meaningful bits of information that are easier to remember. For example, take out a credit card and look at the number. Notice how it is divided into chunks of four numbers each. For security reasons, most companies that have your credit card number on file will ask you only for the last four digits. If you use your card often, you probably have memorized this number. In other words, to make the transfer of information from sensory memory into your working memory takes attention and action. Focus on what you want to remember—a name or a number—then say it a few times. Remember this rhyme: *Recitation and repetition aid recording and retention.*

EXERCISE 8.6 Work Your "Working" Memory

Imagine that you are at a party surrounded by strangers. Near the end of the evening, you have met many people and have learned a great deal about them. How much can you remember? Study the facts about the people listed below for three or four minutes. Then cover up the facts and try to answer the questions. If you prefer, you can do this exercise with a partner. Take turns timing each other and asking the questions.

Name:	Matt	Claudia	Bill
Age:	34	29	23
Eye color:	Brown	Blue	Brown
Favorite book:	*The Da Vinci Code*	*Twilight*	*Digital Fortress*
Favorite place:	Disney World	Grand Canyon	Wind River
Favorite film:	*Quantum of Solace*	*Casablanca*	*The Matrix*
Favorite activity:	Traveling	Hiking	Blogging
Favorite color:	Purple	Red	Sky blue

1. Whose favorite activity is hiking? _____
2. How old is Matt? _____
3. Who has blue eyes? _____
4. Who loves to travel? _____
5. Who would love to hike in the Grand Canyon? _____
6. Who is the youngest? _____

Now uncover the facts and check your answers. How accurate was your short-term memory? If you got fewer than three answers right, you probably did not use a memory aid such as recitation or grouping of similar items. For example, did you notice that Claudia's favorite activity, hiking, could be done at her favorite place, the Grand Canyon? Bill's favorite book, film, and activity are all related too.

Recording information in your short-term memory takes concentration. To help you focus your attention, build background for new ideas or concepts, relate what you are trying to remember to something that you already know. Placing new information in a familiar context not only makes it easier to remember but also establishes a mental network that you can expand with related concepts as you learn.

Suppose you have been assigned a chapter on stress in your psychology text. Before reading, assess your prior knowledge. Ask yourself what stress means to you. Imagine yourself in stressful situations, and recall what you have done to overcome stress. If you have not successfully managed stress in the past, the chapter may suggest a new method to try. Read to find out whether the author's ideas about stress confirm what you already know or give you new information.

Now here are some more tips to improve recording:

▼ Become more attentive and observant. Stay alert in class and manage your distractions.

▼ Engage as many of your senses as possible. During a lecture, *look* at the speaker. *Listen* attentively to what he or she says. *Take notes* to help you remember. These strategies make full use of your visual, auditory, and tactile senses.

▼ Ask questions, as needed, to aid understanding. Remember: *You can't recall what you don't understand.* Make sure that you understand the information.

▼ Before you read a textbook chapter, survey (or preview) it to get an overview of its content and to establish a purpose for reading. This step is especially helpful when the chapter covers a topic that is new to you. As you will see in Chapter 9, surveying is the first step in the SQ3R study system: *survey, question, read, recite,* and *review.*

Long-Term Memory: Retain and Recall

Your short-term memory lets you hold information for a brief time so that you can work with it. What makes it possible for you to follow a lecture, keep up your end of a discussion, or read without losing your place? That's your short-term memory at work with a little bit of help from selective attention. But what if you need to retain a chemistry formula, the rules for solving an algebra problem, or the details of a famous experiment explained in your psychology textbook? This information will have to be transferred from your short-term memory to your long-term memory and stored there. If the transference is successful, you will be able to retrieve the information when needed to answer an exam question or complete an assignment. Think of your long-term memory as a computer that contains the files of all the information you have saved. As you add new information, you update your files. Information that you don't use a lot gets deleted. Information that you forget to save gets lost. Like a computer, your long-term memory is only as good as its programmer—that's you.

Long-term memory has a vast capacity, is more or less permanent, and retains information such as learned skills and personal experiences.

Long-term memory is more or less permanent and can hold a vast amount of information—everything from names, dates, facts, and images to learned skills and personal experiences. Stored information falls into three categories. *Verbal information* comes from books and other printed sources. Verbal information that is oral, such as music or a lecture, is transmitted through your auditory sense. To improve retention of verbal information, become an active reader and listener. *Visual information* includes everything you see—paintings and other artwork, photographs, dance, the world around you. To improve retention of visual information, become more observant, attentive, and involved in what you are learning. *Physical and motor information* includes things you learn by doing: writing, drawing, participating in sports, and operating machines, for example. To improve retention of physical and motor information, practice new skills or activities until they become automatic.

Do you see a relationship between the categories of stored information and learning style? Which kind of information is easiest for you to remember? Which is the hardest? For example, some visual learners may find it easier to remember visual information than physical or motor information. Imagine a person who is learning to drive a vehicle with a standard transmission. Whereas a strongly tactile/kinesthetic learner would be able to feel or sense where the gears are, a strongly visual learner would do better with a diagram that illustrates the positions of the gears. You can see in this example that the diagram enables the visual learner to adapt to a physical learning task. As explained in Chapter 2, you can find effective ways to learn any kind of information, no matter what your learning style is.

Some information—your name, your birthplace, your birthday—you remember for life. Such information is part of you, although you may not remember when you first learned it. You retain other information—the multiplication tables, how to ride a bicycle—through use or practice. With enough practice, some skills become *internalized*, meaning that we know how to do them so well that they seem automatic. Swinging a golf club or tennis racquet, pitching a baseball, doing the backstroke, driving a car, and cooking a meal are a few examples of internalized skills. You do not easily forget information that you have internalized. Like your name, it has become part of you.

Bike riding is one example of a skill internalized in long-term memory.

Don Mason (RF)/Jupiter Images

Anything you really want to learn is going to stay with you because you are motivated to remember it. The key to retaining academic information is to first *make a conscious effort to remember* and then use an active learning strategy. Here are some ways to make retention an active and effective process:

▸ **Motivate yourself.** *Why* you study is as important as *what* you study. You will be more attentive, more receptive to learning, if you have a goal—even if it's simply a desire for a better grade. Try to get beyond the immediate reward of a good grade. Instead, think about what you are studying and how the skills you are learning will bring you closer to your goals.

▸ **Listen and read actively.** Before a lecture and before reading, assess your prior knowledge about the topic as an aid to comprehension. During a lecture or reading, concentrate, ignore distractions, take notes, and think critically about the ideas and their meaning. During your review, reflect on what you have learned and try to think of practical ways to apply it.

▸ **Recite and review.** Reciting aloud during review activates your aural sense and opens another pathway into your brain. The more senses you involve, the greater will be your retention. Review immediately after studying and frequently thereafter. Schedule daily and weekly reviews so that you don't have to cram before an exam. Cramming isn't learning. Although you may pick up a few points on a test by cramming the night before, you will quickly forget the information.

▸ **Do all assigned work and then some.** The more you use new information and practice new skills, the more you will retain. Frequent practice helps you internalize rules and procedures.

What happens when you try to remember a date, a name, a concept, or a procedure for working an algebra problem? Just as you would open a file on your computer, you will search through the stored knowledge in your long-term memory and try to recall the information you need. For some information, recall is immediate: Frequently

Memory cues are triggers that aid your recall.

dialed numbers and your zip code are two examples. If you've ever had trouble remembering a name or one of the steps required to solve a math problem, then you have experienced recollection in action. Your brain is searching for the information much as a computer searches through files.

Why are essay questions more difficult to answer than multiple-choice questions? The essay question requires you to construct your answer from memory without any help (Bloom's categories of analysis and synthesis). The multiple-choice question lists several answer choices, some of which will contain **memory cues**—certain words, phrases, or ideas that act as triggers to help you recognize the correct answer (Bloom's categories of knowledge and comprehension). To improve recollection, try these suggestions:

▸ **Prepare for tests.** Study and review to ensure understanding. Do not memorize your notes. Instead, recite from your notes in your own words or discuss concepts with a study partner or group. This may help you recognize concepts when you see them in different contexts.

▸ **Choose your memory cues.** Use key words to recall concepts. For example, can you describe the characteristics of a reachable goal as explained in Chapter 4? Two key words are *realistic* and *flexible*. Do you remember any others? A diagram can also serve as a memory cue. Study the diagram; then picture it in your mind to recall the process it illustrates.

▸ **Study similar subjects separately.** When two subjects are similar, you may confuse their concepts, and doing this can cause problems at both the storage and retrieval stages of memory. Because your understanding is incomplete, your recall will be sketchy as well. To avoid this problem, do not study for two similar courses back to back. In other words, put a little mental distance between the two similar courses so that you don't confuse their concepts.

▸ **Make and take practice tests.** Practice is the key to long-term retention. Anticipate test questions and quiz yourself. Better yet, study with a partner and quiz each other.

In conclusion, retaining information in your long-term memory requires your active involvement, a desire to remember, and regular practice. Actions such as using study systems, reciting and reviewing, and making study guides all help you to retain and recall what you have learned.

Forgetting and Remembering

Forgetting is not only normal, it's also necessary. If you never forgot anything, your mind would be so crammed with useless information that you wouldn't be able to think. Do you remember the addresses of every place you have lived or the names of everyone you have ever met? Obviously, you don't. Information that you stop using soon passes out of your memory unless it has special significance. *Your mind stores only what you need and discards the rest.* In fact, even when you have made a serious attempt to learn something new, forgetting starts within an hour. After several days, you remember very little of the new information unless you take action to combat forgetting.

The three Rs of memory—record, retain, and recall—work throughout the three stages of memory to help you combat forgetting. Your *sensory memory*, *short-term memory*, and *long-term memory* determine what you remember and for how long. As you now know, you have some control over the way your memory processes information. Figure 8.3 on the next page illustrates the process. Now read the next section for some specific tips and strategies to combat forgetting and boost your memory.

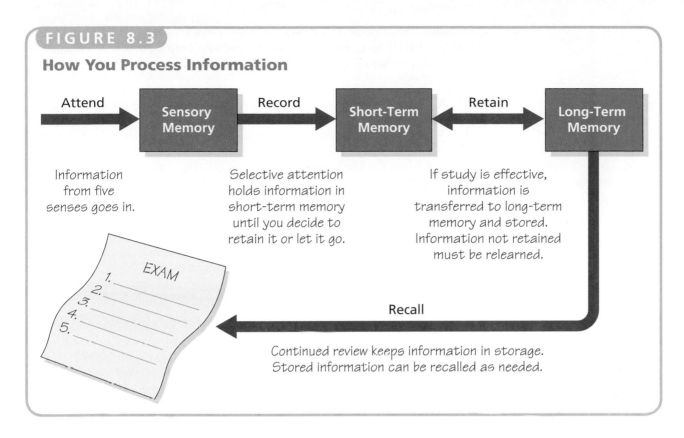

FIGURE 8.3

How You Process Information

Attend → **Sensory Memory** → Record → **Short-Term Memory** ↔ Retain ↔ **Long-Term Memory**

Information from five senses goes in.

Selective attention holds information in short-term memory until you decide to retain it or let it go.

If study is effective, information is transferred to long-term memory and stored. Information not retained must be relearned.

EXAM
1.
2.
3.
4.
5.

Recall

Continued review keeps information in storage. Stored information can be recalled as needed.

Power Your Memory: 10 Tips

- Use common memory techniques to focus your study and enhance learning.

The strategies that follow have worked for many students. Perhaps you already use some of them, or maybe you'll discover a new technique to try.

▼ **Decide to remember.** Resist passivity. Become an active learner by making a conscious, deliberate decision to remember. Follow through on this decision. This is the most important step you can take. Unless you *decide* to remember, none of the other techniques will work.

▼ **Review regularly.** Don't wait until the last minute before a test to do your reviewing. If you try to cram at the last minute, you may be forced to memorize isolated facts. Any information is difficult to understand, much less remember, outside of a meaningful context. By reviewing often, you are more likely to remember both the meaning and significance of what you have learned, and this will aid your recall.

▼ **Stay relaxed.** When you are studying for a test or doing an assignment that is difficult and frustrating, it is normal to become tense. However, stress is a distraction that can interfere with learning. Practice the desktop relaxation technique explained in this chapter's *Confidence Builder*. Also, see Chapter 13 for more information on how to manage stress.

▼ **Combine review with a physical activity.** Each sensory pathway that you open aids retention. Recite, either silently or aloud, while riding a bicycle, doing

Concept Check 8.2

How does stress affect your ability to study? If you are feeling anxious, does your classroom performance suffer? What ways have you found to reduce the stress that is associated with being in an academic setting where you are expected to achieve?

aerobics or calisthenics (floor exercises like sit-ups and jumping jacks), and while walking and running. Feel good about yourself for keeping fit *and* exercising your mind. This technique works well for anyone but is especially good for student athletes.

Mnemonics (ne-MON-ix) are memory strategies that involve linking something you want to learn with something you already know. They include rhymes and acronyms.

▼ **Use mnemonics. Mnemonics** can be games, rhymes, lists of words, or letters in a certain order that aid memory. You may know the rhyme that begins with "Thirty days hath September" to help you remember the number of days in each month. Here is one that you probably haven't heard: "Tyranny nixed in '76." This rhyme recalls the year the Declaration of Independence was signed. A sentence in which the first letter of each word or the words themselves might serve as memory cues is another kind of mnemonic. Have you ever heard this one? "The quick brown fox jumped over the lazy dog." This sentence helps people learn to type faster. By typing the sentence over and over without looking at the keyboard, you will soon memorize the positions of the letters, and this helps increase your speed. An acronym is another kind of mnemonic. Perhaps when you were taught about the Great Lakes your teacher used HOMES to help you remember Huron, Ontario, Michigan, Erie, and Superior. Each of the letters helps trigger your memory for the first letter of a lake's name.

An **Acronym** is a word or expression made from the first letters of a group of words that stand for something. CPR is an acronym that stands for "cardio-pulmonary resuscitation."

▼ **Use acronyms.** An **acronym** is a word formed by the first letters of other words. COPE, a problem-solving method, and GRAB, a time-management technique, are just two examples of acronyms used in *The Confident Student.* You probably know many others such as ASAP, a business acronym that means "as soon as possible," and NASA which stands for National Aeronautics and Space Administration. An acronym may help you remember the steps in a process. Choose a key word to remind you of each step. Then, using the first letter of each key word, create your own acronym.

Association is a memory aid whereby you connect a familiar idea with a new idea.

▼ **Associate to remember. Association** is the process of connecting new information that you want to remember to something that you already know. An association is often personal. For example, a student who wanted to remember the particles of the atom—proton, electron, and neutron—associated the names of the particles with the names of her brothers—Paul, Eric, and Norman. Her brothers' names and the particle names begin with the same letters, and they form the acronym *PEN.*

To recall the three stages of memory, you could associate the mind with a computer and associate the three Rs of memory (record, retain, and recall) with three computer processes (input, storage, and output). If your instructor asks you to describe the three stages of memory, think of how a computer works, and you should be able to recall the three Rs and relate them to the way your sensory memory, short-term memory, and long-term memory work to process information. Similarly, try to think of some familiar process, object, or situation to associate with any new knowledge that you want to retain.

Visualization involves forming a mental picture or image to associate with something you want to remember.

▼ **Visualize.** Form an image, or picture, in your mind of something that you want to remember. **Visualization** is an especially good way to link names with places or parts with locations. In geography, visualize places on a map. In physical science, draw an idealized continent that could stand for any continent and fill in climate zones. When reviewing this information or recalling it during a test, picture the continent and visualize the zones. In anatomy, label the bones on a drawing of a human skeleton. When reviewing or recalling, close your eyes and see the skeleton with your labels.

▼ **Sleep on it.** Reviewing before sleep helps you retain information. Because you are relaxed, your concentration is focused. The information stays in your mind while you are sleeping, and interference from conflicting sounds, images, or ideas is minimal. When you wake, try to recall what you reviewed the night before. Chances are good that you will remember.

▶ **Dump Data.** Suppose you have an upcoming exam and you know that some of the questions may require you to remember the names of people or places, dates, steps in a process, mathematical rules, formulas, or other material. As soon as you get your test paper, dump your data: Jot down some memory cues or key words in the margin that will help aid your recall. Because you can get nervous during an exam and forget some of what you've learned, the data dump is a hedge against forgetting.

You might be thinking, "What about memorization?" This too is a legitimate memory strategy, although some educators have reservations about memorization. Critics say that memorization is not learning because it is usually done out of context or in order to cram for an exam. Students may not be able to recall items memorized in a certain order if the instructor puts them in a different order on a test. Critics also say that memorization is an inefficient technique and that memorized items are difficult to recall. Yet memorization does work for learning some kinds of information. What is nine times nine? You probably know the answer.

Memorization can be a useful technique, especially if it is combined with another memory strategy and is not the only technique you know how to use. Of course, you cannot expect to remember anything that you do not understand. First, make sure you comprehend any new information well enough to link it to knowledge you have already acquired. Memorization works best on information such as the spelling and definition of words, math and chemical formulas, poetry, and facts that belong in a certain order—such as historical events, life cycles, or food chains.

To review the three Rs of memory and how they work through the three stages to process information, see Figure 8.4.

FIGURE 8.4

The Stages of Memory Compared

Stages of Memory	What is it?	How does it work?	How long does it last?
SENSORY MEMORY	Registers all perceptions, both internal and external	Through your five senses: sight, sound, smell, taste, and touch	Automatic from second to second; forgetting is almost immediate
SHORT-TERM "WORKING" MEMORY	Enables you to focus on and record specific ideas or images long enough to work with them	Through selective attention, some information is saved and some is discarded	For a short time, up to two minutes, then quickly lost
LONG-TERM MEMORY	Enables you to retain ideas or images transferred from short-term memory so they can be recalled later	By integrating new information with your stored knowledge	Up to an hour before forgetting sets in, but with review, practice, and use, ideas and images last indefinitely

CRITICAL THINKING

Choose Your Best Strategy

Exercise Overview

This exercise will help you practice selecting appropriate memory strategies and memory aids.

Exercise Background

As explained in this chapter, memory is a three-stage process by which the brain takes in information through the senses and sorts it either for discarding or storage. You can manage this process by deciding to remember, by concentrating, and by using various active learning techniques, strategies, or aids that enhance memory. What this means is that learning and remembering are not random acts. You have the power to improve the way you learn.

Exercise Task

Listed next are some typical learning activities required of college students. Choose one that you think may be difficult for you. Then review the memory strategies explained in this chapter. Using the questions that follow the list, decide which strategy would best help you complete the activity. Write your answers on your own paper and then share them in a class discussion.

- Reading a chapter from a biology textbook
- Listening to a lecture
- Taking notes from a lecture
- Learning the names of the bones of the human body
- Matching the names of artists with examples of their work
- Solving an equation that has two unknowns

1. Which activity did you choose, and why do you think it may be difficult for you?

2. Does the activity require you to process verbal, visual, or physical/motor information?

3. What memory strategy will help you *record* the information, and how?

4. What memory strategy would improve your ability to *retain* the information, and how?

5. What memory strategy would improve your ability to *recall* the information, and how?

Guided CHAPTER REVIEW

The following checklist summarizes this chapter's key terms and strategies. After reading the chapter, how confident are you that you can apply the information you have learned? To assess your level of confidence, respond to each statement with one of the following: *very confident* (3 points), *fairly confident* (2 points), *not very confident* (1 point), *not confident* (0 points). Write your number of points in the box beside each statement. Then add your score and read the analysis that follows. When you have finished, take the chapter quiz.

SUMMARY CHECK

How confident are you about applying these strategies?

Points

1. Understanding the role attention and attitude play in learning and memory
2. Knowing what you can do to take control of your attention
3. Eliminating or minimizing your internal and external distractions
4. Knowing the characteristics of a good study environment
5. Finding your own best place to study
6. Understanding the three Rs of memory and how they help you process information
7. Knowing what happens at each stage of memory
8. Understanding why you forget and what you can do about it
9. Being able to choose among the 10 memory tips the ones that will best aid your retention and recall

How confident is your understanding of this chapter's key terms?

10. concentration
11. internal distractions
12. external distractions
13. memory
14. record
15. retain
16. recall
17. sensory memory
18. selective attention
19. short-term memory
20. long-term memory
21. memory cues
22. mnemonics

☐   23. acronym

☐   24. association

☐   25. visualization

Total

Add your score. The highest possible score is 75. The closer your score is to 75, the higher your level of confidence. Use your *Summary Check* results to help you determine which parts of the chapter to review.

YOUR WEBSITE RESOURCES

This chapter's resources include the following items. To access them, go to The Confident Student premium website.

- **Video Skillbuilder: "Memory Strategies"**
- **Chapter Exercises**
- **Forms to Download**
- **Chapter Summary of Topics**
- **Thinking Ahead About Career**
- **Confidence Builder Web Search**
- **Self-Test**
- **Article: *"Internal/External Distractions"***

CHAPTER REVIEW Quiz

Answer the following questions from memory. Then return to the chapter to check your answers. As a final activity, complete *Show Your Confidence* at the end of the quiz.

1. What is the value of the desktop relaxation technique as it applies to concentration and memory?

_____

_____

2. What is the difference between an internal and an external distraction? Give an example of each.

_____

_____

3. What effect does your attitude have on concentration and memory?

_____

_____

4. This chapter explains several characteristics of a good study environment. Explain at least two of the characteristics and why they are important.

_____

_____

5. What is one of the active learning strategies explained in this chapter that you have used successfully and would recommend to a friend?

_____

_____

6. What can you do to improve your ability to record, retain, or recall information? Choose one of the three Rs of memory and explain what you would do.

_____

_____

7. At what stage of memory is it possible for information to last a lifetime? Give two or more examples of your own lifetime memories.

_____

_____

8. What is your sensory memory?

_____

_____

9. Why do we forget some things and not others?

_____

_____

10. What is a mnemonic? Give an example.

_____

_____

SHOW YOUR CONFIDENCE

This chapter is about the relationship between attention and memory. A major point made in the chapter is that both concentration and memory can be managed and controlled. Do you agree or disagree? What success, or lack of success, have you had with maintaining your attention while studying or being able to recall information or construct good answers to test questions? Be prepared to share your opinions either in writing or in class discussion.

YOUR REFLECTIONS: YOUR MEMORY IS YOUR EXPERIENCE

Reflect on what you have learned from this chapter about attention, attitude, memory, and how they shape your experience of what you know and are able to remember. Use the following questions to stimulate your thinking; then write your reflections. Include in your writing specific information from the chapter.

- What in your life or in your courses gets most of your attention, and why?
- After reading this chapter, is your attitude toward memory and learning positive or negative, and why?
- What is one thing you learned from this chapter that you think will be most helpful to you, and why?

_____

_____

9 Creating Your Study System

SimoJarratt/Corbis (RF)/Jupiter Images

This chapter encourages you to:

- Identify and use the common parts of textbooks and chapters as convenient learning and study aids.

- Learn the role that textbook graphics play, and follow guidelines for reading graphics with understanding.

- Start with a basic system like SQ3R and adapt it to your learning style.

- Meet the reading demands of all your courses by knowing what to study in the different academic disciplines.

Confident students are **committed**. They have pledged their time and effort to learn and will do what it takes to improve their performance.

How often do you finish reading a textbook chapter wondering what you were supposed to learn? How often do you skip a table, chart, or diagram either because you don't think it's important or because you're in a hurry to get done? If your answer to these questions is "frequently" or "all the time," then you probably also have trouble deciding what to study and are often unprepared for tests. You can turn all this around by studying with a system. Adopt a proven system such as SQ3R, which is explained in this chapter, or create a system that fits your learning style and meets your course requirements.

As explained in Chapter 2, not everyone learns in exactly the same way. Students' preferred learning styles, most productive times of day, and favorite study environments differ. Whatever your preferences, you will learn more and retain information longer if you are actively involved in the process. A **study system** focuses your attention on certain parts of a textbook or chapter where the most important information is contained. A good study system employs active learning strategies such as questioning and note-taking.

Reading and study require your commitment. No study system will work unless you work at using it. One way to commit yourself to improving your grades and performance in all your courses is to become **proactive** about studying. The following *Confidence Builder* explains how.

Study system refers to the learning strategies or a process used to access information from reading. One example of a study system is SQ3R.

Proactive is a term from the world of business that means to take initiative and accept responsibility for what happens. People who are proactive try to foresee problems that could arise, and they take preventive action.

CONFIDENCE BUILDER

Be Proactive About Studying

Stephen R. Covey, author of *The Seven Habits of Highly Effective People*, says that people are either proactive or reactive in their responses to life's circumstances. *Proactive* people take initiative and accept responsibility for what happens to them. *Reactive* people lack initiative; instead of taking responsibility for what happens, they blame other people or outside events. The first and most important of Covey's seven suggested habits is to *be proactive*. Being proactive means being in control of how you feel, what you think, and what you do. Being proactive means accepting responsibility for your own success or failure. Being proactive also means choosing your actions, accepting the consequences, and modifying your behavior as needed to achieve success.

When it comes to studying, are you *reactive* or *proactive*? Language is a key. The language of reactive people, according to Covey, relieves them of responsibility. For example, if you say, "I can't make a good grade in that class," what you are really saying is that you are not responsible. Rather, someone or something is preventing you from making good grades in the class. If you say, "I don't have time to study" instead of managing your time, you are allowing the

factor of limited time to control you. If you say, "I have to study," then you mean that you are not free to choose this action; instead, someone or something is forcing you to do it.

To be proactive about studying, you must first take control of your language. The following is an example of how language can either limit or expand your horizons. When you say, "I can't make a good grade in that class," you convince yourself that there is no reason to try. As a result, you give up. You stop studying. The belief that you can't make a good grade becomes a self-fulfilling prophecy. But if you become proactive and instead say, "I *choose* to make good grades in that class," then you realize that grades are the result of your own decisions and your own effort. You can then accurately assess what your strengths and weaknesses are and choose appropriate study systems or learning strategies that will get you the results you want.

The following chart lists reactive statements about studying and their proactive counterparts. Use the chart to assess your own "self-talk." Ask yourself, "Am I reactive or proactive?" Then take steps to change your reactive language and behavior as needed.

continued

Reactive Statements	Proactive Statements
I don't have time to study.	I can make time for studying.
I have to study.	I can choose whether, when, and how to study.
I must pass this test.	I will study and do my best to pass this test.
I'm just no good at math.	I can improve my math skills.
I can't understand this chapter.	I will use a study system to understand this chapter.
My instructor gave me a B on the test.	I earned a B on the test.

How does Covey's advice, *be proactive*, relate to motivation? Those who are externally motivated are *reactive* because they expect others to motivate them. Those who are internally motivated are *proactive* because they are self-motivated. How does proactivity relate to goal setting, time management, and problem solving? In every case, the proactive response of selecting a desired outcome and taking the steps necessary to achieve it puts *you* in control of your life and learning. With control comes confidence and increased self-esteem.

Follow Up: To explore this topic further, visit *The Confident Student* premium website for an online search activity about Stephen R. Covey's books and ideas.

SQ3R: The Basic System

- Identify and use the common parts of textbooks and chapters as convenient learning and study aids.

It's easy to see why students who don't read textbook assignments make poor grades. It may be a little harder to see why students who *do* read all assigned material may still not make the grades they want. There is a big difference between reading and studying. You can't merely read a chapter from first word to last and expect to retain the information. Instead, read *actively* by underlining, making notes, asking questions mentally, and then looking for the answers. Studying with a system guides your reading so that you can find the information you need to complete assignments and prepare for tests.

Perhaps you've heard of **SQ3R**. Developed by Francis P. Robinson in 1941, SQ3R is a classic system that millions of students have used successfully to improve their reading and studying. SQ3R is not just a study system; it is a recipe for active learning that includes these five steps: *Survey, Question, Read, Recite,* and *Review*. Before you read about these steps in detail, take *Awareness Check* 9.1 to find out whether you are currently getting the most that you can from your textbooks.

SQ3R is an acronym that stands for *survey, question, read, recite, review*. SQ3R is a study system that promotes active reading and learning.

Survey Books and Chapters

A **survey** is a quick review or brief overview of an entire textbook or a single chapter. A survey is intended to give you the big picture—what the book or chapter covers. Surveying a book or chapter before you read helps you build background for the author's ideas and also helps you assess your prior knowledge on the topics covered. You can survey a textbook in about ten minutes, and you need to do it only once to determine what it covers and what helpful aids it contains. This knowledge will help you begin your courses with confidence. Surveying also has a practical advantage beyond the classroom: You can survey *any* book that you are thinking of buying. To survey a work of fiction, read the title and the plot summary to get an idea of what it

Survey means "preview" or "overview." The first step of SQ3R is to take a quick survey of a book or chapter to see what it covers.

AWARENESS CHECK 9.1

Are You Using Your Textbooks Efficiently?

Part I

Can you identify and use the parts of a textbook? Match the textbook parts in Column A to their functions in Column B.

Column A

_____ 1. title page

_____ 2. copyright page

_____ 3. contents

_____ 4. introduction

_____ 5. glossary

_____ 6. index

_____ 7. appendix

_____ 8. bibliography

Column B

A. contains supplementary material

B. lists topics, terms, names of people, and their page numbers

C. tells when a book was published

D. lists chapter titles, main headings, and page numbers

E. lists author's sources or references

F. tells author's purpose for writing the book

G. identifies title, author, and publisher

H. contains terms and definitions

Part II

Can you identify and use the common parts of most textbook chapters? Match the chapter parts in Column A to their functions in Column B.

Column A

_____ 1. title

_____ 2. introduction

_____ 3. heading

_____ 4. graphic aid

_____ 5. summary

_____ 6. questions and exercises

Column B

A. restates and condenses author's ideas

B. helps explain or illustrate

C. identifies overall topic covered

D. used for review or skill practice

E. identifies section topic or main idea

F. states author's purpose and gives overview

Part III

Do you have a study system? Respond yes or no to the following statements.

Yes   No

☐   ☐   1. When I sit down to read or study, I often have trouble getting started.

☐   ☐   2. My studying is hit or miss. I don't have any set way to study; I do it when and if I have time.

continued

3. I underline or highlight when I read.

4. I know how to tell what is important in a chapter.

Check your answers to Part I: 1. G, 2. C, 3. D, 4. F, 5. H, 6. B, 7. A, 8. E. The answers to Part II are: 1. C, 2. F, 3. E, 4. B, 5. A, 6. D. In Part III, if you checked yes for either statement 1 or 2 and no for either statement 3 or 4, you will benefit from learning how to use a study system.

is about. The plot summary appears on the back of a paperback or inside the jacket of a hardcover book. Read any comments from reviewers to find out what they think of the book. Read the first paragraph to see if the author's style and subject matter arouse your interest. Your survey will help you determine whether you want to read the book. You can also survey books online at sites like http://www.amazon.com or http://www.barnesandnoble.com.

Surveying also has a practical application in the workplace, where reading books, manuals, reports, and other materials may be required. Surveying printed or online resources is a quick way to assess their importance or usefulness.

How to Survey a Textbook. Survey a textbook one time only—as soon as you buy it—before the first chapter is assigned. Then you can start the class with an advantage: You will already know what topics the course is likely to cover. You will also have determined which of the eight common parts your textbook has and how they may be useful to you. For example, if you are taking a biology course and you find out by surveying your textbook that the book has a glossary, then you know that you will be able to save time while studying. It is much quicker and easier to look up specialized terms in a glossary than in a dictionary. Also, glossary definitions fit the author's use of terms within the context of a book's subject matter.

Before you sign up for a course, visit the campus bookstore to survey the text the instructor has chosen. This will enable you to see what the course will cover and whether the level of the material is suited to your background and skills.

Bill Aron/PhotoEdit

To survey a textbook, examine its parts in the order in which they appear as you leaf through the book from beginning to end. Exercise 9.1 below will allow you to practice this skill. Figure 9.1 on the next page lists features common to most textbooks, their purposes, and questions to ask during your survey. Your answers to the survey questions will give you a good idea of what the book covers.

How to Survey a Textbook Chapter. Survey a chapter before you read it for the first time. Then resurvey chapters that you are reviewing for a major exam. Resurveying material that you have not read for a while will refresh your memory. Your chapter

---

EXERCISE 9.1 Practice Surveying Textbooks

BORROW A TEXTBOOK FROM A friend who is taking a course that you plan to take. Survey the textbook from beginning to end and then respond to the following items. Use Figure 9.1 for reference if necessary.

Book Title: _____

Name of Course: _____

1. **Can you tell from the title and introduction whether the book is an introductory text or an advanced text? Explain your answer.**

   _____

   _____

2. **How current is the information in the text? In what part of the book did you find your answer?**

   _____

   _____

3. **What is the author's purpose? In what part of the book did you find your answer?**

   _____

   _____

4. **Where are chapters listed? Write the title of a chapter whose topic interests you.**

   _____

   _____

5. **Does the book contain a glossary? If so, on what page does it begin?**

   _____

   _____

6. **Does the book contain a bibliography? If so, on what page does it begin?**

   _____

   _____

FIGURE 9.1

Survey Your Textbook: Questions to Ask and Answer

Textbook Feature	Purpose	Questions to Ask and Answer
Title Page	Lists title, author, publisher	• What is the book's topic? • Who published the book? • What are the author's qualifications (degree or college affiliation)?
Copyright Page	Lists publication date	• How current is the information? • What edition is the book?
Introduction	States author's purpose and intended audience	• Why did the author write the book? • What are readers expected to learn? • Is the book for beginning students or more advanced students?
Contents	Lists the book's parts and chapters	• How many chapters are there? • What topics are covered? • What do I already know about these topics?
Glossary*	Contains an alphabetical listing of terms and definitions	• Is there a glossary? • Is it a single list or are terms sorted by chapter?
Appendix*	Contains tables or other supplemental materials	• Does the book contain an appendix? • What kind of information does it contain?
Bibliography*	Lists author's source material	• Is there a bibliography or list of references? • How extensive is the list? • What kinds of resources are listed?
Index	Lists topics alphabetically and page numbers where they can be found	• Where is the index? • How many pages does it contain?

*May not be present in some textbooks

survey will not take long, it will focus your attention, and it will help you determine a purpose for reading. To survey a chapter, examine its parts in the order in which they appear. Figure 9.2 on page 220 lists the parts of most chapters, their purposes, and questions to ask during your survey. Your answers to the questions will give you a good idea of what the chapter covers. In addition, complete Exercise 9.2, a collaborative activity that will teach you how to survey a textbook chapter.

Surveying helps you make assumptions about what a chapter covers. It is a pre-reading activity that focuses your attention on a topic. By relating the topic to what you already know, you prepare yourself for the next step in the SQ3R system: asking questions to guide your reading.

Question As You Read

During your chapter survey, as you read each heading, turn it into a question. The heading of a section identifies the topic covered in that section and may serve as a clue to the author's main idea. For example, here are three questions you could ask about the heading "How to Improve Concentration."

FIGURE 9.2

Survey Each Chapter: Questions to Ask and Answer

Chapter Feature	Purpose	Questions to Ask and Answer
Chapter Title	States the chapter topic	• What is the chapter about? • What do I already know about this topic?
Objectives or Learning Goals*	List what you are expected to learn	• What does the author want me to learn? • What should I be able to do after reading this chapter?
Introduction	Explains the author's purpose and central idea and builds background for the topic	• Why did the author write the chapter? • What is the central idea? • Why is this information important?
Headings and Subheadings	Reveal the author's outline of the topic and show how the ideas are related	• How is the chapter organized? • What questions do the headings raise in my mind? • Which topics arouse my interest?
Graphics	Illustrate topics or key ideas, add visual impact	• Does the chapter contain photographs? • Are there tables, diagrams, and other visual or graphic aids?
Key Words or Terms*	Call attention to terms of the discipline you are expected to learn and use	• Is there a list of terms at the beginning or the end of the chapter? • Are these terms new or familiar to me?
Summary*	Provides an overview of the chapter's key ideas	• Does the chapter contain a summary? • Is the summary a paragraph or a list of topics?
Exercises	Help you apply new knowledge to write, discuss, or solve problems	• Are exercises or problems at the end of the chapter or spread throughout? • Are there questions for discussion, writing, or review?

*May not be present in the chapters of some textbooks.

Computer CONFIDENCE

Survey to Save Time Online

Surveying is an important prereading step not only for textbooks but also for *any* reading you might do. Surveying before reading on the Internet is yet another practical application of this essential prereading strategy. Whether you are reading your email or researching a topic on the web, surveying is a time-saving first step that will help you sift through irrelevant data to find desired information quickly.

A word of caution: Much of your college reading and studying will come from textbooks and other printed sources. But with more and more materials available electronically, you will also find that you're doing reading and studying online. Because being on the computer can distract you from the task at hand, reserve specific computer time for course-related research and separate that from using your computer as a reward *after* studying.

continued

Survey Email

Log on to the Internet and start your mail program. Any new messages are usually listed by date and time, along with the subject lines of their message headers. Survey the subject lines to determine which messages may be urgent and which ones can wait. Then you can decide which messages to read first, saving the rest for a more convenient time. Surveying email will become more relevant in the workplace, as you will want to look out for messages from your boss or others in a supervisory role before anything else.

Survey Websites

As an information-gathering and communication tool, the World Wide Web provides access to resources located throughout the world's libraries, universities, and research institutions. You can browse these resources in search of books, periodicals, and other materials. Because resources are so extensive and because not all Internet connections provide access to the web, tools such as *search engines* and *web indexes* can help you find information quickly.

A search engine collects, categorizes, and indexes information from web pages, allowing you to generate a list of sites relevant to a subject. You are probably already familiar with Google (http://www.google.com) and Yahoo! (http://www.yahoo.com).

Google evaluates websites and Internet documents based on the number of links to them from other sites, and it is the largest search engine on the web. The sites on any list generated are ranked according to their popularity, so the first few listed may be more useful or reliable. Yahoo! is another popular subject directory that classifies thousands of sites. For most purposes, these two search engines may be all you need. Whatever search engine you use, remember two things: When you use a search engine, you are searching only through that engine's collection of documents, not the entire web. Therefore, it is a good idea to use at least two search engines. Second, a search engine selects documents based on the exact words they contain, so the search words you choose are instrumental in generating a list that is truly useful. Here are some tips for enhancing your use of search engines:

- **Be specific.** A focused search will yield the best results. The more specific your search words are, the more likely it is that your results will accurately reflect what you want. For example, the phrase *abnormal psychology* is too general, but *bipolar disorder* focuses the search on one abnormality. Short phrases are usually better than single words, and a phrase that resembles the title of a book or magazine article may produce the best results. Two good examples are *symptoms of bipolar disorder* and *treatments for bipolar disorder.*

- **Use mathematical symbols.** *For most search engines, using the plus sign will allow you to find pages that contain all the words in your search phrase: bipolar disorder + symptoms + treatments. Use the minus sign to indicate that you don't want to see listings containing a certain word: bipolar disorder − symptoms − treatments.*

- **Use quotation marks.** *If you want listings in which your search words appear in exactly the order you specify, put them in quotation marks: "Walt Disney World resort hotels," "World War Two generals," and "Honda motorcycles" are some examples.*

- **Get to know your search engine.** *If you have a favorite search engine, learn everything you can about its features and how they work. The more you know about a search engine, the more proficient you will become in using it. Most search engines have a Help function that explains their use.*

Not all searches are fruitful. If you don't find exactly what you need at first, keep modifying your search words until you get the results you want. Survey your list, looking for words and phrases in the listings that suggest that a site may contain the information you need.

1. What is concentration?

2. How can I improve my ability to concentrate?

3. Why is concentration so important?

The first question asks you to read for a definition. In Bloom's Taxonomy (see Chapter 3), definition questions are at the *knowledge* level. The second question calls for an *application*, which is Bloom's third level of thinking. By asking how you can improve your own concentration, you are looking for ways to use the information. The third question stimulates you to think critically about the value of concentration. In Bloom's Taxonomy, questions about value are at the *evaluation* level. In each case, the three example questions formed from the heading "How to Improve Concentration" provide a focus and a purpose for reading. In your own questioning, challenge your thinking by trying to use all six of Bloom's levels. To review Bloom's Taxonomy, see Chapter 3.

Turning headings into questions guides your reading so that you can find important details and examples. Later, as you read each section carefully, try to find the answers to your guide questions. You may discover that some of your questions are off topic; but even if they are, you will win. Right or wrong, your questions can help you follow the author's ideas and correct errors in your comprehension.

EXERCISE 9.2 | Collaborative Activity on Surveying Textbook Chapters

THE PURPOSE OF THIS EXERCISE is for you to practice surveying a textbook chapter with group members. Follow the guidelines for group discussion that appear on the inside back cover. Your tasks are as follows: Select from *The Confident Student* a chapter that you have not yet read. Each person must survey the chapter and write answers to items 1–7 within a time limit of 10 minutes. Let one group member serve as timekeeper. Discuss your answers and compile the best ones on a separate sheet of paper to be handed in along with the group evaluation. Or you can visit *The Confident Student* premium website to download the form.

Chapter Title: _____

1. **What are the chapter goals or objectives?**

   _____

   _____

2. **According to the introductory section or paragraph, how will the information contained in this chapter help you?**

   _____

   _____

3. **List three major headings and turn each one into a question to guide your reading.**

   Heading   **Question**

   _____   _____

   _____   _____

   _____   _____

continued

4. How many visual aids are there? What kind?

   _____

   _____

5. List two key words or terms that you should remember.

   _____

   _____

6. List a major point that is emphasized in the summary.

   _____

   _____

7. What skill or topic is covered in the first exercise?

   _____

   _____

Group Evaluation:

What have you learned about surveying? Is surveying a strategy that you will use? Why or why not? Did your group complete its tasks successfully? What improvements can you suggest? What additional questions do you have about surveying? How will you find answers to your questions?

Read Actively

We have already talked a lot about active reading in Chapter 7, so this step in the SQ3R system will be very familiar to you. Read slowly and carefully, concentrating on one section at a time. Don't worry about how long you take. Although you may wish you could read faster, it takes time to absorb new ideas. Do not skip unfamiliar words or technical terms. If you can't infer their meanings from context, look them up in the book's glossary or in a dictionary. Then reread the sentence in which each new word appears to make sure that you understand it. Carefully examine each diagram, chart, illustration, table, or other visual aid. Often, ideas that are hard to understand when you first read about them become clear when you see them illustrated in a diagram or other graphic.

After reading, try to determine the main idea of the section. Summarize this idea in a marginal note that will aid your recall when you review. Read through the section again and underline the main idea and key details or examples. If you have difficulty deciding what is important, review Chapter 7 for a complete explanation of how and what to underline or highlight.

If a section seems particularly technical or complex, you may have to read it more than once. You may also have to restate the author's ideas in your own words to get the information into your long-term memory. Chapter 10 explains how to make study guides to aid your recall.

Making notes, underlining or highlighting, and constructing study guides are essential steps of active reading. These activities help you think critically about what you read, they make studying a productive activity, and they enhance memory.

Recite to Focus and Record

Recitation is an essential aid to memory. As explained in Chapter 8, forgetting takes place almost immediately without some intervention on your part. Recitation helps you focus on an idea so that you can record it in your working memory. Continued practice and review will aid the transfer of new information into your long-term memory. After reading a section, try to state—aloud or silently—the important ideas covered in that section. Then scan the section to check your accuracy. If you find this hard to do, you probably have not understood the section and need to reread it. Talking it over with a study partner may also help. You can quiz each other on the section's important ideas as part of your recitation. Continue in this manner—reading, marking, reciting—one section at a time until you finish the chapter. Take breaks from your reading as needed to stay focused.

Review to Aid Retention and Recall

Review a chapter immediately after reading it. One quick way to review it is by resurveying the chapter. Go over any notes you made in the margins and see if they still make sense to you. (Again, refer back to Chapter 7's suggestions about marking up text.) Recite from any underlined or highlighted passages. Also, review a chapter before you take a test. It is a good idea to review a chapter at least once between your first reading and your last pretest review. With practice, you will discover how often you must review a chapter in order to retain the information in your long-term memory. In addition, try these review strategies:

� Answer any end-of-chapter questions even if they have not been assigned. Reading the questions and looking up the answers helps you practice using the ideas or skills you have learned.

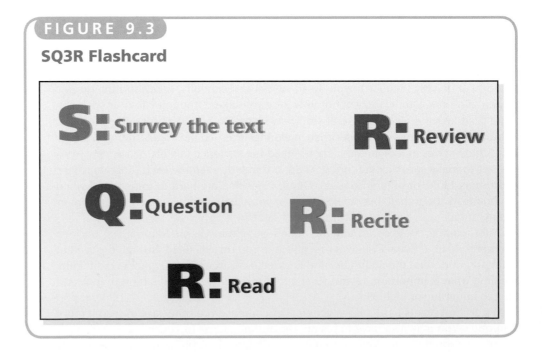

© 2011 Wadsworth, Cengage Learning. All Rights Reserved.

FIGURE 9.3

SQ3R Flashcard

S: Survey the text

R: Review

Q: Question

R: Recite

R: Read

▼ Recite your answers to the questions you asked during the "question step" of SQ3R.

▼ Write your own summary of the chapter. See Chapter 7 for instructions on how to write a summary; then compare your summary to the one printed in the textbook.

▼ Make study guides such as charts or diagrams. Chapter 10 provides plenty of examples.

This concludes our discussion of the SQ3R study system. The system may seem time intensive, but it is a very effective way to master course content. Use the SQ3R flashcard on page 224 to remind you of the steps. Copy this flashcard, cut it out, and place it at your desk or preferred study area. You can also tape it on your favorite notebook or binder. The flashcard may also be downloaded from Chapter 9 on *The Confident Student* premium website.

Understanding Graphics

- Learn the role that textbook graphics play, and follow guidelines for reading graphics with understanding.

Textbooks and other printed sources of information are filled with graphics that are essential to your understanding of what you read. **Graphics** condense and summarize a great deal of information. Graphics illustrate relationships among ideas, and they provide a visual supplement to the text they accompany. Make reading graphics an important part of your study system. Figure 9.4, on pages 226–227, shows five common types of graphics you can learn to recognize.

Graphics are written or pictorial representations of data. Pie charts, line or bar graphs, diagrams, charts, and tables are types of graphics commonly used to illustrate textbooks and other materials.

Circle or "Pie" Charts. Pie charts illustrate part-to-whole relationships. Slices of the pie represent amounts and percentages. The size of each slice in relation to the other slices and to the whole pie indicates its significance. For example, where a student's monthly income goes could be illustrated on a pie chart, with each slice representing a different expenditure.

Bar Graphs. Bar graphs illustrate relationships between *variables*, or quantities, such as time and amount. They also show trends such as an increase or decrease in amount over a period of time. One variable is measured on a vertical axis; the other variable is measured on a horizontal axis.

Line Graphs. Like bar graphs, line graphs illustrate relationships among variables. Trends are represented by lines instead of bars or columns. Voter turnout among different age groups over several presidential elections could be illustrated by either a line graph or a bar graph.

Diagrams. Diagrams are drawings that illustrate functions or processes. A *process diagram* may illustrate the steps and stages of a process or trace a sequence of events. The stages of pregnancy and the events that occur during cell division are two examples. *Function diagrams* illustrate parts of a whole, such as the separate bones of a skeleton.

Concept Check **9.1**

Graphics are used extensively in the workplace for illustrating presentations and reports. What other uses can you think of for graphics?

Tables. Tables are organized lists or rows of numbers or text. They classify and compare large amounts of information or statistical data. A table that lists contraceptive methods and their rates of effectiveness is one example.

FIGURE 9.4

Textbook Graphics: Some Common Types

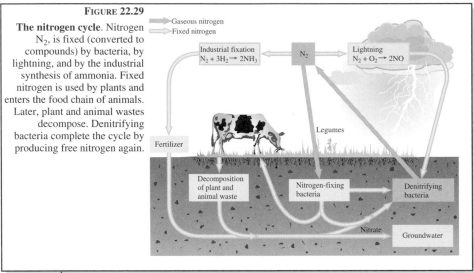

FIGURE 22.29

The nitrogen cycle. Nitrogen N_2, is fixed (converted to compounds) by bacteria, by lightning, and by the industrial synthesis of ammonia. Fixed nitrogen is used by plants and enters the food chain of animals. Later, plant and animal wastes decompose. Denitrifying bacteria complete the cycle by producing free nitrogen again.

Gaseous nitrogen
Fixed nitrogen

Industrial fixation
$N_2 + 3H_2 \rightarrow 2NH_3$

N_2

Lightning
$N_2 + O_2 \rightarrow 2NO$

Fertilizer

Legumes

Decomposition of plant and animal waste

Nitrogen-fixing bacteria

Denitrifying bacteria

Nitrate

Groundwater

diagrams

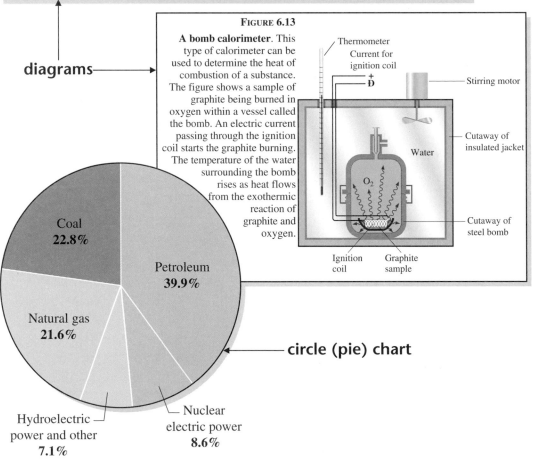

FIGURE 6.13

A bomb calorimeter. This type of calorimeter can be used to determine the heat of combustion of a substance. The figure shows a sample of graphite being burned in oxygen within a vessel called the bomb. An electric current passing through the ignition coil starts the graphite burning. The temperature of the water surrounding the bomb rises as heat flows from the exothermic reaction of graphite and oxygen.

Thermometer

Current for ignition coil

Stirring motor

Water

Cutaway of insulated jacket

O_2

Cutaway of steel bomb

Ignition coil

Graphite sample

Coal
22.8%

Petroleum
39.9%

Natural gas
21.6%

circle (pie) chart

Hydroelectric power and other
7.1%

Nuclear electric power
8.6%

Figures from Darrell Ebbing and Steven D. Gammon, *General Chemistry*, Ninth Edition. Copyright © 2010 by Cengage Learning. Reprinted by permission of Brooks Cole/Cengage Learning.

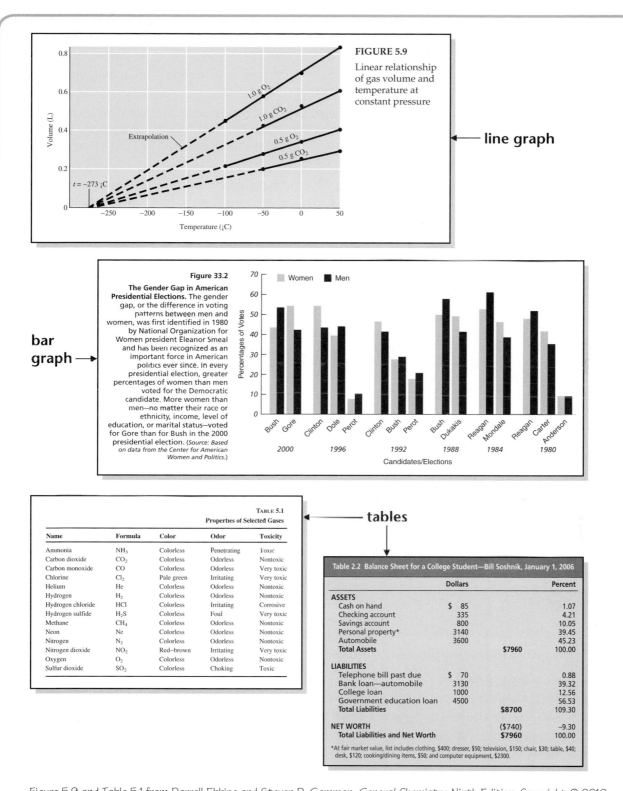

FIGURE 5.9
Linear relationship of gas volume and temperature at constant pressure

line graph

Figure 33.2

The Gender Gap in American Presidential Elections. The gender gap, or the difference in voting patterns between men and women, was first identified in 1980 by National Organization for Women president Eleanor Smeal and has been recognized as an important force in American politics ever since. In every presidential election, greater percentages of women than men voted for the Democratic candidate. More women than men—no matter their race or ethnicity, income, level of education, or marital status—voted for Gore than for Bush in the 2000 presidential election. (*Source: Based on data from the Center for American Women and Politics.*)

bar graph

tables

TABLE 5.1
Properties of Selected Gases

Name	Formula	Color	Odor	Toxicity
Ammonia	NH_3	Colorless	Penetrating	Toxic
Carbon dioxide	CO_2	Colorless	Odorless	Nontoxic
Carbon monoxide	CO	Colorless	Odorless	Very toxic
Chlorine	Cl_2	Pale green	Irritating	Very toxic
Helium	He	Colorless	Odorless	Nontoxic
Hydrogen	H_2	Colorless	Odorless	Nontoxic
Hydrogen chloride	HCl	Colorless	Irritating	Corrosive
Hydrogen sulfide	H_2S	Colorless	Foul	Very toxic
Methane	CH_4	Colorless	Odorless	Nontoxic
Neon	Ne	Colorless	Odorless	Nontoxic
Nitrogen	N_2	Colorless	Odorless	Nontoxic
Nitrogen dioxide	NO_2	Red–brown	Irritating	Very toxic
Oxygen	O_2	Colorless	Odorless	Nontoxic
Sulfur dioxide	SO_2	Colorless	Choking	Toxic

Table 2.2 Balance Sheet for a College Student—Bill Soshnik, January 1, 2006

	Dollars	Percent
ASSETS		
Cash on hand	$ 85	1.07
Checking account	335	4.21
Savings account	800	10.05
Personal property*	3140	39.45
Automobile	3600	45.23
Total Assets	**$7960**	100.00
LIABILITIES		
Telephone bill past due	$ 70	0.88
Bank loan—automobile	3130	39.32
College loan	1000	12.56
Government education loan	4500	56.53
Total Liabilities	**$8700**	109.30
NET WORTH	($740)	–9.30
Total Liabilities and Net Worth	**$7960**	100.00

*At fair market value, list includes clothing, $400; dresser, $50; television, $150; chair, $30; table, $40; desk, $120; cooking/dining items, $50; and computer equipment, $2300.

Figure 5.9 and Table 5.1 from Darrell Ebbing and Steven D. Gammon, *General Chemistry*, Ninth Edition. Copyright © 2010 by Cengage Learning. Reprinted by permission of Brooks Cole/Cengage Learning. Figure 33.2, "The Gender Gap in American Presidential Elections," from Norton, *A People and a Nation*, Volume 2: Since 1895, Seventh Edition. Copyright © 2008 by Houghton Mifflin Company. Reprinted by permission of Cengage Learning. Table 2.2 from Garman, *Personal Finance*, Ninth Edition. © 2008 South-Western, a part of Cengage Learning, Inc. Reproduced by permission. www.cengage.com/permissions.

To read a graphic with understanding, determine its *purpose*, discover what *relationship* of ideas it illustrates, and read the *text* that accompanies it. To help you recall these steps, remember the acronym **PRT:**

1. To determine the **purpose**, read the title of the graphic and its caption for any clues they may provide.

2. To help you discover the **relationship**, determine the graphic's type. For example, if you have identified a graphic as a process diagram, then determine what process is illustrated, trace the steps, and understand what happens at each stage.

3. For an explanation of the graphic, read the **text** that accompanies it. For each part of the explanation in the text, find its counterpart in the graphic. To test yourself, recite the explanation in your own words while looking at the graphic. Then close your eyes and visualize the graphic.

CRITICAL THINKING

Apply the PRT Strategy

Exercise Overview

This exercise will help you apply what you have learned about the importance of graphics and how to read them.

Exercise Background

Charts, tables, diagrams, and photographs are not just fillers. They play an important role in a textbook chapter, illustrating complex ideas in a visual way that makes them easier to remember. A single graphic may summarize and condense concepts or idea relationships that take pages to explain in detail. However, you need to read both the graphic and its explanation in the text to get the full picture.

Exercise Task

Choose a graphic from one of your textbooks. Using PRT (purpose, relationship, text), read the graphic and interpret its meaning by answering the following questions.

1. What is the graphic's title?
2. Is there a caption? If so, summarize its contents.
3. Based on your answers to questions 1 and 2, what is the graphic's purpose?
4. What type of graphic have you chosen: pie chart, bar graph, line graph, diagram, chart, or table?
5. Based on your answer to question 4, what idea relationship does the graphic illustrate?
6. What is the connection between the graphic and the text that accompanies it? For example, what does the text tell you that the graphic does not? What does the graphic help you understand that the text does not?

Create Your Own Study System

- Start with a basic system like SQ3R and adapt it to your learning style.

No one has discovered the best way to learn because no system works best for everyone all the time. Most systems are variations on the basic one, SQ3R. The best system for *you* is one that reflects your learning style and is a good fit for the material that you need to study. Most important, be committed to active learning and use your system consistently. Try SQ3R as is or make slight variations in its steps to create your own best system for studying the material in any course. Ways to vary SQ3R may take into account whether you prefer to study alone or with someone else and whether you prefer visual, verbal, auditory, or tactile modes of learning. For example, if you prefer to study with someone, try these steps:

1. Survey the chapter together. Determine what the chapter is about and what you are expected to learn.

2. Start with the first section. Discuss the heading and formulate some questions to guide your reading. Write down your questions.

3. Each of you should read the section on your own and highlight, annotate, or take notes.

4. When you have finished the section, discuss what you have read. Answer your guide questions. Share what you have underlined or annotated. Quiz each other from your notes. Then move on to the next section and repeat steps 2–4.

5. When you have finished the entire chapter, review separately, then quiz each other.

6. As a final step, do the end-of-chapter questions together, unless your instructor is collecting them for a grade. In that case, you should each do them on your own.

If you prefer auditory modes of instruction, record the material you want to review—a list of special terms and definitions, for example—and then listen to the recording. Many cell phones have this capability!

Or have someone quiz you. If you prefer visual modes of learning, make charts, diagrams, and illustrations for review. If taking notes from textbooks and outlining are strategies that work for you, by all means use them. You will have to resort to these strategies if you are studying from library books or materials your professor has put on reserve.

As part of your review for any course, **connect and reflect**. Make connections between what you already know and what you have learned. How does the new information add to or change what you already know? Reflect on ways to use new information or apply it in different contexts. For example, use the research and writing skills acquired in a composition class to write papers and compile reports due in other classes. Use the information learned in one course as a source of topics for writing papers in other courses. The interpersonal skills that you learn in a business course may improve your relations with others at work. The skills learned in an accounting course may help you improve the way you keep track of your spending. Through connection and reflection, you can personalize what you have learned, making the information your own so that you are less likely to forget it.

Once you have decided upon a study system that works best for you, use it consistently. Knowing that you have a study system will make you feel confident that you can learn and remember. Also, if you are like many students and have trouble getting

Connect and reflect is a review process. Connect new information with prior knowledge and reflect on ways to use the information.

Concept Check **9.2**

Can you connect and reflect? Think about a skill or process that you have learned recently. How has your new knowledge affected the way you think or act? How will you use the skill or process? What will it help you accomplish?

EXERCISE 9.3   Learning Styles Application on Using SQ3R

READ THE NEXT ASSIGNED CHAPTER in one of your textbooks and try out the SQ3R study system. When you have finished, answer *yes* or *no* to questions 1–7; then write your answers to questions 8–10.

Yes   No

☐   ☐   1. Did surveying the chapter before reading it give you an idea of what the chapter would cover?

☐   ☐   2. Were you able to formulate questions from the headings to guide your reading?

☐   ☐   3. Did you find answers to most of your questions as you read each section?

☐   ☐   4. After doing the reading, did you know what to underline?

☐   ☐   5. Did you make any marginal notes?

☐   ☐   6. Did you find any material that would be easier to understand if you were to diagram it to make it more visual?

☐   ☐   7. After reciting and reviewing, did you have a thorough understanding of the information contained in the chapter?

8. Did you vary the SQ3R system? If so, how and why?

_____

_____

9. Given your learning style, is SQ3R an effective system for you? Why or why not?

_____

_____

10. How would you adapt SQ3R to fit your learning style?

_____

_____

started when you try to study, a study system will provide the starting point you need. As you become more comfortable using a study system, you will think of ways not only to adapt it to fit your learning style but also to help you meet the different demands of courses in every discipline, as explained in the next section.

Studying for Different Disciplines

• Meet the reading demands of all your courses by knowing what to study in the different disciplines.

Discipline refers to an academic field of study such as social science, history, or mathematics.

As you already know, your college courses are categorized by academic discipline. A **discipline** is a body of knowledge or field of study. Familiar disciplines include the natural sciences such as biology and chemistry; the social sciences such as psychology and sociology; the humanities such as literature and history; and many others. The reading in some of your courses will be more difficult for you than in others for two reasons: You may have little experience with a discipline and the terms used to talk about the subject may be new or unfamiliar to you. Every discipline has its own terminology, its own theories and assumptions, and its own big names in the field—people who made important discoveries or contributions. You may not like every course you take, and certainly learning is easier when the material is both familiar and interesting to you. Knowing what to study in different disciplines may serve as a guide to empower you while reading difficult materials. In the process, you may even develop a new interest in the subject.

Composition and Literature

Courses in these areas combine reading and writing. The difference is that in a composition course your focus is on producing your own writing. In a literature course, your focus is on reading and comparing the creative work of others. In a composition course, you may also read essays and articles as models or examples of good writing. In a literature course, you may be assigned to write papers that call for you to interpret, analyze, criticize, or react to a poem, short story, or novel. In a composition course, your focus will be on skill development that includes the use of standard English grammar, vocabulary building, sentence structure, and the basics of planning, organizing, and writing paragraphs and essays. Research skills may also be included. Composition textbooks contain many helpful aids in the form of examples to follow and exercises that help you build skill. When reading an assigned chapter, pay attention to step-by-step instructions, do the exercises, keep a list of questions to ask in class, and spend time reading and thinking about the example paragraphs or essays that are included in the chapter.

In a literature course, you may study the different *genres*, or types, of literature such as poetry, short stories, plays, or novels; the *periods* of literature such as romantic, Victorian, or twentieth century; or *critical theories* of literature. Figurative language is the soul of literature: Symbols, images, and multiple meanings help develop characters, arouse emotions, and engage imagination. Knowledge of literary terms can unlock the reading in any literature course. Figure 9.5 shows a few terms you will encounter and may already know.

You may find yourself reaching for a tool that provides plot summaries, analysis, and criticism of many works of fiction, like CliffsNotes or SparkNotes. Some students like to review these resources first to guide them through a novel. However, once you have read what someone else says about a story, it is hard to form an original viewpoint.

FIGURE 9.5

Four Frequently Used Literary Terms

Term	Definition	Example
Alliteration	A repeated sound in a series of words—often as the first letter	The city seduces the senses with sounds and sights.
Metaphor	A direct comparison that is more poetic than logical	Her teeth were rows of pearls.
Personification	Assigns human characteristics to animals or objects	"Rosy fingered dawn," Homer
Simile	A comparison that contains "as" or "like"	"My love is like a red red rose," Robert Burns

Therefore, it is probably better if you read an assigned novel first and form your own opinion before reviewing additional sources. Outside resources should never be used as a substitute for reading the original materials. Remember too that your instructor is familiar with these tools, so beware of trying to pass off any ideas gathered from these sources as your own.

Every short story or novel is developed through five elements of fiction. A good way to read fiction is to look for, pay attention to, and take notes on these elements:

1. **Plot:** The action of the story moves along through various events and story lines to a *climax*, or moment of high drama, where all the various story lines come together and are resolved. To study plot, make a time line of the major events.

2. **Characters:** Usually there is a main character, or *protagonist*. Often there is a villain, or *antagonist*, and several minor characters. Take notes on characters' gender, physical characteristics, personalities, and motives—why they do what they do.

3. **Setting:** The setting is the place where all the action occurs. Weather and time are part of the setting and may serve as a backdrop to some of the action. For example, a character's traits may reflect where he or she comes from. Take notes on the story or novel's setting: When does the action take place—within hours or days or over a longer span of time? What year or century is it, and are there any details of history that may be important to the story's development or the characters' lives?

4. **Theme:** The theme is the story's meaning or significance. Literature is a reflection of our lives and tends to deal with major themes such as relationships, spiritual growth, and the cycle of life from birth to death. To understand a story or novel, pay attention to the way characters deal with the situations in which the author places them. Often, the theme will be revealed through the interaction of characters as the plot moves along. Underline words or phrases that you think may reveal the theme or the story's meaning. When you finish a story or novel, read your notes and try to state in your own words what you think is the theme.

5. **Point of View:** A story's point of view is the perspective of the storyteller. The storyteller is also called a *narrator*. The narrator's point of view can be first person (I, me, mine); second person (you); or third person (he, she, they). The narrator can be a character in the story or an omniscient or all-knowing "voice" that seems to come from outside the story. You can usually identify the narrator within the first few paragraphs of a story or novel. Take notes on the narrator's point of view and attitude.

Many students say that they have a hard time taking notes when reading a story or novel because they can't tell what is important. Identifying and following the five elements of fiction as you read not only helps focus your attention but also gives you something to mark or underline for review. See Figure 9.6 for a diagram of the five elements of fiction.

In addition, try these strategies for studying literature:

▶ **Visualize the characters and setting.** Imagine that the story is playing out in your mind and try to "see" what is taking place as if you were watching a movie. Visualization will help you remember details of the plot.

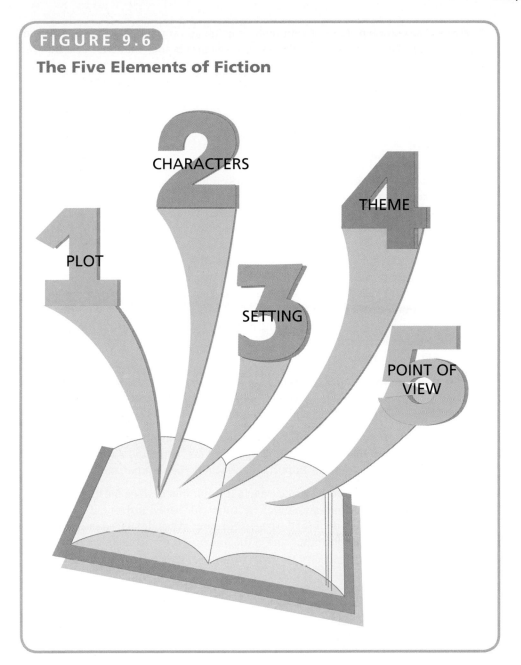

FIGURE 9.6

The Five Elements of Fiction

1 PLOT

2 CHARACTERS

3 SETTING

4 THEME

5 POINT OF VIEW

▶ **Make a list of characters.** When reading stories or novels, take notes on their physical characteristics, background, and values as they are revealed in the story.

▶ **Keep a list of literary terms.** Learn the terms that scholars use to talk and write about literature and use them in class discussions, in the papers you write for the course, and in your responses to test questions.

▶ **Follow the plot.** Note major events and either mark them in the margin or take notes on what happens as the story moves to a climax. When you have finished reading, use your notes to make a time line that traces the plot from beginning to end. Use your time line as a study guide for reviewing the story.

▶ **Research the author.** Most authors have a website, or you can Google the name. Reading about the author may give you an insight into his or her themes or other work.

▼ **Predict as you read.** To keep your interest going and your attention focused, try to anticipate what will happen next, based on past events and characters' actions.

▼ **Discuss the story with a partner or group** outside of class. Share notes and ideas. Talking about what you read not only aids comprehension but also strengthens memory.

The Social Sciences

Courses in the social sciences include many different areas of study such as anthropology, business, criminal justice, finance, law, marketing, and psychology. Courses in these areas examine human behavior, relationships, and societies. These topics are fascinating to most people because they help us understand our own motives and actions as well as those of others. However, the terminology and theoretical perspectives can also make social science courses seem difficult. The good news is that the textbook for a psychology course or other course in the social sciences has standard features that help to make it as student-friendly as possible. Therefore, become familiar with your textbook. If it has a glossary, use it. Take advantage of chapter features such as a chapter outline on the opening page and list of objectives, which focus your attention on the important topics and learning goals for the chapter. Read the summary to determine in advance what the most important ideas are.

In addition, do the following:

▼ **Pay attention to graphics.** Graphics are important in any textbook, but are especially helpful when reading information that is unfamiliar or complex. Graphics help clarify difficult concepts and may appeal to your visual sense.

▼ **Take notes** on names that are repeated often and the theories, discoveries, or accomplishments that made these people famous. Experimental data—who did what, when, and why—is also important and should be summarized in your notes.

▼ **Draw time lines.** Illustrate how one event led to another or trace the history of a significant development. To draw a time line, turn your paper horizontally and draw a straight line across the middle of the page. Plot dates at evenly spaced intervals along one side of the line. On the other side of the line opposite each date, jot a brief note to explain what happened. Give your time line a title that explains what it covers.

Using flashcards or recitation with a partner can help you remember important concepts in courses across many disciplines.

Alejandro Rivera/Real Latino Images/PhotoLibrary

EXERCISE 9.4 A Strategy for Every Discipline

Choose one of the courses you are taking and try out one of the strategies suggested for reading and learning in the disciplines. For example, if you are taking a literature course, make a list of characters for a story you are reading. If you are taking a social science course, read an article or watch a news segment on a related topic and write a summary of it. If you are taking a math course, make flashcards of example problems and solutions to study. The course and strategy are up to you, but be prepared to share your results in writing or in a class discussion.

▸ **Make it your own.** Imagine how you would react to the situation being described. If you are reading about an experiment, determine how you would have responded. If you are reading about a historical event, try to picture yourself in the place and time.

▸ **Reinforce what you are learning.** If a topic really interests you, find out more about it. Search the Internet or your library for another book or article. If references are listed at the end of the chapter or in a bibliography, these may give you ideas for additional sources to explore.

▸ **Make flashcards of terms and definitions** to study, and review them either on your own or with a friend who is also taking the course. Flashcards are convenient to carry around, so you can use them anywhere.

▸ **Make real-world connections.** If you are taking a criminal justice course, watch the news for stories about crime and follow the events as they develop. Following political events in the news can add insight to a course in political science or history. Watch one of the market analysis shows on TV to flesh out what you are learning in a course in finance or economics. Try to work in some reading related to your social science course. Magazines like *Psychology Today* or *BusinessWeek* portray real people dealing with the issues you are studying.

The Natural Sciences

Courses in the natural sciences are among the most challenging because of their technical terms; their use of numbers, measurements, and statistics; and the complexity of the ideas that are presented. You are probably most familiar with biology, but the natural sciences also include physics, chemistry, engineering, geology, environmental science, computer science, and many other fields. Courses in the natural sciences will help you develop an understanding of the scientific method, a knowledge of various laws and theories of science, and the ability to reason inductively and solve problems. Laboratory work may also be required. When reading your textbook, pay attention to graphics as you would in any other text. Compare what you see in the graphic with the textbook explanation. Always survey the chapter before reading, keep a terms list, and build background with supplementary reading in magazines or on the Internet. In addition, try these strategies for reading in the natural sciences:

▸ **Read slowly and carefully,** one section at a time. Types of information to watch for include theories, formulas, explanations and examples, experimental data, terms and definitions, and predictions and projections of future developments in the field.

▸ **Relate lab assignments to coursework.** Lab assignments often clarify and expand on information presented in lectures, covered in class discussion, and explained in your textbook. When doing a lab assignment, determine its purpose and what scientific principles or laws it illustrates.

▶ **Read the chapter summary** because it highlights the essential concepts and ideas you are expected to learn. Reading the summary should alert you to any concept or idea that you don't remember reading or that you don't understand. If this happens, take the time to reread the section of the chapter that contains the information. Some students like to read the summary first. Knowing in advance what ideas are most important will guide your reading.

▶ **Pay attention to numbers.** Measurements, statistics, and mathematical formulas are an essential part of courses in the natural sciences. If numbers make you nervous, get used to them. Whenever numbers are mentioned, spend extra time determining what they mean and why they are significant.

▶ **Make study tools** such as charts, diagrams, and outlines—whichever of these help you condense and summarize information for study. Write chemical formulas on flashcards. Flashcards are also good for summarizing experimental data and for listing names of important people in the field and their discoveries. Chapter 10 explains how to organize information for study.

Mathematics

Chances are you will be required to take algebra, statistics, or another math course, depending on your major or program of study. If you like math, have an aptitude for it, and have always performed well in math, then this should be no problem. But if you are like many students who dislike math, you may have had a bad experience in the past and may even have some math anxiety. Face up to those challenges because studying math need not be difficult if you remember two things:

1. Any math course follows a linear learning pattern—one skill builds on another.

2. Learning algebra or any other mathematical system is like learning a foreign language—it requires some translation, helps if you can immerse yourself in the culture, and takes practice, practice, practice.

In a math course, one skill builds on another. For example, you can't do algebra without a solid foundation in the basic mathematical operations of addition, subtraction, multiplication, and division. If you have trouble solving word problems or problems involving fractions, then you will have trouble in algebra. That said, it is possible to go back and pick up missed or misunderstood information. Math labs, math tutors, and basic math courses exist to provide help for students who need it.

As mentioned, learning math is like learning a foreign language. Your new vocabulary consists of rules, formulas, mathematical operations, and mathematical terms. Learn the terms. Use them during class discussion to make them your own. To immerse yourself in the "culture" of math, try to understand what attracts people to this field of study. Ask your instructor why he or she chose teaching math as a profession. Read a math-themed article or book. Some good ones to try are: *A Mathematician Reads the Newspaper*, by John Allen Paulos, which is about the misuse of statistics; and *Freakonomics*, the best seller by Steven D. Leavitt and Stephen J. Dubner in which the authors use economics and humor to explain some of life's mysteries. Did you know that music, games like poker, and even poetry all incorporate some mathematical ideas? Rhythm, rhyme, and "beat" in music and poetry are math based. People who excel at poker must be able to keep track of numbers in their heads. Just as you have to visit a foreign country to immerse yourself in its culture, you have to do math to learn math—so practice, practice, practice. In addition, keep these tips in mind.

▶ **Never get behind.** Remember that math follows a linear progression from one level to another. Do not skip a class; if you do, then you will miss an essential step. If you have to be absent, make arrangements to get the notes from a classmate. Keep up with the assigned work.

FIGURE 9.7

Vary the Steps of SQ3R to Meet Specific Needs

Discipline	What to Study from the Textbook	Steps to Add or Expand
Math	• Sample problems and solutions • Mathematical rules and procedures	• Add a **practice** step for solving problems. • Expand the **recite** and **review** steps for making flashcards of rules, terms, and procedures to study.
Science	• Scientific theories and breakthroughs • Scientists and their discoveries • Laws and principles of science • Experiments that illustrate key concepts	• Add a **draw** step for making diagrams of processes that you can use as study guides. • Expand the **recite** and **review** steps by making flashcards of terms, formulas, and principles to study. • Add a **write** step to summarize experiments: who did it, what they found, and why.
Social Science	• Theories of behavior and personality • Names of people who developed the theories • Key experiments that test the theories	• Add a **write** step for summarizing theories: Briefly explain the theory, who developed it, and its significance and limitations. • Expand the **review** step to include experiments: who was involved, what they found, and why it is important.
History	• Important people and events • Important documents and their significance • Laws and policies	• Add a **draw** step for making time lines that help you trace events. • Add a **write** step for summarizing the significance of documents, laws, or policies.
Literature	• Names of authors and their works • Types of fiction: similarities and differences • Literary terms • The elements of fiction: plot, characters, setting, theme, point of view, style, and tone	• Expand the **recite** and **review** steps by making flashcards of literary terms to study. • Add a **draw** step for making plot time lines to review. • Add a **write** step for explaining themes and their significance.
Languages	• Words and meanings • Pronunciation • Verb conjugations • Spelling and grammar rules	• Add a **draw** step for making conjugation charts. • Add a **write** step to practice translating from one language to another. • Expand **recite** and **review** to include flashcards of words and meanings, spelling, and grammar rules to study.

- **Study math first.** If math is your hardest subject, study it first, before you get tired. Plan to give math your full attention, because your working memory needs time to take in new information and attach it to previously learned material.

- **Find a reason to like math.** The problem with math for many students is that they can't see an immediate use for it. Do whatever you can to relate mathematical concepts to your daily life. Perhaps you will see a connection to your major or career. Marketing, accounting, engineering, computer science, and many other fields all require the use of math to some degree. If you can see a use for math, you will be more inclined to make the effort to learn it.

▼ **Give yourself time.** Math is one body of knowledge that you have to apply to really get it, and this takes time and practice. You need to study every day, work as many problems as you can, assigned or not. The more you practice, the more likely it is that the operations and rules involved will become internalized.

▼ **Seek help if you really get bogged down.** Get a tutor or get yourself into a study group. Talk to the instructor. Determine why you are having difficulty and what you need to do to get back on track.

▼ **Use these steps to get the most out of reading your math textbook:** Survey the chapter. Before you begin your careful reading, review the previous chapter so that you will know how the new topic builds on previous material. During reading, spend time working through the example problems. After reading, review the chapter, then do the exercises. If there are rules or formulas to learn, recite them, write them down, and keep reviewing and reciting until you learn them.

All of the discipline-specific reading and study strategies explained previously can be incorporated into your study routine or system. Figure 9.7 on page 237 lists ways to vary the SQ3R study system to meet the specific needs of courses in several disciplines.

Guided CHAPTER REVIEW

The following checklist summarizes this chapter's key terms and strategies. After reading the chapter, how confident are you that you can apply the information you have learned? To assess your level of confidence, respond to each statement with one of the following: *very confident* (3 points), *fairly confident* (2 points), *not very confident* (1 point), *not confident* (0 points). Write your number of points in the box beside each statement. Then add your score and read the analysis that follows. When you have finished, take the chapter quiz.

SUMMARY CHECK

How confident are you about applying these strategies?

Points

☐ 1. Recognizing the value of a study system

☐ 2. Being proactive about studying

☐ 3. Understanding the steps of SQ3R

☐ 4. Surveying a textbook, chapter, or website before reading

☐ 5. Asking questions to guide your reading

☐ 6. Using active reading strategies such as underlining and annotating

☐ 7. Reciting and reviewing as part of your study system

☐ 8. Using the PRT strategy to read graphics in your textbooks

☐ 9. Creating a study system that reflects your learning style

☐ 10. Choosing appropriate strategies for reading and studying your textbooks in different courses

How confident is your understanding of this chapter's key terms?

☐ 11. study system

☐ 12. proactive

☐ 13. SQ3R

☐ 14. survey

☐ 15. graphics

☐ 16. connect and reflect

☐ 17. discipline

Total

Add your score. The highest possible score is 51. The closer your score is to 51, the higher your level of confidence. Use your *Summary Check* results to help you determine which parts of the chapter to review.

YOUR WEBSITE RESOURCES

This chapter's resources include the following items. To access them, go to *The Confident Student* premium website.

- **Video Skillbuilders: Textbook Note-taking: Student Methods**
- *SQ3R Flashcard*
- **Chapter Exercises**
- **Forms to Download**

- **Chapter Summary of Topics**
- **Thinking Ahead About Career**
- **Confidence Builder Web Search**
- **Self-Test**

CHAPTER REVIEW Quiz

Answer the following questions from memory. Then return to the chapter to check your answers. As a final activity, complete *Show Your Confidence* at the end of the quiz.

1. What does it mean to be proactive about studying?

_____

_____

2. In your own words, what is a study system and how does SQ3R fit in this category?

_____

_____

3. What is the purpose of surveying a chapter?

_____

_____

4. How does turning headings into questions guide your reading of a chapter section?

_____

_____

5. What is one type of information for which recitation is an appropriate strategy?

_____

_____

6. What is your own system for reviewing a chapter that you have read?

_____

_____

7. What is the PRT strategy, and what is its purpose?

_____

_____

8. What have you done, or could you do, to adapt your study system to your learning style?

_____

_____

9. What is one strategy you would use for learning the material in a math course?

_____

_____

10. Why is it important to do the exercises at the end of a chapter, even if they are not assigned?

_____

_____

SHOW YOUR CONFIDENCE

This chapter is about study systems. What have you learned that reinforces what you already have been doing when you study? What have you learned that will help you change the way you study? Be prepared to share your opinions either in writing or in class discussion.

Your REFLECTIONS: YOUR STUDY SYSTEM

Reflect on what you have learned from this chapter about study systems and how you can use them and vary them to acquire information and enhance learning. Use the following questions to stimulate your thinking; then write your reflections. Include in your writing specific information from the chapter.

- What course gives you the most trouble? What have you learned from this chapter that will improve the way you study for that course?
- Are you taking a course in a discipline that is not listed in Figure 9.7? If so, how can you adapt SQ3R to improve the way you study?
- Are you proactive about studying? Explain your answer.

_____

_____

_____

_____

_____

_____

_____

_____

_____

_____

_____

10 Studying and Learning from Textbooks

iStockphoto(RF)

This chapter encourages you to:

- Create graphic organizers and other tools that will take you beyond note-taking to the next level of studying.

- Use visual formats to organize ideas and show their relationship.

- Construct charts or tables that categorize or compare ideas.

- List details under a key idea or essential concept to show their relationship.

- Make three types of flashcards to use for study and review.

Confident students are **pragmatic**. They take a practical approach to learning that involves trying new strategies to see what works.

Do you often finish a study session wondering if you have studied the right information? Do you ever give up studying in frustration because your notes don't seem to make sense? If you have ever felt that strategies such as underlining, taking notes from your textbook, or writing questions in the margin are not getting the job done, then perhaps it's time to take your studying to the next level. You can transform your notes into practical study guides and tools that will help you master the information. Also, you will get much more out of studying if you approach it with the right attitude. The following *Confidence Builder* explains how to adjust your attitude for a **pragmatic** approach to learning that involves commitment and persistence.

Pragmatic means "practical," "realistic."

CONFIDENCE BUILDER

Adjust Your Attitude

Reading and studying take time; there are no short-cuts, only efficient study techniques. The pragmatic approach to studying involves using proven strategies and adopting the confidence-building attitudes of commitment and persistence. What are these attitudes and what do they have to do with studying?

Commitment. You may recall from Chapter 5 that a *commitment* is a pledge. For example, in marriage, a couple pledge to love one another. Similarly, people who pledge their money and time to support a cause are committed to that cause. In academic terms, an *attitude of commitment* means a willingness to pledge your time and effort to reach your goals. For example, if you are committed to success, then you will adopt the behaviors that promote success, such as regular attendance, sufficient preparation, and studying. Commitment also involves desire. Therefore, if you know what you want and how to get it and you are willing to set goals, then you have the attitude of commitment.

Persistence. Persistence is *the willingness to sustain effort over time, even in the face of difficulty.* Remember when you learned to ride a bicycle or drive a car? These skills took time to master. But no matter how many times you fell off the bike or how many times you had to practice parking and backing up the car, you learned to ride or drive. Finally, you got your license. That took persistence. Moreover, you were committed to learn because you *desired* having those skills and the freedom

they would give you. In academic terms, an attitude of persistence means a willingness to try out new strategies and to practice new skills as often as necessary until you achieve mastery. Persistence means not giving up in the face of failure but, instead, analyzing your mistakes to see what went wrong, then trying again. Through commitment and persistence, you can take control of your learning. Here are seven suggestions:

1. Choose success. Commit yourself to the idea that you will succeed.
2. Be self-motivated. Think about why you are in college. Look to the future. Where do you want to be in five years? What is your dream job or career? Let your desires be your motivators.
3. Set goals. Dreams don't come true without planning and effort. Set long-term goals (complete requirements for my major), set short-term goals (attain a 3.0 GPA this semester; earn an A on the next assignment), and make action plans to reach them. Commit yourself to the plans and then follow through.
4. Remember that each day, each assignment or test brings you closer to achieving your goals. Make them all count. Put forth your best effort.
5. Try out the strategies that you are learning. They won't do you any good if you read about them and then forget them. For SQ3R or any study system to work, you have to use it consistently so that it becomes second nature. When

continued

surveying before you read becomes a habit, when you read with a pencil or other marker in your hand, and when you take time to review after *every* time you read, you will see your understanding grow and your memory increase. Like SQ3R, making study guides is an *active* process that involves you in learning. The value of both of these methods is that they involve all your concentration, making it less likely that a part of your brain will be on vacation while you are attempting to study.

6. Don't give up. Suppose you have made a bad grade or you think you aren't making progress. Perhaps more practice is needed, or perhaps you need to try a new strategy. Seek help and be persistent.

7. Turn to your learning community. You are not alone. Other students are experiencing the same successes and failures that you are. Join a study group if you have not already done so. Find out from others what works and doesn't work for them. Then revise your plans or methods as needed. Remember, *you* are in control.

The attitudes of commitment and persistence also have a workplace connection. Being committed to a company's goals and being persistent in your efforts to reach them make you a valued employee.

Follow Up: To explore this topic further, visit *The Confident Student* premium website for an online search activity about attitudes and how they affect your academic, personal, and career goals.

From Notes to Study Guides

- Create graphic organizers and other tools that will take you beyond note-taking to the next level of studying.

Memorizing lists of facts, concepts, and other important information may not be the most effective way to study. For example, you could memorize the definitions of the terms *id*, *ego*, and *superego*, but would that help you understand Freud's theory of personality and how the id, ego, and superego interact to affect human behavior? Would learning only the definitions of Freud's terms help you explain how Freud's theory compares with other personality theories or what the limitations of his theory are? Probably not.

One good way to study Freud's theory is to make a chart that lists his components of personality, a brief explanation of each, and an example showing how each affects behavior. In making such a chart, what have you done? You have restructured the information in a format that gives it meaning.

Diagrams, charts, and other self-made study tools have three advantages. First, they condense a lot of information into smaller, meaningful chunks. Second, they help you visualize relationships among ideas; as explained in Chapter 8, visualization is a powerful memory aid. Third, the process of going through your notes and deciding what information is important and how best to organize the ideas forces you to review the material and think critically about it.

As you have probably guessed by now, you can't make a useful chart, table, or diagram without having some information to work with. Where do you get that information? You get it from your textbooks. This is why we have placed so much emphasis on active reading and the necessity of interacting with your textbooks by underlining, annotating, writing questions in the margins, making outlines, and anything else you can think of that will help you highlight a chapter's key ideas and terms. To assess the strategies you are currently using to read and study from your textbooks, take *Awareness Check* 10.1.

AWARENESS CHECK 10.1

How Do You Study from Textbooks?

The following Awareness Check *will help you determine whether you are getting all the information you can out of your textbooks and using it effectively for studying, reviewing, and retaining what you have learned. Check the statements that apply to you.*

☐ 1. Part of my textbook study includes making some type of study guide to help me remember important information.

☐ 2. I rarely, if ever, underline or annotate a textbook chapter.

☐ 3. When I make notes from textbooks, I don't copy the information directly; I put it into my own words.

☐ 4. If I make notes, I usually copy directly from the textbook.

☐ 5. I have used or heard about mapping techniques and other ways of organizing information.

☐ 6. I am not aware of ways to organize information. I study by rereading textbook chapters or reviewing my lecture notes.

☐ 7. I underline or annotate key ideas in a chapter and I study from my markings.

☐ 8. I have difficulty deciding what to underline or mark, so I try to study everything.

☐ 9. Overall, I would say that my method of studying from textbooks is effective.

☐ 10. Overall, I think that my method of studying from textbooks needs improvement.

If you checked mostly odd-numbered statements, you are probably already using an effective method of organizing information from textbooks, but this chapter may introduce you to some new strategies to try. If you checked mostly even-numbered statements, you are probably not using your textbooks as effectively as you could. Using this chapter's strategies will no doubt help you improve the way you study.

So how do you take your studying to the next level? How do you go beyond reading and marking a textbook chapter to create study guides and tools? Moreover, what are your options for organizing key ideas from chapters in meaningful ways? As a starting point, let's review some of the suggestions made in Chapters 7 through 9 for marking and annotating your textbooks:

▼ Underline or annotate the main idea or topic sentence of a paragraph.

▼ Underline or highlight key words or phrases from the sentences that support the main idea.

▼ Underline or highlight major headings and subheadings.

▼ Turn headings into questions and write the answers in the margin.

▼ Circle key terms and write their definitions in the margin or keep a separate list.

▼ Take notes on the chapter in one of two ways: (1) Briefly outline or list the key ideas in each section—in your own words; (2) Write a short summary paragraph of each section.

▼ Outline or summarize steps in a process or the details of an important experiment.

After reviewing your notes, select the information that you need to study in more depth or that you think will be on a test. Then transform this information into one of several formats, such as a diagram, a chart, or an idea cluster. These types of study tools and how to make them are explained in the sections of this chapter that follow.

Graphic Organizers

- Use visual formats to organize ideas and show their relationship.

You probably know from experience that studying from a textbook chapter—even if you have marked it effectively—can be difficult and time consuming. Suppose you have several chapters to study for a test. By the time you get through reading all your marked parts of the first chapter or two, you are probably too tired to study the others. You go to the test unprepared. Also, it is difficult to remember material that you have under-lined or highlighted. For one thing, the words are the author's, not your own. Second, you end up resorting to memorization, which as you know by now is not an effective way to study complex ideas. But what if you could isolate the most important ideas in a chapter and condense them into a format that is both meaningful and visual? Then you would have a study guide that you could review many times before a test, fixing it in your mind so that you could call it up from memory when needed. What are these "visual formats"? They are called **graphic organizers** and they include the following types. The diagrams beside the organizers listed below will give you a skeleton idea of what they look like.

A **graphic organizer** is any type of chart, table, diagram, or other format for arranging ideas to show their relationship.

▟ Concept Map

▟ Hierarchy Diagram

▟ Process or Function Diagram

▟ Branches or Clusters

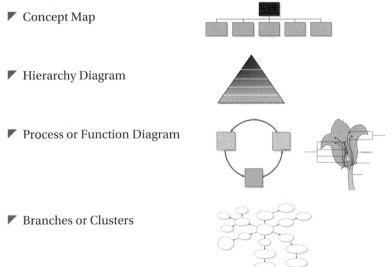

Concept Map

Unlike an outline—which is a *linear*, or sequential, listing of main ideas and supporting details—a **concept map** is a *spatial*, or visually organized, breakdown of a topic that may not be sequential. But like an outline, a map breaks down a main idea into more specific ideas or details that support it. If your learning style is visual, concept maps and the other graphic organizers explained in this chapter may appeal to you. To construct a concept map, first identify the main idea and write a key phrase from it in a box. Identify key ideas from the sentences that support the main idea and write them in connecting boxes to show their relationship to the main idea.

Read the following paragraph. Then study the concept map shown in Figure 10.1. Notice how the concept map in Figure 10.1 reflects the way that the paragraph is high-lighted and annotated.

A **concept map** diagrams a topic or main idea by breaking it down into one or more levels of detail.

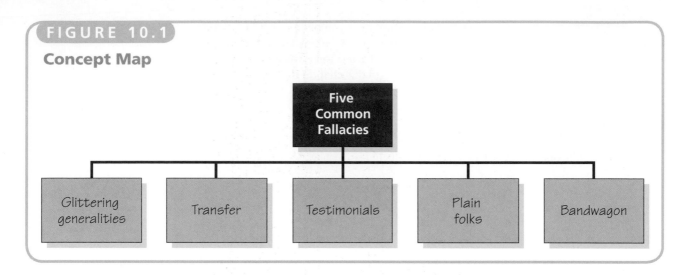

FIGURE 10.1

Concept Map

Main Idea

To avoid being manipulated by advertising, learn to separate facts from fallacies

> [*Television advertisers use five common fallacies, among others, to manipulate viewers' attitudes toward their products and to get them to buy.*] **Glittering generalities** *are* <u>*words and phrases that make viewers respond favorably*</u> *to a product. Phrases such as "no preservatives," "low fat and cholesterol," or "97% fat free" associated with food products make people believe they're getting something that is healthful.* **Transfer** *is a fallacious type of reasoning whereby a* <u>*product is related to an idea or activity with which the viewer is likely to identify.*</u> *Restaurant commercials are a good example of transfer. Families are shown having a good time in a restaurant or a young couple is depicted in a romantic cafe. Viewers are supposed to get the idea that if they eat at these restaurants, they will become like the happy families and couples in these ads. Many advertisers use* **testimonials** *of* <u>*famous people to endorse their products.*</u> *A film star advocates the use of one brand of shampoo. A sports celebrity endorses a company's athletic shoes. Some advertisers use* **plain folks***,* <u>*people the audience can identify with,*</u> *to* <u>*sell products;*</u> *others encourage viewers to jump on the* **bandwagon** *and buy a product because* <u>*"everybody does it."*</u> *Viewers need to pay attention to ads and sift the hype from the facts. Of course, they can always press the mute button on their remote control unit.*

The map shown in Figure 10.1 is very simple. It breaks down the main idea that advertisers use "five common fallacies" into its five major supporting details, providing the key term for each one. For a more detailed map, you could attach two more boxes to each of the five detail boxes. In one, you could write a definition of the term; in the other, you could write an example of your own that is similar to one given in the paragraph. Concept maps can break down ideas as far as you need to in order to show their relationship.

To study from your map, look at it and recite from it until you can visualize the map and recall from memory what is written in each box. In addition, you should be able to explain from memory the terms or phrases you have written on your map. For instance, if you were studying the map in Figure 10.1 for a test, you should be able to explain what a "glittering generality" is and give an example of one.

Hierarchy Diagram

A **hierarchy** is an arrangement of ideas by their order of importance or rank.

In some of the material you will read in your textbooks, an order of importance, or **hierarchy**, is stated or implied. Levels of government form a hierarchy from the highest offices to those that are subordinate to them. Animals are classified according to a hierarchy based on their species. Bloom's Taxonomy, explained in Chapter 3, is a hierarchy that ranks thinking skills from least complex (knowledge) to most complex (evaluation).

Your diagram of any hierarchy must show how the ideas are ranked in order of importance from lowest to highest or from first to last. See Figure 10.2 for two ways to diagram Maslow's hierarchy of needs, a topic you will encounter in an introductory

FIGURE 10.2

Two Ways to Diagram Maslow's Hierarchy of Needs

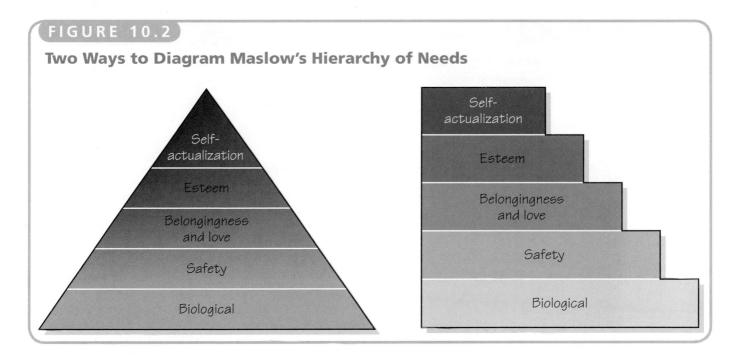

psychology class. The diagrams in Figure 10.2 reflect the key ideas that are highlighted and annotated in the next paragraph.

[*Abraham Maslow was a psychologist who believed that five basic needs motivate human behavior.*] *In Maslow's view, <u>low-level needs have to be at least partially satisfied before higher-level needs can be met.</u> At the bottom of Maslow's hierarchy are* ①**biological** *needs for food, oxygen, water, and sleep. At the next level are* ②**safety** *needs: the need for shelter and clothing and the need to protect oneself from harm. Working to satisfy safety needs consumes the energy of many people. When safety needs are met, the need for* ③**belongingness and love**—*the desire for affection and the need to feel part of a group or society—asserts itself. At the next-to-highest level is the* ④*need for* **esteem**, *or recognition by others of one's self worth and achievements. At the top of Maslow's hierarchy is* ⑤**self-actualization**, *the need to achieve one's fullest potential as a human being. Maslow believed that <u>only a few people,</u> such as Jesus or Gandhi, have ever <u>achieved self-actualization,</u> though everyone has the potential to do so.*	Main Idea Lowest level: biological Highest level: Self-actualization

Notice how the pyramid and the staircase shown in Figure 10.2 above effectively illustrate the hierarchy of needs that Maslow described. First of all, Maslow's needs are listed on different levels of the pyramid, suggesting that they are not equal in rank. For example, biological and safety needs have to be met for survival, but you can live without having the other needs met, even though it is preferable to find love and develop self-esteem. Second, the lowest level of need is at the base of the pyramid and the highest level of need is at the top, showing how they are ranked. Third, the fact that each level of the pyramid gets smaller as you ascend to the top illustrates the idea that fewer and fewer people reach the higher levels of need satisfaction. As Maslow theorized, only a very few people become self-actualized. Similarly, the staircase, like the pyramid, shows the levels of needs and their rankings. See also Chapter 3, Figure 3.6, on page 62, which ranks Bloom's Taxonomy on a staircase diagram. The staircase and pyramid are common formats that you can use to represent any hierarchical arrangement of ideas.

To study from a hierarchy diagram, look it over a few times. Read the information you have listed. Then close your eyes and try to picture the diagram. If you were studying the staircase of Maslow's needs, for example, you would picture the staircase and visualize each need falling into place on the appropriate stair. During a test, you would visualize your map to recall the key words, which in turn would cue your memory to recall the more detailed explanation of each level of need.

Concept Check 10.1

Hierarchy within organizations refers to the ranking of jobs or positions. Your college administration is a hierarchy with the board of trustees at the top, followed by your college president, and so on. What other hierarchies can you describe?

EXERCISE 10.1   Experimenting with Hierarchies

FROM ONE OF YOUR TEXTBOOKS, select some material that is hierarchically arranged—that is, arranged in a certain order from lowest to highest or from most important to least important. Diagram this information to clearly show the hierarchy. Use the pyramid or staircase format illustrated in Figure 10.2, or devise a format of your own that clearly shows the levels and ranking of key ideas. Then share your diagram with the rest of the class.

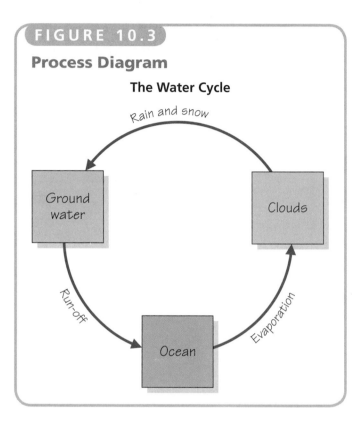

FIGURE 10.3

Process Diagram

The Water Cycle

A **process diagram** illustrates the steps or stages of a process such as digestion or the circulation of blood.

A **function diagram** illustrates parts of a whole in a relationship of interdependence, such as the parts of an automobile engine.

A **branching diagram**, like an idea cluster, is a visual format for organizing ideas.

Concept Check 10.2

Why would a branching diagram *not* be an appropriate format for illustrating a hierarchy such as Bloom's Taxonomy or Maslow's hierarchy of needs?

Process or Function Diagram

A **process diagram** illustrates steps or stages in a procedure or method, showing how they interact and whether they follow a sequence. Processes are an essential part of most courses. In a biology class, you learn how diseases are transmitted or how food is digested in the human body. In a political science class, you learn how a bill becomes a law. In an economics class, you learn how periods of inflation and recession develop. In a social science or psychology class, you read about experiments that explain certain aspects of human behavior. A chart that visually represents a complicated process may make it easier for you to learn and remember each step or stage. The process diagram shown in Figure 10.3 illustrates the natural movement of water from the ocean to freshwater sources and back to the ocean.

A **function diagram** illustrates the parts or functions of an organism or object and may suggest how they work together to ensure the smooth operation of the whole. A diagram of the human skeleton with labels showing the names of the bones is a function diagram. Other examples of the type of information that could be illustrated with a function diagram include the parts of a flower, the three branches of government, or the way the shutter on a camera operates. Function diagrams may include labeled parts along with a brief explanation or arrows to indicate movement—if movement is involved in the function. For an example of a function diagram, see Figure 10.4 on page 252 and see also Chapter 11, Figure 11.5, on page 282, which labels the muscles of the human body.

Whether studying from a process diagram or a function diagram, be sure that you understand exactly the process or function that your diagram represents. Look at your diagram and read your labels. Then close your eyes and visualize the diagram. Try to mentally affix the labels in the right places. At the same time, recite in your own words what happens at each step or stage of a process or what purpose each part or function serves. You can also try to draw and label your diagram from memory. Either way, a combination of visualization and recitation opens sensory pathways that aid information retention.

Branches or Clusters

An idea cluster was first introduced in Chapter 5 as a visual format for taking notes from a lecture. To refresh your memory, see Figure 5.8 on page 123. You can also create an idea cluster from your textbook notes or markings to use as a study guide. In a **branching diagram**, as in a cluster diagram, ideas radiate outward on lines drawn from a central circle. To create a branching diagram, draw a circle in the middle of your page. Inside the circle, write a key word or phrase that summarizes the author's main idea. Draw lines from the circle like the spokes of a wheel, but don't put them too close together. On these lines write the major details that support the main idea. Draw more lines coming off these lines and write in additional examples that support each of the

EXERCISE 10.2 Collaborative Activity on Diagrams

WORK WITH GROUP MEMBERS to identify and read a process diagram or a function diagram. Follow the guidelines for group discussion that appear on the inside back cover of this textbook. Search through all the textbooks you have with you to find a good example of a process diagram or function diagram. These types of diagrams are typical of science and social science textbooks but may also appear in other texts.

Process diagrams are easy to recognize. Look for drawings connected by arrows showing the direction of the process. Look for stages illustrated by connected boxes or circles, as in the diagram of the water cycle (Figure 10.3). Whereas process diagrams illustrate procedures or methods, function diagrams illustrate parts and how they connect or work. In a process diagram, look for labels of parts and brief explanations of how they depend on each other. When you have found a process or function diagram, examine it carefully and read the textbook explanation that accompanies it. Use the following questions to guide your discussion. Record the group's answers to the questions and the group's evaluation, and be prepared to share your results in a class discussion.

1. **Does your diagram illustrate a process or a function? What is the process? What is the function?**

_____

_____

_____

2. **Choose *a* if you chose a process diagram; choose *b* if you chose a function diagram. (a) What are the steps or stages of the process? List and explain. (b) What are the parts and how do they connect? What function do they make possible?**

_____

_____

_____

3. **Does the textbook explanation about the process or function provide additional information that is not illustrated in the diagram? Briefly explain your answer.**

_____

_____

_____

4. **What have you learned from the diagram about the process or function that you did not already know?**

_____

_____

_____

Group Evaluation:
How will you use what you learned about process diagrams? Did your group complete its tasks successfully? What improvements can you suggest? What additional questions do you have about process diagrams? How will you find answers to your questions? Write the evaluation on your own paper or visit *The Confident Student* premium website to download the form.

FIGURE 10.4

Function Diagram

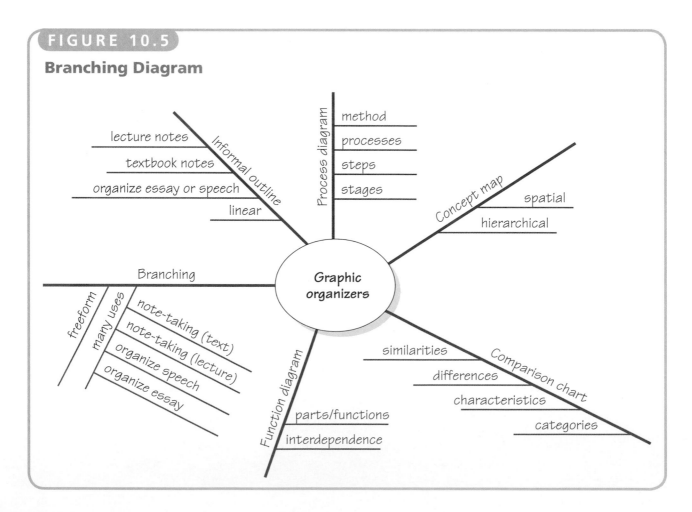

The Parts of a Flower

details. Draw your branches as level as you can so that you don't have to turn the page upside down to write on or read your diagram. Figure 10.5 shows a branching diagram of the six types of tools and organizers explained in this chapter.

Like clustering, branching can also be used as a format for planning an essay or a speech and for taking notes. To brainstorm a topic for writing, draw a circle in the center of your paper around your topic. Add branches to the circle as ideas occur to you. Unlike outlining, branching does not require that you list your ideas in order. You can branch all over your paper, leaving one branch when you think of an idea to connect to another branch. You can also use branching to diagram the major points of a speech. Copy your diagram onto a 5 × 7-inch note card for easy reference during your speech. Finally, branching is a good note-taking method to use when listening to a speaker who does not explain ideas sequentially. Add a new branch whenever the speaker makes another point. If the speaker returns to a previous point that you have already branched, add another line to that branch.

To study from your branching diagrams or clusters, read them over several times. Make sure that you understand how the ideas relate. Then turn your diagram over and, on a clean sheet of paper, try to re-create it. When you've finished, check your new diagram against the original, filling in any details you might have missed.

FIGURE 10.5

Branching Diagram

EXERCISE 10.3 — Learning Styles Application on Making A Study Guide

READ THE FOLLOWING PASSAGE ABOUT the five objectives of financial planning. Underline, highlight, or annotate the passage to make the key ideas stand out. Then make a study guide for the passage, using a graphic organizer that (1) appeals to your learning style and (2) is an appropriate format for the information presented in the passage.

> *For most people, effective financial planning takes into account five lifetime objectives.*
> **Making money** *is a goal that can be reached either through employment or investments.*
> **Managing money** *so that there is some left over for savings after spending is a goal people can reach by becoming effective consumers. Preparing and following a budget, using credit wisely, choosing good investments, buying economical insurance, establishing inexpensive bank accounts, and keeping accurate records of all transactions are all part of being an effective consumer.*
> **Living well** *is a goal many people strive for, in part by trying to achieve financial success. Personal achievement, a challenging career, good health, satisfying relationships, community service, and material comforts are among some of the factors most people equate with living well. The decisions people make about all these factors determine the level of income and savings needed to achieve the quality of life they desire.*
> **Becoming financially secure** *is a goal best achieved through effective money management. People who are financially secure are free from debt and concerns about money. They have enough to buy the things they need plus occasional luxuries. They have savings, investments, and insurance to maintain their quality of life in the future.*
> **Planning for the future** *is a primary reason for saving money and making investments. It is a goal of many people who want to save money for their children's education, to live well in retirement, and to leave an estate for their heirs. This, like the other four, is a lifetime objective.*
> *Making money, managing money, living well, becoming financially secure, and planning for the future are related goals in the sense that achieving one usually requires achieving the others.*

Comparison Chart

- Construct charts or tables that categorize or compare ideas.

A **comparison chart** sorts facts and other information into categories according to similarities and differences or group characteristics. A comparison chart enables you to take information out of context and reorganize it in a way that condenses it and makes it easier to review. If your learning style is visual, you may benefit from using color in your charts or adding small pictures or illustrations. Read the following annotated paragraph and examine the comparison chart shown in Figure 10.6. The annotations show how one student thought through the information explained in the paragraph before making a comparison chart.

A **comparison chart** organizes information in columns and rows to show the similarities or differences between two or more subjects.

> An author may have one of three major purposes for writing. Authors who want to ①inform the reader present facts in an objective way and cover all sides of a topic. Their language is usually formal, and their goal is to explain or instruct. Informational writing is characteristic of textbooks, periodicals, and scholarly journals. Authors whose purpose is to ②entertain are, primarily, storytellers. Their language may be formal or informal, but it is always descriptive. To amuse, delight, and engage the reader's imagination are goals of writers who want to entertain. They write short stories, novels, essays, and poems. Authors whose purpose is to ③persuade have taken a stand on an issue of importance to their readers. These authors may attempt to inflame their readers with emotional language. Their prose is a mix of fact and opinion, and they may slant evidence in their favor. Their goal is to change readers' minds; they speak out from books, from the editorial pages of newspapers, and from popular magazines. Authors' purposes may determine what they write, how they write, and for whom they write.

Main Idea:
3 purposes for writing

1st: inform
2nd: entertain

3rd: persuade

Purpose determines
language, goals,
type of material.

FIGURE 10.6

Comparison Chart

An Author's Three Purposes

	Inform	Entertain	Persuade
Language	Usually formal	Formal or informal; descriptive	May be emotional, slanted
Goals	To explain or instruct	To amuse, delight, engage imagination	To change reader's mind
Type of Material	Textbooks, periodicals, journals	Short stories, novels, poems, essays	Books, editorials, magazine articles

Figure 10.6 above shows the relationship among three purposes for writing and compares their similarities and differences in three categories: the language, goals, and type of material best suited to each purpose. Read down the chart for purposes; read across for a comparison of similarities and differences.

A comparison chart lets you organize a lot of information into a relatively small and compact format that you can put in a notebook for frequent review. You may be able to

---

EXERCISE 10.4   **Charting Key Ideas**

READ THE PASSAGE THAT FOLLOWS. Then organize the important information on the comparison chart, which is partially filled in to get you started. Give the chart a title that indicates what the passage is about.

Several types of social groups play important roles in our lives. Sociologists study two major types of social groups.

Primary groups *are small, and people's relationships within these groups are intimate and personal. Examples of primary groups include families, teams, friends, and lovers. The function of these groups is to act as a buffer against the larger society. You can always come back to a primary group and find security and acceptance.*

Secondary groups *may be either small or large. They are usually organized around a task or a goal, and relationships within them are usually impersonal. Examples of secondary groups include the military, businesses, colleges, and universities. The purpose of these groups is to help you reach a goal or accomplish some type of work. These groups remain fairly impersonal in order to get their work done, but it is possible to develop close relationships with members of your secondary group.*

Title: _____

Type	Size	Relationships		
Primary groups				Families, teams
		Usually impersonal		

draw comparison charts on 5×7-inch note cards, which are even easier to carry with you. Also, comparison charts are easy to make on your laptop, using the "table" feature in your word processing program.

Informal Outlines as Study Tools

- List details under a key idea or essential concept to show their relationship.

Like many students, you probably use some form of outlining to take notes during lectures, to organize your ideas before writing, or to plan a speech. As previously mentioned, outlining a portion of a chapter might also be a first step before making a graphic organizer. For students who are more print oriented than visually oriented, an *informal outline* listing key ideas or essential concepts and the examples or other details that explain them can be a convenient study tool.

Suppose that you are taking a psychology course. You have just finished reading a chapter on motivation and listening to a lecture in class on theories of motivation. During the lecture, your instructor listed some theories on the board and said, "This is important." You have a test in a few days, and you know what you should study: theories of motivation. Your study guide for Maslow's theory might look like the outline shown in Figure 10.7 on page 256. The outline has four key ideas indicated by the numbers 1, 2, 3, and 4. Stars and indentations signal material that supports or explains each of the four key ideas.

You could also write the outline on a 5×7-inch note card. You could make outlines on note cards for all of the theories and cover the same four points: the name of the originator, the gist of the theory, its weaknesses, and what makes the theory useful. How would you study from your outline? You could read and recite the information listed. You could mentally try to fill in details. For example, can you explain each level of need in Maslow's hierarchy without looking back at the chapter? Suppose you get to esteem

Computer CONFIDENCE

Your Computer as a Study Buddy

Once you become comfortable using your computer to organize notes, you can use it to create study guides as well. If you like concept maps, experiment with ways to arrange your notes onscreen. Some software programs like PowerPoint, Microsoft Word, and Inspiration allow you to place boxes and circles around type. You can also use your tabs and margins to set off words or blocks of type in an ordered way; then pencil in boxes or circles on the hard copy.

If you want a concept map that shows a hierarchy, your word processing tools should allow you to use various type sizes to represent levels. Start with the largest type for the most important concept and reduce the type size for each step, ending with the least important stage in the smallest type. You can also use type style functions to diagram differences. Use capitals, boldface, italics, underlines, double underlines, and plain text to make up your own hierarchy, selecting a different style for each idea on your map. Write a key to remember your choices. For example: ALL CAPS = most important idea; **boldface** = secondary idea; *italics* = supporting detail. Comparison charts are easy to make using the Table feature in Microsoft Word. If you have a color printer, you can add a visual element to your chart or table by creating different sections in different colors.

If you already use a laptop to take notes in lectures or make informal outlines from class discussions, you can begin constructing a study guide by

continued

inputting chapter titles and headings from your textbook in outline form. Then, using the Copy and Move functions on your computer, pick up portions of your class notes or lecture notes and insert them in appropriate places in the chapter outline.

Try using numbers for main ideas and asterisks (stars) for details. Or make up your own symbols to set off main and supporting ideas. You can also use different spacing, type styles, or type sizes to make distinctions. Some programs give you a choice of typeface or font so that you can even change the look of the letters. Have fun experimenting with different treatments for important ideas until you find one that helps you visualize your outline at test time.

FIGURE 10.7

Informal Outline as Study Tool

Maslow's Hierarchy

1. Originator: Abraham Maslow

2. Theory: Five basic needs motivate human behavior
    and form a hierarchy from lowest to highest.
    Lower-level needs have to be met first.
    *   Biological, physiological needs (lowest level)
    *   Safety
    *   Belongingness and love
    *   Esteem
    *   Self-actualization (highest level)

3. Weaknesses of theory:
    *   People don't always act
        according to the hierarchy.
    *   A higher-level need might be satisfied
        before a lower-level need.

4. Strength of theory: Researchers agree theory useful
    because it describes motivation in general.

needs and draw a blank. Suppose you can't even remember Maslow's definition of *esteem*. The value of your study tool becomes clear: It tells you what information you need to review or reread. Now look back at the two diagrams of Maslow's needs in Figure 10.2 on page 249 and the highlighted paragraph about Maslow's needs also on page 249. Can you now see how your textbook markings, graphic organizers, and other study tools (such as an informal outline or comparison chart) can all work together to provide a comprehensive review? In the next section, you will learn how to use flashcards—another useful study tool.

Flashcards

• Make three types of flashcards to use for study and review.

Flashcards are an all-purpose study tool, useful for reviewing all kinds of information. They are portable—you can take them anywhere and use them to study from or for review. When you have some time to kill—while waiting in a doctor's office, for example—use that time wisely to review your flashcards.

To make your flashcards, get lined or unlined index cards, colored ones or white ones, and different-sized cards for different purposes. The small 3 × 5-inch cards are good for recording terms and definitions. The larger 5 × 7-inch cards are useful for drawing graphic organizers or brief outlines for study. Listed below are three types of flashcards you can use to round out your study routine. For examples of each type, see Figure 10.8 on page 258.

▼ **Term and Definition Card:** Use this type of card for learning and studying special terms or other vocabulary and chemical formulas and other expressions. Write the term on the front of the card, along with its pronunciation if necessary. On the back of the card, write the definition. For some terms, you might want to add a sentence using the term or give an example.

▼ **Concept Card:** Use this type of card for concepts such as Bloom's Taxonomy, for processes such as the COPE problem-solving strategy, and for the explanation of rules and principles such as how to factor in math or the properties of zero. Write the concept on the front of the card and write the explanation on the back. Keep your explanations brief, and if it has several parts, then use a bulleted or numbered list.

▼ **Question-and-Answer Card:** To make this type of flashcard, write a question on the front and its answer on the back. Questions can come from your reading or from class or lecture notes. Try to anticipate test questions and how you would answer them. Remember to use Bloom's Taxonomy to help you come up with questions on different levels of thinking. Use your question-and-answer flashcards to quiz yourself before a test. If you have a study group, each member should make flashcards. Then you can shuffle all of them together and quiz each other.

To study from your cards, turn them all so that the terms are facing up. Look at a term and try to recite the definition. Turn the card over to check. If you get it right, remove the card from your stack. Follow the same procedure for concepts or questions. If you get it wrong, place the card at the bottom of the stack to review again. Continue in this manner until you have no cards in the stack. You can review your cards silently or aloud, alone or with a partner. After you have reviewed your cards several times, you can remove from the stack the ones you know without question. Then concentrate your efforts on the ones that need further study. From time to time, put all the cards back in the stack and review again to combat forgetting.

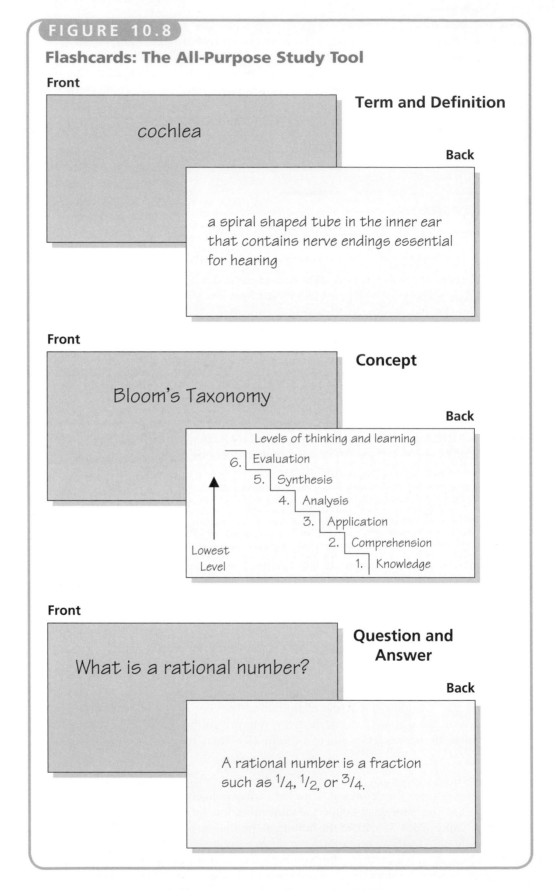

FIGURE 10.8

Flashcards: The All-Purpose Study Tool

Front

Term and Definition

cochlea

Back

a spiral shaped tube in the inner ear that contains nerve endings essential for hearing

Front

Concept

Bloom's Taxonomy

Back

Levels of thinking and learning

6. Evaluation
5. Synthesis
4. Analysis
3. Application
2. Comprehension
1. Knowledge

Lowest Level

Front

Question and Answer

What is a rational number?

Back

A rational number is a fraction such as $1/4$, $1/2$, or $3/4$.

CRITICAL THINKING

Study Tools Teach-In

Exercise Overview

This exercise will help you think critically about and apply what you have learned about the graphic organizers and other study tools explained in this chapter.

Exercise Background

Graphic organizers, comparison charts, informal outlines, and flashcards have many uses. As study guides or tools, they condense a lot of information into formats that are easy to review. As illustrations for your speeches and presentations, graphic organizers provide the audience with a visual example. As examples in reports and research papers, diagrams, charts, and tables help explain complex ideas. As a portable, convenient study tool, a stack of flashcards is a valuable aid.

Exercise Task

Working with a partner or small group, follow these instructions to plan, rehearse, and present an oral presentation in which you teach your classmates how to use one of the study tools explained in this chapter.

1. Decide among yourselves which one of this chapter's study guides or tools you want to demonstrate. If possible, choose something that one or more of you have used successfully so that your presentation will have practical value.
2. Your presentation should explain how to use your study tool and what its purpose is.
3. Present your study tool in a demonstration, skit, or other creative way.
4. Illustrate your presentation with graphics that you make.

Guided CHAPTER REVIEW

The following checklist summarizes this chapter's key terms and strategies. After reading the chapter, how confident are you that you can apply the information you have learned? To assess your level of confidence, respond to each statement with one of the following: *very confident* (3 points), *fairly confident* (2 points), *not very confident* (1 point), *not confident* (0 points). Write your number of points in the box beside each statement. Then add your score and read the analysis that follows. When you have finished, take the chapter quiz.

SUMMARY CHECK

How confident are you about applying these strategies?

Points

☐ 1. Taking a pragmatic approach to studying that involves finding strategies that work

☐ 2. Being committed and persistent

☐ 3. Choosing and using the best graphic organizer for a specific purpose

☐ 4. Selecting key ideas from textbooks to map, diagram, or chart

☐ 5. Knowing how to make a comparison chart

☐ 6. Making informal outlines as study tools

☐ 7. Using three types of flashcards for study and review

How confident is your understanding of this chapter's key terms?

☐ 8. pragmatic

☐ 9. graphic organizer

☐ 10. concept map

☐ 11. hierarchy

☐ 12. process diagram

☐ 13. function diagram

☐ 14. branching diagram

☐ 15. comparison chart

Total

Add your score. The highest possible score is 45. The closer your score is to 45, the higher your level of confidence. Use your *Summary Check* results to help you determine which parts of the chapter to review.

YOUR WEBSITE RESOURCES

This chapter's resources include the following items. To access them, go to *The Confident Student* premium website.

- **Video Skillbuilder: Textbook Note-taking: Traditional Methods**
- **Chapter Exercises**
- **Forms to Download**
- **Chapter Summary of Topics**
- **Thinking Ahead About Career**
- **Confidence Builder Web Search**
- **Self-Test**

CHAPTER REVIEW Quiz

Answer the following questions from memory. Then return to the chapter to check your answers. As a final activity, complete *Show Your Confidence* at the end of the quiz.

1. In your own words, what does it mean to be *pragmatic*, *committed*, or *persistent*? Choose one of these terms to explain.

   _____
   _____

2. What type of study guide lists items according to their order of importance?

   _____
   _____

3. Where do you get the information for making graphic organizers and other study tools?

   _____
   _____

4. What is one type of graphic organizer that you have noticed in one of your textbooks? Explain where you saw the graphic organizer and how it was used.

   _____
   _____

5. What is one graphic organizer you have used successfully, and for what kind of information did you use it?

   _____
   _____

6. What is the difference between a *process diagram* and a *function diagram*?

   _____
   _____

7. What type of study tool illustrates categories, similarities, and differences?

   _____
   _____

8. How does an informal outline differ from a formal outline?

   _____
   _____

9. What are at least two uses of outlining?

   _____
   _____

10. What is one type of flashcard that you have used or would like to try, and why?

   _____
   _____

SHOW YOUR CONFIDENCE

Based on what you have learned from reading Chapters 7 through 10, how would you now rank your own personal study system: excellent, good, fair, or poor? How will using the new strategies you have learned from Chapter 10 either keep your studying at its current level of success or help to improve it? Be prepared to share your answers to these questions either in writing or in class discussion.

Your REFLECTIONS: TAKE THE RISK TO COMMIT AND PERSIST

Reflect on what you have learned from this chapter about studying and learning from textbooks and how you can use this information to improve the way you study. Use the following questions to stimulate your thinking; then write your reflections. Include in your writing specific information from the chapter.

- Would you define yourself as someone who persists despite setbacks? Give an example of a time when you overcame some difficulty in order to succeed.
- Do you currently use graphic organizers or flashcards as study tools?
- How can you incorporate this chapter's study guides and tools with the SQ3R system?

_____

_____

_____

_____

_____

_____

_____

_____

_____

_____

_____

_____

_____

_____

_____

11 Preparing for Tests

Hemera Technologies/AbleStock.com(RF)/Jupiter Images

This chapter encourages you to:

- Use three types of reviews to prepare for tests.

- Know what to do before, during, and after a test to improve your performance.

- Use appropriate strategies for taking objective tests, including standardized tests.

- Identify the instruction words that tell you what kind of information an essay question is seeking, and know how to write an effective answer.

- Identify the causes of test anxiety and work to eliminate them.

- Practice relaxation techniques and positive self-talk to reduce test anxiety.

Confident students are **persistent**. They never give up. They remain focused on their goals despite setbacks.

f you ask college students what their most persistent academic worry is, many will say, "grades." Like most college students, you may be looking for ways to improve your grades and may even wish there were a secret formula or shortcut to success. Although there are no shortcuts, there *is* a key to good grades, and it's no secret: preparation.

Time management, planning, and the use of appropriate study skills are your keys to preparing for tests. This chapter explains how to prepare for tests, how to take tests, and how to reduce test anxiety if that is a problem for you. Many students are especially anxious when it comes to math. Are you a math-anxious student? Help is on the way in the following *Confidence Builder*.

CONFIDENCE BUILDER

Help for the Math-Anxious Student

If you ask students what their most difficult subject is, more often than not, they will say, "math." Estimates of the percentage of entering college students who are underprepared in math may run as high as 60 percent or more at some institutions. It is no wonder that many students suffer from math anxiety.

Math anxiety is mental disorganization, fear, or panic associated with math courses and other math-related situations. Are you a math-anxious student? If so, the fear or panic that you feel may produce physical or mental symptoms, or both. Physical symptoms include sweaty palms, nausea, headaches, and jittery feelings. Mental symptoms include the fear of failure and mental disorganization during a test, such as confusing one concept with another, forgetting what you have studied, or writing down one answer when you really mean to write down another. Does any of this sound familiar?

Math anxiety is a learned response that you can unlearn, but be patient because it may take some time. The best defense against math anxiety is to be prepared. Keep up with assignments and give yourself plenty of time to review for all tests. In addition, try these tips:

- Understand that you can't be relaxed and anxious at the same time, so practice relaxation techniques before you sit down to study and before a test. The desktop relaxation technique explained in Chapter 8, the chair-seat relaxation technique explained in Chapter 13, and the visualization technique explained in this chapter are all helpful strategies.

- As soon as you receive a test, jot down memory cues—rules and formulas that you will need to use but are likely to forget if you become anxious.
- Learn mathematical terms. Math has its own language. Numbers, symbols, and formulas stand for ideas and relationships. Review these often until you know them; then you will be less likely to forget them on a test.
- Always do all the problems at the end of a textbook chapter even if they have not been assigned. Practice develops skill, and with skill comes confidence.
- Learn from your mistakes. Know the differences among concept errors, application errors, and careless errors. Concept errors occur when you haven't learned a rule or principle needed to solve a problem. Application errors occur when you do know the concept but you apply it incorrectly. Careless errors are often proofreading errors, such as dropping a plus or minus sign.
- If more than one math course is required for your program, take them in consecutive terms to prevent loss of skill from one course to the next.
- Above all, attend class regularly and keep up with assignments. A math course develops sequentially and gets more difficult toward the end of the term.

Follow Up: To explore this topic further, visit *The Confident Student* premium website for an online search activity about math anxiety.

Know When, What, and How to Study

- Use three types of reviews to prepare for tests.

If you walk into a test knowing that you are well prepared, you will feel confident that you can succeed. If you do not prepare sufficiently, you will probably feel a lack of confidence and perhaps even some anxiety that you will not earn a good grade. Preparation is your best defense against test anxiety. The strategies explained in the next few sections can help you prepare for tests with confidence.

You may already use some strategies to prepare for tests, but is there more that you could do? Find out by completing *Awareness Check* 11.1.

When to Study

To prepare for tests takes time. To avoid running out of time, make room in your schedule for daily, weekly, and pre-exam reviews. These three types of reviews not only aid retention but help reduce the anxiety and feelings of unpreparedness that result from having to cram the night before a test.

Daily Reviews. In addition to the time you spend studying new material, take five to ten minutes per day to review each course. Begin your review by looking over your notes and assignments from the previous class. Immediately, or as soon as possible after class,

AWARENESS CHECK 11.1

How Well Do You Prepare for Tests?

Choose one of the following as your response to each statement: *always* (4 points), *usually* (3 points), *occasionally* (2 points), *rarely* (1 point). Write your number of points in the box beside each statement. When you are finished, add your score.

Points

☐ 1. I allow enough time for daily, weekly, and pre-exam reviews.

☐ 2. I am good at figuring out what I should study for a test.

☐ 3. I use SQ3R or another system for studying.

☐ 4. I am satisfied with my grades.

☐ 5. When reviewing my mistakes, I can tell what kinds of errors they are.

☐ 6. I do not become distracted during a test.

☐ 7. I enter a testing situation feeling mentally and physically prepared.

☐ 8. I have a test-taking routine: There are certain things I do before, during, and after any test.

☐ 9. I am good at taking objective tests (true-false, fill-in, multiple-choice).

☐ 10. I know how to plan and write an effective answer for an essay exam.

Total   *Add your score. If your total is 35–40, you have developed some strategies that help you prepare for tests. If your total is 29–34, you may be prepared most of the time, but you could do better. If your total is 10–28, you probably are not satisfied with your grades and would benefit by being better prepared for tests. Whatever your level of skill, this chapter's strategies will help you improve the way you prepare for tests.*

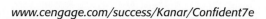

review new material and try to relate it to what you have learned in the course so far. In doing this, you will make connections among topics and gain a broad perspective on the course.

Weekly Reviews. In addition to the time you spend doing assignments, spend about an hour at the end of the week reviewing each subject. Review lecture notes, textbook notes, and your study guides and try to anticipate test questions. A weekly review is an in-depth look at what you have covered in a course during one week. Relate the current week's work to the previous week's work and determine how the new material fits into the course.

Pre-Exam Reviews. About one week before a test, conduct a major review. Exam reviews will take longer than weekly reviews because they may cover several weeks' material. To prepare for exams, review lecture notes, textbook notes, graphic organizers and other self-made study guides, flashcards, instructors' handouts, and previous tests, papers, or graded assignments. If you have been doing your daily and weekly reviews, the material will seem familiar so that you may notice a pattern in the topics you are studying and may also think of possible test questions.

Your study schedule should allow five to ten minutes a day per course for daily reviews, an hour per course for weekly reviews, and two hours or more for a specific exam review. Pre-exam reviews are the hardest because they take the longest and cover the most material. Try these tips for improving concentration when you have to study for two or more hours:

▼ Review at the time of day when you are most alert.

▼ Study for your hardest exam first.

▼ About once every hour, take a short break. Stand up and walk around or do something unrelated to studying.

▼ Reward yourself for getting the job done. Plan to go out with friends or relax when you have finished your review.

Relaxing and talking with others for a few moments is a good way to break from an exam review.

EXERCISE 11.1 Your Exam Schedule

MAKE OUT A NEW WEEK'S schedule. Include time for daily reviews and for one weekly review. After you have completed this schedule, update your semester or quarter calendar. Schedule times for major exam reviews one week before each test date. Visit *The Confident Student* premium website to download a copy of the weekly schedule form that was introduced in Chapter 6 (on time management).

What to Study

Test questions can come from a variety of sources. To study for a major test, review lecture notes, textbook chapters, textbook notes and study guides, previous tests, papers, homework, and instructors' handouts. Don't waste time reviewing information you already know; study material you have not fully grasped. Study the most difficult material first. If you study the easiest topics first, then by the time you get to the hard ones, you will probably be tired and unable to give them your best effort. Study the most complex or technical concepts when you are most alert; be willing to look up definitions and reread sentences until you grasp their meaning. Later, when you are tired, take a short break and then study less challenging material. Your understanding of the subject will lead to improved confidence and productivity. Listed below are some tips that will help you decide what to study.

Lecture Notes. Lectures often supplement information presented in textbooks. They are usually organized around a major topic in the course outline. If your instructor gives weekly lectures, the lecture topics probably build on weekly assigned chapters and the week's topic listed in your syllabus.

Textbook Chapters. Review your underlining and marginal notes. If you have underlined or annotated the most important ideas, your review will be both efficient and thorough.

Textbook Notes and Study Guides. Review any additional notes, maps, outlines, flashcards, or other study materials you have made. Since your own notes and guides are summaries of textbook material written in your own words, they will be the easiest for you to remember.

Graded Tests, Papers, Homework, and Other Assignments. Your previous tests are useful for two reasons. First, you can determine from these tests the kinds of questions your instructor asks. Second, you can learn from your mistakes. Questions that you missed enable you to spot weak points in your studying—information that you forgot, ignored, or didn't understand. Instructors' comments on papers and other graded assignments may also point out strengths and weaknesses and provide clues about what you should study.

Instructors' Handouts. Anything your instructor hands out is bound to be important. Instructors frequently summarize information on handouts. Don't overlook these important study aids when you review for a major test.

Course and Instructor Websites. If applicable, visit your instructor's website and course website to see if anything is mentioned about upcoming tests or material that should be studied prior to the test. In addition, many textbooks offer companion websites that include interactive testing and quizzing to help you practice for upcoming exams.

Figure 11.1 is a checklist showing what to study for tests. Make your own checklist. Before a test, check off the items you need to study. Organizing your materials beforehand establishes a framework for studying and builds confidence.

FIGURE 11.1

What to Study for Tests: A Checklist

☐ Lecture notes

☐ Underlining, highlighting, marginal notes

☐ Graphic organizers, note cards, and other study aids

☐ Graded tests and exercises

☐ Instructor's comments on papers

☐ Instructor's handouts

☐ Terms and definitions

☐ Formulas and sample problems

☐ Broad concepts and theories

☐ Lab notes

As mentioned in previous chapters, you may benefit from studying with another student. Comparing your notes with someone else's can help both of you. What one of you misses the other may have in his or her notes. Also, students vary in their understanding of lectures and textbook chapters. A topic that gave you trouble may have been easy for a friend. Talking it over gives you another perspective on the subject.

How to Study

Once you have decided *what* to study, *how* you study will determine the effectiveness of your review. Don't study in a hit-or-miss fashion, and don't reread chapters. Instead, use a system. By now you may have tried the suggestions in Chapter 9 for using SQ3R or for adapting a system to your learning style. If your system is working, use it. If you would like to try a different strategy, follow these steps to prepare for a major test in one of your courses:

1. One week before the test, schedule two or more hours of time to review all chapters and topics that the test will cover. Do not attempt to study for two hours straight without taking a break, because you will lose interest and concentration. Instead, plan your study time to review specific material in several short sessions, taking a break in between.

2. Organize your materials. Sort lecture notes, textbook notes, study guides, handouts, and previously graded tests and assignments by chapter or topic; then make a list of the important topics, kinds of problems, or other specific information you think will be on a test.

3. If you must review a lot of facts, terms, formulas, steps in a process, or similar material, make flashcards to carry in your pocket or purse. Recite from these cards, silently or aloud, at every opportunity. Keep your cards simple; write just enough to serve as a memory cue. For examples of three types of flashcards to make, see Chapter 10, Figure 10.8 on page 258.

4. Make graphic organizers or study guides of any information that you think will be difficult to remember. As explained in Chapter 10, graphic organizers such as maps and diagrams visually represent the relationship among ideas. Graphic organizers are convenient; they summarize a lot of information in a little space. When studying for or taking a test, close your eyes and visualize your maps or diagrams. Reconstruct them in your mind and try to "see" what you have written or drawn.

5. Once a day until you take the test, review your study guides and other materials. Review them again the night before the test, just before you go to sleep. Research shows that studying before sleeping improves retention. Then review once more on the day of the test.

Knowing when, what, and how to study will help you prepare for a test, but when the day of the test arrives, is there anything more you can do to help you stay focused during the test and ensure your best performance? You will find the answer in the next section.

CRITICAL THINKING Pre-Exam Checklist

Exercise Overview

This exercise will help you think critically about the material covered in one of your courses and determine what to study for the next test.

Exercise Background

Many students say they are often not prepared for tests because they do not know what to study. As a result, they may not study at all, or their studying may be hit or miss. The easiest way to determine what a test will cover is to ask the instructor. Most instructors conduct a review before a test anyway, and most are happy to tell you what chapters to review. Some may emphasize specific skills or concepts to practice. Therefore, there is really no excuse for not knowing what to study.

Exercise Task

Choose a study partner who is in one of your other classes—algebra or psychology, for example. Discuss what your class has covered recently and when your next test will be. Look through all of your course materials together and make a checklist similar to the one in Figure 11.1 on page 268. Beside each item on your checklist, write something specific to study. For example, if "textbook notes" is on your list, write down the chapters that you need to study. Plan a time to study with your partner. When you get your test results, evaluate your checklist to determine whether your studying was effective.

Develop a Test-Taking Routine

• Know what to do before, during, and after a test to improve your performance.

You can improve your grades on tests by developing a routine to follow that helps you stay calm, avoid distractions, and demonstrate your knowledge. The following list of suggestions is a test-taking routine that focuses your attention on what to do before, during, and after a test to ensure your best performance. These strategies may help prevent anxiety from sabotaging your efforts.

Before the Test

Let's say that you have reviewed sufficiently and are well prepared on test day. You have had a good night's sleep, fortified yourself with a nutritious breakfast, and are ready for the test. Now here are five things you can do before the test to calm yourself, focus, and ensure your best performance.

Arrive on Time. If hearing other students discuss the test beforehand makes you nervous and distracted, don't arrive too early. Arrive on time and try to sit near the front of the room, where you are less likely to be distracted. If you feel a little nervous, close your eyes, take a few deep breaths, and think positive thoughts. If anxiety either before or during tests is a problem, you will benefit from the suggestions given later in this chapter for reducing anxiety.

Jot Down Memory Cues. If you are likely to forget facts, formulas, dates, names, terms, or other items, write them in the margin or on the back of the test as soon as you get it.

For example, math students tend to get nervous when they are working on a difficult problem or can't remember the next step in a mathematical operation. This anxiety can cause them to forget other concepts and applications. The facts, formulas, and other items that you jot down on your test are memory cues. Knowing that the cues are there will boost your confidence. You won't be worried about forgetting the information, and you will be able to concentrate on taking the test.

Survey the Test. As soon as you receive your test and after you have jotted down your memory cues, survey the test to determine how many questions there are, how many points each is worth, and what kinds of questions you must answer: true-false, multiple-choice, fill-in, or essay. If it's not clear from the test how many points each question is worth, ask your instructor. A quick survey of the test will let you know what you must accomplish within the time limit so that you can plan your test-taking time.

Plan and Use All Your Time. Plan to spend the most time answering the questions that are worth the most points. If 25 multiple-choice questions are worth one point each, and two essay questions are worth 25 points each, and you have 50 minutes to complete the test, answer as many of the multiple-choice questions as you can in 10 minutes. That will leave you 40 minutes to complete the two essay questions. Spend 15 minutes answering the first question; then stop and go on to the next one, even if you have not finished. Spend 15 minutes on the second question. You will now have 10 minutes left. Use the 10 minutes as needed. You can return to the multiple-choice questions if you have completed the essays, or you can work more on your essays if you have finished the multiple-choice questions earlier. Save a few minutes to proofread the whole test and answer any multiple-choice questions that you may have skipped.

Although there are many ways to plan your time, the one suggested here will help you gain some points for each part of the test, even if you are unable to finish all of the questions. If you plan your time and stick to your plan, you will not have to rush. Use all of your time, even if you don't need it. The extra care you take may help you spot mistakes or think of a better way to state an answer.

Read Directions. It may seem obvious that you should read test directions before beginning, but a surprising number of students skip directions. Perhaps they think that reading directions wastes time or that they already know what to do. To avoid needless mistakes, always read directions and ask the instructor to explain anything that you do not understand.

During the Test

Jotting down memory cues, surveying the test, planning and using all your time, and reading directions as soon as you get your test will take only a couple of minutes. These strategies should boost your confidence by giving you an overview of what is to come. So that you don't waste your remaining test time, follow five more suggestions for taking the test.

Do Easy Questions First. When you survey the test, you will probably spot questions that will be easy for you to answer. Do those first because you have a good chance of getting the answers right. In addition, doing the easy questions first will raise your confidence in your ability to answer the rest of the questions.

Skip and Return to Difficult Questions. Don't spend too much time on a difficult question. Skip it and return to it later. If something you read or recall as you answer the other questions triggers your memory, you can go back to the one you didn't answer and then resume taking the test where you left off.

Guess If There Is No Penalty. If there is a penalty for wrong answers, the test directions will probably say so. If you are in doubt, ask the instructor. If there is no penalty, guess. Don't leave questions blank; even if you don't think you know the answer, write something anyway. You may pick up a few points. If you guess the answer to a multiple-choice question that has four choices, your chances are one in four that you will get the right answer. If you don't answer, your chances are zero.

Control Your Feelings and Attention. Remain in control of your feelings and attention throughout the test. To avoid becoming distracted, focus your attention on the test. Keep your eyes on the test and don't look up or around. If you don't know what other students are doing, you're not likely to be disturbed by them. You won't notice what page someone else is on or whether someone finishes early.

Maintain a Positive Attitude. Don't let negative thoughts undermine your work. Counteract them with positive ones. Say to yourself, "I have studied, and I am doing fine." If you become anxious, close your eyes, breathe deeply, and relax. When you feel calm, return to the test and give it your full attention. See later in the chapter for more suggestions on how to reduce test anxiety.

After the Test

When you finish your test, you are not done. If you have not successfully planned your time, you may have to rush to the finish before time is up. Rushing may cause you to make careless errors. With no time left to proofread your answers and find these

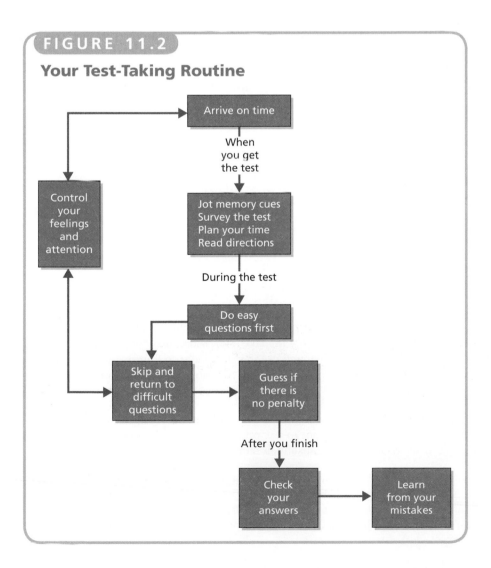

FIGURE 11.2

Your Test-Taking Routine

EXERCISE 11.2   Learning Styles Application on Test-Taking

DISCOVER YOUR OWN BEST WAY to prepare for a test by answering the following questions about test preparation and your learning style.

1. **Based on your answers to *Awareness Check* 11.1, what are your strengths and weaknesses in preparing for tests?**

   _____

   _____

2. **What relationship do you see between your body's reactions and the way you prepare for tests? For example, when is your best time to study, and how do you accommodate your body's reactions to hunger, tiredness, stress, and so on when preparing for tests?**

   _____

   _____

3. **What is your preferred learning style (visual, auditory, tactile/kinesthetic), and how does it affect the way you prepare for tests?**

   _____

   _____

4. **Are you self-motivated or other-motivated, and how does your source of motivation affect your ability to study for tests?**

   _____

   _____

5. **What changes can you make in the way you prepare for tests that will help you take advantage of your learning style preferences?**

   _____

   _____

mistakes, you could lose enough points to lower your grade significantly. Also, think of a test as a learning experience. If you make a low score, it is not the end of the world. Figure out what you did wrong, and use the knowledge to improve your studying and strengthen your test-taking routine. Here are two more things you should do when you finish the test.

Check Your Work. Always save time to proofread your test for careless errors and for questions you skipped or forgot to answer. Because first choices are usually correct, change answers only if you're absolutely sure your first answer was wrong.

Learn from Your Mistakes. The next time your instructor returns a graded test, determine what kinds of mistakes you made. Look for a pattern. If you are like many students, you probably make the same mistakes over and over again. If you can prevent these errors, you will improve your test scores.

Master Objective Tests

- Use appropriate strategies for taking objective tests, including standardized tests.

Objective tests include true-false, multiple-choice, and fill-in-the-blank tests. An **objective test** requires you to recognize the correct answer among a list of choices (multiple-choice) or based on information that is given (true-false), or to complete an answer that is partially given (fill-in-the-blanks). In other words, you do not have to construct the answer entirely from memory as you would when taking an essay test. If you are well prepared for a test, you should be able to answer the questions successfully no matter what type of test it is. However, when you are confronted with questions you cannot answer, try to gain points by making informed guesses.

An **objective test** requires you to recognize the answer among the choices given rather than having to recall the answer entirely from memory. Examples of objective tests include multiple-choice and true-false tests.

True-False Tests

If you have studied the information, it is likely that you will know the answer to a true-false question. What if you haven't studied, or what if you *have* studied but you still don't know the answer? Because a true-false question has only two possible answers, you have a 50 percent chance of choosing the right one if you guess. Use two strategies for guessing the answer to a true-false question when you are sure that you don't know the answer:

1. Assume a statement is false if it contains absolute words.

2. Assume a statement is false if any part of it is false.

Mark a statement *false* if it contains **absolute words** such as *always, never, invariably, none, no one, all,* and *everyone*. Absolute words tend to make statements false because they do not allow for exceptions. For example, you should mark the statement

Absolute words like *always* and *never* rule out exceptions.

EXERCISE 11.3 Which Is True or False?

USE THE GUESSING STRATEGIES YOU just learned to mark the following statements *T* for *true* and *F* for *false*. Work with a partner or complete the exercise on your own.

	T	F
1. The heart contains a left and right ventricle.	☐	☐
2. You can look up the meaning of a word in a glossary, index, or dictionary.	☐	☐
3. All fears are acquired at an early age.	☐	☐
4. Making note cards is the only way to study vocabulary.	☐	☐
5. Whenever there is a fatal accident on the highway, drinking is invariably involved.	☐	☐
6. It is doubtful whether there is human life on other planets.	☐	☐
7. College graduates will always be able to find good jobs.	☐	☐
8. Most violent crime today is drug related.	☐	☐
9. Carl Jung has been called "the father of modern psychology."	☐	☐
10. The *numbers 1, 3, 5,* and *9* are prime numbers.	☐	☐

"It never gets cold in Florida" *false* because the word *never* means "never in the history of the world." It is highly unlikely that there is a place on Earth where it has never gotten cold even once. Is the next statement true or false? "A statement that contains an absolute word is always false." The statement is false. Remember, absolute words *usually* make statements false, but not always.

Mark a statement *false* if any part of it is false. If part of a statement is untrue, then the whole statement is untrue. For example, the statement "*Hamlet, Macbeth,* and *The Dream Merchant* are three of Shakespeare's most famous tragedies" is false. Although Shakespeare did write *Hamlet* and *Macbeth,* he did not write *The Dream Merchant.* If you don't know whether a statement is true or false, but you're certain that part of it is untrue, mark it *false.*

Multiple-Choice Tests

Stem refers to the question part of a multiple-choice item.

Options refers to the answer choices in a multiple-choice item.

Distractors are the wrong options in a multiple-choice item.

A multiple-choice item on a test consists of a question followed by several answer choices. The part of a multiple-choice item that asks the question is called the **stem**. The answer choices are called **options**, and only one of them is correct. The incorrect options are called **distractors** because they distract your attention away from the correct option. Usually there are four options, though there might be three or five. Your job is to identify the one correct option. You can do this in several ways.

▸ If you know the material, first answer the question mentally and then read all the options and choose the correct one.

▸ If you know the material but cannot answer the question mentally, read the options, eliminate those you know are incorrect, and choose the answer from those remaining. The more wrong options you eliminate, the more likely your choice will be correct.

▸ If you do not know the material, or if you cannot figure out the answer, guess.

Options that contain the phrases "all of the above" or "none of the above" are frequently the correct choices. If two options are similar—for example, "Northern Hemisphere" and "Southern Hemisphere"—one of the options is probably the correct answer. Finally, if one option is more complete or contains more information than the others, it may be the correct one.

An option that contains an absolute word such as *all, always,* or *never* is probably a distractor—an incorrect answer. An option that contains an unfamiliar word may also be a distractor. Many students assume that an unfamiliar term is probably the correct answer, but it is more often a wrong answer. When you are guessing, you are more likely to choose the right answer if you choose an option that is familiar to you. Finally, if the list of options is a list of numbers, middle numbers tend to be correct answers, and the highest and lowest numbers in the list tend to be distractors. These strategies are not foolproof, but they may be useful as a last resort if you must guess the answer to a question.

One final word of caution: A well-written multiple-choice test makes guesswork difficult because a good test writer knows all the guessing strategies. Thorough preparation is still your best strategy for taking any kind of test.

Fill-in-the-Blank Tests

A fill-in test may require you to recall an answer from memory or choose an answer from a list of options. Choosing an answer from a list is easier than recalling an answer from memory. In either case, the information given in the incomplete statement may provide clues that will help you decide what to write in the blanks. Three strategies can help you fill in the blanks correctly.

First, decide what kind of answer the statement requires. Read the statement carefully and decide whether you are required to supply a name, a date, a place, or some other kind of information. Knowing what the question asks will help you recall or select the right answer.

EXERCISE 11.4 Collaborative Activity on Using Guessing Strategies

THIS EXERCISE ASKS YOU AND the members of your group to practice the guessing strategies that are appropriate to use when you do not know the answer to a multiple-choice item. Your tasks are as follows:

1. First, each person should answer questions 1–10.

2. Next, discuss your answers and come to a consensus about the best answer choice for each question. Be able to explain why you think your answer is correct and the strategy you used to arrive at it. Review the guessing strategies explained in this chapter as needed.

3. Finally, summarize your answers and explanations on a separate piece of paper to be handed in along with the group evaluation. Visit *The Confident Student* premium website to download an evaluation form. Also, don't forget to follow the guidelines for group discussion that appear on the inside back cover of the book.

Multiple-Choice Questions:

1. A marriage may have a better chance of succeeding if the spouses have which characteristic in common?
   a. a similar level of education
   b. similar social and economic backgrounds
   c. shared interests and goals
   d. all of the above

2. Most of the assignments college students are asked to do require them to use
   a. left-brain capacities.
   b. right-brain capacities.
   c. learning styles.
   d. visualization.

3. Which of the following are examples of fallacious reasoning?
   a. glittering generalities
   b. plain folks
   c. bandwagon
   d. glittering generalities, plain folks, and bandwagon

4. A balanced diet should include
   a. milk, cheese, and fruit.
   b. bread, cereals, and whole grains.
   c. milk, fruit, vegetables, meat, and whole grains.
   d. vegetables, fruit, and meat.

5. Most of the world's population is situated
   a. in the Pacific Islands.
   b. in the Northern Hemisphere.
   c. in the Southern Hemisphere.
   d. near the equator.

6. Approximately what percentage of immigrants to the United States between 1971 and 1984 came from Asia?
   a. 60 percent
   b. 30 percent
   c. 40 percent
   d. 15 percent

7. Which of the following words is a synonym for *intractable*?
   a. synergistic
   b. acerbic
   c. exacerbating
   d. stubborn

8. Television commercials
   a. always attempt to deceive viewers.
   b. are sometimes interesting to viewers.
   c. are never in the public interest.
   d. influence only people who listen to them.

9. The first quiz programs were televised
   a. in the 1970s.
   b. in the 1950s.
   c. in the 1940s.
   d. before 1920.

10. A smile
   a. may mean different things in different societies.
   b. always signifies happiness.
   c. occurs among the people of only some societies.
   d. never occurs involuntarily.

Group Evaluation:

What advantages do guessing strategies offer? What is the best way to avoid having to guess? Did your group complete its tasks successfully? What additional questions do you have about taking multiple-choice tests? Write the evaluation on your own paper, or visit *The Confident Student* premium website to download the form.

EXERCISE 11.5 Fill in the Blanks

THE FOLLOWING FILL-IN-THE-BLANK test covers the section you have just read: "Master Objective Tests." First, review the information contained in this section. Next, close your book and complete the test for practice. When you have finished the test, open your book and check your answers. Any questions that you missed indicate material that needs additional review.

1. **Three common types of objective tests are ____________, ____________, and ____________.**
2. **Words such as *always, never,* and *only* are called ________________________.**
3. **These words generally indicate a wrong answer because ________________________ ____.**
4. **A statement is false if any part of it is ________________________.**
5. **The question part of a multiple-choice item is called the ________________________.**
6. **____________ are the possible answers to a multiple-choice question.**
7. **Incorrect answer choices to a multiple-choice question are called ________________________.**
8. **Three strategies to use when taking fill-in-the-blank tests are ____________, ____________, and ____________.**

Second, the way that a statement is written may help you decide how to complete it. Your answer should complete the statement logically and grammatically. For example, if you are asked to choose options from a list to fill in the blanks and the statement you are working on requires a verb to complete it, scan the list for verbs and choose the one that best fits the context.

Third, key words in statements may help you determine what topic the question covers. Knowing the topic will help you recall information needed to complete the statement. For example, if a question asks you to briefly describe Piaget's third stage of development, the key words *Piaget* and *third stage of development* let you know that the topic is Piaget's stages. If you can't recall the third stage, mentally reconstructing the other stages may jog your memory.

Standardized Tests

You can't study for a standardized test, but there are ways to prepare yourself for success. First of all, commercial study guides are available for tests like the GRE. Your campus bookstore or local bookstore may have a guide for the test you need to take. Also, find out if your college offers a prep course or review session that will help you get ready for the test. In addition, try these suggestions:

- Know how many sections there are on the test and what each section covers. Find out whether you will be required to write one or more essays.
- Find out whether the test will be timed, how long it will last, and how much time you will have to complete each section. If the test will last longer than two hours, take a snack that you can eat during a break for a quick energy boost.
- If you must write an essay as part of the test, practice writing in a timed situation. Choose a topic, set a timer or alarm clock, and write your essay. If you practice writing within a time limit, you are less likely to become anxious when taking a timed test.

▼ Find out if you will be allowed to use a dictionary, calculator, or other learning aids or reference tools during the test.

▼ Find out whether the test is administered online or with examination booklets. Then purchase any special materials you will need.

▼ Get a good night's sleep, eat a nourishing breakfast, and arrive at the testing site on time, rested, and in a positive frame of mind.

▼ To increase your chances of scoring well, apply the test-taking strategies you have learned from this chapter. Use guessing strategies if there is no penalty for guessing and if you do not know the answer.

▼ During breaks between sections of the test, stand up and move around to increase your circulation. This little bit of exercise will make you feel more alert when you return to the test.

▼ Whether working online or on an answer sheet, use any remaining time to proofread and correct your answers.

Don't worry if you are unable to complete a section of the test. On some standardized tests, hardly anyone finishes. Also, you can miss many of the items and still make a passing score. Finally, even if you score below a cutoff on a standardized test, you may be allowed to retake the part of the test on which you scored low.

Banarastock(RF)/Jupiter Images

Come to a test prepared, nourished, rested, and in a positive frame of mind.

Answer Essay Questions with Confidence

- Identify the instruction words that tell you what kind of information an essay question is seeking, and know how to write an effective answer.

You can expect to see two kinds of essay questions—those that require a short answer and those that require a longer, more developed answer. You can often tell how much you are expected to write by the number of points a question is worth or the amount of space left between questions. Sometimes the directions will be specific: "Answer any two of the five questions that follow and devote no more than a page to each." If you are not sure how much you should write or how detailed your instructor expects your answer to be, ask. In general, follow these guidelines for composing answers to essay questions of the short-answer type:

▼ Read the question carefully and make sure you understand what the question asks.

▼ Watch for instruction words. Short-answer questions often ask you to supply definitions, examples, or other specific pieces of information.

▼ Concentrate on answering the question briefly and precisely.

▼ Stay on the topic and avoid stating your opinion or making judgments unless the question asks you to do so.

▼ Restate the question in your answer. Doing this makes it easier for your instructor to read and follow your explanation.

If you do not know the answer to a question, go on to another part of the test and return to it later. Information you read in another question may jog your memory. In any case, don't leave a question unanswered. Try to write something. Essay questions are often worth several points, and you have nothing to lose by attempting to answer. Read the following sample test question and its answer:

> **Question:** Define *memory* and illustrate your definition with examples.
>
> ***Answer:*** *Memory is a mental process that occurs in three stages: record, retain, and recall. Information comes in through your five senses. Most of this information you will forget unless you record it in your short-term memory through selective attention. Short-term memory is fleeting. It enables you to remember a phone number you have looked up long enough to dial it or the name of someone you met at a party long enough to introduce him or her to someone else. To retain information for even longer periods of time you must transfer it from short-term memory to long-term memory. You can do this by using or reviewing the information. Long-term memory can be permanent. For example, you never forget your birthday. In the recall stage, you retrieve information you have stored, much as you would retrieve a file from a computer's directory.*

Instruction words are terms that tell you how to answer a question.

This answer responds to both **instruction words** in the question: *define* and *illustrate*. The student defines memory as a three-stage process, names and explains each stage, and gives examples of each. Figure 11.3 contains a list of instruction words that are frequently used in essay questions and their meanings.

Some essay questions require a longer answer that may cover several points. You will stand a better chance of getting a good grade if your answer is detailed but not rambling, if you stick to facts and information and avoid opinions and judgments, if your answer follows a logical plan of development, and if you state your ideas clearly in error-free sentences. In general, apply the same skills you use for writing essays in your composition class to composing answers to essay questions. Be sure to look for instruction words in each question that will tell you what kind of answer to write.

FIGURE 11.3

Instruction Words Used in Essay Questions

INSTRUCTION WORDS	MEANINGS
Compare	Explain similarities and differences.
Contrast	Explain differences only.
Criticize or evaluate	Make a judgment about strengths and weaknesses, worth or merit, or positive or negative aspects.
Define	Give a precise and accurate meaning.
Describe	Give a mental impression, a detailed account.
Discuss or explain	Give reasons, facts, or details that show you understand.
Enumerate or list	State points one by one and briefly explain.
Illustrate	Explain by using examples.
Interpret	Explain in your own words and discuss significance.
Justify or prove	Construct an argument for or against and support with evidence.
Outline	Describe in general and cover main ideas.
Relate	Show a connection among ideas.
Summarize	Condense main ideas; state them briefly.
Trace	Describe a series of steps, stages, or events.

The following general guidelines will help you compose good answers to longer essay test questions. See also Chapter 12 for more information on how to improve your writing not only for answering essay questions but for other tasks as well.

▼ Read the question carefully. Watch for instruction words and make sure you understand what the question asks you to do. Ask the instructor for an explanation if necessary.

▼ Think about what you will write. Plan your answer and allow yourself enough time to write thoughtfully.

▼ Jot down a rough outline of the important ideas you will cover so that you don't forget them.

▼ Incorporate the question into your first sentence and briefly state your answer to the question.

▼ In the rest of your essay, provide enough details to explain your answer and to demonstrate your knowledge of the material.

▼ Save time at the end of the exam to proofread your essay and correct errors.

Now that you know how to prepare for all kinds of tests, do you still feel a little test-anxious? If so, the rest of this chapter will help you tackle that problem and find a solution.

The Causes of Test Anxiety

• Identify the causes of test anxiety and work to eliminate them.

Test anxiety is stress that is related to a testing situation, and it may affect students in different ways. Test anxiety is of two types: situational and chronic. **Situational test anxiety** is the most common and may occur only when you are unprepared or when the test has a lot riding on it. Final exams, certification or board exams, and other tests of skill that determine whether you move forward or stay behind are anxiety provoking for most students. Some situational test anxiety is both rational and expected. **Chronic test anxiety** is more severe and less common. Students who have this type of anxiety get nervous at the mere mention of a test. Their fear of testing may be so paralyzing that it affects their performance. Chronic test anxiety that does not respond to relaxation techniques combined with adequate test preparation is best dealt with by professionals who can provide the kind of help needed to overcome the anxiety.

Test anxiety is recognizable by various physical and mental symptoms. Do you have any of these symptoms? Take *Awareness Check* 11.2 to find out.

The best way to overcome test anxiety is to understand its causes and to realize that the specific triggers and effects of test anxiety may vary. As explained earlier in this chapter, the most common cause of most test anxiety is lack of preparation. Test anxiety may result from three other common causes as well:

▼ Fear of not meeting expectations

▼ Equating grades and self-worth

▼ Feelings of helplessness

Fear of Not Meeting Expectations

Many students' **perceptions** of what their parents or important others expect may be inaccurate. If you worry that you will alienate people you care about unless you do well in college, you may become fearful and anxious that you will disappoint them or make them angry. If you believe that you can't live up to the expectations of others, tests may make you especially anxious. Suppose your parents or important others become angry

Test anxiety is stress that is related to testing. It can occur before a test or during a test or may be triggered by thinking about tests.

Situational test anxiety commonly results when you are insufficiently prepared for a test or when the test is an important one.

Chronic test anxiety is less common, but those who have it may become anxious even though they are well prepared for a test.

Perceptions involve an awareness or understanding gained through the senses. Perceptions may or may not reflect reality.

Awareness CHECK 11.2

Do You Have Test Anxiety?

Never	Sometimes	Usually	**Check the response that seems most characteristic of you.**
☐	☐	☐	1. I have trouble sleeping the night before a test.
☐	☐	☐	2. During a test, my palms sweat.
☐	☐	☐	3. Before a test, I get a headache.
☐	☐	☐	4. During a test, I become nauseated.
☐	☐	☐	5. Because of panic, I sometimes cut class on a test day.
☐	☐	☐	6. I often have pain in my neck, back, or legs during a test.
☐	☐	☐	7. My heart pounds just before or during a test.
☐	☐	☐	8. I feel nervous and jittery when I am taking a test.
☐	☐	☐	9. During a test, I have trouble breathing.
☐	☐	☐	10. I lose my appetite before a test.
☐	☐	☐	11. I make careless errors on tests.
☐	☐	☐	12. My mind goes blank during tests.
☐	☐	☐	13. I worry when other students are finished before I am.
☐	☐	☐	14. I feel pressed for time when I am taking a test.
☐	☐	☐	15. I worry that I may be doing poorly on a test but that everyone else is doing well.
☐	☐	☐	16. When I am taking a test, I think about my past failures.
☐	☐	☐	17. During a test, I feel as if I have studied all the wrong things.
☐	☐	☐	18. I can't think clearly during tests.
☐	☐	☐	19. I have a hard time understanding and remembering directions when I am taking a test.
☐	☐	☐	20. After a test, I remember answers to questions I either left blank or answered incorrectly.

Items 1–10 refer to physical symptoms of test anxiety, and items 11–20 refer to mental symptoms. If you checked sometimes or usually 10 or more times, you may have some test anxiety. To be sure, you might want to talk to your advisor about how you feel before, during, and after taking tests.

if you earn any grade lower than an A or a B. You need to talk this over with them to determine the source of their anger. Perhaps they feel that a grade lower than an A or a B means that you aren't trying hard enough or that you aren't committed to getting an education. But there may be other reasons why you are not performing as expected in a course. You may have been unprepared for the level of the course, or illness or other hardships may have affected your ability to perform. It is unreasonable to expect a student to achieve someone else's ideal grade, but it is not unreasonable to expect a student to do his or her best. Try to separate yourself from others' expectations of you. Focus instead on what you expect from yourself and work hard to achieve it.

Equating Grades and Self-Worth

Test anxiety can result from placing too great an emphasis on grades. A low grade for some students translates into "I don't measure up." The result is a loss of self-esteem. One way to reduce test anxiety is to emphasize performance instead of grades. Rather than letting grades control your feelings, take control of your performance.

Turn each testing situation into an opportunity for self-assessment. Use tests to track your performance in a course. Keep a record of the number and type of items you missed, your level of anxiety during the test, your level of preparation, and what you now need to review. Over a period of time, you may see a pattern in your study and testing behavior. For example, if you consistently miss the same type of question or if your level of anxiety goes up when you haven't prepared sufficiently, then you will know what and how much to study for the next test.

When you emphasize performance over grades, a test becomes a personal challenge, a chance for you to apply your knowledge and skill to new problems and tasks, an opportunity for you to discover your strengths and weaknesses. Improved performance is the goal. Grades are not a measure of self-worth. They are merely a way to keep score.

Feelings of Helplessness

Are you self-motivated (internally motivated) or other-motivated (externally motivated)? Other-motivated students often do not see a connection between studying and grades. They blame their poor grades on the perceived unfairness of the instructor or the difficulty of the test instead of blaming their own lack of preparation. As a result, they feel helpless and out of control and experience test anxiety. The more self-motivated you are, the more likely you are to see a connection between your preparation and your grades. When you are well prepared for a test, you are in control of your emotions and of your reactions to the testing situation. As a result, you enter the classroom feeling calm and confident, ready to do your best.

By identifying the cause of your test anxiety, you can do what is necessary to eliminate it. Figure 11.4 lists common causes of test anxiety and how to eliminate them. The next section explains some specific ways to reduce test anxiety.

FIGURE 11.4

Test Anxiety: Causes and Eliminators

Causes	Eliminators
Lack of preparation and resulting guilt	So you weren't prepared for your test this time. Keep your goals in sight and resolve to do better.
Fear of not meeting expectations	Decide whether others' expectations are the same as your own. Set your own goals and live up to your own expectations.
Equating grades and self-worth	Who you are as a person has nothing to do with your grades. Emphasize performance over grades. Failure is a temporary setback, not a permanent condition.
Feelings of helplessness	Feelings of helplessness may be a learned response or may be the result of looking to others for motivation. Accept responsibility for your own successes and failures. Find the motivation within to prepare yourself for success.

How to Reduce Test Anxiety

• Practice relaxation techniques and positive self-talk to reduce test anxiety.

The good thing about test anxiety is that it is a learned response; therefore, it can be unlearned. Through the use of relaxation techniques, you can counteract the test anxiety response. Relaxation is a proven way to reduce the physical and mental discomfort caused by test anxiety. By consciously trying to relax, you take the attention away from your anxiety and refocus it on the task of taking the test. This works because you can't be relaxed and anxious at the same time.

Muscle relaxation exercises can help you control the physical symptoms of test anxiety. Become aware of the 16 muscle groups of your body (see Figure 11.5) and practice a technique that will help you relax each muscle group. When you are in a relaxed state, you can then program yourself for success.

FIGURE 11.5

Sixteen Muscle Groups

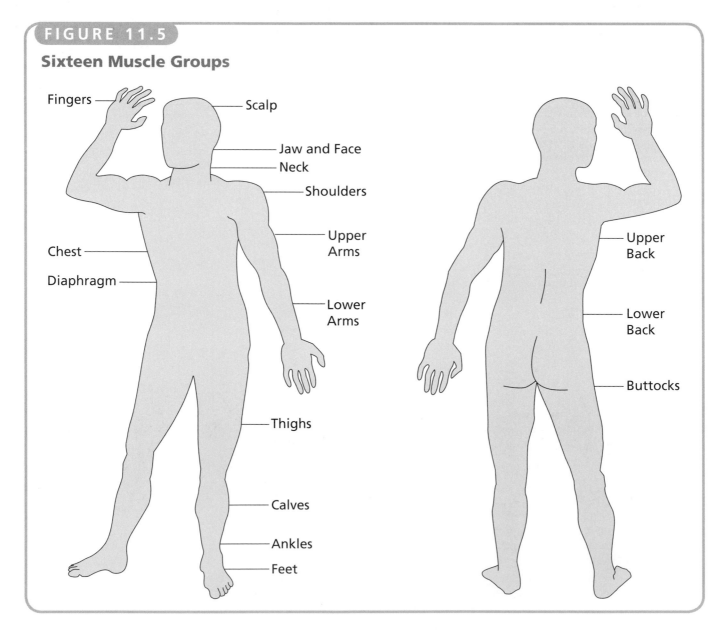

Learn to Relax

Some people don't even know when they are tense. As you locate each of the 16 muscle groups in Figure 11.5, try to sense whether you are holding any tension in your own muscles at each site. Try this simple six-step exercise:

1. Close your eyes and search for the tension in your body.

2. Are you clenching your teeth? If so, open your mouth slightly and relax your jaw.

3. Are your shoulders hunched? Lower your shoulders and feel an immediate sense of relief.

4. Now breathe deeply and slowly, in and out. Try to empty your mind of negative thoughts and replace them with a feeling of calm optimism.

5. Uncross your legs if they are crossed and press your feet flat on the floor. Relax your leg muscles if they are tense.

6. Settle comfortably into your chair and enjoy how good you feel when your muscles are relaxed. Imagine taking a test when you are this calm.

To feel the difference between tension and relaxation even more, try this exercise: Clench your hand into a fist. Squeeze as tightly as you can until you feel your fingers pressing uncomfortably into your palm. Hold that position for a few seconds. Feel your pulse pounding in your fingertips. Very slowly, open your hand. Uncurl your fingers and let go of the tension. When you are experiencing test anxiety, your mind is like your clenched fist. When you relax, your mind is like your hand opening and letting go of the tension.

Here is another relaxation exercise you can do the evening or morning before a test. Either sit or lie down comfortably; close your eyes and breathe deeply for a few seconds. Beginning with your feet, focus on each muscle group, one at a time; tense and then relax the muscles so that you feel a sharp difference between tensing and letting go. While you are relaxed, visualize a pleasant scene. For example, imagine yourself lying on a beach in the warm sun. Hear the waves washing up on the shore. Enjoy this scene for a few seconds; then let it fade. Concentrate on relaxing your body even more. Breathe slowly and deeply for a few more minutes; then open your eyes.

To relax yourself in a classroom situation, try these two simple but effective exercises:

1. Take a deep breath and relax your shoulders. Put your hands in your lap and clench your fists to feel the tension. Slowly open your hands and let them drop down at your sides, letting go of the tension.

2. With your elbows on the desk, bow your head over your open book or test paper while resting your forehead on top of your hands. Either close your eyes or leave them open but unfocused. Breathe slowly and deeply until you feel calm.

You can do these exercises without calling attention to yourself. Instead, it will seem as if you are simply concentrating or relaxing.

Talk Positively to Yourself

Although you may sometimes think that your mind is blank, it really is not. A mental dialogue plays like a radio in your mind, no matter what else is going on. While you are listening to a lecture, you are also thinking ahead to what you will do when class is over, or recalling something that happened earlier, or thinking about a problem that has been on your mind. When you have a conversation with someone, while you are listening, you are also thinking about what you will say next. Your inner voice is talking to you, and it is extremely persistent.

EXERCISE 11.6 — Visualize to Relax

CANDACE IS OVERWHELMED WITH TEST anxiety when she thinks about her biology midterm. Read about her attempt to overcome this problem; then answer the questions.

> *Even though the exam is more than three weeks away, Candace is already waking up at night, panicked by the thought of her biology midterm. She knows that she is always well prepared for class. She does all the reading. Why does she feel so anxious about the exam? In desperation, she decides to try a visualization technique that her psychology professor explained to her. Here is what she does:*
>
> *Each day for about twenty minutes, she sits alone in her room. Closing her eyes, she begins to breathe deeply and then, through a process of tensing and relaxing each muscle individually, she relaxes her entire body. When she feels totally relaxed, she imagines herself sinking into the overstuffed pillows of a lovely old chair in a beautiful garden. Feeling the warmth of the sun on her face, she breathes in the fragrances that surround her. She enjoys this imaginary scene for a few long seconds, then lets the scene slowly fade and replaces it with another scene. She is sitting in her biology class, about to begin taking her exam. She feels totally relaxed and prepared for the test. Calmly, she opens the test booklet and begins to write. Again, she imagines how prepared she is, how good she feels at that moment. She knows she can pass the exam. She feels confidence flow through her body. After lingering for a few moments on this image, Candace imagines one last scene. Her professor is handing back the test booklets. Confidently accepting hers, Candace opens the cover and reads the hand-written note at the top of the page: "Great work. You should be proud of your success on this exam." Candace concentrates on her intense feelings of success and then allows the scene to fade. She breathes deeply for a few more moments, then slowly opens her eyes.*

1. **How does Candace begin her visualization technique?**

   _____

   _____

2. **Why does she imagine a beautiful garden?**

   _____

   _____

3. **What other pleasant or peaceful scenes might she imagine?**

   _____

   _____

4. **Why do you think she visualizes the garden scene before visualizing the classroom scene?**

   _____

   _____

5. **What is the final image that Candace visualizes?**

   _____

   _____

continued

6. **Why is it important for Candace to visualize this final scene?**

_____

_____

7. **How might this visualization exercise help reduce Candace's test anxiety?**

_____

_____

8. **If you were to try this exercise, what scene would you visualize and why?**

_____

_____

Take a few minutes right now to listen to that inner voice. Try this simple exercise: Sit or lie down comfortably; close your eyes and breathe deeply. Concentrate on making your mind go blank. You will probably find it very hard to think about nothing because your inner voice will keep interrupting. What are your thoughts? Are they positive or negative? Do you praise or belittle yourself? Students who have test anxiety are frequently troubled by negative thoughts such as these:

"I'm going to fail this test."

"I hate this class."

"This course is doing nothing for me."

"The instructor doesn't care whether I pass or fail."

"Everybody in this class is doing better than I am."

Examine each negative thought and see how it hurts you. If you think and believe, "I am going to fail this test," then you probably will because you will become more anxious and less able to focus your attention on the test. If you say to yourself, "I hate this class" or, "This course is doing nothing for me," you are wasting time indulging thoughts that keep you from concentrating on recalling information you need to answer questions. Saying to yourself, "This instructor doesn't care whether I pass or fail" or, "Everybody in this class is doing better than I am" causes you to focus attention on other people instead of on the test. To combat negative thoughts, become task oriented. Block out all but positive thoughts specifically related to the task of taking and passing the test. Negative thinking can become a habit. To break the habit and program yourself for success, do three things:

1. Become aware of all the negative messages you may be sending yourself.

2. Replace negative thoughts with positive ones such as these:

"I'll pass this test."

"I'm learning something in this class."

"The instructor wants me to succeed."

VISIT YOUR COLLEGE WEBSITE TO learn whether your counseling office, psychology department, or other campus service offers help with test anxiety. Find out if there is a support group for students who have anxiety or stress issues. Then find a contact person who can tell you more about what is available. Share the results of your search in a class discussion.

"This course is a step toward my goals."

"I am well prepared, and I will do my best."

3. Change your inner voice into one that is calm and confident.

You may have to apply conscious effort for a long time before you learn to control your inner voice. Chances are good that your negative thoughts about yourself go back to your early childhood; they are probably so automatic that you hardly even notice them when you are involved in an activity such as taking a test. But learning to silence those thoughts and to replace them with positive, supportive ones will have a positive effect on other areas of your life besides test-taking. You may find yourself having more fun in your classes and in activities such as sports, hobbies, and work if you aren't so critical of your performance. Studying will become easier too, and your chances for success in college will improve. Thinking positively about yourself can even change the expression on your face. If you look and feel confident, people will assume that you are.

Once you have learned to focus all of your attention on taking a test, speak positively to yourself, and feel confident that you will be able to demonstrate your knowledge, test-taking may become an enjoyable intellectual challenge for you. Now do Exercise 11.8 to practice some positive self-talk.

Find Your Best Solution

Test anxiety is an individual problem. Anxiety differs in degree and kind from student to student. It is important to remember two things. First, a little anxiety won't hurt you and may even be the incentive you need to do your best. Second, even if you have a great deal of anxiety that causes you considerable discomfort, you are not a hopeless

LISTEN TO YOUR INNER VOICE. In the first column, list any negative thoughts you are having. Then, in the second column, rewrite them as positive self-directions. For example, the negative thought, "I'm going to fail this test," becomes the positive direction, "I'm well prepared for this test, so I will earn a good grade."

Negative Thoughts	Positive Self-Directions
1.	1.
2.	2.
3.	3.
4.	4.
5.	5.

case. Furthermore, you have a lot of company. For many students, test anxiety has become a way of life, but it doesn't have to remain so.

The coping strategies discussed in this chapter have worked for many students. Here are six more tips for reducing test anxiety:

1. **Be prepared for tests.** Most test anxiety is the result of irrational fears. The only real cause for fear is insufficient preparation for a test, which almost always does result in a poor grade. If you know you are not prepared, then you can expect to have some anxiety. Allow sufficient time to prepare for tests and remember to follow your test-taking routine during the test. We've said it before and it's worth repeating: Preparation is your best defense.

2. **Listen to your body.** Your body will tell you when you are becoming anxious during a test. Learn to recognize the signals that may be signs of stress: increased pulse rate, excessive perspiration, shallow breathing, sweaty palms, upset stomach, headache, and mental confusion.

3. **Dress comfortably for tests.** Wear loose-fitting clothes and comfortable shoes. Dress in layers so that you can put something on or take something off if the temperature in the room is too cold or too hot.

4. **Remember to relax.** Try the relaxation techniques suggested in this chapter either before you go to class or during the test if you become anxious.

5. **See test anxiety for what it is**—a learned response that you can unlearn, a habit that you can break.

6. **Seek help.** Talk to your instructor or academic advisor about professional resources on campus that are available to help with test anxiety, such as the campus counseling center. See Exercise 11.7 on page 286 to further explore this option.

Guided CHAPTER REVIEW

The following checklist summarizes this chapter's key terms and strategies. After reading the chapter, how confident are you that you can apply the information you have learned? To assess your level of confidence, respond to each statement with one of the following: *very confident* (3 points), *fairly confident* (2 points), *not very confident* (1 point), *not confident* (0 points). Write your number of points in the box beside each statement. Then add your score and read the analysis that follows. When you have finished, take the chapter quiz.

SUMMARY CHECK

How confident are you about applying these strategies?

Points

☐ 1. Using three types of reviews to study for tests

☐ 2. Anticipating test questions and choosing the right information to study

☐ 3. Knowing when, what, and how to study for tests

☐ 4. Developing and using a test-taking routine

☐ 5. Using appropriate strategies for each type of test

☐ 6. Knowing what test anxiety is and what causes it

☐ 7. Using relaxation techniques to reduce test anxiety

☐ 8. Identifying and replacing negative thoughts with positive self-talk

How confident is your understanding of this chapter's key terms?

☐ 9. objective test

☐ 10. absolute words

☐ 11. stem

☐ 12. options

☐ 13. distractors

☐ 14. instruction words

☐ 15. test anxiety

☐ 16. situational test anxiety

☐ 17. chronic test anxiety

☐ 18. perceptions

Total

Add your score. The highest possible score is 54. The closer your score is to 54, the higher your level of confidence. Use your *Summary Check* results to help you determine which parts of the chapter to review.

YOUR WEBSITE RESOURCES

This chapter's resources include the following items. To access them, go to *The Confident Student* premium website.

- **Video Skillbuilder:** *Test-Taking: Understanding Tests*
- **Video Skillbuilder:** *Test-Taking: Preparing for Tests*
- **Article:** "Stress: A Common Denominator"
- **Chapter Exercises**

- **Forms to Download**
- **Chapter Summary of Topics**
- **Thinking Ahead About Career**
- **Confidence Builder Web Search**
- **Self-Test**

CHAPTER REVIEW Quiz

Answer the following questions from memory. Then return to the chapter to check your answers. As a final activity, complete *Show Your Confidence* at the end of the quiz.

1. What are the three types of reviews and the purpose of each?
_____
_____

2. What are at least three types of materials that you would study from to be well prepared for a test?
_____
_____

3. As part of a test-taking routine, what should you do before the test? Explain any two strategies.
_____
_____

4. As part of a test-taking routine, what should you do during a test? Explain any two strategies.
_____
_____

5. What is a good strategy to use for taking true-false tests?
_____
_____

6. What is a guessing strategy you have used when you didn't know the answer to a multiple-choice question?
_____
_____

7. Explain the purpose of instruction words in an essay question, and give an example of an instruction word.
_____
_____

8. What is one cause of test anxiety and what can you do to eliminate this cause?
_____
_____

9. What is one relaxation technique explained in this chapter or another chapter, that you have tried, and how did it work?

_____

_____

10. What is *positive self-talk*, and why is it important?

_____

_____

SHOW YOUR CONFIDENCE

Read the following statement from this chapter: "The good thing about test anxiety is that it is a learned response; therefore, it can be unlearned." Do you agree or disagree? What does the statement mean to you? Be prepared to share your answers to these questions either in writing or in class discussion.

Your REFLECTIONS: YOUR RESPONSE TO TESTING

Reflect on what you have learned from this chapter about preparing for tests and reducing test anxiety. Use the following questions to stimulate your thinking; then write your reflections. Include in your writing specific information from the chapter.

- Which type of test explained in this chapter is the most challenging for you?
- To what extent has each of the following affected your grades and how: preparing for tests, test anxiety, attitude, motivation?
- What is one strategy you have learned from this chapter that you will definitely use?

_____

_____

_____

_____

_____

_____

_____

_____

_____

_____

_____

_____

12 Building Skills for Confident Communication

Bananastock(RF)/Jupiter Images

This chapter encourages you to:

- Improve the way you communicate and manage your relationships.

- Listen to, communicate with, and work cooperatively with others in groups.

- Use communication technology effectively and appropriately.

- Improve your ability to give speeches and make presentations.

- Understand the basics of researching and writing so that you can use these skills with confidence.

Confident students are **empathetic**. They are good communicators who can identify with the situations, feelings, and motives of others.

ollege, so far, has probably been an eye-opening experience for you. Making new friends, meeting people from all sorts of backgrounds, ethnicities, and nationalities, being exposed to new ideas and different perspectives, taking courses in subjects you never dreamed of, and beginning to recognize the opportunities that are unfolding before you—all of these must at times be overwhelming, at times exhilarating. To paraphrase poet Emily Dickinson, you grow newer every day.

Obviously, college is not only about adding new information to your store of knowledge or about preparing for a career, but it is also about learning how to learn and learning how to get along with and work with others. Chapters 1 through 11 of this book have been about learning how to learn. This chapter and the next two chapters are about building skills for living well—both in and beyond college—and for getting along with others. That includes learning how to communicate your ideas in ways that are helpful, civil, but also expressive of the unique person that you are.

What are the communication skills that employers seem to value above all others and that the professors of all your courses emphasize? They include *listening*, *speaking*, and *writing*. It is through these activities that you interact with others and during which the interpersonal skills of cooperation, respectfulness, civility, and teamwork come into play. Some or all of these skills may be on display whether you are interacting with an individual, contributing to a class discussion, giving a speech, making a presentation, or expressing your opinion in writing.

Now here is an important question for you to consider: Are you comfortable with expressing your opinions, or do you get butterflies in your stomach when you are called on to speak? In the last chapter, we explored the topic of test anxiety. Many students have some **speech anxiety**. Are you one of them? If so, don't worry. The following *Confidence Builder* explains how you can overcome any anxiety you may have about speaking before a group.

Speech anxiety is stress that results from having to speak in front of a group.

CONFIDENCE BUILDER

How to Reduce Speech Anxiety

As explained in Chapter 11, test anxiety is test-related stress, and math anxiety is math-related stress. Similarly, speech anxiety is stress that is brought about by having to speak in front of a group. Also known as "stage fright," speech anxiety is quite common. If you have it, you are not alone. Although you probably have no trouble carrying on a conversation with your friends or even joining a casual discussion in a group that includes people you don't know, you may experience anxiety, or stress, in more formal speaking situations. For example, does one or more of the following make you feel anxious or tongue-tied: asking a question in class, sharing your opinion in a small group discussion, making a formal speech, or giving a presentation?

As with test anxiety or math anxiety, a little speech anxiety is a good thing because it motivates you to do your best. On the other hand, don't let

speech anxiety silence you. The best way to fight speech anxiety is to recognize its symptoms, understand its causes, and use confidence-building strategies to overcome it. You can do this.

What does speech anxiety feel like? Like other forms of stress, speech anxiety has both physical and mental symptoms. Physical symptoms include feelings of tension or nervousness, sweaty brow or palms, increased pulse, dry mouth, and a shaky voice. Mental symptoms include confused or disorganized thoughts, forgetting what you had planned to say, feelings of inadequacy, and negative self-talk. Some people experience these symptoms before speaking and become tongue-tied. Others are nervous or uncomfortable until they begin to speak, but then they do fine once they get going. So why do people have speech anxiety?

continued

What causes speech anxiety? Like test anxiety, speech anxiety may be situational or chronic. Situational speech anxiety is usually the result of not being prepared. If you are caught off guard when asked a question, or if you have to give a presentation for which you are unprepared, you may become anxious. If merely thinking about having to speak in front of a group gives you butterflies or other more serious symptoms, then your anxiety may be chronic. Some of the common causes of speech anxiety include the following: not knowing what is expected of you, lacking confidence in your ability or your ideas, not knowing how the audience will respond, fearing that you will forget what you meant to say, or worrying about how you will be evaluated.

What will relieve or reduce speech anxiety? Preparation and practice are the keys to feeling confident about giving a speech or presentation. But even when you can't prepare your remarks—such as when speaking up in class discussions or contributing your ideas in a small group—three strategies have worked for many students: positive self-talk, relaxation, and visualization (some of the same strategies you use to reduce test anxiety or math anxiety).

- *Positive self-talk*: Say to yourself, "My ideas are good. I can contribute something useful to this discussion" and other self-affirming thoughts.
- *Relaxation*: Take a deep breath before speaking. If you have a few minutes before it is your turn to give a speech or contribute your part to a group, do one of the relaxation techniques explained in Chapter 11.
- *Visualization*: Form a mental picture of yourself speaking confidently while your classmates and instructor respond favorably to your opinions. Visualize this image while you are relaxed and thinking about what you are going to say.

If you are a serious student, you will probably always have some speech anxiety because you care enough to make a good impression. Remember to take a deep breath and know that many of your classmates feel the same way you do.

Follow Up: To explore this topic further, visit *The Confident Student* premium website for an online search activity related to speech anxiety.

Building Interpersonal Skills

- Improve the way you communicate and manage your relationships.

When you have a conversation with someone, do you ever feel misunderstood? Has a friend or roommate taken something you said the wrong way? Do you find it hard to get along with some people no matter what you do? Most of us have had experiences like these, but we have also enjoyed positive relationships where conversation flows smoothly and getting along together seems effortless. Why is that so? Why do some relationships work while others do not? Differences in personalities, backgrounds, and values can affect our ability to get along with others, and so can attitude and behavior. Not only what we say but the way we say it has a powerful effect on people. Good communication is the key to good relationships. Now let's take a closer look at what communication is.

Communication Defined

Communication is a process that involves at least two people: a sender and a receiver. During this process, information is exchanged. The sender delivers a message and the receiver interprets the message. A "message" can be **verbal** (stated or said) or **nonverbal** (unstated, delivered through expressions, gestures, tone of voice). So far this seems very technical, doesn't it? Here's what it means. When you start a conversation with your friend, you are the sender and your friend is the receiver. The words that pass between you are the message. However, the message does not consist of words alone. Your expression, the tone of your voice—whether depressed or upbeat—and the way

Communication is the process in which both verbal and nonverbal information is exchanged between a sender and a receiver.

Verbal messages are stated or spoken.

Nonverbal messages are unstated or delivered by various cues such as expressions, gestures, and tone of voice.

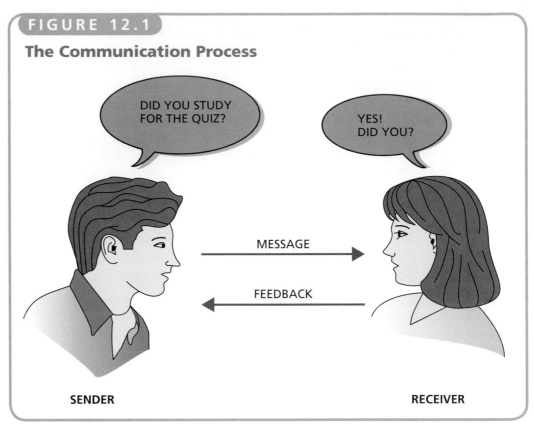

FIGURE 12.1

The Communication Process

DID YOU STUDY FOR THE QUIZ?

YES! DID YOU?

MESSAGE

FEEDBACK

SENDER

RECEIVER

you hold your body all send nonverbal cues that may or may not be consistent with the spoken words. A lot can happen during the information exchange between a sender and a receiver. Even though only a few seconds may elapse, a misunderstanding of the verbal message or a misreading of the nonverbal cues can cause a breakdown in communication. But when the process works as it should, everyone is happy. Figure 12.1 illustrates the communication process.

What can you do to become a more effective sender or receiver in the communication process? Develop the following interpersonal skills to help you improve your ability to communicate and manage your relationships: Be a good listener, avoid several common communication barriers, practice civility, and learn to resolve conflicts. Now take *Awareness Check* 12.1 to assess your interpersonal skills before completing the rest of this section.

Concept Check **12.1**

The communication process and memory process are intentional processes. What else do they have in common?

Awareness CHECK 12.1

Are You a Confident Communicator?

To assess your interpersonal skills now, check all of the following statements that apply to you.

☐ 1. During a conversation, I may find myself thinking about what I am going to say next instead of listening to the other person.

☐ 2. When someone is speaking to me, I listen attentively and try to relate to the conversation.

☐ 3. If I think someone's opinion is wrong, I will say so no matter what.

continued

- [ ] 4. I am respectful of another person's opinion even when I don't agree.
- [ ] 5. I often have a hard time relating to people who don't think or act as I do.
- [ ] 6. I am generally known for my ability to get along with anyone.
- [ ] 7. I am not a mind reader, so I think people should say what they mean.
- [ ] 8. I am good at reading both verbal and nonverbal cues.
- [ ] 9. I have been called down for interrupting or talking too much.
- [ ] 10. I tend to do about the same amount of listening as I do talking.
- [ ] 11. If I don't like someone, it is difficult for me to hide my feelings.
- [ ] 14. I can be polite to someone even if we aren't the best of friends.
- [ ] 15. It's not easy for me to get along with one or more of my instructors.
- [ ] 16. I have good relationships with all my instructors.
- [ ] 17. I don't know how to deal with aggressive or unpleasant people.
- [ ] 18. People often turn to me to settle arguments or misunderstandings.

If you checked mostly even-numbered statements, you are probably already a confident communicator, and this chapter's strategies will add to your store of knowledge. If you checked mostly odd-numbered statements, you may lack confidence in some areas of communication and will benefit from developing your skills.

Are You Listening?

Remember that in Chapter 5 we said that hearing and listening are two different things. *Hearing* means that the sound of the words is registering in your brain. *Listening* means that you are paying attention to and thinking about what the words mean. Passive listeners do more hearing than listening. Passive listeners also do more talking than listening. They hog conversations and interrupt. At times, they may appear to be listening when they are really thinking about what they are going to say next. As a result, they may change the subject or make comments that are unrelated to the topic under discussion. Passive listeners rarely ask questions and often seem to be focused only on themselves. Do you know someone like that?

On the other hand, active listeners are engaged. They look at the speaker, nod when they agree, take notes or ask questions when appropriate, and give feedback. For example, suppose a friend is telling you about the hard time she had studying for an exam, staying up all night and worrying that she did not do well on the test. As an active listener, you might share your own experience with studying and offer some encouragement. In other words, your response sends the message that you are listening and that you understand.

Not only are good listeners *active* listeners, they have other characteristics as well. Active listeners are creative. They relate their experience to what is being said. If a student is telling a humanities class about his trip to Europe on a student visa, active listeners will recall their own experiences as travelers. Those who have never traveled abroad will use their imaginations to put themselves in the student's place. Active listeners use selective attention, as explained in Chapter 8, to focus on a speaker's key words or ideas. In a discussion, use your selective attention to focus on ideas that

FIGURE 12.2

Listening with All Your Senses

SPEECH TODAY: Exploring Alaska

interest you and comment on these when giving feedback. Active listeners use all their senses, knowing that the more sensory pathways they keep open while listening, the more likely they are to remember what they hear. A person's tone of voice appeals to your aural sense. Gestures and expressions create a visual impression. The words themselves may evoke strong sensations or feeling. See Figure 12.2, which illustrates listening with all your senses.

When you are talking, you hope that your listener will pay attention and be responsive. One way to ensure a positive response is to be a good listener yourself. Here are a few more things you can do to improve your listening habits—or develop new ones.

▼ **Fight distractions.** All sorts of internal and external distractions compete for your attention, as you will remember from Chapter 8. Noise, an annoying gesture or speech habit such as saying "uh" every few words, random thoughts, emotions, or various physical sensations such as hunger or tiredness can distract you. Recognize these distractions for what they are and try to ignore them by focusing on the person who is speaking and the message.

▼ **Be open-minded.** No one will argue the fact that you have a right to your own opinion. However, try to keep an open mind when listening to someone—even when you disagree. Be open to different perspectives and the opportunity to learn new things.

▼ **Listen for content.** Focus on the topic and the opinions being expressed. One way to do this is by relating what you are hearing to your own experience. For example, if the topic is a popular film that you have seen, then you can add your opinion to the conversation.

▼ **Paraphrase.** Restate in your own words what you think someone has said, especially if you are in doubt. Paraphrasing can help clear up misunderstandings. Begin your paraphrase with words like "What I'm hearing is . . . " or "If I understand correctly . . . ," followed by what you think the person said.

▼ **Summarize.** A lot of ideas can get tossed about in a discussion. It helps to stop and pull some of these ideas together. Summarizing key points that have been covered is a good way to refocus a discussion that has gone off on a tangent. A summary statement might begin with these words: "Let's review . . . " or "So far we've said . . . ," followed by the points that were made.

By following these suggestions, you will show that you are listening and trying to hold up your end of a conversation. In addition, watch for nonverbal cues and be

CRITICAL THINKING

What Kind of Listener Are You?

Exercise Overview

This exercise will help you identify four different types of listening that you can use to focus your attention more clearly on a speaker's message.

Exercise Background

Researchers define several different kinds of listening. Though their terms may differ, here are four types of listening that you may recognize. Read the descriptions and then complete the exercise task.

1. **Empathetic:** As an empathetic listener, you are attentive to people's emotions and the feelings they arouse in you. For example, as you listen to someone discuss working with native peoples in a tropical rainforest, you try to put yourself in that person's place. You listen for details that tell you what life there was like, and you try to imagine how you might have felt if you were there.

2. **Appreciative:** As an appreciative listener, you show your enthusiasm. You focus on parts of a conversation or presentation that make you laugh or arouse your enjoyment. The way you feel and react when listening to music with your friends is one example of appreciative listening. Also, when you respond favorably to jokes and other bits of humor that add enjoyment to a conversation, you are expressing your appreciation.

3. **Information-Gathering:** As an information gatherer, you focus on facts and details. If someone is talking about a new store that gives good prices on clothing, you want to know where it is, what brands they sell, what kind of prices to expect, and so on. If your instructor announces a test for the following class meeting, you want to know what it will cover and how you will be graded.

4. **Critical:** As a critical listener, you make judgments and evaluations—not in a negative way, but because you are trying to understand the message and how you can use it. When someone expresses an opinion, a critical listener might ask, "How do you know?" or "Where did you hear that?" Critical listeners are also interested in the soundness or practicality of the ideas. They want to know "What's in it for me?"

continued

You might be better at some types of listening than others, and in some situations a particular type of listening may seem more appropriate. However, remember that good listeners use all their senses, and they will also try to use all four types of listening when possible.

Exercise Task

Using what you now know about the four types of listening, answer the following questions and be prepared to share your answers in class.

1. During an election year, you listen to several candidates' speeches. What kind of listening do you use?

   _____

   _____

2. A professor is giving a lecture on reproduction among plants. What kind of listening do you use?

   _____

   _____

3. At a memorial service, several people give their impressions of the person who has passed on. What kind of listening do you use?

   _____

   _____

4. Your friend is taking a speech class and wants to practice a humorous speech with you as audience. What kind of listening do you use?

   _____

   _____

5. Of the four types of listening, which one(s) do you use most often in your college courses?

   _____

   _____

6. Which type(s) of listening do you use most often when talking with friends outside of class?

   _____

   _____

7. Which type of listening do you find easiest? Which one is most difficult, and why?

   _____

   _____

8. Describe a situation in which you used all four types of listening.

   _____

   _____

aware of your own body language when interacting with others, whether in a one-to-one relationship or in a group discussion.

The Posture of Involvement

The next time you are in class, look around and see if you recognize any of these students: Two students are texting to each other, ignoring what is going on. A student in the back of the room is slouching in the seat, eyes closed, with one foot sprawled out into the aisle. Another student is busy doing an assignment for a different course. Several students are quietly carrying on an animated conversation, but not about anything related to the class discussion. Imagine that you are speaking to your class. You have worked hard on your presentation but are feeling a little anxious. As you look around the room, hoping for some positive feedback, you see students acting like the ones just described. How would you feel?

This is the communication process in action: the flow of ideas between sender and receiver.

Now put yourself in the place of a classmate whose turn it is to speak. This time, you are the receiver of this sender's message. You know that as a speaker, you want your listeners to be attentive and responsive. Therefore, you display the kind of listening behavior that you expect others to assume. This "golden rule" of listening is also known as *the posture of involvement*, and it is one of the essential classroom skills explained in Chapter 5. What is amazing about the posture of involvement is that even if you are not particularly interested in what someone is saying, by assuming the posture, you may become interested. This is so because the posture of involvement focuses your attention on the speaker and promotes listening. When you are listening instead of merely hearing, you begin to engage with the speaker: to question, relate, and identify with the speaker's words and feelings. As a result, your understanding grows, and so does your interest. This is the communication process in action: the flow of ideas between sender and receiver.

What is the posture of involvement? Think of someone you know who always listens to you attentively; someone who appears interested in what you say; someone whose expression is positive and encouraging. To assume the posture of involvement, do the following and remember that these guidelines are appropriate for any listening situation, from lectures and class discussions to small group activities and even one-on-one conversations with friends.

▼ **Posture:** In class or other formal situations, sit up straight, leaning forward slightly. No slouching—it sends a message of disrespect. With friends, you can be more casual, but turn your face toward the one to whom you are speaking.

▼ **Eye Contact:** In class or other formal situations, look at the speaker, but be ready to shift your attention to graphics or other materials when they are displayed. With friends, remember to look into their eyes. Looking down or off to the side sends a message of distrust.

▼ **Attention:** In class or formal situations, give the speaker your full attention. Refrain from doing anything else while listening—with the exception of taking notes. With friends, even though you may be eating, watching TV, listening to music, or engaging in other activities while carrying on a conversation, they should never feel as though you are not being attentive—it's part of your job as a friend.

▼ **Feedback:** In class or other formal situations, react honestly to the speaker. Laugh if something is funny. When you agree with the speaker, nod your head. Similarly, don't be afraid to look surprised or confused if you are. Your expression will alert the speaker

Concept Check **12.2**

One way to improve communication is to put yourself in the other person's place and ask yourself, "How would I feel in this situation?" Demonstrate the behavior that you expect from others.

that more information or a clarification is needed. With friends, your responses may vary depending on how well you know them, but honest reactions are always best.

The posture of involvement describes how to behave while listening. Although the specifics of posture, eye contact, attention, and feedback may vary depending on how formal or casual the situation is, the point is to remind you that good listening is a whole-body experience. Not only that, the posture of involvement is good for interpersonal relations because it shows respect. Speaking of respect, we turn now to what you say and how you say it.

Let's Be Civil

Civility means good manners or polite behavior, and it is the opposite of rudeness.

Instructors talk a lot among themselves about civility. **Civility**, pure and simple, means politeness or good manners. Civility is the opposite of rudeness. Unfortunately, civility among the general population has declined. We see this in politics when candidates attack each other personally instead of debating the issues. We see it everywhere—people talking during a movie, using their cell phones in restaurants and other public places, pushing and shoving in lines, and yelling at each other in traffic. Too often people act before they think and speak without thinking. The use of inappropriate language has filtered down to middle-school-aged children, and respect for others seems a thing of the past. No wonder your instructors are talking about civility! They are seeing less of it among the students they teach. However, there is one place where civility still rules—the workplace. Employers expect—and usually get—polite conduct from their employees.

Civility is an interpersonal skill that is encouraged by and developed through class and group interaction. Civil behavior is as essential to one-on-one relationships as it is to group interactions. Because we tend to take our friends for granted, we can let civility lapse. No doubt you have said things to your friends or family members that you would like to take back. Unfortunately, some people have a habit of speaking in ways that offend others, and, what is worse, they may not even be aware of it. Although no one would discourage you from saying what you honestly think or from expressing a strong opinion, there is an appropriate way to say it. Basically, civil speech requires that you avoid common barriers to effective communication.

Communication Barriers. A communication barrier can be verbal or nonverbal. Verbal communication barriers include name-calling and other inappropriate speech. Profanity, for example, is widespread in casual conversation, and celebrities have pushed it into the mainstream of communication. This is unfortunate because profanity is still unacceptable in classrooms, the workplace, and many other settings. To the extent that it makes people feel uncomfortable, profanity may act as a communication barrier. Other communication barriers include domineering or judgmental behavior. People don't like to be told that they are wrong—even when they are. Instead of adopting a preachy or condescending tone, simply point out the mistake. For more examples of communication barriers and how to transform inappropriate language into more civil speech, see Figure 12.3.

Nonverbal Cues and Communication Barriers. When you say one thing and your body says another, the result is confusion at best and mistrust at worst. In other words, your verbal and nonverbal messages should be consistent. For example, saying you agree while shaking your head "no" is confusing to the listener. Looking off to the side or down at your feet suggests that you are not telling the truth. Folding your arms across your chest suggests that you are putting up a wall between yourself and the other person and discouraging intimacy. If that is the message you want to send, fine. But if intimacy is what you are after, then uncross your arms. Leaning toward someone when you speak shows you are interested. However, don't get too close because some people have issues with personal space and may feel crowded. Psychologists have made a study of body language, but the rest of us have to use our instincts. You can usually tell whether your body language is either attracting people or repelling them. Watch for cues in their facial expressions and in their own body language.

Concept Check 12.3

What is another verbal or nonverbal communication barrier that you have noticed? What attitudes or behaviors are most likely to come between you and someone with whom you have a relationship?

FIGURE 12.3

Barriers to Communication

Communication Barrier	What It Is	Example	A More Civil Way to Say It
Name-calling	Belittling or ridiculing other people or their ideas	"That's a stupid question."	"I'm not sure I understand what you mean."
One-upmanship	Downplaying the other person's ideas in order to boost your own	"You think you had a good vacation? Wait until I tell you what I did in Las Vegas."	"Sounds like you had fun in Las Vegas; I'd like to go there sometime."
Preaching	Trying to make people feel bad about what they have done instead of trying to be helpful	"You should have done the reading; then you would know what we are talking about."	"This is covered on page 19. You can skim over it quickly and catch up."
Negative criticism	Evaluating someone or an idea in a negative rather than a constructive way	"You are going about this all wrong."	"Here, let me help you with this."
Commanding	Demanding that someone do what you want, your way	"This is what we have to do first."	"Where would you like to begin?"
Controlling	Using threats to manage a person's behavior or a situation	"If people aren't going to do their share of the work, then I'm leaving this study group."	"Why don't we each agree to do part of the work by a certain time?"

Effectively Manage Your Relationships

The most influential people in your life may include your parents, your spouse or other intimate partner, your children, your roommate, and your friends. Your relationships with these people can span the entire range of emotions, from great happiness to extreme disappointment. What makes a relationship succeed or fail? Educators, philosophers, psychologists, writers, and many others have explored this question. Every relationship is based on a complex system of need satisfaction, and each type of relationship has characteristics that distinguish it from other types. Yet most people would agree that we expect certain basic things from each other in any relationship: respect, civility, honesty, openness, good humor, a willingness to listen. What are some other qualities you would add to this list? Figure 12.4 lists 20 things you can do to build better relationships.

Everyone has some advice to give about relationships. People will tell you to "be yourself," and this is good advice, because sooner or later the real you is going to come out anyway. It is better to be open about who you are and what you want at the beginning of a relationship so that no one is surprised later on. Some people

EXERCISE 12.1 Overcome Communication Barriers

REVIEW THE SIX COMMUNICATION BARRIERS listed in Figure 12.3 and the examples. Do you see yourself in any of the examples? Do you know someone else who speaks in ways that create barriers to communication? Describe a situation in which you or someone else communicated ineffectively. What was said, and what would have been a more civil way to say it?

FIGURE 12.4

Twenty Ways to Build Better Relationships

1. Do more listening than talking.
2. Listen without judging.
3. Give all your attention to the person you are with.
4. Understand that a conversation is an exchange of ideas.
5. Don't "hold forth," and don't interrupt.
6. Be receptive to new ideas.
7. Seek points of agreement.
8. Respect opinions that are different from yours.
9. Everyone wants "someone I can really talk to." Be that person.
10. Create opportunities to have fun together.
11. Laugh a lot.
12. Go someplace new.
13. Try a sport or activity together that neither of you has ever done.
14. Encourage the other person's dreams.
15. Share each triumph and disappointment as if it were your own.
16. Be supportive when your partner needs to talk.
17. When a friend turns to you for help or comfort, be there.
18. Don't assume that the person you love knows you care.
19. Let your feelings show.
20. Call your parents; they miss you.

advise choosing friends and partners with whom you have "something in common." But then others will remind you that "opposites attract." So which is it? Psychologists tell us that common interests, backgrounds, values—the things that count—are the firm foundation of a relationship. But we also seek out people who complete us in the sense that they have qualities we don't have. A man who has no business sense marries a woman who does. A woman who is quiet and reserved chooses friends who are more outgoing. In each case, the relationship works because each person fulfills a need that the other has. In sum, it is possible to have successful relationships with all kinds of people.

Relationships break down when there is not an equal give and take in the partnership. If one person seems to be doing all the giving, he or she may feel taken advantage of. Some relationships turn abusive or manipulative. When this happens, the wronged person should get out of the relationship. Though it may not be easy to end a bad relationship, there is help available. Family members, close friends, a family physician, or a public agency are some of the resources people in abusive relationships will turn to in need. For information on maintaining healthy relationships, see Chapter 13. Now let's see what suggestions you have for the couple in Exercise 12.2.

Relationships at College

Unlike your relationships with the influential people in your life—many of whom you will be involved with permanently—your relationships with most classmates, roommates, and instructors may be only temporary. Nevertheless, treat these

EXERCISE **12.2**   Collaborative Activity about Interpersonal Communication

APPLY WHAT YOU HAVE LEARNED about interpersonal skills by completing this exercise either on your own or with a partner. Read the following scenario, discuss the questions if you're working with a partner, and write your answers on the lines provided.

> *Jack was exhausted. He had three college courses on Mondays and worked the lunch shift at the cafeteria. Then he had to rush to pick up his girlfriend Bonnie, a music major, at her part-time job. Today Bonnie seemed particularly disgruntled. "I hate my job. I hate my professors," she said. "I just want to be home practicing my guitar."*
>
> *"Your professors work hard all day too," Jack snapped.*
>
> *"Why don't we stop for coffee on the way home?" asked Bonnie.*
>
> *Jack sighed and answered, "Not today. I have a research paper to finish and so do you."*
>
> *Bonnie turned her back and looked out the window.*

1. **At what point could Jack have listened more actively to what Bonnie was saying?**

   _____

   _____

2. **What could Jack have said to start a positive conversation with Bonnie?**

   _____

   _____

3. **How could Bonnie have been supportive of her boyfriend?**

   _____

   _____

4. **What would have been a better way for Jack and Bonnie to spend their time together before going home to do their work?**

   _____

   _____

temporary relationships as you would all others, in the sense that openness, civil behavior, and respect are something you owe to everyone. Here are some guidelines to follow.

Classmates. The key to getting along with classmates is to realize that you have common goals. You want a good grade in the class, you have some similar reasons for coming to college, and you want to succeed. You also share some of the same fears and misgivings. Through communication and interaction, you will discover in what ways you are similar to or different from your classmates, and the differences will not be a barrier if you keep an open mind. If there is one thing that most people agree on regardless of race, background, ethnicity, or nationality, it is that everyone wants to be treated fairly. Everyone wants an equal chance to succeed. Remember that in your dealings with classmates. Remember too that whatever you may think of a classmate, somebody values that person. It may seem obvious, but like you, your classmates have families, friends, and lives outside of class. In a society that makes much of our differences, it is all too easy to forget the many ways in which we are alike.

Roommates. Your roommate might be a friend you knew before coming to college, but more likely your roommate will start out as a stranger. As the term wears on, you may become good friends, or you may remain only casual acquaintances even though you live together. Living together throws people into intimate contact. You sleep in the same room, share bath and laundry facilities, and share space. Disagreements can arise when you want to sleep and your roommate wants to study, or when neither of you likes the other's friends. Early on, you should work out a sleep and study schedule that is agreeable to you both. Lay some ground rules for bringing friends into the room. It is very fortunate if you and your roommate like each other and get along. In that case, you will have a live-in study partner and someone to walk with to classes and meals.

What if your roommate is noisy, borrows your clothes and other items without asking, has disgusting personal habits that you can't live with, and you have tried everything you can to solve the problem but without success? Then you have three choices: Seek advice from your resident advisor, try to move in with someone else you know, or make the best of the situation until the term is over and you can make a change.

Instructors. When it comes to getting along with instructors, it's up to you to make the first move. To most instructors, you are one of many students. The only way you are going to stand out is to either be exceptional or to get on their bad side. Obviously, exceptional is the way to go. Exceptional students come prepared to class, arrive on time, and are absent only in emergencies. Exceptional students participate, ask questions, and treat their classmates fairly and with respect. Exceptional students pay attention in class. The quickest way to get on an instructor's bad side is to arrive late, not do the assignments, socialize when you should be working, and engage in annoying behaviors such as texting or IMing your friends. Sarcasm or attempts at humor are usually not appreciated either. The classroom is a training ground for the workplace. You are expected to be professional in your attitude and behavior. Figure 12.5 lists tips for building positive relationships with your instructors.

Here is an additional tip for improving relationships and classroom performance. Sit near the front of the room. Students who sit up front show that they are interested and ready to learn, as opposed to the back-row-sitters who may appear to be avoiding interaction. If you can get along well with instructors and classmates on a one-to-one basis, chances are that you will be able to interact successfully with your classmates in small group activities.

FIGURE 12.5

Building Positive Relationships with Instructors

Attitude		Preparation	
Act interested. Be positive. Make no excuses. Accept responsibility. Motivate yourself.		Do the assignments. Buy/bring the right materials. Use the syllabus. Stay on task. Attend regularly.	
Manners		**Professionalism**	
Arrive on time. Avoid sarcasm. Be civil. Use instructor's name with title. Turn off electronic devices in class.		Pay attention. Listen and take notes. Ask relevant questions. Make appointment before visiting office. Practice academic honesty.	

EXERCISE 12.3   Visiting Your Instructor

CHOOSE AN INSTRUCTOR OF A course other than your student success course. Make an appointment to visit this instructor during office hours. Your purpose for the visit can be to review a test, to answer questions about an assignment, or for some other reason. The choice is up to you. The visit will also give you an opportunity to establish a working relationship with the instructor. Complete the following items to prepare for your visit.

1. **Contact your instructor either in person or by email to make an appointment. Provide several alternatives so that the instructor can schedule the appointment at his or her convenience. When you have an appointment, write the day and time here:**

   _____

2. **What will be the purpose of your visit?**

   _____

3. **You don't want to overwhelm the instructor with questions. Two or three specific questions are enough, because the visit will probably last only 15 minutes. Write your questions here:**

   a. _____

   b. _____

   c. _____

4. **List any materials you will need to take with you to the visit.**

   _____

5. **After the visit, evaluate the outcome by checking off the items on the following list and writing your comments.**

   _____ a. **Did you start the conversation by asking a question or stating your purpose?**

   _____ b. **Did you let the instructor do most of the talking?**

   _____ c. **Did you follow up the instructor's points with relevant comments or questions?**

   _____ d. **Did you refrain from revealing your personal problems?**

   _____ e. **Did you remember to thank the instructor for taking the time to meet with you?**

   Comments:

   _____

   _____

Guidelines for Successful Group Interaction

- Listen to, communicate with, and work cooperatively with others in groups.

By this time, you probably have had some experience working in groups. Some of your professors may rely on collaborative activities as their primary mode of instruction. A lot of research supports the idea that students learn more when they interact with each other. Also, don't forget that a primary purpose of getting a college education is to prepare you for a career, and teamwork is a valued skill in the workplace.

Very little work today is done in isolation. Collaboration is the rule in the professions, in the corporate world, and in many other jobs and careers. Whatever your

Radius Images/Jupiter Images

In some ways, a small group convened for a particular task in a college classroom is like a sports team.

life's work happens to be, it is likely that you will be working as part of a team. Teamwork requires good communication and interpersonal skills, cooperation, and civility. Now let's consider how you can use your interpersonal skills for successful group interaction.

A good place to begin is with a sports analogy. No doubt you have either played a sport, enjoyed watching sports events, or both. But even if you are not interested in sports, you know that without teamwork, the game is lost. In some ways, a small group convened for a particular task in a college classroom is like a sports team. Each member of a group is important and has a contribution to make, just as each player on a team is important and has a position to play. A group member who monopolizes the conversation is like a player who hogs the ball. A group member who fails to do a share of the work is like a player who drops the ball. Sportsmanship is a team's brand of civility. Fans and TV viewers don't like it when players lose their tempers, commit intentional fouls, or display improper conduct either on or off the court or field. When players or group members are uncivil and don't communicate effectively, everyone loses. But when they work cooperatively in a spirit of good humor and respect, the work gets done, the game is won, and everyone feels good—like the team that high-fives each other at the end of a game.

Working in small groups does not appeal to everyone. Personalities differ, and some students value themselves more as individuals than as part of a team or a group. These students may resent being held personally accountable for the work of the group, especially if some group members don't do their share. Conflicts can arise and communication can break down unless goals are clear and everyone in the group is committed to the task. Have you ever participated in a group where one person does most of the work? Have you ever done your part but felt resentful because someone else did not contribute, yet everyone got the same grade? These problems and others can be resolved with good leadership and by making sure that everyone in a group has a specific task or takes on a portion of the work.

Collaborating

To **collaborate** means to work together cooperatively.

Collaboration is another word for teamwork. To **collaborate** means to work together cooperatively, as on a sports team. The following guidelines suggest ways in which you can interact with others for the successful completion of a group task. These guidelines both summarize and expand on what has already been said in this chapter and in previous ones. To remember the guidelines, think of them as *the four "Be's"* of successful group interaction.

1. **Be supportive** of group members. By practicing this chapter's strategies for listening actively, speaking civilly, and avoiding the communication barriers listed in Figure 12.3, you will show your support. In addition, watch your body language. Assume the posture of involvement, and keep your expression friendly and encouraging.

2. **Be considerate.** Do not monopolize the conversation, interrupt when others are talking, stray from the topic, or begin socializing instead of working. Stay on task, and when you ask a question or add your opinion, make sure that it is relevant and to the point. Acknowledge the contributions of group members. Say encouraging words such as "That's a good idea" or "I hadn't thought of that."

3. **Be accepting.** In working with students from diverse backgrounds, remember that their perspectives and behavior patterns may differ

from yours. Students who come from cultures that do not value individualism may hold back from participating in a group setting for fear of standing out. Reach out to these students and show them that their ideas are important to the group as a whole. You can also point out to international students that in American colleges and workplaces, everyone is expected to have an opinion and to express it. Another way to be accepting is to focus on similarities rather than differences. Look for ways to connect with others through shared ideas and interests.

4. **Be organized.** As soon as the group has an assignment, choose a leader, divide up the work, and assign each person a role or a task. The inside back cover of this book lists some possible group roles and responsibilities. Make wise use of the time available. For example, if you have 30 minutes to complete the task, appoint someone as timekeeper and divide the time according to what must be done. Allow the last few minutes to assess what you have accomplished and compile a report.

Resolving Conflicts Within the Group

In any group, conflicts may arise, and they are generally of two types. *Procedural conflicts* occur when one or more group members are confused about who is in charge, what the task is, how to do the work, and so on. That is why organization, the fourth "Be," is so important. As soon as a group is formed, the first order of business is to appoint a leader and assign a portion of the work to each group member. If you will do this, then procedural conflicts may not arise.

Behavioral conflicts are the second type. These conflicts fall into three categories, and they describe types of behavior that cause verbal and nonverbal communication barriers: aggressive behavior, passive behavior, and manipulative behavior. **Aggressive behavior** is rude, domineering, and intimidating. Students who behave aggressively may try to impose their ideas on others or to monopolize the conversation. They may react hostilely to those who question their ideas or may show insensitivity to others' feelings. **Passive behavior** is submissive and dependent. Students who behave passively wait for others in the group to tell them what to do. Some may not participate at all, and most of them will refrain from expressing their feelings or opinions. At times it may be hard to tell whether a student is passive because of shyness or for some other reason, or because he or she comes from a culture where speaking out in class is neither valued nor rewarded. **Manipulative behavior** is devious. For example, a manipulative student plays the victim. The manipulators are the ones who always have an excuse for not getting their work done, yet they somehow manage to make you feel sorry for them.

One way to deal with conflicts is by being assertive with those whose behavior interferes with the group's work or makes people feel uncomfortable. **Assertive behavior** is polite, strong, and independent. Being assertive means standing up for your rights without denying the rights of others. For example, if someone in your group gets angry and starts using profanity and you don't like it, say so calmly and firmly. If an aggressive student is monopolizing the conversation, an assertive group leader will say something like "Thank you for sharing your opinion, now let's hear from someone else." To deal assertively with a passive student, all group members should try to draw this person into the conversation. At the same time, they should recognize that a student's seeming passivity may simply be a cultural difference. If this is the case, perhaps after class someone could reach out to the student in a spirit of friendliness and explain the rules. When manipulative students try to get out of doing work, don't take no for an answer. Insist that they do their share, but do so in a polite way.

Aggressive behavior is domineering, intimidating, and inconsiderate behavior.

Passive behavior shows submission, dependence, and avoidance of responsibility.

Manipulative behavior is shrewd and devious.

Assertive behavior is polite but forceful, independent, responsible, and considerate behavior.

EXERCISE 12.4   Collaborative Activity about Group Communication

APPLY WHAT YOU HAVE LEARNED about communication by completing this exercise with group members. Follow the guidelines for group discussion listed on the inside back cover of this book. Read the following scenario; then discuss and answer the questions and evaluate your work. A group evaluation form is available for downloading at *The Confident Student* premium website.

> *Where Mya grew up, students listened while the teacher talked and were not expected to speak until they were recognized. Because of this background, Mya hesitates to voice her opinions during class discussions. In addition, she feels self-conscious when her instructors assign small-group activities as most of them do. Mya is intelligent, makes excellent grades on her written work, and is a good listener, but she tends to react passively in a group. Often, she has a question that goes unanswered because she will not raise it and no one else has thought of it. Many times during a discussion, Mya has an idea or an opinion that would really add to the discussion, but she can't bring herself to speak up. Whenever Mya has to work in a group, she can tell by their body language and remarks to each other that some of the students think she is not doing her share. Mya would like to get over her fears and contribute more, but she doesn't know how.*

1. **What are Mya's strengths and weaknesses as a student?**

    _____

    _____

2. **How can she build on her strengths to overcome her weaknesses?**

    _____

    _____

3. **What barriers to communication have some of Mya's classmates shown?**

    _____

    _____

4. **What type of conflict is Mya's behavior causing and how can it be resolved?**

    _____

    _____

5. **What can the group leader do to promote civility within the group?**

    _____

    _____

6. **What can group members do to help Mya feel more comfortable in the group?**

    _____

    _____

7. **What is one or more constructive ways to encourage Mya to participate?**

    _____

    _____

Group Evaluation

Evaluate your discussion. Did everyone contribute? Did you accomplish your task successfully? What additional questions do you have about interpersonal and group communication?

Using Communication Technology

- Use communication technology effectively and appropriately.

Although you have probably grown up with the Internet, not too long ago the only means people had for maintaining relationships, other than face-to-face encounters, were the telephone and letters sent through the mail. Obviously, long-distance relationships were hard to maintain. Similarly, college students living in dorms usually had to fight to use the one pay phone at the end of the hall. Now pay phones have fallen on the ash heap of history, replaced by cell phones. Look around campus or any public place and you will see that more people than not are talking on cell phones or texting on a BlackBerry or iPhone. Communication technology has changed how we relate to each other in ways that are both positive and negative.

Some of the technology with which you are probably familiar and have used are email, instant messaging, Internet communities such as blogs and chat rooms, and social networking sites such as Facebook and MySpace. A question to consider: Has the use of this technology interfered with relationships as many people once feared that it would? A number of studies report that communication technology has helped people develop social networks, connect globally with others in ways never imagined, and may have actually improved relationships by making it easy for people to keep in touch. Although you may not be able to see a certain relative or friend every day, you can send an instant message several times a day. Another positive effect of computer-aided communicating is that gender, ethnic, and age differences are obscured when all you have in front of you is text. It becomes much easier to express opinions and share views with people whose faces you can't see.

Now here is the negative side. Without question, using communications technology can become time consuming, if not addictive. Students suffer attention deficits—especially when they Twitter or text in class. Nothing is more annoying than a cell phone that rings in a lecture or during a test, which is why many instructors are telling students to check their electronic devices at the door. To avoid making a nuisance of yourself, unplug, turn off, and store your electronic equipment in your backpack before entering the classroom. The exception would be a laptop that you are using to take notes. Still, you should make sure that the instructor doesn't mind if you use your laptop in class. Take off your earphones too. Instructors who think that wearing a hat in class shows bad manners will feel the same way about earphones. Also, be warned about the following:

- Communications technology, convenient as it is, can also be a big time waster. How many times has a text message or instant message interrupted your studying? Do you have the discipline to say no? Are you able to postpone answering until later? If not, then you could find yourself engaged in a long messaging session, forgetting all about your other obligations. Assertiveness can help here. Tell your friends "I can't talk now," and be assertive with yourself too. Put the devices away until your studying is done or unless you are using them to contact a classmate or study partner with a legitimate question regarding the assignment.

- Many instructors use email to keep in touch with their students. They may post the syllabus, assignments, and announcements online. They may expect you to email them if you are absent, if you have questions, or if you want to set up an office appointment. When emailing instructors, keep your message brief, formal, and to the point. The instructor is your superior, not your contemporary. Avoid slang and follow conventional rules of spelling and grammar. Keep your message businesslike and professional; do not be chatty with instructors. By following these guidelines, you will show your instructors that you realize how valuable and limited their time is. See Chapter 1, pages 9–10, for more rules of online etiquette.

▼ Once personal information is posted on a social networking site, you may not be able to retrieve it. If you post questionable comments or pictures of yourself on sites such as Facebook, you may be sorry later. Employers use these sites to check up on applicants.

▼ When you consider how many predators lurk on the Internet, you should be cautious about whom you connect with in chat rooms and on blogs. Too often we hear on the nightly news that the victim of a kidnapping, or worse, was targeted online. Be careful—enough said.

Only you can decide how you will use communication technology. A good rule of thumb is to manage the technology rather than letting it manage you. Make good decisions about the time, place, and frequency of your online communications. Most important, remember that the Internet is not a substitute for face-to-face contact.

EXERCISE 12.5 Computer Application on Using Online Communication

INSTRUCTORS AND OTHERS HAVE WORRIED that communications technology might interfere with communication, leading to an ever more impersonal society in which people feel alienated and disconnected. However, recent studies suggest that because of the ease, convenience, and frequency of online communication, many people believe that their relationships have improved. What do you think? Express your opinion by answering the following questions.

1. **Which one of the following do you use most often, least often, or not at all: email, instant messaging, text messaging, online chatting, blogging, other online communicating?**

2. **Has using communication technology helped or hurt your relationships with instructors? Explain how.**

3. **How have you used communication technology in your relations with classmates or in your studying?**

4. **Have you had a relationship that developed as a result of social networking?**

5. **What advantages and disadvantages of using communication technology have you seen in your own life?**

Developing Your Public Voice

- Improve your ability to give speeches and make presentations.

Speaking and writing have much in common. Both are essential communication skills and both are your primary means of self-expression. Not only are good speaking and writing skills highly valued in the workplace, they greatly improve your chances for success in most jobs and careers. Many of your courses require you to write papers and give speeches or presentations.

What precisely are the similarities between speaking and writing? Whether you are preparing a speech or presentation or writing a paper, you will have to do the following:

▼ Select a topic

▼ Determine a purpose

▼ Consider the audience

▼ State your thesis (main idea)

▼ Support your thesis

▼ Plan and organize what you will say or write

▼ Have a good introduction and conclusion

Despite so many similarities, speaking and writing differ in important ways. When writing a paper, you can edit and revise it many times until you get it right, but you have only one chance to say what you mean in a speech or presentation. When you speak, your facial expression, gestures, and tone of voice supplement your words with nonverbal cues. However, your words alone have to provide all the cues in writing. Finally, when you are giving a speech, no one will know, or care, whether you are a good speller. In writing, spelling counts.

Your public voice is different from your private voice. With friends and family, you can say what you want, the way you want. When making a formal speech or presentation or when writing a paper, your voice is more formal. For the most part, you will avoid slang. You will be mindful of the audience and choose topics that will interest them. If you tackle controversial issues, you will have an opinion, but you will remember that there is another side, and you will acknowledge opposing viewpoints. In this section, you will learn strategies for developing your public voice.

Planning Your Speech or Presentation

Sometime during your college years, you will take a speech course devoted entirely to planning and delivering speeches and presentations. But until then, you may still be required to give an oral report or make a speech or presentation in one of your classes. In a nutshell, here is what to do.

A good speech or presentation begins with a plan. Writing an outline will help you organize your ideas into an introduction, a body, and a conclusion—the three essential parts of any speech or presentation. As explained in Chapter 5, the introduction states your topic, purpose, and thesis. The body is the largest part of your presentation or speech, and this is where you support your thesis with information from your own experience or gathered from research. Your conclusion can be a brief summary of what you have said, along with its practical value or significance to your audience. See also Chapter 5, Figure 5.9, for a list of specific items to include in the three parts of your speech or presentation. In addition, try these strategies for planning your speech or presentation:

Topic: You may be assigned a topic or you may get to choose your own topic. In either case, find something in the topic to interest you, because if you are enthusiastic about the topic, your audience will be interested too. Choose a topic that you know something about, or research the topic if it is one you have been assigned and with which you are unfamiliar.

Audience: The more you know about your audience, the easier it will be to choose a topic and determine a purpose. Fortunately, most of your speeches and presentations in college will be for your classmates. For the most part, their interests, level of knowledge, attitudes, and values will resemble your own. However, remember that you will have students from diverse cultural and international backgrounds in your classes, and their interests should be considered too. Here are two questions to ask about your audience:

▼ What does my audience already know about this topic?

▼ What more do they need to know?

Purpose: As with writing a paper, there are three general purposes for speaking: to inform, to entertain, and to persuade. Once you have settled on a general purpose, the next step is to determine a specific purpose. For example, suppose you have chosen "hurricanes" as your topic and your general purpose is to inform. Let's say that you are interested in hurricane preparedness. Your specific purpose, therefore, is to inform the audience of what they need to do to prepare for a hurricane.

Thesis: The thesis of your speech or presentation is your main idea. Your thesis is a statement that combines your topic and your specific purpose, and it also suggests what response you want from your audience. For the hurricane presentation, your thesis statement might be this: *When a hurricane is coming, you need to prepare for the worst because your life may depend on it.* This statement makes clear that you want the audience to feel a sense of urgency about what you are going to say.

Support: The support for your thesis may include facts, reasons, and examples from your own experience or from information you have gathered through research. You can also support your presentation with media such as PowerPoint or Keynote slides, a handout that you prepare for the audience, or other materials. For the hurricane speech, you might bring in an emergency kit, a battery-powered lantern, or a list of public buildings that serve as shelters in your area during an emergency.

Organization: Don't expect to speak off the top of your head. The more well-organized your speech, the better it will be. Make an outline of what you will say in your introduction, body, and conclusion. Plan to have three or four major points in the body of your speech or presentation. Don't try to write down every single word—just hit the high points in your outline. Then practice from it. If you are using media, list on your outline what you plan to use and when you will demonstrate or show it.

Before reading the next section, see Figure 12.6, page 313, which illustrates the process of giving a speech or presentation.

Presenting Your Ideas to an Audience

To reduce any speech anxiety you may have, practice your speech or presentation until you know it well and feel comfortable giving it. Practice alone at first, then in front of your roommate or a couple of friends who can give you honest feedback. If you are using media, work on ways to integrate it with your presentation. Knowing your introduction and conclusion well is a trick that many professional speakers use both to relieve anxiety and to get off to a good start. Knowing that you have a good conclusion is a confidence booster because even if you begin to run out of time, you can move quickly to the end and leave the audience with a good impression. Make three note cards and number them. On the first card, write the introduction. On the second card, outline the major points that support your thesis. On the third card, write the conclusion. Arrange your cards in order and use them for reference if you need them. In addition, follow these guidelines.

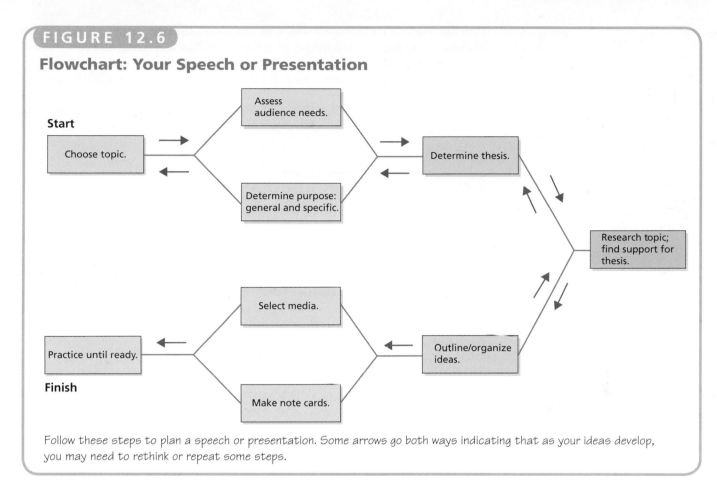

FIGURE 12.6

Flowchart: Your Speech or Presentation

Follow these steps to plan a speech or presentation. Some arrows go both ways indicating that as your ideas develop, you may need to rethink or repeat some steps.

▼ Dress comfortably in an outfit that looks professional. Although you may dress in jeans and an old tee shirt on most days, you can still dress casually but nicer on the day of your speech or presentation.

▼ Arrive a few minutes early, especially if you are the first to speak and if you have media or other materials to set up.

▼ Relax by taking a few deep breaths. Do not look at your notes while you are waiting for your turn to speak. Reading your notes again may only make you nervous. If you have practiced your speech, then you won't need to look at your notes one last time anyway.

▼ When it is time for you to speak, think positively and focus on the audience. Remember that they are on your side. They know that sooner or later, they will be in the same position that you are.

Soon after you have finished speaking, evaluate your performance. Asking yourself four questions may help you determine what you need to do to improve the next time you speak.

1. Did you remember to say everything you had planned?

2. If you made notes, did you use them and were they helpful?

3. Were you able to successfully present any media that you had brought with you?

4. Did the audience react favorably?

One way to gauge audience reaction is by expression and body language. Nodding in agreement, laughing when appropriate, paying attention, and taking notes are some of the behaviors to watch for. Asking questions is also a good sign. On the other hand, if you do not invite your audience to ask questions, then don't take it as a bad sign if they don't ask any.

Like speaking, writing is another skill that only gets better with practice. The next section explains the basics of researching and writing.

Researching and Writing

- Understand the basics of researching and writing so that you can use these skills with confidence.

If this is your first year in college, you may not yet have taken a writing course. Even so, the courses you are now taking may require you to write papers or essay exams. In fact, many of your instructors may assume that you have had some experience researching a topic or writing a paper. Have you? Don't worry if you haven't had much experience in these areas, because this section of the chapter will acquaint you with the basics of researching and writing.

Finding Information

When you **research** a topic, you study it carefully or investigate it thoroughly.

To **research** a topic means to study and investigate it carefully. When you research a topic, you gather information from several sources such as books, periodicals, websites, and even interviews with experts in the field. The kind of information to look for includes facts, figures, expert opinions—whatever you need to build background for your thesis and support for your ideas. Through research, you can add interest and credibility to your paper. Don't forget: The same sources and methods can also be used to research a topic for a speech or presentation.

Where do you find information? Many resources are available to you, and which ones you choose are up to you, unless your instructor has specific requirements. Your college library contains a wealth of information in its online catalogs and databases and in its collection of books and periodicals. If you are doing research for the first time, then your college library is a good place to begin. A librarian can help you navigate the library and all of its holdings. What are your library's resources? Figure 12.7 is a general guide to the resources that you are likely to find in any library.

Should you do your research on the Internet? Your instructors may prefer that you get most of your information from print sources such as books, periodicals, and peer-reviewed journals. Why? The reason is that the reliability of these sources is much easier to check than material that is found on the Internet. As mentioned in Chapter 3, anyone can post anything on a website, and it may be difficult for you to evaluate a source's credibility. For tips on how to evaluate online sources, see Chapter 3, pages 77–78. If you do use information from the Internet, be able to ask and answer these questions about it:

EXERCISE 12.6 Learning Styles Application on Using Your Library

TAKE A TOUR OF YOUR college library. Your purpose is to find out what resources are available for your use. Make a list of the resources, services, and locations. Then be prepared to share your information in class. You can do this assignment in one of several ways, depending on how you learn best. If you like hands-on activity, ask a librarian to give you a walking tour. If you are more visually oriented, check your library's website for a map that shows the library's layout and a listing of resources and services. Do this exercise with a partner, or by yourself if you prefer to work alone.

FIGURE 12.7

A Library's Resources

RESEARCH AREA	USUAL LOCATION	RESOURCES/SERVICES AVAILABLE
Circulation	Near main entrance	Book checkout and return
Reference	Main floor	Dictionaries, encyclopedias, almanacs, indexes, yearbooks, guides, and other reference books—both print-based and electronic
Catalog	Main floor, near circulation or reference area	Computer terminals for accessing print, audiovisual, and electronic information sources
Stacks	Bookcases that may be housed on several floors	Books and other bound volumes, arranged according to Library of Congress or Dewey Decimal system
Current periodicals	Display racks or shelves	Magazines, newspapers, and journals
Government documents	May be separated from general collection	Statistical and other information on a wide variety of subjects—both print and online
Microfilm	A section housing film cases and readers (projectors)	Collections of special materials such as back issues of periodicals and newspapers—many stored electronically
Media center	An area identified as "Multimedia," "Audiovisual," etc.	Films, records, videotapes, CDs, DVDs, CD-ROMS, etc.
Preshelving	An area on each floor	Recently returned books stored temporarily before being reshelved
Special collections/ libraries	In main library or another building on campus	Rare and oversized books, Braille editions, specific collections such as medical or law books, etc.
Interlibrary loan	Near circulation desk	Checkout and return of materials borrowed from other libraries
Reserve desk	Near circulation desk	Books, periodicals, etc., reserved by instructors or groups for a limited time
Computer area	Terminals may be on each floor	Internet access for students; email, word processing, or other services

Source: Carol C. Kanar, *The Confident Writer* 5th ed., Cengage Learning, 2009; p. 165

▶ Is the site hosted by a respectable person or group?

▶ Did an expert in the field write or provide the information?

▶ Is the source free from bias?

▶ Is the information current or updated regularly?

A librarian can suggest websites and sources that are known to be reliable and may be able to help you evaluate any sources that you have found on your own. To avoid plagiarism, take good notes from sources and remember to write down the complete reference for each source, including author, title, page where you found the information, publication date, and Internet address.

Avoiding Plagiarism

You may remember from Chapter 5 that *plagiarism* is the use of someone else's ideas and word choices without giving proper credit to the source. See also *Confidence*

Builder: Academic Honesty and You, pages 108–109. Copyright laws protect an author's work but allow you to use it within limits if you give credit to the source. Plagiarizing another's work is unethical. Acknowledging sources demonstrates that you are academically honest and has four more advantages as well:

1. Provides more information for readers

2. Allows readers to check your evidence

3. Shows readers that you have researched the topic

4. Adds credibility to your writing

An instructor can usually tell if a student's paper has been plagiarized. For example, the vocabulary, sentence structure, and complexity of ideas may be beyond the level demonstrated in the student's other work. As mentioned in Chapter 5, instructors are familiar with sites that provide "canned" papers. Some instructors will use plagiarism detection software to check suspicious papers. The most popular are TurnItIn and MyDropBox. Do you want to know more about ways to avoid plagiarism? To link to a site on plagiarism prevention, visit *The Confident Student* premium website.

If you don't know how to document sources and can't wait until you take a composition course to find out, check with your instructor or a librarian. The two most popular documentation styles are the MLA (Modern Language Association) style and the APA (American Psychological Association) style. Your college bookstore probably has manuals or style sheets available for purchase. A good handbook will also contain many examples of how to document all kinds of sources, and there are also websites that contain the information. Your librarian can point you in the right direction.

Planning and Writing a Paper

When a paper is assigned, start on it right away, especially if the assignment requires you to do research. Allow plenty of time to choose a topic, gather your information, plan your paper, and write it. Writing, and the thinking that goes with it, takes time. If you wait until the last minute, your work product will be poor, or you may give up and not do it at all. Don't get in this situation. Follow these steps to plan and write your paper. Figure 12.8 is an overview of the researching and writing process from start to finish. If your writing assignment does not require research, simply ignore steps 6 and 11. For steps 5 and 8, "information" will consist of your own ideas—facts, reasons, examples, opinions—gathered from your own knowledge, experience, or observations.

Taking Essay Exams with Confidence

Not all the writing that you do in college consists of research papers or other types of papers your instructors may assign. Many instructors use essay exams as one means of evaluation. Writing an essay exam requires you to think on the spot, and the ideas come from the information you have stored in your long-term memory. But like other papers, your answer for an essay exam should have a main idea that you support with facts. Keep your opinion out of it unless your instructor specifically asks for your opinion. The purpose of an essay exam is to demonstrate your knowledge. Therefore, you want to state your ideas clearly and stay on the point—no rambling.

First, read the question and make sure that you understand what is required. As explained in Chapter 11, instruction words in the question will tell you what to do. For example, "describe" means to give a mental impression or detailed account. If the question asks you to "compare," then your answer should show similarities and differences. Figure 12.9 shows how to plan an effective answer to an essay question. The instruction word is in bold type and the topic is in italics.

FIGURE 12.8

How to Plan and Write a Paper

Steps to Follow	What to Do at Each Step
1. Choose a topic.	Unless a topic is assigned, choose one that interests you and allows you to use your knowledge and experience.
2. Narrow the topic.	Make the general topic specific by turning it into an issue to be discussed, a problem to be solved, or a question to be answered.
3. Determine audience and purpose.	Decide who will read the paper and why; determine whether you will inform, entertain, or persuade the audience.
4. Write a working thesis statement.	The working thesis helps you determine what to look for when you do your research. Depending on the information you are able to find, you may keep the working thesis as is or revise it later.
5. Gather and evaluate information.	Gather information on your topic from at least five sources. Places to look include books, periodicals, journals, and websites. Personal interviews with experts and documentary films are also good sources.
6. Compile a list of preliminary sources (working bibliography).	Use index cards for recording complete information about your sources, including type of source, title, author, publisher, publication date, URL, or other source information; and seek help if you need it.
7. Write your final thesis statement.	After you have researched your topic, you may want to refine your thesis so that it more clearly reflects your narrowed topic and the point you want to make about it.
8. Synthesize (put together) your information.	Compile the information you have gathered, plus your own ideas, into an outline. This is the evidence that will support your thesis. Remember that in Bloom's Taxonomy, *synthesize* means to compile information from more than one source to create something—in this case, a paper—that is your original work.
9. Draft your paper.	Write a rough draft of your paper and don't worry about grammar or mechanics at this point. Your purpose is to develop and organize your ideas.
10. Revise your paper.	Revise your paper, write the final copy, proofread it, and make any final changes before you are ready to hand it in.
11. Compile your final bibliography.	The final bibliography is a list of the sources from the working bibliography that you actually used in the paper.

FIGURE 12.9

Plan Your Answer to an Essay Question

Essay Question:

What can a student do to *improve time management?* **Discuss** the effective use of scheduling.

A Plan for Your Answer:

Paragraph 1: Briefly introduce and restate the question and provide a brief answer.

Paragraph 2: Discuss how and why to make a semester schedule.

Paragraph 3: Discuss how and why to make a weekly schedule.

Paragraph 4: Discuss how and why to make daily lists.

Paragraph 5: Summarize three types of schedules and how they help you manage time.

As you can see in Figure 12.9, the topic is how to improve time management, and the student plans to explain three types of schedules. The instruction word "discuss" suggests that the answer calls for facts, reasons, or examples.

When your test paper is returned to you, read over your answers to the essay questions. Notice how many points you gained, how many you lost, and the reasons for each. Check for these three common mistakes: First, did you read the directions carefully? If not, your answer may be off topic. Second, did you cover all parts of the question to receive full credit? Third, did you include enough details? If not, you may have lost points. Read your instructor's comments to determine what you need to do to improve your grade on the next test. If you scored poorly on the essay portion of the test and you do not understand why, make an appointment with your instructor to discuss your grade. Be sure to ask your instructor what you can do to improve.

Guided CHAPTER REVIEW

The following checklist summarizes this chapter's key terms and strategies. After reading the chapter, how confident are you that you can apply the information you have learned? To assess your level of confidence, respond to each statement with one of the following: *very confident* (3 points), *fairly confident* (2 points), *not very confident* (1 point), *not confident* (0 points). Write your number of points in the box beside each statement. Then add your score and read the analysis that follows. When you have finished, take the chapter quiz.

SUMMARY CHECK

How confident are you about applying these strategies?

☐   1. Listening with all your senses

☐   2. Using different types of listening

☐   3. Listening with "the posture of involvement"

☐   4. Recognizing and overcoming barriers to communication

☐   5. Getting along with classmates and instructors

☐   6. Collaborating effectively with others in small groups

☐   7. Being able to resolve conflict

☐   8. Using communications technology appropriately

☐   9. Planning and giving a three-part speech or presentation

☐ 10. Using basic research skills to find information

☐ 11. Knowing what plagiarism is and how to avoid it

☐ 12. Planning and writing a paper that develops a thesis

☐ 13. Planning and writing an answer to an essay question

How confident are you about this chapter's key terms?

☐ 14. speech anxiety

☐ 15. communication

☐ 16. verbal

☐ 17. nonverbal

☐ 18. civility

☐ 19. collaborate

☐ 20. aggressive behavior

☐ 21. passive behavior

☐ 22. manipulative behavior

☐   23. assertive behavior

☐   24. research

Total

Add your score. The highest possible score is 72. The closer your score is to 72, the higher your level of confidence. Use your *Summary Check* results to help you determine which parts of the chapter to review.

YOUR WEBSITE RESOURCES

This chapter's website resources include the following items. To access them, go to *The Confident Student* premium website.

- **Video Skillbuilder: Persuasive Communication: Effective Strategies**
- **Video Skillbuilder: Persuasive Communication: Communicating in a Group**
- **Chapter Exercises**
- **Forms to Download**

- **Chapter Summary of Topics**
- **Review Exercise**
- **Thinking Ahead About Career**
- **Confidence Builder Web search**
- **Self-Test**

CHAPTER REVIEW Quiz

Answer the following questions from memory. Then return to the chapter to check your answers. As a final activity, complete *Show Your Confidence* at the end of the quiz.

1. Why is it important to listen with all your senses?

_____
_____

2. What are two or more of the physical or mental symptoms of speech anxiety?

_____
_____

3. What is "the posture of involvement," and what is one of its advantages?

_____
_____

4. What is one barrier to communication that you have suffered from and overcome?

_____
_____

5. Of the guidelines for successful group interaction explained in this chapter, what is one guideline that you have found to be especially effective?

_____
_____

6. What is one type of conflict explained in this chapter, and how would you resolve it if you were a group leader?

_____
_____

7. What type of communication technology do you use most often and why?

_____

_____

8. What are two questions to ask about the audience for your speech or presentation?

_____

_____

9. What are three types of sources to consider when gathering information for a speech or a paper?

_____

_____

10. Of the three parts of a paper, which one is easiest for you to write and why?

_____

_____

SHOW YOUR CONFIDENCE

How well do you get along with instructors? Think of one instructor with whom you get along well. What makes this a good relationship? Now think of another instructor with whom you do not have such a good relationship. What can you do to improve your relationship with this instructor? Be prepared to share your strategy either in writing or in class discussion.

Your REFLECTIONS: COMMUNICATION AND YOU

Reflect on what you have learned from this chapter about developing your interpersonal and communication skills. Use the following questions to stimulate your thinking; then write your reflections. Incorporate in your writing specific information from the chapter.

- Are you more comfortable in one-on-one relationships or interacting in a group?
- Do you value face-to-face communication or electronic communication more, and why?
- Of your communication skills (listening, speaking, and writing), which are your strongest, which need improvement, and which one of this chapter's strategies will help you the most?

_____

_____

_____

_____

_____

_____

13 Maintaining Your Health and Well-Being

Somos/Veer(RF)/Getty Images

This chapter encourages you to:

- Understand the connection between success in college and your health and well-being so that you can make good choices.

- Determine what causes your stress and find ways to reduce it.

- Learn how you can manage your feelings and regain your perspective if emotions cause you to lose sight of your goals.

- Develop and follow guidelines that will help you maintain healthy relationships with your friends and intimate partners.

Confident students are **emotionally intelligent**. They control their impulses rather than allowing their impulses to control them.

O ne of the values of a college education is that it exposes you to diverse students and ideas. It offers you a chance to develop socially, culturally, and intellectually—to become well-adjusted. *A well-adjusted person has achieved a balance among physical, emotional, and social needs.* Some students are not managing their lives as well as they could. Other students' emotional and physical well-being are out of balance. Some may place excessive emphasis on their friends' and family's needs and neglect their studies. Still others may be a little too conscientious, neglecting the importance of social relationships and leisure-time pursuits.

Your *physical self* is linked with health, diet, fitness, and stress management. Your *emotional self* involves your feelings, your degree of satisfaction in life, and your source of motivation. Your *social self* is expressed in your relationships and your behavior. Keeping your physical, emotional, and social selves all in balance takes self-management and **emotional intelligence**. How emotionally intelligent are you? Read the *Confidence Builder* below to find out.

CONFIDENCE BUILDER

Emotional Intelligence—Another Way of Being Smart

Why do some highly intelligent people fail? Why do some less intelligent individuals still manage to succeed? What makes one person moody and another person more even-tempered?

Emotional intelligence, or EQ, may be the answer. Daniel Goleman, author of *Emotional Intelligence*, draws on Howard Gardner's theory of "multiple intelligences," Peter Salovey's definition of *emotional intelligence*, and the research of many others to explain why your EQ may be more important than your IQ.

According to Goleman, "IQ contributes about 20 percent to the factors that determine life success, which leaves 80 percent to other factors." One of those factors is emotional intelligence: the qualities that enable you to control your emotions instead of letting them control you. For example, you can have the IQ of an Einstein and still find yourself on academic probation if you cannot control the emotions that make you want to party instead of study.

What exactly is emotional intelligence, and can it be developed? Goleman says it can. Emotional intelligence adds up to *character*, and it includes these qualities:

- Self-motivation. You alone are responsible for paying attention, maintaining concentration, and relieving yourself of boredom.
- Persistence. Following through on schedules and commitments, living up to obligations, and continuing to make progress despite temporary setbacks will help you achieve your goals.

- The ability to control impulses and delay gratification. Now and then we all do things on a whim or "in the heat of the moment." But some people let passion rule, with disastrous results: the student who drinks too much, has unprotected sex, or acts first and thinks later. To control your impulses, you have to think ahead to the consequences and ask yourself, "Is it worth it?"

- The ability to regulate moods. How fast can you bounce back from disappointment and frustration? Do you allow yourself to be overcome by sadness, anxiety, or anger? Constantly giving in to your emotions produces stress that has harmful physical and mental effects. If your inclination is to say, "But I can't help how I feel," think again. The answer is to know yourself. Learn to recognize what your feelings are and what causes them. If you know *why* you are depressed, for example, you may be able to figure out how to eliminate the cause.

- Empathy. *Empathy* is another word for *caring*, and it is a valuable interpersonal skill. People who are empathetic have a high degree of self-awareness that enables them to sense the feelings of others. They are able to put themselves in another's place so that they can tell what he or she wants or needs.

continued

- Hope. You have to believe that things will get better, that life is basically good, and that with hard work and persistence, you will achieve your goals. Without hope, it is unlikely that you will have either the will or the self-discipline to make a plan and follow it through.

Do you see a connection between Goleman's emotional intelligence and intrinsic motivation? Remember that internally motivated people take responsibility for their own successes and failures. They manage their lives, as opposed to allowing life's circumstances to manage them. Goleman's qualities of persistence and hope are also characteristic of those who are internally motivated.

Follow Up: To explore this topic further, visit *The Confident Student* premium website for a search activity about emotional intelligence.

Health, Well-Being, and Success in College

- Understand the connection between success in college and your health and well-being so that you can make good choices.

Getting an education means more than gaining academic skills. If you are a first-time college student, you are also learning how to live on your own, and you can take advantage of unique opportunities for establishing good health habits, building self-esteem, and forming close friendships. If you are an adult learner, college is one more responsibility you are adding to those you already have. Your health, relationships, and self-esteem may be put to the test as you struggle to cope with the challenges of being a student.

Whatever your age, health and well-being can affect your ability to do well in college. If you don't eat sensibly, stay physically fit, manage your stress, and avoid harmful substances, then your health and grades will suffer. Similarly, if you have troubled relationships, allow your emotions to rule, and resist change, then you will not have the sense of **well-being** that keeps you optimistic, hopeful, and motivated. *To do well academically, you need a good balance among the physical, emotional, and social factors that contribute to your sense of well-being.* This first section of the chapter focuses on your physical self and keeping it healthy. To begin thinking about how you can keep your life in balance, take *Awareness Check 13.1* now.

Well-being refers to your emotional state. High self-esteem, confidence, optimism, and positive feelings about your health and abilities—all contribute to your sense of well-being.

Awareness CHECK / 13.1

Are You Leading a Balanced Life?

Check the statements in each part that describe you.

Part I: Your Physical Self

☐ 1. I exercise regularly, three times a week or more.

☐ 2. I think that I am getting enough sleep most nights.

☐ 3. As far as I know, I eat a balanced diet.

☐ 4. I limit my intake of foods that are high in fat, salt, and sugar.

☐ 5. I feel well most of the time.

continued

☐ 6. I believe that I am not under a great deal of stress.

☐ 7. When I do have stress, I am able to manage it.

☐ 8. I am neither overweight nor underweight.

☐ 9. I do not smoke.

☐ 10. I do not abuse alcohol, caffeine, or other drugs.

Part II: Your Emotional Self

☐ 1. Basically, I am a confident person.

☐ 2. Generally speaking, I am happy.

☐ 3. When I am angry or depressed, I can get over it quickly and go on with my life.

☐ 4. My outlook for the future is positive.

☐ 5. I am rarely, if ever, overcome by nervousness, stress, or anxiety.

☐ 6. Overall, my self-esteem is high.

☐ 7. For the most part, I believe that I am in control of what happens to me.

☐ 8. I am not a fearful person by nature.

☐ 9. I am able to take criticism.

☐ 10. I can cope with change.

Part III: Your Social Self

☐ 1. It is fairly easy for me to make friends.

☐ 2. I have several friendships that mean a lot to me.

☐ 3. I am not uncomfortable if I am at a party where I don't know many people.

☐ 4. People would probably not describe me as shy.

☐ 5. I am a good listener.

☐ 6. I can also contribute to a conversation.

☐ 7. Most of the time I get along well with the significant people in my life.

☐ 8. I understand and accept my responsibilities in a sexual relationship.

☐ 9. I believe I am assertive about what I want without being overbearing.

☐ 10. If a friend points out a fault that I have, I don't take offense; instead, I try to change my behavior if I agree with my friend.

All of these statements are positive ones, so if you have checked most of them, you may be managing your life successfully. The statements are grouped into three parts, reflecting the physical, emotional, and social aspects of your health and well-being. Therefore, fewer checks in one section could indicate a need for greater balance in that part of your life. Of course, this checklist is an informal survey that does not begin to cover all of the possible aspects of adjustment, but your responses should give you a starting point for improving your health and well-being.

Health is a basic need. If your body doesn't work properly, your mind can't function at its best. Good or bad health is rarely something that just happens; it is partly the result of choices and actions. The four questions that follow embody four goals of healthful living that can lead to improved brain functioning. Think about your life and your habits; then, mentally answer the following questions *yes* or *no*.

1. Do you eat nutritionally sound, balanced meals?

2. Are you physically fit?

3. Are you able to manage stress?

4. Do you avoid the use of harmful substances?

Eat Sensibly

A nutritionally sound, balanced diet is one that includes more fish and poultry than red meat, plenty of fruits and vegetables, whole grains, nuts, and low-fat dairy products. A balanced diet contains a variety of foods. It also contains more complex carbohydrates than protein and less fat than either carbohydrates or protein. A fast-food meal of a hamburger, french fries, and a soft drink, for example, is not a balanced meal because it contains too much fat. A more balanced meal would consist of broiled lean meat (chicken or fish), two cooked vegetables or a cooked vegetable and a salad, a whole grain roll, and a piece of fruit for dessert. For more nutritional guidelines, see Figure 13.1.

Not only should you eat balanced meals, but you should also eat at regular intervals spaced throughout the day so that your brain is continually supplied with the nutrients it needs to function properly. Skipping breakfast, for example, or going into an exam hungry can interfere with your concentration and memory function and make you feel drowsy and less alert. Your brain responds to highs and lows in your blood sugar levels. When you haven't eaten, the level of glucose in your blood is low, and your mental alertness is diminished.

Glucose is a sugar best synthesized from proteins and fats. Eating a candy bar before a test will temporarily raise the level of glucose in your blood, but the burst of energy you get from it will be short lived and will leave you feeling sluggish. Instead, eat balanced meals three times a day, with snacks in between. A piece of fruit, which is high in fructose (another sugar), or a cup of yogurt is a good high-energy snack.

Glucose is a sugar and is the body's main energy source.

FIGURE 13.1

Nutrition Chart: Guidelines for Good Eating

GUIDELINES	FOODS	REASONS
Eat some of these foods every day.	Fruits, vegetables, fish, poultry, nuts, beans	To achieve a varied, balanced diet that supplies enough energy and essential nutrients for optimum brain functioning
Increase complex carbohydrates.	Fruits, vegetables, nuts, whole grains	For maintaining energy throughout the day
Avoid simple carbohydrates.	White flour, refined sugar	To reduce risk of diabetes, heart disease
Choose good sources of protein; limit red meat.	Lean meat, fish, chicken, eggs, peas, and beans	For the growth and repair of tissue and to help fight infections
Choose *good* fats over *bad* fats, and limit fat intake.	Vegetable oils instead of butter; low-fat dairy products instead of whole-milk products	To reduce risk of high blood pressure, heart disease, and diabetes

What can you do to maintain a healthful diet while you are in college? Try these 10 suggestions:

1. Schedule your classes and other activities so that you have time for meals.

2. Eat balanced meals. You may be able to get a nutritious meal in your college's cafeteria. A variety of vegetables is usually available, and you can select your own combination of foods. If you live off campus, select foods according to the guidelines listed in Figure 13.1.

3. Avoid rich, high-calorie snacks. If you get hungry between meals, eat an apple or another fruit; carrot or celery sticks; or unbuttered, unsalted popcorn. For an energy boost, try low-fat yogurt or a few unsalted nuts instead of sugary or salty snacks.

4. If you live off campus, go home for lunch or bring your lunch. Be in control of what you eat.

5. If you go to parties, go easy on the snacks and alcoholic drinks. You may not know this, but alcohol converts to sugar in the bloodstream and is stored as fat. Apart from its other dangers, too much alcohol can make you gain weight, and it can interfere with your body's absorption of essential nutrients.

6. Don't make a habit of skipping meals. Fatigue, fuzzy thinking, and diminished concentration are among the problems this habit can cause.

7. If you are overweight and would like to reduce, ask your doctor to help you select an appropriate weight-loss program.

8. Exercise regularly; it will increase your level of fitness, make you feel positive and energetic, and help reduce stress. If you are trying to lose weight, combining a sensible diet with exercise will speed up the process and help keep the weight off.

9. Put food in perspective. Eat for good health. Don't eat because you feel depressed, because you want to celebrate, or as a social activity.

10. Drink eight to ten glasses of water a day to aid the digestive process, help eliminate wastes and toxins from your body, and supply needed moisture to the tissues.

Aerobic exercise is continuous muscular activity that elevates the heart rate. Running and walking are examples.

Walking is one of the simplest forms of aerobic exercise. Thirty minutes of brisk walking daily can raise your fitness level.

Jim Cummins/CORBIS

Get Fit, Stay Fit

Exercise has many benefits; fitness is just one of them. Regular exercise strengthens your heart, improves circulation, and helps reduce your risk of cardiovascular illness or death from a heart attack or stroke. Exercise can make you strong and able to withstand other diseases, and it can relieve stress. In addition, it helps you lose weight and improves your appearance.

The best exercise is aerobic. An **aerobic exercise** lasts for a minimum of 20 minutes, during which your heart rate is elevated and your muscular activity is continuous. You should not do aerobic exercises without checking your pulse frequently and without first receiving instructions on how to perform the activities. Overstressing your heart can have serious, even fatal, effects. "No pain, no gain" is a dangerous myth. "FIT" is a much better guideline.

EXERCISE 13.1 — Are You Eating a Balanced Diet?

FIND OUT WHAT YOU EAT and whether your diet is as balanced and healthful as it could be. Keep a record of what you eat for one week; then determine ways to eat more sensibly if necessary. For example, if you discover that most of your calories are coming from fats, decrease your intake of fatty foods such as butter, cheese, ice cream, margarine, salad dressings, and luncheon meats or other meats rich in fat and increase your intake of whole grains, fruits, vegetables, lean meats, fish, and poultry. Keep recording your meals and attempting to adjust what you eat until you achieve a balanced diet.

Make copies of this chart so that you can record what you eat throughout the day. (If you wait until evening, you may forget what you've eaten.) Visit *The Confident Student* premium website to download copies of the chart.

	Sunday	Monday	Tuesday	Wednesday	Thursday	Friday	Saturday
Breakfast							
Lunch							
Dinner							
Snacks							

F = Frequency	How often you exercise—three times a week is the generally recommended starting frequency
I = Intensity	Your target heart rate, based on your age and present level of fitness
T = Time	The amount of time you spend exercising—start with 15 minutes or less, depending on your age and condition, and then gradually increase the time as you are able

Exercise is great for you if you do it correctly. An excellent place to get started is in your college's athletic department. Exercise classes and individual consultation may be available at a lower cost than you are likely to find at one of the commercial health clubs or spas, and may even be offered free of charge. If you don't have time for exercise that requires a change of clothes or a special place or type of equipment, try walking. You can walk anywhere; just 30 minutes a day of brisk, uninterrupted walking greatly

Concept Check 13.1

Would you like to see more information on improving diet and fitness? Go to http://www.Nutrition.gov for the latest U.S. Government nutrition guidelines. WebMD (www.webmd.com) is another great source for finding information on health, nutrition, and fitness.

aerobic activities
✓ rowing
✓ swimming
✓ bicycling
✓ running
✓ walking
✓ jumping rope
✓ dancing

reduces your risk of heart problems and improves your overall level of fitness. See the list of aerobic activities to the left, some of which you may already be doing.

Avoid Harmful Substances

When it comes to drugs, both legal and illegal, it's best to take a realistic approach. What are the facts and misconceptions surrounding alcohol, tobacco, caffeine, and illegal drugs such as marijuana and cocaine? What are the risks and perceived benefits of using one or more of these substances? Arming yourself with knowledge enables you to deal with issues of substance use and abuse on your own terms.

Tobacco. Smoking places you at risk of getting lung cancer, heart disease, and a host of other illnesses, according to the American Cancer Society, the American Lung Association, the American Heart Association, and many other health organizations and professionals. Because secondhand smoke poses similar risks for nonsmokers, smoking is prohibited or limited in all public buildings, many

EXERCISE 13.2   Choose Your Exercise

FIND AN EXERCISE PROGRAM THAT works. Choose a form of exercise that you enjoy and can easily fit into your schedule. Try out some of the aerobic exercises listed above; then use the following chart to summarize and comment on your experiences. The chart will help you determine which type of exercise works best for you and why. To download extra copies of the chart, visit *The Confident Student* premium website.

Type of exercise	Aerobic dancing				
Time of day	7:00 p.m.				
Amount of time spent	1 hour				
Reaction	I went to an aerobics class with a friend, and I liked it so much that I decided to join too.				

restaurants, and other establishments. Public awareness about the dangers of smoking has increased, and a growing social stigma against smoking prevails. All states have laws prohibiting the sale of tobacco products to minors. Those are the facts.

A misconception some people have is that they can quit smoking whenever they want to. However, the National Institute on Drug Abuse (NIDA) has published numerous articles on tobacco addiction. The NIDA has called the cigarette a drug delivery system for nicotine and other chemicals that activate the brain's pleasure centers, causing effects similar to those of illegal drugs. Although quitting is difficult, it is not impossible. If you smoke, ask yourself this question: What is this habit doing for me? If, after considering the risks and benefits, you decide to quit, ask your doctor to suggest a smoking cessation program.

Caffeine. How many students do you know who can't face the morning without a cup of coffee? How many students need caffeine to keep them going throughout the day or to keep them awake during late-night study sessions? Here are the facts about caffeine: It is present in coffee, tea, chocolate, some sodas, and certain over-the-counter drugs. When used in moderation, caffeine reduces drowsiness and increases energy. When abused, caffeine can produce anxiety and tremors and may aggravate certain conditions such as heart disease and high blood pressure. Caffeine can be addicting; an abrupt decrease or cessation of use produces withdrawal symptoms such as headaches and jitters, but one or two cups a day may produce few, if any, negative side effects. As you weigh the health benefits and risks of using caffeine, consider two alternatives to morning coffee: switch to decaffeinated, or manage your time so that you get enough rest, eliminating the need for a caffeine boost.

Illegal Drugs. What is the allure of drugs such as marijuana, cocaine, heroin, amphetamines, and crystal meth? They stimulate the brain's pleasure centers, generating feelings such as alertness, euphoria, or relaxation. But the "high" users get is short lived and may be followed by feelings of depression or anxiety. Because these drugs are both psychologically and physically addicting, abuse can lead to a habit that is extremely hard to break. Because the drugs are illegal, the Food and Drug Administration has no control over their manufacture. As a result, they may be produced in unsanitary conditions and may contain toxic additives that increase users' health risks.

Some students who have experimented with illegal drugs have experienced few, if any, ill effects. But some have become addicted, some have died of overdoses, some have been sexually assaulted while under the influence, and others have served jail terms and have had their academic careers and future prospects forever curtailed as a result. Keeping these facts in mind, ask yourself whether the short-term benefits students may think they are getting from drug use are really worth the considerable risks involved and their long-term consequences.

Alcohol. We have saved this drug for last because its use and abuse are of greatest concern to college students. Because binge drinking among college students, alcohol abuse at campus social events, and alcohol-related deaths and other incidents during spring break get a lot of media attention, it's easy to get the impression that "everybody does it." The reality is that many college students do not drink, and many who do drink do so

If you choose to drink, do so responsibly and be aware of the risks and consequences.

responsibly. But for others, alcohol abuse has resulted in dangerous behavior—and even death. Because students are often pressured to drink in social situations and because the opportunities to abuse alcohol are readily available, your best defense is knowledge.

Ingram Publishing(RF)/Jupiter Images

Why do students drink? Psychologists and other professionals cite several reasons. For one thing, children of alcoholics and children who grew up in homes where alcohol was used at family occasions may be more prone to use alcohol. Also, some experimentation with "the forbidden" is a normal part of growing up. Drinking, for some students, is a rebellious act through which they establish their independence. Third, despite the risks of drinking, some students turn to alcohol to relieve stress or to escape unpleasantness. Peer pressure is another reason. Students may feel that they must drink in order to be accepted. Finally, the media and the campus atmosphere exert powerful influences. The media are filled with images that make drinking seem glamorous. Beverage companies sponsor social events that make alcohol consumption by young people seem normal, average. Social organizations on campus, Greek organizations in particular, may sponsor events that revolve around drinking. Too often, college administrators look the other way, ignoring the underage drinking that may be occurring on campus.

Binge drinking is the consumption of four to five or more drinks within a short time period.

Although light drinking may pose few health risks, binge drinking is dangerous. What is binge drinking? According to the NIAAA Advisory Council, ingesting five or more drinks (males) or four or more drinks (females) within a time period of about two hours constitutes **binge drinking**. This behavior can result in injury, illness, and even death from alcohol poisoning. Binge drinking has negative academic effects as well, impairing performance and judgment.

What are your choices? As a student, you must make your own decisions about alcohol use. You don't have to drink, but if you choose to, know the risks. Know the difference between light-to-moderate drinking and abusive or binge drinking. Consider also your religious beliefs and personal values. Be aware of legal limits and campus policies regarding alcohol use and make ethical choices. If you do drink, the following guidelines may help you drink safely and responsibly.

▶ Know what you're drinking. It's easy for someone to slip a drug into a drink and easy for someone to spike a drink with more alcohol than you had intended to consume. Therefore, do not accept a drink from anyone. Get your own drink.

▶ Time your drinking. Don't drink too much too fast. Drink slowly, making one drink last at least an hour.

▶ Do not drink on an empty stomach. Eat or nibble while drinking. Eating slows the absorption of alcohol into the bloodstream.

▶ Opt out of drinking games. Games such as chug-a-lug contests are risky because they introduce too much alcohol into your system too rapidly.

▶ Say no when you've had enough. A simple "no" is all you need to say to refuse a drink. You don't owe anyone an explanation.

▶ Do not drink and drive. If you and your friends are out drinking, let someone who has not been drinking be your designated driver. Do not drive drunk, and don't ride with a driver who is.

Choosing not to drink is a valid option. If you make this choice, you can still attend parties and other social events where alcohol is consumed without participating in drinking. Take someone with you who is also a nondrinker. In addition, choose other, positive ways to find escape, relaxation, excitement, and pleasure. For example, plan activities with your friends that involve physical and mental stimulation. Attend sports events, take bicycle or hiking trips, go to the beach for a day of surfing and sunning, or go to a movie. Solitary pursuits that provide escape, adventure, and excitement include reading, writing, various arts or crafts, and individual sports.

Like everything else, deciding whether or not to drink is *your* choice. In this behavior, as in all others, by being informed and by making responsible choices, you are taking control of your life.

EXERCISE 13.3 Survey on Alcohol Use and Abuse

HOW PREVALENT IS DRINKING ON your campus? Take this informal survey to gather information about your own habits and assumptions. Do not identify yourself on the survey. Your instructor will compile all students' answers and report back to the class.

To take the survey, read each question and circle your answer.

1. **Do you drink?**

   a. **never**   b. **occasionally**   c. **regularly**

2. **How many drinks do you have in a week?**

   a. **none**   b. **1 or 2**   c. **more than 1 or 2**

3. **When are you most likely to drink?**

   a. **at social events**   b. **on special occasions**

   c. **with meals**   d. **whenever I'm with friends**

4. **How many drinks do you usually have at a social event or during an evening spent with friends?**

   a. **1 or 2**   b. **2 to 5**   c. **more than 5**

5. **Have you ever engaged in binge drinking?**

   a. **never**   b. **occasionally**   c. **regularly**

6. **Have you ever engaged in drinking games?**

   a. **never**   b. **occasionally**   c. **regularly**

7. **To the best of your knowledge, how prevalent is binge drinking among the students on your campus?**

   a. **not prevalent at all**   b. **somewhat prevalent**   c. **very prevalent**

8. **In general, what would you estimate to be the percentage of students on your campus who drink regularly?**

   a. **fewer than 50 percent**   b. **about 50 percent**   c. **more than 50 percent**

9. **Do you believe that a student on your campus has to drink in order to be accepted or to have a social life?**

   a. **not at all**   b. **in some cases**   c. **definitely**

10. **Based on your own experience, how would you describe college students' drinking behavior?**

    a. **Most students do not drink.**

    b. **Most students engage in light-to-moderate drinking.**

    c. **Most students drink to excess.**

11. **How does drinking behavior on your campus compare with that on other campuses?**

    a. **There is less drinking among students on my campus.**

    b. **About the same amount of drinking occurs among students on my campus as on others.**

    c. **Students on my campus drink more than students on other campuses.**

continued

12. If you are out with friends, how likely is one of you to abstain from drinking so that he or she can be the designated driver?

    a. not likely   b. somewhat likely   c. very likely

13. How much underage drinking do you see at campus events or other social events at which college students are present?

    a. hardly any   b. some   c. a great deal

14. Among the students on your campus, how much pressure is there to engage in drinking?

    a. none   b. some   c. a great deal

15. Do you know anyone on your campus who has been involved in one or more of the following while drinking? Circle all that apply.

    a. acquaintance rape   b. an automobile accident

    c. a serious injury   d. unsafe sexual activity

16. Do you know anyone on campus whose drinking has led to one or more of these outcomes? Circle all that apply.

    a. missed class or was late   b. scored poorly on a test

    c. failed to hand in course work   d. had a loss of memory

Managing Stress

- Determine what causes your stress and find ways to reduce it.

Some stress won't hurt you. In fact, you should expect to experience stress now and then. For example, in Chapter 12, you learned that it is normal to feel a little anxious before getting up in front of a group to speak. You want to do your best, and you may be wondering whether you will be able to remember everything you want to say. Once you get started, this anxiety should pass quickly as you begin to focus your attention on giving the speech. As explained in Chapter 11, it is also normal to feel a little anxiety on the day of an exam. But once you have the exam in front of you and get down to the business of taking the test, the anxiety should pass. Real **stress** is unrelieved anxiety that persists over a long period of time. Stress is especially harmful if you are unable to manage it. Unrelieved stress can weaken you physically so that you become vulnerable to disease, and it can impair your ability to think clearly so that your performance in class and at work suffers.

Stress is persistent, unrelieved anxiety that interferes with normal functioning.

Many warning signs can tell you if your stress is getting out of control. Look at the brief list that follows, and see whether you have any of these common symptoms of stress. The more of these symptoms that you have, the more likely it is that you need to learn some strategies for coping with stress.

Depression	Loss of pleasure in life
Difficulty falling asleep	Increase or decrease in appetite
Extreme tiredness, fatigue	Muscular aches for no apparent reason
Feelings of anger or resentment	Stomach or intestinal disturbances

Sweaty palms	Frequent absence from work or classes
Impatience	Tension headaches
Inability to concentrate	Test anxiety

Many students find adjusting to college and meeting course requirements extremely stressful, especially if they are also working, raising a family, or trying to cope in an environment in which they feel out of place. Some students are chronically anxious about tests, and their nervousness prevents them from doing their best. Test anxiety is a special kind of stress related to testing situations. Chapter 11 explains test anxiety and how to overcome it.

It is important that you find ways to manage stress so that you can reach your goals and enjoy yourself in the process. Try the following tips for managing stress.

Ten Stress Beaters

1. **Be realistic.** You know what you can and cannot do. Don't waste energy worrying about matters that are out of your control. Instead, use your energy to alter those situations that you have the power to change. Unrealistic goals, perfectionism, and believing you have to do everything right the first time will set you up for failure. Be reasonable about what you expect of yourself, and don't be afraid to make mistakes.

2. **Exercise tensions away.** When you are under stress, your muscles tense involuntarily. Exercise has a natural calming effect that is accompanied by a positive feeling. For example, you may have heard about or experienced "runner's high," the feeling of euphoria and the sudden burst of energy runners get after they have been running for a long time.

   To help you relax, try the desktop relaxation technique explained in Chapter 8. Also try this simple deep-breathing technique for calming yourself in any situation: Breathe slowly through your nose, filling your lungs. Then slowly exhale through your mouth. As you take 10 deep breaths in this manner, think to yourself: "I am relaxed; I am calm." Another stress reliever to try is the chair-seat relaxation method, demonstrated in Figure 13.2 with four photographs. As shown in the first photo, sit up straight with your feet together on the floor. As shown in the second photo, close your eyes and pull up hard on the chair seat with your hands. At the same time, press your feet firmly into the floor until you can feel all your muscles tensing. While you are doing this, count slowly to 10 as you breathe deeply in and out. When you get to 10, relax as shown in the third photo. Let your arms hang limply at your sides; but with your eyes still closed, visualize yourself as calm and stress-free. Then, as shown in the fourth photo, open your eyes and return to your work feeling positive and relaxed.

3. **Learn to say no.** For whatever reason, many of us have difficulty saying no. When you are under stress because of work, family, course requirements, and other obligations, the last thing you need is to take on more responsibilities. When someone makes demands on your dwindling time, ask yourself, "Do I really want or need to do this?" If the answer is "no," don't be afraid to say so. If you have trouble saying no, you may need to become more assertive, as explained later in this chapter.

4. **Ask for help.** Some problems may be more than you can handle by yourself, so you may need to seek financial, medical, or some other

FIGURE 13.2

The Chair-Seat Relaxation Method

1   2   3   4

type of help or advice. If you are the kind of person who hates to ask for help, try to get over this attitude. Many times we worry needlessly and cause ourselves even more stress by living with problems that we consider unsolvable when asking for and getting help might bring a solution. For example, see the nearby *Computer Confidence* box about Internet addiction. Help is available for these kinds of issues.

5. **Learn to deal with negative people.** People who display negative attitudes, a pessimistic outlook on life, and a constant state of nervousness can make you experience negative feelings that add to your stress. If you can eliminate negative people from your life, do so. If they are friends or family members, try to counter their negative remarks with positive ones of your own. When they do behave in a more positive way, comment on what you like about their behavior, thereby positively reinforcing a behavior that you want them to continue.

6. **Lose yourself in activity.** When you are under stress, engage in some positive and healthful activities that cause you to lose all track of time. During those moments, you can forget your worries and experience happy, calming feelings. Reading, playing a sport, and spending time pursuing a hobby or special interest are all activities in which you can lose yourself.

7. **Reward yourself.** Ideally, you should always be prepared for tests, complete assignments on time, and follow your study schedule.

Computer CONFIDENCE

Are You Spending Too Much Time Online?

Internet addiction is a student health issue that causes concern on college campuses. Cruise by your college's computer lab at any time of day, and you are likely to see all stations occupied. What are these students doing? Some undoubtedly are researching and writing. Many, however, are playing games and chatting with friends online. Though harmless in themselves, when taken to extremes, these activities can put students at risk for failing grades and failed relationships. College counselors are troubled by the attrition rate of students whose misuse of the Internet has disrupted their lives and curtailed their education.

Why do people become addicted to the Internet? When spending time online, one can escape from reality and the complexities of real-world human relations. People can create new identities, concealing their real names, ages, personalities, and socioeconomic status. The intimacy that develops between friends who meet online is, therefore, an illusion. Real intimacy comes from closeness with another person. But online- -or virtual—relationships are, by their nature, at arm's length.

Who is at risk? The same risk factors that apply to drug and alcohol use apply to Internet addiction. Depression, anxiety, or lack of self-confidence and self-esteem may cause people to seek relief online. People who have abused drugs, alcohol, or tobacco may have an increased susceptibility to Internet addiction.

What can you do? As with any other activity that has a potential for abuse, use caution. Have a purpose for using the Internet, and schedule your online time so that it doesn't interfere with your other activities. Use the Internet as a research tool or for an occasional game, but don't let it become a substitute for social interaction. Email also can get out of hand if reading and sending messages consumes too much of your time or if you use email not as a convenience but rather as a way to keep the people closest to you at a distance. If you are concerned that your Internet use may be excessive, seek help at your campus counseling center.

The Internet is a helpful tool for researching and fact finding; it can also be a pleasant distraction similar to watching a movie or a favorite TV program. But when your Internet use becomes obsessive, it may also become addicting. Watch for these warning signs:

- Internet activities are on your mind more often than not.
- The amount of time you spend online has gradually increased.
- After deciding that you were spending too much time online, you tried to stop or cut back but were unsuccessful.
- Just the thought of limiting your Internet time makes you feel anxious or depressed.
- Friends, family members, or others close to you have expressed concern about the amount of time you spend online.
- You often turn to the computer for relief from stress, life's problems, or feelings of depression.

Do four or more of these warning signs apply to you? If so, you may be spending too much time online.

Realistically, however, you may fall short of meeting these goals. When that happens, get back on track as soon as you can; then reward yourself with a break or another treat. A completed task followed by a reward is a great stress reducer.

8. **Get your life in order.** You've probably been meaning to do this anyway. If you are off schedule or behind in your courses, resolve

to get organized. Make out a new study schedule that includes time to catch up on work you've missed. Make a list of all the other tasks that need doing; then tackle them one at a time. Don't worry if it takes you a while to get organized. After all, it took a while to get off schedule.

9. **Make a wish list.** We all have a tendency to say to ourselves, "If only I had the time, I'd do _____." How would you complete this sentence? Make a list of all the things you'd do if you had the time. When stress has become more than you can handle and you have to get away for a while, do one of your wish-list activities.

10. **Help someone else.** It's no secret that doing something for someone else can make you feel good and can take your mind off what is worrying you. Take the opportunity to help a friend who has a problem. Volunteer or participate in service learning projects. The things you do for others not only help them but also help you build self-esteem, an important personal quality.

Concept Check 13.2

People experience stress from many sources. What makes you feel stressed? How do you cope with the stress in your life? What works best for you?

CRITICAL THINKING   What Stresses You?

Exercise Overview

What are the most common sources of stress? What can people do to cope with stress? This exercise will help you think through these questions to find answers.

Exercise Background

Stress affects people in different ways. A situation that is a major stressor for one person may not be a source of worry for another. However, some events are universally stressful because they disrupt the orderly pattern of our lives and relationships. How we handle the stress following one of these events determines how well we are able to move on with our lives and reach our goals.

Exercise Task

Listed next are some life-changing events that can upset the balance of a person's health and well-being and cause stress. Have you experienced one of these events within the last six months or year? Write a short essay about the changes in your life resulting from the event, and explain what you are doing to adapt to your new circumstances. If you prefer, you can write about a stress-causing event that is not listed.

Death of a spouse or partner	Loss of a job or financial support
Death of a parent	Breakup of a relationship other
Death of other close family member	than marriage
Divorce	Serious argument with someone
Unwanted pregnancy	Legal problem
Major injury or illness (self)	Academic difficulties, probation
Major injury or illness (family member or partner)	Relocation of residence

Managing Your Emotions

- Learn how you can manage your feelings and regain your perspective if emotions cause you to lose sight of your goals.

Although you may be faced with a situation you cannot change, you *can* change how you react to it. For example, if you are having trouble getting along with a roommate, you may be losing study time because of arguing or worrying about the problem. Soon your grades will suffer if you can't resolve your differences and get back on schedule. Obviously, you can't change your roommate's behavior, but you can change your feelings about that behavior. You can decide not to let it get to you. Focus your attention on doing well in your courses. Concentrate on meeting every requirement, completing every assignment, and preparing for every test. Do most of your studying in the library or some other place away from your roommate. Try to resolve your differences, but if you cannot, make the best of the situation until you can make other living arrangements. Avoid getting into arguments, and say to yourself, "I am in charge of my feelings, and I will not let my conflict with my roommate interfere with my success in my courses."

Similarly, if you are an older student who lives off campus, you may have a family member or friend who tries to undermine your efforts to be successful by making comments such as "You'll never make it" or "You shouldn't put yourself through this." Negative comments like these don't have to upset you. Your emotions belong to *you*. People cannot control how you feel unless you give them that power.

Understand Your Feelings

To begin taking control of your emotions, determine what causes you to feel one way or another. Begin by listening to yourself think and talk. Are your thoughts and words dominated by statements that begin with *they, he, she,* or *you*? Do you often make statements such as these?

▶ *You* make me angry because you don't listen to what I say.

▶ *She* doesn't care how I feel.

▶ *He* really hurt my feelings.

▶ *They* make it hard for me to get the schedule I want.

▶ *She* gave me a D on that paper, but I deserved better.

When you make statements like these, you place all the blame for your feelings on someone else. You place yourself at the mercy of others' whims. If they choose to, they can make you feel great. If they choose to, they can make you feel terrible. You never know where you stand with people, and consequently, your self-esteem is undermined.

Chapter 2 explains sources of motivation as being either extrinsic or intrinsic. For example, if you expect someone or something to motivate you, then your source of motivation is extrinsic or external. If you are self-motivated, then your source of motivation comes from within. These motivating factors may also explain, in part, what controls your feelings. Externally motivated students tend to blame others for the way they feel. Internally motivated students are more likely to examine their own behavior as the cause of their feelings.

One way to take control of your emotions is to replace any statements of feeling that begin with *they, he, she,* or *you* with statements that begin with *I*. You will then be able to determine what actually caused the feeling. For example, here are the same statements you read before, but the word *I* has replaced the first word, and the statement has been altered to shift the cause of the feeling to the person making the statement.

▼ *I* get angry when I think you're not listening to what I say.

▼ *I* believe she doesn't care how I feel.

▼ *I* feel hurt by some of the things he does.

▼ *I* find it hard to get the schedule that I want.

▼ *I* made a D on that paper, but I could have done better.

Pretend for a moment that you made these statements. Notice how you have accepted responsibility for the feelings. For example, by accepting that the D is the grade that you earned, you are likely to do better next time. But if you blame someone else for the D, then you are off the hook and have no control over your future in the course. Similarly, if *they* are not responsible for your schedule, then you must determine what actions *you* should take to get the schedule you want. This kind of thinking puts *you* in control of the outcome.

For example, in the first three statements, you accept responsibility for your feelings that seem to result from others' actions. The value of doing this is that it opens a discussion about behavior you don't like without blaming someone else. For example, if it turns out that your friend really doesn't listen, doesn't care how you feel, or does things that hurt you, then you can decide what you are going to do about the situation, whether it is worthwhile to try to improve the relationship, or if you should end it. In either case, you open the way for communication rather than for more arguments and bad feelings.

EXERCISE 13.4   Learning Styles Application on Taking Responsibility

IN THE FOLLOWING STATEMENTS, THE pronouns *they*, *he*, *she*, and *you* suggest that the people making the statements are not taking responsibility for their feelings and behavior. Rewrite each statement so that the focus is on the person making the statement. Replace any pronouns with the first-person pronoun *I* and change any other wording as needed.

1. **You didn't tell us we had to do the exercises.**

   _____

   _____

2. **They told me the department chair would let me in the course even though it's full.**

   _____

   _____

3. **You are not paying attention to me.**

   _____

   _____

4. **Professor Brown is a boring lecturer.**

   _____

   _____

5. **Professor Greene is never in the office when I go there.**

   _____

   _____

Find Purpose in Your Life

When you control your emotions and accept responsibility for your feelings, you increase your chances for happiness and decrease your chances for disappointment. A sense of well-being results from having goals to reach and making plans to achieve them. As explained in Chapter 4, setting reachable long-term and short-term goals will give you a purpose for attending college, completing your tasks at work, and realizing your dreams and plans. When your purpose is clear, you are more likely to schedule your time, follow through on your action plans, and avoid procrastination.

If your life seems to lack purpose, examine what you are doing in your courses, at work, or at home. Ask yourself, "Why am I doing this?" Answers may not come right away, but when they do, they may remind you of your goals or indicate a need to make some changes in your life. This knowledge will give you a renewed sense of purpose. You can also discuss these important issues with a trusted friend, parent, academic advisor, or counselor.

Managing your emotions and relationships does not have to be a solitary task. You can always seek help from professionals and peers.

When it comes to exploring your life goals and purposes, don't underestimate the value of spiritual or religious beliefs. Throughout time, people in all societies have felt a yearning for something greater than themselves. These feelings often express themselves in religious observances. If you have always been a religious person, don't let college change that. Continue to practice your faith. On the other hand, if you are not a religious person, you may still have spiritual urgings that express themselves in a love of music or art. Your sense of purpose may come from doing something you love.

Accept the Need for Change

Negative feelings, a sense of helplessness, and lowered self-esteem result when something you are doing isn't working out, but you are afraid to make a change. An unhappy wife or husband may continue without help in a relationship that makes both partners miserable because one or the other is afraid of the changes that marriage counseling might require. A person who has been offered a new and better job or a transfer to a higher-paying job out of state may turn down the offer because he or she fears change. You may keep working on a research paper—even though you may realize that you have chosen an unworkable topic—because you don't want to start over. If you are "test anxious," you may avoid seeking help because you believe the problem will go away or there is nothing you can do about it. Trying to avoid change by ignoring a problem can be self-destructive. Negative feelings breed more negative feelings, encouraging the mistaken belief that a bad situation can only get worse.

Accept the need for change when it becomes clear that you have done all you can do in a situation that is not working. Acceptance is the hard part. Once you're committed to making a change in your life, exploring your options and deciding what to do next can be fun and challenging. The next exercise will give you more practice with managing your emotions and engaging in self-reflection.

EXERCISE 13.5 **Value Who You Are**

LIKE MOST PEOPLE, YOU PROBABLY have times in your life when you feel disappointed, depressed, angry, frustrated, lonely, incompetent, or unloved. Like many people, you may tend to blame others for making you feel this way. In fact, no one needs to have that much power over you if you assume responsibility for your own well-being. Complete the statements that follow to remind yourself of what you have and the things that make you feel good. Think about these positive qualities and accomplishments whenever you lack confidence.

continued

1. **My finest character trait is** _____.
2. **My favorite possession is** _____.
3. **My closest friend is** _____.
4. **I am proud of myself for** _____.
5. **I feel happiest at home when I** _____.
6. **I feel most comfortable at work when I** _____.
7. **The course in which I am doing my best is** _____.
8. **Something I enjoy doing by myself is** _____.
9. **A skill I have mastered very quickly is** _____.
10. **One thing I can really do well is** _____.
11. **On my next vacation I will** _____.
12. **One of my plans for the future is** _____.

Maintaining Healthy Relationships

- Develop and follow guidelines that will help you maintain healthy relationships with your friends and intimate partners.

As explained in Chapter 12, college offers the opportunity to build new relationships and to test old ones. Your well-being depends, in part, on the relationships you are able to establish and maintain. When you are new in college, you may have trouble meeting people at first, but don't be discouraged. Many students are in the same situation as you are, and they are just as eager to make friends. In the student center or cafeteria, resist the temptation to sit by yourself. Join a group at a table and introduce yourself. Offer to exchange phone numbers or email addresses with one or two people in each of your classes so that you can compare notes if one of you should be absent. Participate in as many campus activities as you can. You will meet people who share your interests, which is the basis of any long-lasting relationship. If you live in a residence hall, introduce yourself to the students living on either side of you and across the hall. Invite someone to go home with you one weekend. As you extend these offers of friendship to others, you will find them responding to you with similar offers of their own.

Chapter 12 explores ways to build relationships that are mutually beneficial—healthy relationships, in other words. In this section, we are concerned with keeping an intimate relationship healthy. This means knowing how to manage your sexuality and how to deal assertively with acquaintance rape and sexual harassment.

Your Sexuality

Sex takes a relationship to a new level of physical and emotional intimacy. Whatever your sexual orientation, you probably want the same thing that most people want from an intimate relationship: mutual acceptance, trust, respect, and—given the prevalence of **sexually transmitted diseases (STDs)**—honesty about past relationships. Although some people may profess a desire for recreational sex or sex without emotional intimacy or commitment, the truth is that sex is rarely, if ever, "just physical" for both

Sexually transmitted diseases (STDs) are contracted through sexual activity. Some examples are herpes, genital warts, and AIDS.

EXERCISE 13.6   Healthy Relationships

COLLEGE OFFERS A VARIETY OF situations and settings for meeting new people. But college students often spend hours in solitary studying and miss out on or ignore many opportunities for socializing. Imagine that you are a new transfer student at your college and don't know a soul. How would you go about meeting new people? Using your college website, student handbook, college newspaper, and posted flyers as resources, list places and situations for meeting new people. Find examples in the following three categories.

1. **Academic activities**

   _____

   _____

2. **Social events**

   _____

   _____

3. **Recreational activities**

   _____

   _____

Are you the kind of person who meets new people easily, or do you take a long time to "warm up" to someone? Think about the three newest friends in your life. Describe where and how you met these people. Can you draw a conclusion about what kinds of situations you find most conducive to meeting new friends? Write your conclusion in one or two sentences.

Friend 1: _____

_____

Friend 2: _____

_____

Friend 3: _____

_____

Conclusion: _____

_____

_____

people involved. Sexual behavior carries with it emotional issues of self-esteem, self-respect, and self-confidence. Moral values and ethics, too, play an important role. In fact, the kind of person you are and your character—or lack of it—are revealed in the way you handle *all* your relationships. Here are some guidelines to follow:

▼ Don't rush sex. If you become physically involved with someone for whom you don't feel real affection, you will probably suffer a loss of self-esteem.

▼ Listen to your feelings. Anxiety before sex, guilt afterward, and a lack of desire or pleasurable feeling at any point along the way signal that something is wrong.

▼ Stand by your values. Don't let someone pressure you into any type of sexual activity if you don't want it or if it goes against your morals, and don't pressure others. Sexual activity should be mutually desired by both partners. Anything less is sexual harassment or acquaintance rape.

▼ Practice safe sex. Take precautions to avoid pregnancy and disease. Either of these can limit your possibilities for the future. Remember that no birth control method, short of abstinence, is 100 percent effective. To guard against STDs, condoms offer some protection, but, again, they are not 100 percent reliable. Your risk of contracting an STD increases with the number of sexual partners you have had. If you and your partner are honest about past relationships, you will both be in a better position to make a wise decision about whether to become sexually involved.

Understanding Acquaintance Rape

Acquaintance rape is forced sexual intercourse involving people who know each other.

Acquaintance rape is forced sexual intercourse involving people who know each other. Statistics on acquaintance rape are hard to pin down. Studies done on college campuses vary as to the percentage of women who may become the victims of rape or attempted rape before they graduate. According to the U.S. Department of Justice, about 25 percent of college women have been victims of rape or attempted rape since their early teens. In any case, acquaintance rape is a risk of which you should be aware.

In any discussion of acquaintance rape, you need to keep in mind three things. Rape is a crime, no matter who is involved. A person who forces sexual intercourse on an acquaintance is just as guilty of a crime as someone who sexually assaults a stranger. Second, a person has a right to say no to sex at any point during a date or in a relationship, regardless of any previous sexual activity that may have occurred. Finally, because alcohol lowers inhibitions, acquaintance rape may be more likely to occur in situations where one or both parties involved may have had too much to drink. The following guidelines should serve as a first step toward acquaintance rape prevention:

▼ Set standards for sexual conduct. Decide how far you will go both physically and emotionally before getting involved with someone.

▼ Communicate with each other. Talk with each other about your expectations. Don't expect your partner to read your mind. Sex is too important to leave to chance.

▼ Stand your ground. If you don't want to respond to someone's sexual advances, your responsibility is to be assertive. Say no and mean it. Don't be hesitant, and don't back down. Even if you *do* want to have sex, your responsibility is to listen when your date says no and to believe that no means no, even if your date's nonverbal signals seem to say yes.

▼ Treat each other with respect. You have a right to your opinions and should trust your feelings. When something feels wrong, it probably is. Demand respect from your partner. At the same time, respect his or her choices as well. Don't let sexist notions or social pressures determine your behavior. Stick to your standards.

If you are a victim of rape, realize that you are not at fault and that you have options. Seek help immediately. Get medical attention. Do not shower or change clothes. Then call the police. To help yourself cope with the aftereffects of sexual assault—which may include nightmares, depression, mood swings, feelings of guilt or shame, and various physical symptoms—call a rape crisis center.

Dealing with Sexual Harassment

Sexual harassment is unwanted teasing, touching, or inappropriate remarks.

Sexual harassment is any kind of unwanted teasing, touching, or inappropriate remarks. Sexist jokes, sexist remarks, unwanted touching, or unwelcome requests for sexual favors are forms of sexual harassment and are inappropriate behaviors in any relationship. Your college probably has a policy on sexual harassment, which may be stated in a pamphlet, student handbook, college catalog, or website. Your college may have a designated advisor or other official on campus who deals with sexual harassment issues and complaints.

Once sexual harassment starts, it will probably continue until you demand that it stop. Dropping a course to get away from an offending instructor or switching dormitories because you are the recipient of sexist remarks and behaviors from another student are short-term and ineffective ways of coping with sexual harassment. Instead, you should speak up at the first sign of sexism and confront the harasser by making it clear that you want the behavior to end.

Don't keep sexual harassment to yourself. Talk to an advisor or report the behavior to the person at your college who handles complaints of sexual harassment. Make sure you have kept a record of the date, time, and place where the harassment occurred and of those people present who can act as witnesses.

Sexual harassment is everyone's business, and creating a friendly, nonsexist environment is everyone's responsibility. Speaking out against sexism is one way students can let their instructors and each other know that sexism has no place in the classroom or on the campus and that harassers will be held accountable.

EXERCISE 13.7 Collaborative Activity about Assertiveness

APPLY WHAT YOU HAVE LEARNED about assertiveness as a way to keep relationships healthy by doing this exercise with group members. Remember to follow the guidelines for successful collaboration listed on the inside back cover. First, read and discuss the list of 10 behaviors typical of assertive people. Choose one of the behaviors from the list and act it out. Create a scenario that demonstrates the behavior, rehearse it, and then present it to the rest of the class. When you have completed the exercise, evaluate your work. Write your evaluation on your own paper or visit *The Confident Student* premium website to download the group evaluation form.

1. **Assertive people are able to turn down invitations without feeling guilty.**

2. **They politely refuse an offer of food or drink if they don't want it.**

3. **They do not let themselves be talked into doing something that goes against their values.**

4. **They make choices and decisions based on what they think is the right thing to do.**

continued

5. **They have little difficulty saying no.**

   _____

   _____

6. **They reserve the right to express their opinions while respecting others' rights to do the same.**

   _____

   _____

7. **They reserve the right to change their opinions.**

   _____

   _____

8. **They are not afraid to speak up, ask questions, or seek information.**

   _____

   _____

9. **They are not afraid to make a mistake or to take action to correct it.**

   _____

   _____

10. **They do not feel compelled to share others' feelings, beliefs, or values that go against their own.**

    _____

    _____

Group evaluation:

Evaluate your discussion and demonstration. Did you accomplish your task successfully? What additional questions do you have about assertiveness in interpersonal relationships? How will you find answers to your questions?

Guided CHAPTER REVIEW

The following checklist summarizes this chapter's key terms and strategies. After reading the chapter, how confident are you that you can apply the information you have learned? To assess your level of confidence, respond to each statement with one of the following: *very confident* (3 points), *fairly confident* (2 points), *not very confident* (1 point), *not confident* (0 points). Write your number of points in the box beside each statement. Then add your score and read the analysis that follows. When you have finished, take the chapter quiz.

SUMMARY CHECK

How confident are you about applying these strategies?

Points

☐ 1. Eating nutritious, balanced meals

☐ 2. Exercising and staying fit

☐ 3. Being able to avoid harmful substances

☐ 4. Using the Internet appropriately

☐ 5. Identifying and eliminating causes of stress

☐ 6. Keeping emotions under control

☐ 7. Finding a purpose in life

☐ 8. Accepting the need for change

☐ 9. Seeking and maintaining healthy relationships

How confident are you about this chapter's key terms?

☐ 10. well-being

☐ 11. glucose

☐ 12. aerobic exercise

☐ 13. binge drinking

☐ 14. stress

☐ 15. sexually transmitted diseases (STDs)

☐ 16. acquaintance rape

☐ 17. sexual harassment

Total

Add your score. The highest possible score is 51. The closer your score is to 51, the higher your level of confidence. Use your *Summary Check* results to help you determine which parts of the chapter to review.

YOUR WEBSITE RESOURCES

This chapter's website resources include the following items. To access them, go to *The Confident Student* premium website.

- **Video Skillbuilder: Keeping Your Mind and Body in Shape**
- **Video Skillbuilder: Healthy Living: Making the Right Choices**
- **Chapter Exercises**
- **Forms to Download**

- **Chapter Summary of Topics**
- **Review Exercise**
- **Thinking Ahead About Career**
- **Confidence Builder Web Search**
- **Self-Test**

CHAPTER REVIEW Quiz

Answer the following questions from memory. Then return to the chapter to check your answers. As a final activity, complete *Show Your Confidence* at the end of the quiz.

1. What does emotional intelligence mean to you?

2. What does this chapter mean by a "balanced life"?

3. What does FIT stand for, and why is it important as a fitness guideline?

4. What is one example of addiction or substance abuse that you have seen among college students on your campus, and how has it affected their academic performance?

5. Of the 10 stress beaters explained in this chapter, what is one that you have used successfully?

6. What advice would you offer a roommate who is having trouble managing stress?

7. What is one thing that gives your life meaning or purpose?

8. Do you think that it is necessary to accept the need for change? Explain your answer.

9. In your opinion, what is a healthy relationship?

_____

_____

10. What advice would you give to a student who is being sexually harassed by another classmate?

_____

_____

SHOW YOUR CONFIDENCE

Many students say they have trouble keeping fit and maintaining a healthy diet while in college. Think about your own issues with diet and fitness. How successfully have you been able to deal with these issues? Be prepared to share your thoughts either in writing or in class discussion.

YOUR REFLECTIONS: GETTING YOUR LIFE IN BALANCE

Reflect on what you have learned from this chapter about health and well-being and how you can find balance in your life. Use the following questions to stimulate your thinking; then write your reflections. Include in your writing specific information from the chapter.

- Are your physical, emotional, and social selves in balance? Explain your answer.
- Do you have a habit that needs changing? What self-improvement goal will you set?
- What do you think is your strongest interpersonal or social skill?

_____

_____

_____

_____

_____

_____

_____

_____

_____

_____

_____

14 Facing Your Future with Confidence

Flying Camera/Corbis

Confident students are **future-oriented**. They look toward the future with the confidence that results from their successes and achievements.

What do you want to be when you grow up? You probably remember being asked this question as a child. What was your answer then? Do you still have the same career goal now? Whether you are a first-time college student or a returning student who has already had some success in the workplace, what are your hopes for the future? Keep in mind that a career is much more than a job. For many people, a career defines who they are and embodies not only what they want to achieve in life but also what they value most. In addition, most people change careers as their values and needs evolve over time.

If you are a recent high school graduate, your skills may be untried and your values uncertain. You may not have decided what your life's work will be. As mentioned in previous chapters, choosing a major will get you started on a career path. If you are an **adult learner** (one who has either postponed college until now or who is returning to college after having left to pursue other goals), you too may need some direction in planning for your future. Are you a highly motivated student who has already selected a major and a career? Then remember that plans change and that life is uncertain at best. College provides the opportunities and resources that will help you make good choices both now and in the future.

In many ways, college is a training ground for success in later life, so take advantage of all it has to offer. Don't be like some students who eagerly await graduation so that they can get out into "the real world." An old saying is "Life is what happens while you are waiting for something to happen." Read the *Confidence Builder* and begin now to face your future with confidence.

Adult learner refers to an older college student who may or may not have attended college in the past.

CONFIDENCE BUILDER

College *Is* the Real World

How many times have you heard remarks like these or made them yourself?

- "Why do I need this course? It won't help me in my career."
- "I'm just marking time until I graduate."
- "My instructors are so out of touch with the real world."

College *is* the real world. Professors are not teaching theory alone. They are helping you lay the foundation for lifelong learning and skill development. Much of what you learn in college is a thought process—a way of approaching problems and making decisions. Any course you take, whether in your major field or not, is the vehicle through which skills such as thinking critically and communicating effectively are conveyed. An equation you solve on a test or a speech you give in class may seem unimportant at the time. However, the logical problem-solving process you learn by working equations and the communication skills you learn by writing and making speeches are transferable skills that employers value.

What are you learning in college, and how does it relate to the skills you will need for career success? What skills do you already possess that will enhance your career readiness? Your courses, assignments, and extracurricular activities have a workplace application, as you can see from the following list. Read the list and determine which skills you already possess and which ones you need to develop.

- Algebra teaches critical thinking within the context of mathematical terms, operations, and procedures. Algebra helps you develop three transferable thinking skills that employers value: logical reasoning, decision-making, and problem-solving skills. Do you make decisions primarily on the basis of feeling or thinking? Can you determine the causes of a problem and find ways to solve it? Do you make logical connections between events and outcomes?
- Psychology deals with human motivation and behavior. The knowledge you gain from a psychology course may lead to self-understanding

continued

and acceptance of others whose values and motivations differ from yours. Psychology also explores the workings of your mind and memory—knowledge that can help you learn how to learn. Employers seek applicants who are flexible and able to quickly pick up new skills as the job requires. Moreover, the personal qualities employers value such as self-management, self-esteem, and personal responsibility are a direct outgrowth of self-knowledge. What personal qualities do you prize in yourself, and how will they help you in your career? What personal qualities do you need to develop?

- Composition helps you develop the writing skills of selecting and organizing details to support a central idea, writing clear and error-free sentences, and expressing ideas that are concrete and concise. Writing is an essential communication skill that employers value. They expect employees to write reports that are readable, meaningful, and useful. How are your writing skills?

- Speech courses teach you the fundamentals of public speaking and active listening, and they provide plenty of opportunities for you to practice these communication skills. Good speaking and listening skills are essential for careers in which you will be required to make presentations; attend meetings, conferences, and seminars; or conduct tours or training programs. Do you know how to plan a purposeful, well-organized speech? How are your listening skills?

- Researching print and online resources for reports or term papers teaches you to acquire, evaluate, organize, interpret, and synthesize information. Just as these skills demonstrate to an instructor that you understand and can apply what you have learned, they also demonstrate to employers that you know how to find and manage information relevant to a specific need or work assignment. Do you need to develop your research skills? Do you have good computer skills?

- Extracurricular activities such as playing a sport, joining an organization, volunteering your service to the community, and holding a student government office help you build interpersonal skills such as teamwork, leadership, and working with others from diverse backgrounds. These skills are essential in any job or career, especially those that require you to interact directly with coworkers, clients, or customers. How would you rate your interpersonal skills?

Do not underestimate the value of your courses. By identifying a skill or concept that has a direct application to your major or career for each course you are taking this semester, you will find the motivation for doing your best. Think of college as an apprenticeship in learning how to learn. If you are marking time until you graduate, you are missing the point. College is not the end of learning. At graduation, you are just beginning.

Follow Up: To explore this topic further, visit *The Confident Student* premium website for an online search activity about careers.

Choose Your Future

- Take control of your future by replacing false career assumptions with career realities, choosing a major or course of study, and writing your action plan.

As you look ahead to graduation from college, think of it as an intersection on the road of life. Where will you go from here? It is not too early to begin making plans. Choosing a major or career is all about planning for your future happiness and success. What do you want to do? What do you want to have? What do you want to accomplish? Seeking the advice of a career counselor or advisor can be helpful, but only you can answer these questions. Knowing what your interests are and clarifying your values will help you begin to narrow down your career choices. The next steps are to examine your career assumptions and determine whether or not they are realistic, choose a course of

Awareness CHECK 14.1

Are You Confident About Your Future?

Choose one of the following as your response to each statement: *always* (4 points), *usually* (3 points), *occasionally* (2 points), *rarely* (1 point). Write your number of points in the box beside each statement. When you are finished, add your score.

Points

1. When I think about the future, I feel optimistic about my ability to have the kind of life I want.

2. I believe that my view of college and my life expectations are realistic.

3. I know what skills employers value, and I know what my strengths and weaknesses in those skills are.

4. I have selected a major or program of study that reflects my values and life goals.

5. I have researched careers and job opportunities in my chosen field.

6. I have a career mentor or advisor on campus.

7. I have workplace or volunteer experience in my chosen field.

8. I consider myself Internet wise and technologically competent.

9. I have thought about my values and how they will affect my career choice.

10. I have set academic, career, and personal goals and am working to achieve them.

Total *Add your score. If your total is 35–40, the skills you already possess should help you make a smooth transition from college to work. If your total is 30–34, you have some workplace knowledge on which to build strong career skills. If your total is 25–29, practicing this chapter's strategies will relieve some of the uncertainty about your career readiness that you may be feeling. If your score is 10–24, supplement this chapter with a visit to a career counselor or career center. Whatever your level of skill, this chapter will help you think critically about your academic and career goals and how they intersect.*

study (major or certificate program), and then write an action plan for achieving your goal. But first, take *Awareness Check* 14.1 to assess your level of confidence about the future.

Your Career Assumptions

As explained in Chapter 3, testing your assumptions is a key component of critical thinking. Assumptions are long-held beliefs or opinions that shape the way we view the world and that influence our decision making. If your assumptions are based on false evidence, untested theories, or unexamined emotions, then your choices and decisions will not operate in your best interests. They may even hold you back, preventing you from achieving the success you deserve. False assumptions about careers are based on commonly held beliefs that don't measure up to reality. Figure 14.1 contrasts each assumption with a reality check. To think critically about choosing a major or course of study, examine your career assumptions and ask yourself, "Am I being realistic?"

FIGURE 14.1

What Are Your Career Assumptions?

FALSE ASSUMPTION:	REALITY CHECK:
Only one career is just right for me.	You possess a range of skills, interests, and abilities that would make you well suited to a variety of jobs and careers.
All the good jobs go to people with experience.	Good communication skills, interpersonal skills, enthusiasm, and a positive attitude make up for a lack of experience, especially in entry-level jobs. You can gain experience through volunteer work, service learning, apprenticeships, fellowships, and part-time employment.
I won't be able to overcome the negative effect of poor grades.	Your transcript is only one part of your résumé, and as you gain experience, it will become less and less important.
I have a spotty work history that will hold me back.	Employers look at the most recent job you held and your reason for leaving. They are more interested in how you deal with setbacks and whether you are persistent in trying to get ahead.
My major or course of study will dictate my career choice.	Majors are not as directly related to specific careers as you might think. A major in psychology or English, for example, is a good background for a career in law. Technical skills are useful in many jobs, and your real education will begin after you are hired through on-the-job training and work-related seminars.
I cannot waste my time taking courses that do not relate to my major.	Employers like well-rounded people who are conversant on a variety of subjects. No course is a waste of time if it broadens your perspective, makes you a more interesting person, or teaches you a new skill that you may use later on.

Your Major or Course of Study

If you are attending a community college, you may be planning to transfer to a four-year college, or you may be enrolled in a certificate program. Before transferring to a four-year college or university, you will earn either an AA (associate of arts) or AS (associate of science) degree. These degrees both require **general education courses**, additional courses in one of the academic disciplines, and **elective courses**. The AS degree requires more courses in the sciences. Certificate programs are career programs that do not prepare you for transfer to a four-year college; instead, they focus on job skills needed for a specific career such as nursing, fire technology, hospitality services, ornamental horticulture, building and contracting, and electrical engineering.

If you are attending a four-year college or university, you will be earning a bachelor's degree in a major discipline such as biology, English, or psychology. If you have chosen to pursue a career in one of the professions such as law or medicine, then your major will prepare you for additional work at the master or doctorate level. Some careers require a specific degree; others may not. The four-year degree requires general education courses that set a foundation for all future courses, plus required courses and electives based on your major.

The following guidelines may help you choose an appropriate major. If you are still not sure what career you want to pursue, choosing a major will narrow the field.

▸ Look at your grades. In what subject area have you consistently done your best? For example, if science courses have been very difficult for you, then you may not want to major in biology.

▸ Be honest about your skills. Does math come easy for you? Do you read and write well? Choose a major that will allow you to use your strengths.

General education courses are foundational courses in the disciplines. They are often required, and their purpose is to give you a broad base of knowledge no matter what your major is.

Elective courses are those you are free to choose in making up your schedule. A certain number of electives may be allowed or even required, depending on your major, and your choices may be limited to courses in certain disciplines.

Concept Check 14.1

Think about a job you have held. What is one skill you learned at that job that will be a career asset for you in the future?

▼ Consider your interests. Choose a major (and a career) based on your interests—the things you enjoy doing most. You are more likely to enjoy your work if you like what you are doing.

▼ Talk to people. Get advice or information from your advisor, from students who are majoring in the field you are considering, and from family or others who know you well and who know what your skills and interests are. Make your own choice, but listen to their suggestions. Also, review the sections on mentors and academic support groups in Chapter 1. Now do Exercise 14.1 to assess your career readiness.

EXERCISE 14.1 Career Readiness Survey

HAVE YOU THOUGHT ABOUT WHAT you want to do for the rest of your life? One of the first steps toward choosing a major or career is to assess your career readiness using six self-image keys. As explained in Chapter 4, career satisfaction depends on finding work that you enjoy doing, that fulfills one or more of your life's goals, and that integrates well with the life you want to lead. Complete the following survey one category at a time. First, read statements 1 through 4. Second, write a statement of your own in the blank provided. Third, rank the statements from *1* (most important) to *5* (least important) in each category. Based on your highest-ranked statements (*1* and *2*) in each category, write a paragraph or short essay describing your readiness for a career you have chosen or one that you would consider choosing.

INTERESTS: WHAT DO I LIKE TO DO?

_____ 1. **I enjoy quiet activities like reading, drawing, or writing.**

_____ 2. **I like to do things with my hands like building something or making handcrafts.**

_____ 3. **I am an outdoors person who enjoys physical activities.**

_____ 4. **I enjoy doing research on the Internet.**

_____ 5. **Write your own statement:** _____

STRENGTHS: WHAT COMES NATURALLY TO ME?

_____ 1. **I am very good at reading people's motives and feelings.**

_____ 2. **I have a natural feel for mechanical things and how they work.**

_____ 3. **I am talented in one or more of the creative or artistic fields.**

_____ 4. **I am an idea person with an aptitude for logical thinking and problem solving.**

_____ 5. **Write your own statement:** _____

VALUES: WHAT IS IMPORTANT TO ME?

_____ 1. **I like money and the things it buys, such as a beautiful home and good clothes.**

_____ 2. **I'd like to be powerful and influential—someone people look up to.**

_____ 3. **I'm concerned about the quality of life today and want to make a difference.**

_____ 4. **I value my family and my relationships with friends.**

_____ 5. **Write your own statement:** _____

continued

CAREER GOALS: WHAT DO I WANT TO ACHIEVE?

_____ 1. I want job security, a comfortable income, and good employee benefits.

_____ 2. I want wealth and a chance for advancement.

_____ 3. I want to travel and get to know other cultures.

_____ 4. I want a career that allows me to work at doing what I enjoy most.

_____ 5. Write your own statement: _____

PERSONALITY: HOW DO I RANK MY PERSONALITY TRAITS?

_____ 1. I am well organized.

_____ 2. I am responsible.

_____ 3. I am sociable.

_____ 4. I am self-disciplined.

_____ 5. Write your own statement: _____

EXPERIENCE: HOW DO I RANK MY WORK EXPERIENCE AS IT APPLIES TO MY CAREER?

_____ 1. I have full- or part-time work experience in the private sector.

_____ 2. I have on-campus work experience.

_____ 3. I have either worked as a volunteer or participated in service learning.

_____ 4. I have had an internship, fellowship, or other work experience.

_____ 5. Write your own statement: _____

This informal survey is meant simply as a guide. For example, if a big-money career is what you want most, then you will need to include postgraduate work in your planning. High-paying careers such as physician, attorney, accountant with CPA license, and many others require advanced degrees. If job security is more important to you, then a service career such as teaching or working in a government agency may be a good choice because of its employee benefits such as health care and retirement plans. If family and relationships are your most important value, then your career choice may take into account factors such as family or maternity leave, vacations and holidays that coincide with school holidays, investment opportunities to provide for children's education, and the amount and frequency of job-related travel that can restrict time spent with family. All of the personal qualities listed are among those employers desire most, so all your rankings in the personality section would mean a plus for you in the job market. Your highest ranking in this category may serve as a clue to your best career choice. For example, sociability is a desired trait in any career, but it is especially desirable in sales, teaching, and other careers where dealing face to face with customers or clients is an important part of the work.

To take a formal interest inventory, visit your academic advisor or college career center. For more help on evaluating your interests and skills, review Gardner's intelligences and your answers to *Awareness Check* 2.1 in Chapter 2.

Your Action Plan

Once you have selected a program or major based on a tentative career choice, deciding what courses to take is only one step in good planning. Continue to explore careers until you settle on what you want to do. Build work experience by taking a part-time job on or off campus. If you take summers off, use them wisely: Study overseas, work or intern in your chosen field, do volunteer work, or engage in other activities to build

Computer CONFIDENCE

Researching Careers on the Internet

Traditional ways to find out about careers include interviewing someone you know who has a job that interests you, going to job fairs, and seeking a part-time job or internship at a company you admire. Spending some quality time on the Internet can provide you with access to hundreds of careers and to career-related information. Here are some guidelines:

- **Visit your college's website.** Find the career services department for your college on your college's website to get you started. They will have information about local events for career seekers and services they offer, many of which may be free to you as part of the fees you pay to be a student. This website should be your first stop for local and on-campus jobs.
- **Research an industry.** Look up industry websites or periodicals for a particular field in which you are interested. You can find an industry's main website by using a search engine such as Yahoo! or Google. Discussion groups may list articles and other information about the industry.
- **Research a company.** To find out everything you can about a company, visit its website. Start by reading the company's press releases to find out about new product launches or services. Learn about the company's history and the job openings to find out about skills you would need to be considered for future employment.
- **Join an online career discussion group.** Visit a major career site such as those listed at right to find a chat room where you can talk about careers with others who share your interests.

Local groups may even have an in-person networking event that you can attend.

- **Check electronic bulletin boards.** Users read notices and post résumés. Most are free and include job listings. Bulletin boards can be found on major career sites.
- **Seek career guidance.** After you look at your local and campus resources for guidance, you can also find national sites that will help you with your career search. Look for sites that may allow you to take interest tests, develop résumés, read articles, and participate in discussion forums.

Two pitfalls to watch out for are the speed with which websites appear and disappear and the fact that anyone can put anything on the Internet. Go to familiar sites, especially those for which you have a trusted recommendation. Evaluate sites using the criteria explained in Chapter 3. A word of caution: Beware of sites that ask for personal information such as your social security number. No reputable site will do this. In this era of identity theft, you need to keep your personal information secure. Now try out your research skills on the following five websites, all of which have been stable for a long time and have a good reputation.

- America's CareerInfoNet, www.acinet.org
- America's Job Bank, www.ajb.dni.us
- Careerbuilder, www.careerbuilder.com
- Careers OnLine, www.careersonline.com
- Hotjobs, www.hotjobs.com

your résumé. During the semester or quarter, make time for clubs and organizations that relate to your major or career, and try to work yourself into a leadership position. In addition, follow six more steps to fulfill the requirements of your course of study.

1. Use your college catalog to determine your degree or program requirements and deadlines. For example, what courses are required? Are your electives restricted to additional courses within your major, or are they free? When must you apply for a degree or transfer credit? Does your program include an internship? Does your program lead to certification in a field? These answers and other important information are contained in your college catalog or on your college website.

2. List all the courses you will need. Map out a tentative guide for each semester or quarter from now until the completion of your program.

3. Work with an advisor to determine which courses you should take first and how best to arrange each term's schedule. Complete required courses as soon as you can to avoid any delays in graduation. For example, some courses may be offered only in alternate semesters or quarters. You might have to retake a course because of a poor grade or other unfortunate circumstance. Some courses, like math, are better taken consecutively to avoid skill gaps. Also, you will do better if you do not try to take too many heavy reading courses in one term.

4. If you will be transferring from a two-year college to a four-year institution, find out which courses will transfer, and plan your program accordingly.

5. Check with your advisor regularly to monitor your progress, to make sure you haven't overlooked anything, and to troubleshoot if you decide to change majors, programs, or degrees.

6. The key to success is to write out your action plan. List your long-term goal and explain how it meets the six characteristics of reachable goals, as explained in Chapter 4. List the short-term goals you will have to meet as you pursue the long-term goal. Finally, explain how you will evaluate whether your plan is working. Your action plan is your commitment to do the work that will impel you toward your goal. Also, when things go wrong, as they probably will, having your plan in writing makes it easy for you to see what you have accomplished, what still needs to be done, and where any problems lie. A good plan is flexible and will accommodate changing circumstances.

Now do Exercise 14.2 to analyze your **work style**, which will add to your self-knowledge and career readiness.

Your **work style** is simply your learning style applied in a work-place context.

EXERCISE 14.2 Learning Style and Work Style

WHAT IS YOUR WORK STYLE? For example, if you are a morning person, do your hardest tasks early in the day when you are most alert. If you like working with others as opposed to working alone, volunteer for team projects and committees. If you like to manage your time and schedule tasks without interference, consider a career that allows you to work from home. To refresh your memory about learning styles, review Chapter 2—especially your answers to the *Awareness Checks*. Then complete Parts I and II that follow.

Part I: Read each question and check each statement that applies to you.

_____ 1. **My energy level is at its highest in the morning.**

_____ 2. **I feel most energetic in the afternoon or at night.**

_____ 3. **I work best when I am physically involved, doing hands-on tasks.**

_____ 4. **I am at my best when mentally challenged.**

_____ 5. **I prefer tasks that require me to interact with others.**

_____ 6. **I would rather do most of my work on my own.**

_____ 7. **I enjoy researching on the Internet and using communications technology.**

continued

_____ 8. **The less time I spend online the better.**

_____ 9. **I think of myself as a people person.**

_____ 10. **I think of myself as an idea person.**

_____ 11. **I want a career that will take me outdoors.**

_____ 12. **I would be most comfortable working in an office.**

_____ 13. **I would be happiest in a career that requires frequent travel.**

_____ 14. **Ideally, I would like to do most of my work from home.**

_____ 15. **I'm a worker bee; just tell me what to do.**

_____ 16. **I like to take the lead; throw out an idea and let me run with it.**

_____ 17. **I work best when tasks and responsibilities are clearly defined.**

_____ 18. **I work best when given the freedom to define my own tasks.**

_____ 19. **I like routine tasks that are pretty much the same every day.**

_____ 20. **I need challenges and opportunities to innovate or create.**

_____ 21. **I am best at teaching, leading, or managing others.**

_____ 22. **I am best at being a team member or filling a niche.**

_____ 23. **I am well organized, a detail person.**

_____ 24. **I tend to look at the big picture, leaving the details to others.**

_____ 25. **I am good at gathering, compiling, and interpreting information.**

_____ 26. **I am best at applying the information others have gathered.**

_____ 27. **Most people would describe me as practical and reality-oriented.**

_____ 28. **Most people would describe me as idealistic and future-oriented.**

Part II: Based on the items you checked in Part I, what is your work style? Write a paragraph or short essay describing your work style. If you have already chosen a career, explain how your work style makes this career a good fit for you. If you are still undecided, then explain how you will use the checklist results as part of your decision-making process.

What Employers Want

- Identify the skills employers value, and work hard to develop those skills.

What are the skills that employers value most? First of all, employers want employees who have good interpersonal and communication skills, who are friendly and sociable, and who are competent in basic skills such as reading, writing, speaking, and computing. Employers seek applicants who are critical thinkers—people who can think for themselves and take the initiative to do what needs to be done. Finally, employers value teamwork. They want employees who can work cooperatively together in a diverse environment. Being career-ready means having these foundational skills and competencies as well as having a mastery of the specific skills and

FIGURE 14.2

Essential Career Skills in Today's Working World

Career Skill	What You Need to Be Able to Do
Basic literacy	Read with understanding and work with figures.
Communication	Listen, speak, and write effectively.
Critical and creative thinking	Make decisions, solve problems, predict outcomes, reason logically, and visualize creatively.
Self-management	Take personal responsibility for what you do; be self-motivated; act with integrity; control your emotions.
Interpersonal skills	Work as part of a team; be able to teach and lead others; know how to resolve conflict and work cooperatively with people from diverse backgrounds and cultures.
Resource management	Use time, money, materials, space, or other resources wisely and efficiently.
Information gathering	Find, evaluate, organize, and interpret information for a specific purpose.
Technology use	Select and use appropriate technology for a specific task; know how to keep the technology in working order and troubleshoot minor problems.

training that qualify you for a job in your chosen field. Figure 14.2 lists the skills that most employers value.

Now let's compare the careers of three different people. These examples illustrate several ways employees in different workplace settings can apply some of the skills listed in Figure 14.2. Michael works for a company that provides food and products to supermarkets. Michael's job is to keep track of the company's inventory using a computerized system. To do this job effectively requires Michael to be competent in the use of technology. He also must have the basic skills of reading and mathematics. In addition, Michael must make decisions and solve problems that require him to think critically and creatively.

Isabel is a high school English teacher. For this job, she needs good interpersonal skills to work with students from diverse backgrounds and to resolve conflicts in the classroom. Her effective listening, speaking, and writing skills help Isabel to communicate to her students. Isabel's love of reading enables her to deliver the course content with enthusiasm. As a critical thinker, she is able to make good decisions about grades and curriculum. Her computer skills are an asset because the school requires all students in English classes to use computers for researching and writing.

Ping manages a landscape nursery. She spends part of her time in the office monitoring employees, assigning work tasks, and troubleshooting with customers. She also spends time out of the office investigating new sources for plants and other products the company uses. To manage the company's resources and employees, Ping must have good personal and interpersonal skills, the ability to make decisions and solve problems, and the mathematical skills needed to spend the company's money wisely.

Did you recognize any of your own qualities and skills in the examples of Michael, Isabel, and Ping? Which of the career skills listed in Figure 14.2 do you feel most confident that you possess? Which ones do you need to develop? Take *Awareness Check* 14.2 to assess your career skills.

Awareness CHECK 14.2

Assess Your Career Skills

Points

Choose one of the following as your response to each statement: *always* **(4 points),** *usually* **(3 points),** *occasionally* **(2 points),** *rarely* **(1 point). Write your number of points in the box beside each statement. When you are finished, add your score.**

- ☐ 1. My reading and math abilities enable me to do many tasks well that require these skills.
- ☐ 2. I know how to plan and deliver an effective oral presentation.
- ☐ 3. I do an excellent job of expressing my thoughts in writing.
- ☐ 4. I do not hesitate to make decisions and tackle difficult problems to find solutions.
- ☐ 5. I have good teamwork skills and am able to interact cooperatively with others of many different backgrounds and cultures.
- ☐ 6. I am a self-starter who can see what needs to be done without being told.
- ☐ 7. When working in a group, I am not afraid to take the lead.
- ☐ 8. I am able to manage the resources available to me, such as time and my personal finances.
- ☐ 9. I am able to use technology both for information gathering and for communication.
- ☐ 10. I try to dress and conduct myself in ways that communicate my respect for others and for myself.

Total *Add your score. If your total is 35–40, your career skills are already well developed. Practice them at every opportunity. If your total is 30–34, the career skills that you have are a good foundation for developing new ones. If your total is 25–29, seek out opportunities to work with others and develop your skills. If your score is 10–24, supplement this chapter with a review of the speaking, listening, and teamwork skills explained in Chapter 12.*

Career Skills to Develop

No matter what you decide to do, basic skills will play a role. Reading—whether from printed or online sources—is one of the primary means of gathering information and keeping up with new research and trends in a field. Being able to understand and apply ideas from reading is an essential skill. Evaluating sources and reporting the information may be part of your duties at work. Good interpersonal skills and the ability to find information are essential competencies for any career. No doubt whatever career you choose will require some understanding of how to manage resources. For example, can you think of many jobs that would not require you to manage your time or to maintain the equipment you use in working order? What career can you imagine where your employer would not expect you to act with integrity and treat others fairly? In other words, all the skills listed in Figure 14.2 on page 361 are essential to a successful career. However, your communication skills are often the ones employers value most for several reasons.

▾ The ability to clearly and concisely express your ideas in an email, letter, report, or other written form is the mark of an educated person—a good point to keep in mind when writing a résumé.

▾ Whether brainstorming ideas in a meeting, giving a formal speech at a conference, or making an oral presentation to coworkers, the ability to state your ideas in a clear, well-organized manner is an asset.

▾ Everyone loves a good listener, and this is true in the workplace, where time is scarce and people don't want to repeat themselves. Listening and hearing are two different things. Listening is an active process; hearing is a passive behavior. To listen actively, focus your attention on the speaker, listen for ideas, and think critically about their meaning. Ask clarifying questions and make appropriate comments. Active listening is a vital communication skill.

College student participating in an internship

Workplace Ethics

Among the personal qualities and interpersonal skills you bring to the workplace are *personal responsibility, self-esteem, sociability, self-management,* and *integrity.* These skills enable people to work cooperatively, treat each other fairly, and interact with others from culturally diverse backgrounds in a spirit of openness and acceptance. In other words, your personal qualities determine how effective your interpersonal relationships will be. Now read the following list of personal qualities and what they mean.

▾ **Personal responsibility.** People who take personal responsibility do not blame others for their own mistakes and do not expect others to do their work. For example, a personally responsible student accepts a bad grade as the result of his or her own misunderstanding or lack of effort. Similarly, a personally responsible manager accepts that his or her subordinates need direction and supervision. If they fail at their tasks, then the manager must accept his or her share of the accountability. To develop personal responsibility, do not make excuses for lateness, bad grades, poorly done assignments, unkind words, or bad behavior. Take the initiative to improve your performance.

▾ **Self-esteem.** Self-esteem means *self-respect.* Students and employees who have self-esteem regard themselves favorably. They think of themselves as essentially good people even when they make mistakes, and they work honestly to correct mistakes. People who have self-esteem have a positive attitude toward themselves and others. To develop your self-esteem, think positively. Focus on the things you do well; be honest with yourself about skills, attitudes, and behaviors that need improving; and make whatever changes you can.

▾ **Sociability.** You don't have to be outgoing to be sociable. Many introverts are sociable people. Being **sociable** means being friendly, pleasant, and agreeable. If you are a sociable student or coworker, then you enjoy the company of others and they enjoy being with you. To become more sociable, listen to others, be encouraging, and make an effort to befriend others—especially those who are culturally diverse.

A **sociable** person is friendly, agreeable, and pleasant. You do not have to be outgoing to be sociable.

▾ **Self-management.** Self-management means *self-discipline.* In many ways, you are your own boss. It is up to you to determine when, what, and how to study. It is up to you to manage your time, control your attention, and say no to invitations that interfere with something important that you need to do. It is also up to you to determine what is and is not important. In other words, a self-managed student or employee is *internally motivated*, as explained in Chapter 2. Daniel Goleman, author of *Emotional Intelligence*, explains several qualities of the self-managed person, such as *persistence, hopefulness,* and the *ability to regulate moods*. For more on this topic, see Chapter 13. To become more internally controlled or self-managed, find ways to motivate yourself and do not expect others to motivate you. Set goals and find incentives such as a higher grade in one of your courses or a promotion at work, and let those provide your motivation. Employers value employees who are self-starters: people who don't have to be told what to do. Be a self-starter.

Integrity means having a moral or ethical code, living according to moral or ethical principles.

▶ **Integrity.** A person who has integrity lives by certain principles. **Integrity** means following a moral or ethical code. Moral codes are often based on religious beliefs. Ethical codes are often based on what is socially acceptable. In either case, such codes provide guidelines for personal and corporate behavior. A person or company that has integrity has these qualities: *trustworthiness, fairness, honesty, respect,* and *obedience to the law*. As a student, you show integrity when you do not cheat on exams or plagiarize others' work. As an employee, you show integrity in little ways when you do not pilfer from the supply cabinet and when you do not make personal

EXERCISE 14.3   Collaborate to Apply Academic Skills

CAN YOU DETERMINE HOW YOU would apply a skill learned in one of your courses to a work-related task? Work with a partner to complete the following comparison chart by filling in the blank spaces. When you get to item 9, you will fill in all the spaces, starting with a course of your choice. You may use a course more than once. Use the *Confidence Builder* at the beginning of this chapter and Figure 14.2 on page 361 as references, and look for clues in the blanks that are filled in. When you are finished, share your work in a class discussion.

APPLYING ACADEMIC SKILLS IN THE WORKPLACE

College Course	Skill Learned/Applied	Workplace Application
1. Freshman Composition	Write a well-organized essay.	Prepare a report.
2. College Study Skills	_____	Take notes in a meeting.
3. _____	Make a speech in class.	Make a presentation at work.
4. Biology	Work with group members to design and run a lab experiment.	_____
5. Personal Finance	_____	Manage a departmental budget.
6. _____	Compare wedding rituals and ceremonies across cultures.	Work with others from diverse backgrounds.
7. Introduction to Psychology	_____	_____
8. _____	Build a working model of an electrical circuit.	_____
9. _____	_____	_____

calls at work. You show integrity in big ways when you do not attempt to undermine others' work in order to advance yourself and when you do not engage in illegal or unethical business practices such as falsifying records or accounts. To develop integrity, use the Golden Rule and the physicians' Hippocratic Oath as guidelines. The Rule says to treat others as you would like them to treat you. The Oath says, "First, do no harm."

In addition to ethical behavior and the other personal qualities listed previously, employers also value flexibility and a positive attitude. These qualities make people pleasant and easy to work with. Flexibility enables you to adjust to the changing circumstances and needs of the workplace. A positive attitude makes you open to new ideas and accepting of others' differences. For more information on the ideas discussed in this section, review the following pages: flexibility, page 2; positive attitude, page 85; values and ethics, pages 85–88 and Figure 4.2.

Concept Check 14.2

Which one of the career skills mentioned in this section and the previous one is your strongest? How do you apply this skill, either at work or in your classes?

From College To Work

- Make a smooth transition from college to work by using the resources that will help you prepare for career success.

Your college has many resources that you can draw on as you prepare yourself for the future. Your courses provide the knowledge and skills you will need to succeed in life and work. The organizations you choose to support, be a member of, or take a leadership role in prepare you for involvement in your professional and community life. Living in a dorm and having roommates afford opportunities for you to build people skills as you interact with others from diverse backgrounds. For example, a residence hall, a sorority or fraternity, or an apartment you share with roommates places you in close quarters with others—some of whom you may not know well or even like. Your adjustment depends on the effort you make to cooperate with your roommates and resolve conflicts. Your college can help you gain work experience through part-time campus jobs, internships, fellowships, and teaching assistantships, and may even put you in touch with prospective employers through job fairs and placement services. No matter how much or how little work experience you have had, your college has resources that can help you prepare for the life you want.

Your college career center or other department that provides career information can tell you where and when a job fair is being held in your area. A **job fair** is an event where companies set up booths and send representatives to collect résumés and screen potential candidates for positions they need to fill. This is a great place to learn about a company you are interested in, check leads on positions for which you may qualify, or learn about a company with which you are unfamiliar or may not have considered. Representatives bring literature about their companies that you can take away, and many set up equipment for viewing videos or visiting their websites, which are also excellent sources of information. Good preparation is the key to getting the most you can out of a job fair. Figure 14.3 is a checklist to help you prepare for the next job fair in your area. Although you may not get the career of your dreams at first, every job you take is a step in that direction.

Job fair refers to an event at which companies gather in one place to attract applicants and fill positions.

Bob Daemmirch/The Image Works

A job fair is an excellent resource for researching careers and networking.

FIGURE 14.3

Job Fair Checklist

☑ **Target companies.** Since many companies will have booths at a job fair, and you can't visit them all, target several that interest you most. Research them ahead of time so that you appear knowledgeable. The Internet, career center, and library are good places to begin your research.

☑ **Be professional.** Dress conservatively, as you would for a job interview. Carry a nice-looking tote bag, briefcase, zippered notebook, or pocket folder for storing copies of your résumé, representatives' business cards, and company literature. This will send the message that you are well organized.

☑ **Make an impression.** Shake hands, make eye contact, state your name and introduce yourself, but keep your comments brief. Think of your introduction as a brief presentation, covering several points: your major or career choice, why you're interested in the company, and your desire for an interview.

☑ **Ask questions.** Questioning representatives about their companies shows interest. Keep your questions brief. Your goal is to find out more about the company and the name of a contact person to whom you can write personally if you decide to make a formal application. Be sure to ask for a representative's business card so that you have a contact to mention in a cover letter.

☑ **Take notes.** You will not remember names, specific information about a company, or helpful tips unless you jot them down. Carry a notepad for this purpose, or write the information on a representative's business card or on a company flyer or brochure.

☑ **Hand out résumés.** Representatives expect to collect résumés from potential applicants, so do not hesitate to hand yours out. Bring plenty of copies. Consider preparing a cover letter that introduces your qualifications and provides the company with a sample of your writing.

☑ **Collect company literature.** The booths at a job fair are usually well stocked with materials such as leaflets, pamphlets, and brochures that contain valuable information about the company's policies and operations. Take whatever literature is available.

☑ **Follow through.** Send thank you notes to the company representatives who expressed interest in you. Following up with a thank you leaves a favorable impression the representative may recall should you decide to formally apply for a position with the company.

CRITICAL THINKING

Your Assets and Accomplishments

Exercise Overview

Self-knowledge is an indispensable tool for academic and career success. This exercise will help you think critically about your assets and accomplishments.

Exercise Background

Many students have difficulty talking or writing about themselves. They may devalue their interests and experience, or they may not be aware of the marketable skills they have developed through working. Now is the time to get over any misgivings you may have and to think confidently about who you are and what you know.

Exercise Task

Make a list of your assets and accomplishments. These might include a skill you mastered quickly, a talent you have developed, an obstacle you have overcome, or an award or special recognition you

continued

have received. Your list might also include a new skill or ability you developed at work—something you thought you couldn't do but were able to accomplish. Do you have a personal skill for which you are well known? Are you a good listener or someone who helps others resolve conflicts? Do people enjoy working with you? Keep your list and add to it over time. Use your accomplishments list to remind yourself of your personal qualities and skills as you think about choosing a major or career and as a guide when it comes time to prepare a résumé.

Build a Firm Financial Foundation

• Manage your finances now to build good habits for a successful future.

If you ask college students what they want out of college, many will be quick to tell you that they want "a better job" or "a high-paying career." They have other goals, to be sure, but financial success is a top priority. Therefore, it is important to understand that financial success begins now, not sometime in the future. How you manage your money today lays the foundation for successful money management tomorrow—not only in your personal life but also in the workplace, where you might be responsible for making decisions about purchases and expenditures and for allocating funds.

Are you in debt, always running a little short of cash, or do you follow a budget? Are you satisfied with your current financial situation, or would you like to keep better track of your earning, spending, and saving? This section explains a few basic principles that will help you improve the way you manage your money.

▼ Set financial goals.

▼ Follow a budget.

▼ Live within your means.

▼ Be credit card wise.

Set Financial Goals

Most financially successful people know how much they make, account for every dollar they spend, and follow a long-term plan for saving and investing in their future. Think of financial success as a pyramid where the foundation rests on a regular income. Each level of the pyramid is a stage in planning and money management that leads to successful achievement at the top, as illustrated in Figure 14.4.

Where are you on the pyramid? What are your long-term and short-term financial goals? Do you have a regular income or savings? Do you budget and manage your money as well as you could? Right now you may be thinking only about how you are going to finance your education for the next four years. But you are probably also looking ahead to your career and the life you want to lead, the kind of home you want to own, and the

FIGURE 14.4

Financial Success Pyramid

Success
Investing
Handling loans and debt
Managing expenses
Setting goals and budgeting
Establishing credit base
Earning income

things you want to have. Financing an education is a long-term goal that you can reach by determining what your earnings are, how much your education will cost, and how you will budget or supplement your income to meet expenses on a monthly basis, year in and year out. You may have to take out a student loan, or you may already have a scholarship that pays for part of your education. The levels of the pyramid in Figure 14.4 represent money-management experience, so no matter what level you are on, making a budget or sticking to one you have already made can help you reach your goals.

Follow a Budget

Budget refers to a summary of earnings and expenditures—your plan for spending and saving.

A **budget** is a plan for spending and saving money based on earnings. A budget has two purposes: (1) to help you live within your means, and (2) to help you keep track of where your money goes so that you can find ways to cut costs and increase your savings. Your first step in making a budget is to determine the source and amount of your income (money in) and your expenses (money out). The chart in Figure 14.5 lists typical sources of college students' income and expenses.

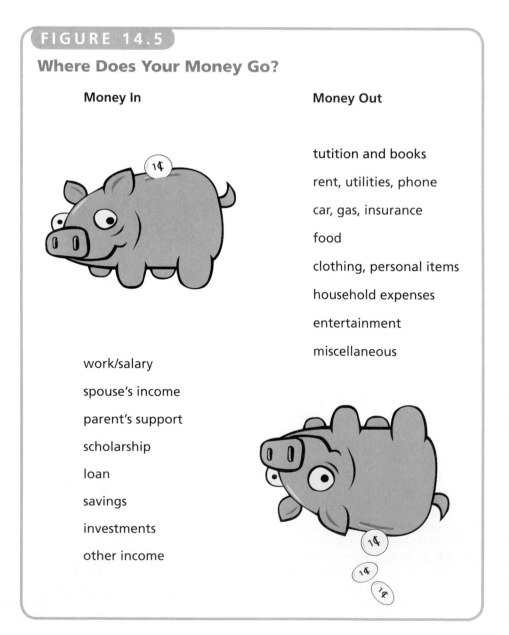

FIGURE 14.5

Where Does Your Money Go?

Money In	Money Out
	tutition and books
	rent, utilities, phone
	car, gas, insurance
	food
	clothing, personal items
	household expenses
	entertainment
	miscellaneous
work/salary	
spouse's income	
parent's support	
scholarship	
loan	
savings	
investments	
other income	

The second step in making a budget is to determine which of your expenses are fixed and which are fluid. *Fixed* expenses recur over time and don't change. Rent, car payments, tuition, and insurance premiums are examples of fixed expenses. *Fluid* expenses may change from month to month both as to type and amount. Food, phone, utilities, entertainment, and clothing are examples of fluid expenses. Although fixed expenses are beyond your control, you do have some control over fluid expenses. For example, you can't make your landlord lower the rent, but you can cut your utility and food costs by using energy-saving methods and fixing your own meals. Suppose your expenses are greater than your source of income. You must find ways to cut expenses. Ideally, a realistic budget should pay your expenses and leave money for savings. Through saving and investing, you can build wealth. In college, your savings may be small and investments may be nonexistent. But as you gain career or work experience, your income will increase, providing the means to save and invest—if you manage your growing income wisely.

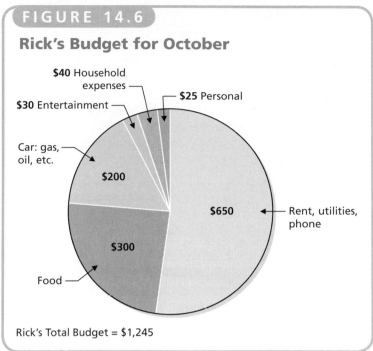

FIGURE 14.6

Rick's Budget for October

Rick's Total Budget = $1,245

Figure 14.6 shows an example of one college student's monthly budget. Rick Morales has a monthly income of $1,295. His budget does not include expenses for tuition and books, which are covered by a scholarship. Rick's income is based on his earnings over several summers, a part-time job, plus a supplement from his parents. He has both a checking account and a savings account. Rick usually keeps his expenses under $1,295. In October, he spent a total of $1,245 and deposited $50 in his savings account. Rick looks for ways to save money. He shares an apartment to reduce his rent and associated costs, rides his bicycle to cut car expenses, and eats most meals at home to save on food costs. By putting money aside each month, he is building a safety net to cover unexpected expenses.

EXERCISE 14.4 Know Where Your Money Goes

Part I. Make a money-in, money-out list of your income sources, expenses, and amounts for one month on the following chart.

MONEY IN		MONEY OUT	
Source	Amount	Expense	Amount

continued

_____   _____   _____   _____

_____   _____   _____   _____

_____   _____   _____   _____

Part II. Based on your income and expenses, make a monthly budget that you can follow. Your budget can be in the form of a pie chart like Rick's budget in Figure 14.6, a simple list, table, or any way that you want to present it. Be creative. As a final step, write a short paragraph explaining how you can reduce expenses.

_____

_____

_____

_____

Live Within Your Means

Self-management and personal responsibility are the keys to living within your means. Unfortunately, advertising and the availability of credit cards make spending seem attractive and affordable. Resist the temptation to buy clothes or personal items that you don't need or to finance big-ticket items that you can do without. In addition, try these 10 money-saving tips:

1. Don't use shopping as a form of entertainment.

2. Don't buy on impulse. Think about purchases based on need rather than desire.

3. Carry cash with you, and leave credit cards at home. If you have to pay cash, you will be less tempted to buy things you don't need.

4. Reduce energy costs by turning the heat down and the air conditioner up. Don't leave lights burning in an empty room. Take quick showers, and don't leave the water running while brushing your teeth. Fill the bathtub only halfway. Use the energy-saving setting on appliances.

5. Cut food costs by eating in, clipping coupons, looking for bargains, and using leftovers.

6. Be creative in finding ways to make extra money. For example, offer to house-sit, babysit, or do odd jobs for pay.

7. Use public transportation, ride a bicycle, or walk wherever you can.

8. If you must drive, shop around for the lowest gas prices.

9. You probably have clothes that you don't wear. Instead of letting them hang in the closet, offer to exchange them with someone of your size. Both of you will have the benefit of a "new" outfit without the cost.

10. For entertainment, search the college or local paper for free concerts, events, and local points of interest such as museums and parks.

No matter how deprived postponing gratification may make you feel, the reward that comes from taking control of your life and spending habits more than makes up for not having everything you want now. In addition, by constantly looking for ways to cut costs, you are building valuable experience for creative money management in the future.

Be Credit Card Wise

The first credit cards, such as Diners Club and Carte Blanche, were available mainly to businesspeople on expense accounts. Major credit cards were introduced to the general public in the 1960s, ushering in an era of unforeseen spending and debt that has steadily increased. Economists cite credit card debt and misuse as a source of many Americans' financial troubles today.

Used wisely, credit cards have several advantages. Buying on credit and paying off your balance on time, every time, is one way to establish a good credit rating. A positive credit history indicates that you are a responsible person, a distinction that can be an asset when you are applying for a loan or a job. Credit cards are convenient and a source of ready cash for emergencies—two advantages that quickly become disadvantages when credit cards are abused.

Credit card companies market to college students, luring them with incredible offers and gifts that often come with a stiff price of annual fees, high interest rates, late fees, and other penalties lurking in the fine print. But the greatest disadvantage is that having a credit card encourages you to spend more than you should. Before you know it, you are living beyond your means and mounting a burden of debt that will be hard to reduce before it ruins your credit rating.

Follow these tips for using credit cards wisely and see also Figure 14.7, which lists credit card issues and questions.

1. Have no more than two credit cards, and preferably only one. The more cards you have, the more you are likely to spend. Do not be tempted by credit card applications that come in the mail. Tear them up and throw them away.

2. Use your card in moderation and save it for emergencies. Charge airline tickets and hotel rooms so that you don't have to carry a large amount of cash when traveling.

3. Do not charge more than you can pay off each month, and pay the full amount on time to avoid finance charges.

FIGURE 14.7

Choosing a Credit Card: Issues and Questions

ISSUES	QUESTIONS
INTEREST RATE	What is the finance charge if I carry a balance?
MINIMUM PAYMENT	What is the minimum I can pay each month? When is it due?
ANNUAL FEE	Is there an annual fee, and how much is it?
LATE FEES AND OTHER PENALTIES	What is the late fee? What other penalties apply?
GRACE PERIOD	Is there a grace period? (If you do not pay the full balance, finance charges may begin immediately, or there may be a grace period of a few days in which no finance charges are assessed.)

4. If you do carry a balance, keep it low, pay more than the minimum each month to reduce interest, and avoid late payment fees. If possible, do not make any additional charges until the balance is paid off.

5. Reduce the need for a credit card by establishing a checking account. When you write a check and note the expenditure in your check register, subtracting it from your balance, it is much easier to see where your money goes.

If you do get into financial trouble, deal with it immediately. The longer you wait, the worse it will get. You want to avoid having your account turned over to a collection agency. Instead, ask creditors for help in developing a payment plan. Also, seek counseling. A reliable source is the National Foundation for Credit Counseling (NFCC), or ask a trusted family member or college financial aid officer for suggestions.

Financial success does not happen by chance; it is the result of good choices. Using proven money management skills such as setting goals, budgeting, living within your means, and using credit cards wisely will start you on your way to the top of the financial pyramid.

To conclude this chapter and this book, think about your life and goals. Where are you now financially, socially, emotionally, and academically? Where would you like to be? Through honest self-assessment and hard work, you can achieve your dreams. Take pride in your strengths; take steps to overcome your weaknesses and you can face your future with confidence.

Guided CHAPTER REVIEW

The following checklist summarizes this chapter's key terms and strategies. After reading the chapter, how confident are you that you can apply the information you have learned? To assess your level of confidence, respond to each statement with one of the following: *very confident* (3 points), *fairly confident* (2 points), *not very confident* (1 point), *not confident* (0 points). Write your number of points in the box beside each statement. Then add your score and read the analysis that follows. When you have finished, take the chapter quiz.

SUMMARY CHECK

How confident are you about applying these strategies?

Points

1. Understanding the relationship between the skills learned in college and their real-world applications
2. Choosing a career that reflects your skills, interests, and values
3. Knowing how to research a career on the Internet
4. Writing an action plan to achieve your career goals
5. Knowing what career skills you possess and which ones you need to develop
6. Understanding the meaning and importance of workplace ethics
7. Setting financial goals and following a budget
8. Living within your means and not misusing credit

How confident is your understanding of this chapter's key terms?

9. adult learner
10. general education courses
11. elective courses
12. work style
13. sociable
14. integrity
15. job fair
16. budget

Total

Add your score. The highest possible score is 48. The closer your score is to 48, the higher your level of confidence. Use your *Summary Check* results to help you determine which parts of the chapter to review.

YOUR WEBSITE RESOURCES

This chapter's website resources include the following items. To access them, go to *The Confident Student* premium website.

- **Video Skillbuilder: Career Planning in College**
- **Video Skillbuilder: Career Planning After College**
- **Video Skillbuilder: Managing Your Finances**
- **Remembering Cultural Differences**

- **Chapter Exercises**
- **Forms to Download**
- **Chapter Summary of Topics**
- **Thinking Ahead About Career**
- **Confidence Builder Web Search**
- **Self-Test**

CHAPTER REVIEW Quiz

Answer the following questions from memory. Then return to the chapter to check your answers. As a final activity, complete *Show Your Confidence* at the end of the quiz.

1. What is one false career assumption and what is the reality?

_____

_____

2. Why is it important to write your action plan?

_____

_____

3. What are two of the skills that employers value?

_____

_____

4. Which skills enable you to get along with others and work successfully in groups or teams?

_____

_____

5. How are academic skills and workplace skills related?

_____

_____

6. What is the meaning of the term "work style?"

_____

_____

7. What is one resource you are able to manage effectively?

_____

_____

8. What is integrity? Give an example of something you do that shows integrity.

_____

_____

9. What is one example of ethical behavior in the classroom?

_____

_____

10. What is one skill you possess that you think will be a career asset?

_____

_____

SHOW YOUR CONFIDENCE

Read again this statement from Chapter 14: "As you look ahead to graduation from college, think of it as an intersection on the road of life." Now look at the photograph on the first page of this chapter. What do the photograph and the statement mean to you? Be prepared to share your answer to this question either in writing or in class discussion.

YOUR REFLECTIONS: BECOMING A CONFIDENT STUDENT

Reflect on what you have learned either from this chapter or from previous chapters that has helped you become a more confident student. Use the following questions to stimulate your thinking; then write your reflections. Include in your writing specific information from one or more chapters.

- In your opinion, what does the term "confident student" mean?
- What attitude, value, or skill makes you feel most confident about your future?
- Would you describe yourself as career-confident? Why or why not?

_____

_____

_____

_____

_____

_____

_____

_____

_____

_____

_____